Inshore
Fly Fishing

"No one I know understands the intricacies of successful fly fishing along the North Atlantic Coast better."

—LEFTY KREH

Inshore
Fly Fishing

A Pioneering Guide to Fly Fishing along Cold-Water Seacoasts

Second Edition

Lou Tabory

Foreword by Lefty Kreh

LYONS PRESS
Guilford, Connecticut
An imprint of Globe Pequot Press

Lyons Press is an imprint of Globe Pequot Press.

Black and white line drawings by Kevin Sedlak
Illustrations by Robert L. Prince
Photographs by Barb and Lou Tabory unless otherwise credited

Text design: Sheryl P. Kober
Project editor: Julie Marsh
Layout: Kevin Mak, Melissa Evarts

Library of Congress Cataloging-in-Publication Data is available on file.

ISBN: 978-0-7627-6434-1

Printed in the United States of America

10 9 8 7 6 5 4 3 2 1

To Barb

A wonderful wife, fishing partner, and friend, whose encouragement, help, and hard work made this book possible

Author's Note on the Structure of this Book

I have kept the revised book's structure the same as the original because the book was written to offer fishing advice to anglers. I've always wondered why most fishing books begin by discussing tackle, knots, or casting. Yes, these are important aspects of the sport, and they need attention, but they are not the heart of most books. A fishing book, after all, is a *fishing* book. That's why I've chosen to discuss fishing first. It's my belief that most anglers who read this book already know what a fly rod is, and what they want is fly-fishing know-how—for inshore saltwater fly fishing. That's why I've placed matters connected to tackle and knots last. Readers who need such basic fly-fishing information might therefore want to read the back sections first.

What makes *Inshore Fly Fishing* unique, I think, is that it deals most in *fishing* know-how, with just enough information about tackle and related fly-fishing techniques to help the beginning angler, while offering new and advanced methods to the veteran. The focus of this book is how to read and fish different waters—from moving water through the many types of fishing locations inshore waters hold. Trout fishermen will notice similarities to some of the waters mentioned, while the saltwater angler will discover how to work a fly in place of a spinning lure—and why the former is often a more effective lure.

I chose to begin with the fishing, ultimately, because that is what's most different for all anglers and what is most unique about what I have to say. This structure starts the reader fishing in the first pages and, without breaks, keeps the emphasis on fishing.

—Lou Tabory

Contents

Foreword by Lefty Kreh. ix

Acknowledgments. x

Introduction xiii

Part One—Reading and Fishing Inshore Waters

  1   The First Cast. 2

  2   Shorelines with Light Surf. 12

  3   Small Creeks 18

  4   Rips and Moving Water. 26

  5   Estuaries 39

  6   Jetties 59

  7   Reefs and Rocky Points. 70

  8   Flats. 81

  9   Ocean Beaches 98

10   Cliff Fishing. 116

11   Chasing Fish in Open Water 127

12   Night Fishing 144

Part Two—The Important Techniques for Catching Fish

13   Saltwater Fly Casting 152

14   Retrieving 167

15   Hooking and Fighting Fish. 177

Part Three—Tackle, Flies, and Gear

16   Tackle 196

17   Rigging Up 218

18   Baitfish and Flies 254

Part Four—Gamefish, Their Habits, and How to Release Them

19   Popular Gamefish and Their Habits 288

20   Releasing Fish 317

Contents

Part Five—Tides, Water Conditions, Weather, and Safety

21 Tides 324

22 Wind, Weather, and Temperature 330

23 Safety and How to Drive on Beaches 336

Appendix One—Conservation 341

Appendix Two—World Records 345

Appendix Three—The Changing Structure along the Coast 346

Glossary 353

Selected Bibliography 360

Index 361

About the Author 370

Foreword

I first met Lou Tabory several decades ago in a shopping mall in New England. There he was, a kid throwing a great deal of fly line, but working at it, and obviously enjoying himself. His enthusiasm was infectious, and as we discussed casting and fishing, I made a vow to get to know him better. Over the years we have fished together, and we've never known an unpleasant moment. I have watched Lou mature from a vibrant young man to a highly skilled, and still enthusiastic, fly fisherman.

There are some anglers who are natural and instinctive fishermen. They seem to know when, what, and how to do what they should to catch fish. Others have to study, practice, and work hard to acquire these skills. Lou is one of the natural fishermen, but he's also a serious student. Innovation is a hallmark of a great angler, and Lou is constantly developing new flies and new ways to catch fish. He is certainly one of the best at landing huge stripers on a fly.

No one I know understands the intricacies of successful fly fishing along the North Atlantic Coast better than Lou Tabory. He has fished these waters night and day, testing his ideas and polishing his already great casting skills. Today there are many writers who are more or less researchers: They fish a little, read a great deal, interview others, and finally, they write a book on the subject. But the information you read here is gathered from a lifetime on the water. If you are a serious angler and want to learn more about fishing this area, you won't find better or more detailed information than lies between these pages.

Tight lines—but not too tight!

—LEFTY KREH

Acknowledgments

As with any book, there are so many people to thank and so little space. I've tried to just include anglers I have worked with in the last several years. To all my friends and fellow anglers who are not listed, thank you for your help.

Anglers I call to get information on fishing, flies, and tackle include Dave Beshara, a longtime friend and a great angler who knows the Merrimack estuary as well as anyone. I did a number of schools with Dave, and it was like working with a big brother. Cooper Gilkes is who I call when I need to know something about fishing Martha's Vineyard. Coop's wealth of fishing knowledge is legendary, and he shares it freely. But mostly it's his generosity, and you will not find a better friend—I feel lucky to know him. Mike Monte, a hard-core New Jersey angler and a great friend, knows the surf fishing on Nantucket like the back of his hand. When I need info about the Island or Jersey, he is my go-to guy. John Posh is a longtime friend and fishing partner. We have spent many hours on the water together with never a bad moment. He is a best friend that I keep learning from—thanks for good memories.

Barry Kanavy is a Long Island guide and gifted angler whose specialty is Montauk and late-season waterfowl. When I need info about Long Island, he is my contact. Tackle pro Frank Catino keeps me informed about fly line development. We worked at Orvis together, and he now guides in Florida. Frank is a pleasure to spend time with, and he can catch fish anywhere. Longtime friend Nick Curcione showed me how to fight big offshore fish. We had some great trips together and many laughs. Nick's specialty is West Coast long-range fishing, but he's another guy who can catch fish anywhere. A special thanks to Pip Winslow for his help with technical photos. We met while working with the Orvis Company and have spent many good days on the water.

John Cumisky and I became good friends through doing fly-fishing schools at the Valley Angler in Danbury, Connecticut. John's strong suit is freshwater, but he is no slouch in salt water. I often pick his brain about fishing the west coast of Florida. Curt Jessup is another guy who became a friend through fly-fishing schools. Curt once owned a shop on Cape Cod but knows the fall albi run on Harkers Island, North Carolina, well and is a great source of info about that fishery. Roger Swiderski attended three of my Orvis Schools and then became a guide fishing the waters in Buzzards Bay, Cape Cod, and wildly chasing bluefin.

Roger, a great friend, keeps me informed about his fishery and is perhaps the best physical therapist known to man—I know because his skills keep me going.

John Merwin is a great friend, great editor, and great writer. Now the fishing editor at *Field & Stream,* John is a constant source of information on the fishing business, tackle, and gear. His counsel on writing books and articles is priceless, and for a big-name writer, he is an excellent angler.

A number of gifted fly tyers keep me supplied with flies. D. L. Goddard, Eric Peterson, Enrico Puglisi, and Dave Skok have developed many different effective patterns. I wish I possessed the tying skills of these good friends. They make a variety of patterns that catch everything from stripers to albies to bonefish, plus many other gamefish. Each of these anglers has developed ways to blend materials that make a fly look alive just sitting in the water. I have only been lucky enough to fish with Dave and Eric, and both are gifted anglers and casters. A day on the water with these two anglers is a learning experience.

Fly shops that keep me busy with fly-fishing schools. Scott Bennett at the Compleat Angler, Jim Bernstein at Eldredge Brothers, Pat Abate at River's End, and Eric Johnson at Westport Outfitters are all easy to work with, fun to be around, and fine anglers.

Thanks to Andy Danylchuck for his help with fish release and fish behavior. Andy is an unusual mix of research scientist, PhD, and fine angler and is also a great friend.

No editor could be better than Mike Mazur—thanks for being so easy to work with.

Special thanks to Lefty Kreh for all his advice and counsel, and for the great friendship for so many years. To this day I often call Lefty "Pop" because he is like a second dad to me. He is never too busy to offer suggestions, and I still have all the letters that he took the time to write. Over the years when I needed help he was there—thanks.

Thanks to Michael Kahn for keeping me employed at Albright Tackle and supplying me with tackle, but mostly for being a fun guy to spend time with, as well as being one hell of an angler. Bill Bowers provided counsel on writing and the fishing business. His special skill is the ability to improve someone's writing without changing the meaning. Doug Cummings at Lee Wulff Fly Lines has been very generous over the years. He is a fine friend who knows the fly business, plus knows how to make fly lines.

Thank you to the Orvis Company and to all my friends there for their help through the years. Working at Orvis was a good run, and we had fun together.

Perk and Dave Perkins allowed me to be myself and always treated me with class. Bill Reed deserves special thanks for his great insight on switch rods and spey casting, and for all the times we talked about hunting with longbows. Tom Rosenbauer has been working at Orvis for decades. When I started working there, he was the first guy I spoke to, and our relationship has lasted to this day. He knows the tackle business well and is an excellent writer as well as a hell of a good angler. Jim Lepage and Paul Fersen are two longtime friends that I could always turn to for sound technique information. We had some great days fishing together.

To Ray Hutcherson, owner of Sea Level Fly Fishing, thank you for supplying me with great tuna reels and for the fine information on West Coast fishing.

Thanks to longtime friend Dan Blanton for all the information on rigging tackle, fly selection, and fishing the West Coast. He is the most knowledgeable West Coast striper angler I know.

Thanks to the Cortland Line Company and Royal Wulff Products for the fine equipment they provided me with over the years. May they never stop producing the fine products they offer to anglers.

Finally a special thanks to Julie Marsh and Elissa Curcio for wonderful editing. Also a special thanks to Ann Seifert for polishing the entire book and making it a smooth read.

Introduction

There have been many tides since I started writing the first edition of this book in 1988. At the time there were relatively few serious, die-hard saltwater fly rodders fishing the Northeast compared to today's number. And I guess I can take some of the blame, or credit, for this rise. When the book hit the shelves, the boom had just started, and now it's not uncommon to see more fly rodders fishing locations than spin anglers. Given the numbers of anglers that reside along the Eastern Seaboard, it's a fly fishery that had to grow. Anglers began to discover a vibrant fishery right in their own backyard, and the fishing was not as difficult as some thought it might be. The freshwater fly rodders found a fishing treasure that gave them a longer season and fish that were big enough to eat some of the trout they were used to catching.

The sea is an intimidating piece of water; it's large and powerful, and the fish are much the same. There is a perfectly descriptive line in a song by Lee Ann Womack: "Do you still feel small when you stand beside the ocean?" I have fished, boated, swam, and surfed in the sea much of my life. Looking up at a 20-foot wave that is about to break on you is something you never forget—surfers call the experience "seeing God." The answer to Womack's question is yes, and it's why I keep coming back. The thrill and challenges never cease to amaze me.

The great thing about saltwater fly fishing from Maine to the Gulf Coast is that there is so much accessible water to fish, in varieties that will fit any skill level. When teaching saltwater fly fishing, I tell my students to select water that they can comfortably fish, and as they become more skilled, fish more challenging waters.

The advantage of fly fishing is the ability to imitate small food types by presenting a lure that is very lifelike, has great action, and will look alive even when the fly is not moving. I have always believed that a fly is more effective than a spinning lure in certain conditions. What fly anglers lose in distance they make up for in presentation. But it's learning where and how to use a fly's advantages that make the angler more effective. Spending time on the water is key to learning the fishery.

This book does not go into detail about southern waters that harbor fish like snook, redfish, and trout. However, many of the techniques used for stripers, bluefish, weakfish, and the ocean speedsters like false albacore are effective on southern species and along the West Coast. In fact, these techniques have worked well on many species that roam the sea all over the world. Fish that live in salt water search for food. If the angler makes a fly look alive and shows it to a hungry fish, the fish will probably eat the fly. A fishing technique that will fool a striper will also work on a snook or a barracuda. It's what makes this fishery so much fun.

We are not using flies that require special eyewear to tie to the leader. In some cases we can just grab several attractor patterns in a few sizes and go fishing. I have caught over twenty species of saltwater gamefish on one pattern—the Snake Fly. Choose a good fly pattern, and find ways to fish it properly. One of the keys is to keep trying different techniques to catch fish. The fun of fishing is developing a new way to fool a fish. The theme of the first edition of *Inshore Fly Fishing* was **time on the water,** and spending time fishing is the way you learn to fish. The theme of this new book is **keep trying different techniques.** Angus Cameron, a dear, departed friend, always believed that he was going to catch a fish on every cast. This philosophy will make you a better angler because it keeps you trying something new until it works. I've fished the sea a long time, and I still keep finding better ways to catch fish—and if I can do it, so can you.

I hope you enjoy this book—good fishing.

PART ONE

Reading and Fishing Inshore Waters

1

The First Cast

Learning something new is not just for beginners, it's for all anglers. Some experienced anglers may never have cast a fly into rolling surf or fished off a rocky cliff. They might be fishing a new area that requires different techniques, or fishing a new fly type. We all make that first cast with a new line type or fly pattern. It's the way we learn something—by doing it for the first time.

Saltwater fly fishing is not rocket science. I've had beginner students catch fish their first day. The ocean can be intimidating—it's big, but it's not one giant piece of water. This book is about breaking that water into pieces, into sections that are easier to fish. A skilled trout angler looks at a river and breaks it into pools, then breaks the pools into small fishable sections. The same approach works well in salt water—break it into small sections, and fish each section according to its depth, current, speed, bait type, and tide. And **keep trying different techniques.**

The selection of fishing water will vary, depending on the angler. Some waters are not for beginners. A novice should choose protected waters such as bowls, open beaches, or rocky outcroppings with deeper water only a short cast away. Stay clear of steep beaches or rocky cliffs with heavy surf, and avoid long reefs or large flats requiring savvy and local tide knowledge. Fish areas that fit your level of proficiency. This will allow you to gain confidence, and in a short while you will be able to fish all water.

Learn to cast on the lawn, and keep working to become a better caster. Casting long distances is not necessary, but improving your casting skills will help improve your fishing skills. I know anglers that have been fishing for many years that still struggle with casting. People who excel in sports do so by practice and honing their skills. I'm constantly telling anglers to practice their casting on the lawn, using a floating line without a fly, and work on throwing loops. You will not learn to cast on the water; that's the time to fish.

A good time to learn fishing skills is during the day, with overhead sun and clear water. Watching the fly work with different retrieves and noting how it moves at different angles to the current is a good way to understand what the fly and line are doing when fishing in low light. It is wise to start with a floating line because it gives better visibility, then change to an intermediate line to see how it gives the fly a different action and reaches deeper into the water column. Try different fly patterns to see how they work with each line type and what action the fly produces in each water type. A brightly colored fly is more visible and will help you see what the fly is doing.

Daytime observation also reveals the type of bait present and how it moves on the changing tide, giving clues to fly pattern choice and what fly action to impart. Spring and fall, when fish might feed all day, are ideal times to investigate places; combine a fishing trip with a learning experience.

Some patterns are better suited to certain line types and work better in particular types of water. A good example is the great action you get from a Snake Fly with a sinking line fished across-current, yet that fly also works well on the surface with a floating line. Patterns like the Snake Fly are attractor flies made with materials that breathe and give good action. Start with a simple fly selection of several different attractor patterns 3 to 6 inches long in different colors. Learning to fish a few good patterns well eliminates the confusion of trying to choose the right fly from several dozen.

Choosing the best fishing location is not always easy. I look for several things when fishing a new spot. Finding a good food source is very important. Bait along a beach or holding in an outflow makes that location a fish magnet. Bait and moving water are an ideal combination to attract fish. Current along a shoreline, water flowing out of a creek or river, or wave action along a beach will move bait and make feeding easier for gamefish. Baitfish holding along a shallow beach is another good feeding situation because the fish can trap the bait against the shoreline. You might find fish at times when there is no food, but they will not stay very long and their return to the area the following day is unlikely. When I find dead bait pushed up along a beach, I will haunt that location until I find fish. Remember that the bait did not swim onto the beach—it was pushed by gamefish.

How to Find Fish

John Posh is one of my closest friends and one of the best fly anglers I know. John does some talks and clinics for local clubs, and he told me some of the questions that anglers ask about finding fish. The one question I found just incredible was, "How did you find fish before there was the Internet?" It's obvious that the angler never thought about finding fish the old-fashioned way—hard work. You can always tell when a fishing spot hits the press because the crowds land. If the location is fragile, the added pressure will often affect or even ruin fishing quality.

Finding fish on your own does take more work, but it is far more rewarding—because you earned it. Now, some Internet sites are great for getting information about the best time of year, bait types, fly patterns, and the different water types you can expect to find, and they help you find new locations. And when a run of fish is on, at least anglers can go online and make a decision about where they plan to fish. But when a place is targeted, expect it to be crowded.

A big part of fishing salt water is hunting—looking for fish activity, bait, and likely water that will hold fish. Stripers are called rockfish because they like structure. Rocky areas are good places to find bass. Not that they don't feed over sand, but they prefer to hold in or near rocky hard bottoms in areas that have good structure. Pockets of deeper water, locations that have a flow into open water, wave action along a beach, and rocky shorelines are all ideal areas to find fish. Unless there is a good food source, fish are reluctant to move into very shallow water once the sun is high. My favorite type of fishing is sight casting to fish in clear, shallow water, but I know that everything must be right to find fish in these conditions. Usually a good food source is necessary for a shallow location to hold stripers in bright sunlight.

Once you learn a location, picking the right tide, wind direction, and time of year will become second nature. However, you need to fish locations at different phases in the tide to know the best tides or wind directions. Some places might be difficult to fish with a strong west-to-north wind, while other areas might collect bait and offer protection under those same conditions. Spending time fishing different places and learning them well pays big benefits when the weather gets tough.

Trout will hold in a particular section of the river and might spend a good portion of their lives in several hundred yards of water, but saltwater fish are constantly moving and hunting for food. Saltwater species might keep returning if there is a good food source, but once the food leaves, they need to find other feeding locations. The smart angler keeps moving until he finds fish. If I know a place should be productive at a certain tide, but after an hour of fishing it's not happening, it's time to move. Beating a dead horse works once in a while, but I prefer to keep hunting.

The obvious signs like breaking fish or bait spraying on the surface are easy to recognize. Watching bird activity is also very useful. When terns are lazily diving, they are often picking up small bait. If they are active, circling in groups over one location, they are usually on feeding fish. When birds become excited, it's a sure sign of fish activity. Even just having birds continuously flying over water means that there is some form of bait holding their attention. Gulls sitting in a group along a beach are waiting for fish to begin feeding, or the fish were feeding before you arrived and the action had stopped. The wise angler checks that section of beach earlier the next day.

Birds can also give clues to the type of bait that fish are feeding on. Terns feed on small baits like sand eels, spearing, or anchovies, while big birds such as herring gulls want a bigger food source, like herring. The big birds cannot catch small live baitfish but will pick up pieces of dead baits that fish kill. Terns will not bother chasing bigger baitfish because they cannot carry or eat them. A good general rule is: small birds, small bait types; big birds, big bait types.

When you are out searching, a good way to find fish is to find other anglers. Popular fishing places will have anglers if the fishing is hot. The outer beaches of Cape Cod are a good example. If one or several of the ocean holes have fish, there will be bait anglers lined up near the parking lot. When I find six to eight

Finding action, at times, can be as simple as seeing surface-feeding fish.

Often angler activity is a good sign that fishing locations are productive.

cars in one lot, I know that there is fish activity. Boats balled up in one spot means that there are surface-feeding fish in that location. And if boats are constantly racing back and forth, shutting down, then quickly moving to another location, they are on feeding fish. This is all part of hunting, and most anglers will share information. But remember to respect that gift and not broadcast it to ten friends.

Part of learning to fish is developing a routine that gives structure to how you fish. I always begin fishing by stretching the line before placing it into the stripping basket. This eliminates some of the tangling that occurs when fly fishing. Pull off the reel only the amount of fly line that you plan to fish—extra line will only end up in knots. If I'm planning to fish a beach in the morning, I'll stretch the line the night before and leave it in the stripping basket, fly on, ready to fish. The next day I'm then set to go, without spending precious time setting up. Always check the drag and be sure that the reel seat is tight and the rod ferrules are snug. The rod connections are very strong, but a loose ferrule can result in a broken rod. I mostly fish with an intermediate fly line if casting from shore. I would choose a fast sinker in big surf, when fishing off a rocky cliff, or when fishing from a boat. Only when fishing a popper or other surface fly or if sight fishing in 1 to 3 feet of water would I fish a floating line. I usually start fishing with an attractor pattern and change if I'm not matching the bait type.

Before you start fishing, choose a section of water and briefly evaluate the surroundings. Is there any water flow, and how deep does the water appear to be? What type of bottom does it have, and what food types, if any, are visible? If wave action or wind is a factor, pick a location or a casting angle that makes fishing easier. Check to see if there are other anglers in the area and where they are fishing. Knowing the tide beforehand is important—if you are planning to wade a long distance where you will be crossing over an uneven bottom, tide information is mandatory. Knowing the tide could save your life!

I generally begin fishing by trying to cover as much water as possible, casting to different locations like a fan. Too many anglers keep casting to one spot, never varying the casting location. In some places it does not matter, but try casting to different sections of water as much as possible. And keep some casts short to move the fly's location around. This is especially effective in a flow where one angle or distance might produce more strikes. Along an ocean beach with wave action, casting at angles along the beach can sometimes be more productive than casting straight out. Maintaining contact with the fly is essential. Using the flow, casting quartering downcurrent or casting with the wind will keep the line tight so you can feel any strikes. Too much

Use wind and or water flow to help keep a straight line. This is very important for anglers learning to cast.

slack in the line is the main reason for missed fish. This is very important when fishing in low light or at night, when feel is the only way to detect when a fish takes the fly. Fishing in the dark is all about touch. This is when good casting comes into play—it is important to cast a straight line so you are in touch with the fly with the first pull of the retrieve. A short, clean cast is much better than a long, sloppy cast. At night only the better anglers can cast directly into a flow and maintain touch with the fly.

Most anglers develop a fishing routine, casting and retrieving to cover water that does not need special techniques. This works well in some locations—let's say a shallow beach, where simply keeping the fly moving through the water will catch fish—and can be very effective when covering large sections of water. But don't get too complacent; remember, **keep trying different techniques.** We all get into ruts, and it is easy to just keep casting and using one retrieve, eventually becoming a one-dimensional angler. This happens to anglers who fish with heavily weighted flies. They just keep working the fly with a steady beat, moving it with hard, sharp pulls. Yes, they catch fish, but in some locations they never cover the water properly. Different techniques work, and the way to learn where and how they work is to try them. There are many ways to fish a location, and there are many ways to fish a fly and line combination. **Keep trying different techniques**—they work.

Water-Finding Checklist

To decide whether a location is worth your while to fish, begin by examining a section of the water at low tide, with enough light to see the bottom's contour (polarizing sunglasses are helpful). Look for holes, drop-offs, structure, bottom cover—anything that will hold bait or fish and that will give a clue as to the best fishing approach to use. Larger sections of deep water keep fish throughout the tide, but note the small dips that may harbor fish along a beach at night or on a certain tide.

Remember that these very elements can cause a broken prop or a swim to shore; boating and wading safety need to be major considerations when studying water. Holes and drop-offs are to the wading angler what rocks, reefs, and bars are to the boat fisherman. Move cautiously!

Check the area at various tides to see how different water levels appear and what effect each will have. Take notice of sections where rips form because of bottom contour and shoreline shape, and places where bait gathers that might offer gamesters easy feeding. Think of moving water and confused bait, and how they combine to bring good fishing. Tides are important, making some places productive for only short periods—determining when these times occur will require some observation and research.

Vast expanses of water are confusing and overwhelming to the inexperienced. The trained trout fisherman knows that a large body of water only needs to be dissected into small, easy-to-fish sections. But salt water has many personalities: rocky points and cliffs, jetties, flats, river and creek mouths, offshore bars, beaches both shallow and deep. Each requires special techniques adapted to the gamefish's changing habits.

Some locations have several different kinds of water in close proximity, at times requiring tackle or equipment changes to fish properly. Other areas may require similar changes because of tide, wind, or different bait or gamefish types. Often the simple switching of a fly pattern, adding a short lead-core section to the line, or using a different retrieve is enough to trigger action. Determining when to make changes is a subject we'll explore in the chapters to follow, but each angler must learn through spending **time on the water.**

I sat on a rock overlooking a Westport, Connecticut, beach one recent fall, explaining to Eric Leiser, an enthusiastic fly rodder and well-known fishing writer, how to fish a particular corner I have enjoyed since I was a kid. I pointed out the different types of water this little area held. Often we take for granted what makes a particular place productive and fish it just to catch fish, never trying to acquire new knowledge from places we claim to know. New light fell on this particular location as I showed Eric the rip that forms on the incoming tide, moving bait from the large sand flat to the hole in front of us, then forming another rip along the rocky point. Studying the water, I realized why this spot produced so many fish. It possessed good structure, a large shallow sand area to hold bait, a tidal creek at one end, and a large river flooding bait and creating water flow at the other. In 1 mile of shorefront it held every type of water imaginable except surf. And regardless of the tide, there was almost always current flowing, giving anglers many opportunities to locate fish.

Similar fish-holding areas exist throughout the Northeast and mid-Atlantic. But finding the good locations is the problem. Learning how to fish a place from a friend or fishing guide is the easiest and most efficient way to go. But learning to read and comprehend water on your own gives you more confidence, helping you discover new fishing spots or understand better the places you already fish. Learning to read and fish a new place is easy with a little common sense and some research. As the trout stream's secrets unfold for you, so the sea's door will

The presence of feeding birds means there is a food source in the location, and if birds get excited, that usually means fish are actively feeding.

open, with a little waterside watching. Remember, to master ocean fly fishing, nothing beats **time on the water.**

A good example of becoming a successful angler comes from my departed friend Angus Cameron. On a fishing trip with John Posh, we watched the eighty-year-old angler fish feverishly, casting his fly time and again into a hard-running rip flowing over a river-mouth gravel bar on Long Island Sound in Connecticut. His determination warmed our hearts; we hoped that we could still fish with such vigor that late in life. I turned to John, our host for the evening, saying, "Angus hasn't stopped casting since we arrived." John replied, "I hope to have that much energy when I'm sixty-five."

Angus was no beginner to fly fishing, but he *was* new to New England's saltwater fly fishing. This was his first night fly rodding for stripers. When asked the secret to his determination, Angus turned to me in the darkness and said, "Lou, you are not going to catch fish if your fly is not in the water!" This is one of the simple codes that made Angus a successful angler.

The sea can at times appear gray and lifeless, giving little encouragement to the angler unfamiliar with the treasures hidden beneath it. Expecting to catch a fish is the key to actually catching one, and a rip, or moving water, is the very best place to start.

Most saltwater fish need two things: an ample supply of bait and moving water. Find these together and you will find fish; either one attracts gamefish, but together they are an unbeatable combination. Fish do feed in calm water, especially at night when they move into sheltered areas. But moving water attracts more aggressive, less wary predators. A baitfish's defense is its ability to stay in a tightly packed school, not giving the gamefish individual targets. Moving water disrupts this ability by breaking up the schools and separating individuals from the pack. Gamefish feed easily on the confused bait.

I once watched a school of southern gamefish, in crystal-clear water, attack bait along a wave-battered rock formation. While I floated motionless, blue runners picked off the tiny minnows separated from the school by the surf action. Never was the importance of motion and confusion illustrated so clearly to me. The fly rodder's focus is a location that holds bait and creates movement. Saltwater fish feeding in moving water need to strike aggressively; thus, just as the normally sly trout will, in faster water, take a fly that is not an exact duplicate, so will a saltwater fish when there is less time to examine the offering. The well-placed fly that flows down a rip and then into a drop-off, or swings from the white water to the trough, need not be a precise bait imitation to bring strikes.

2

Shorelines with Light Surf

Shorelines with little wave action are good fishing locations for all skill levels. They can offer action for many species all season long and are perhaps the most popular fly-fishing areas. Lobsterville Beach on the Vineyard, most of the shorelines in Long Island Sound, Barnegat Bay, and even many ocean beaches when the surf is low are prime examples of easy-to-fish sections of water. Ocean beaches are affected by both strong winds and wave action from offshore low pressure systems. With protected shorelines, only strong winds can disrupt fishing. The ocean beaches will tolerate more wave action before being difficult to fish, while some protected locations quickly become unfishable.

Slow-moving or still-water areas are easy to fish. Many of them have hot fishing as the tide floods, bringing in food followed by gamefish looking to corner the bait for easy feeding. Coves, pockets, or anywhere food collects or is trapped is a potential fishing place. Fish feeding in calm, protected waters are detectable by sound and even sight in low-light periods. At these times the fish show when surface feeding, and once located are easy to stalk.

Any sheltered area or backwater bay will have protected water, and some of these places might offer good fishing even in strong storms. These areas are ideal for wading or boating, and the boat angler will be able to cover more water and reach areas inaccessible to the wading angler.

During the fall shorelines such as Lobsterville on the Vineyard see activity all day long, with bluefish, false albacore, and bonito feeding just beyond the surf fisherman's reach. Many anglers fish these areas exclusively from boats, finding their range far greater than that of the shore fisherman. Any number of craft will work, providing there is ample casting room and the boat is safe and seaworthy. Some fishermen even use small craft like canoes, kayaks, and prams, weather permitting, to reach the productive areas beyond the shore angler's casting range. Beaches throughout the Northeast have seasonal all-day offshore fish activity, offering the small-boat owner extended fishing opportunities.

The boating angler needs to be cautious, using oars or a pole to get close to working fish in still, shallow water. Always assume that there are fish in

Along with wading, calm shorelines are ideal boating locations, but be respectful if there are wading anglers fishing along a beach.

the area and approach any fishing location in this manner, even when there is no apparent action. Even anglers using canoes and kayaks need to move slowly and try to keep noise to a minimum. Deeper water also requires a careful approach to avoid spooking feeding fish. The boatman must calculate wind and tide, using them to quietly position the craft for easy casting.

The wading angler, however, can still fish quiet shores, for many times fish push bait onto the beaches in a feeding frenzy. Certain beaches lend themselves perfectly to light surf fly rodding because of their large shallow areas, making the quiet entrance of a shore fisherman more productive.

Both boat and wading anglers can fish this kind of water with the same technique. The only difference is casting direction, and here the wader has an advantage. A fly swimming from shallow to deep water gives the fish ample time for investigation. A fly moving toward shore looks like an escaping baitfish, possibly prompting a gamefish to hit.

In the absence of significant tidal flow, use a retrieve to give the fly a lifelike appearance. Retrieves may vary in speed and length of stroke depending upon fly pattern, bait type, species of fish sought, and water conditions. On calm

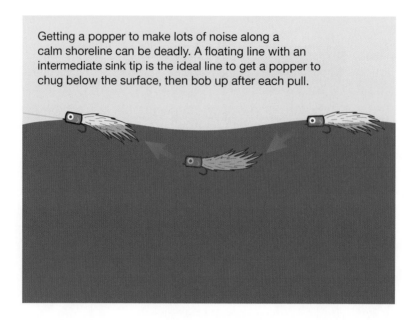

Getting a popper to make lots of noise along a calm shoreline can be deadly. A floating line with an intermediate sink tip is the ideal line to get a popper to chug below the surface, then bob up after each pull.

nights a slow-working top-water pattern, such as a Snake Fly or foam-headed fly, that leaves a surface wake is deadly. Pulsating flies with plenty of action, worked with short jerks, are also effective. Work small patterns like shrimp or worm flies this way, using a floating line. Fish larger flies with an intermediate line to enhance the action. The line will pull the fly under on every strip, giving it a struggling appearance as it bobs up, then dives below with each pull. This technique works in any flat, calm situation and even enhances fly action in moving water. Poppers also work well with this method on calm mornings or evenings, bringing fish from great distances to investigate the sound. For this reason, long casts are generally more effective with top-water bugs, because the gamefish require time to locate them. Depending on the line type, some intermediate lines will work a popper, but usually a floater or sink tip is a better choice when fishing a surface bug.

Without top-water activity, and if the water is deep enough, try fishing a high-density line with a 7½- to 9-foot leader and a buoyant fly. This combination keeps the fly off the bottom but will still fish the lower section of the water column. In shallower water, use the same leader and fly system with an intermediate line. Try to cover as much water as possible, concentrating on any structure located along the beach. Weedless or inverted flies on keel hooks are a good choice in locations with rocky bottoms.

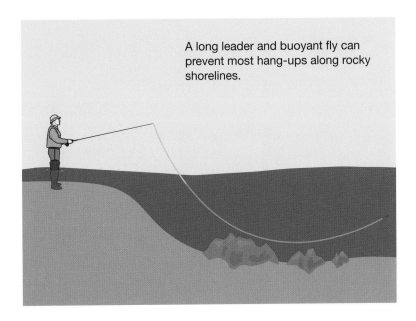

A long leader and buoyant fly can prevent most hang-ups along rocky shorelines.

Deep fishing in calm areas can also be productive at night if the gamesters are foraging for bottom baits or feeding deep on schooling baitfish. Employ the same methods used during the day, but use bushy, dark fly patterns. Bottom-bouncing can be productive on those slow, seemingly fishless nights. But remember to also try fishing a floating line with a buoyant fly along the surface. Try to move the fly slowly so it leaves a surface wake. When you think the fly is moving too slowly, cut the retrieve speed in half—a slow crawl can be deadly at times if you have the patience.

On beaches where they frequent, keep looking for bonito or albacore. These daytime feeders are not shy of sunlight and can hit a beach with the right water depth at any time. Below the Frisco pier on the Outer Banks in North Carolina, I once ran into a school of albacore on a calm, bright morning. The fish worked up and down the beach for over an hour, feeding wildly on bait. Always expect action along a beach.

The ocean speedsters can be tough foes when they are spot feeding, moving quickly up and down a beach. I have watched anglers try to cast to feeding fish with little success. Fly tackle is not suited to making casts that quickly—there are times when even spinning gear is not fast enough. When fish keep popping up along a shoreline, just keep casting, working the fly along the shore. Often the fish will pass by when the fly is in the water and you will hook up while

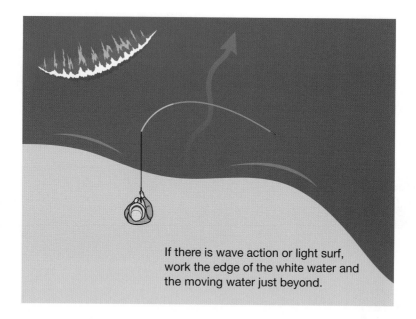

If there is wave action or light surf, work the edge of the white water and the moving water just beyond.

fishing blind. There have been times when I've hooked a fish with no surface action, or the action started after I was already onto the fish.

If there is any wave action, keep working the edge just outside the white water. Many beaches offer ideal fishing when 1- to 2-foot waves are rolling along a shoreline. Unless the beach is very shallow, work the deeper water with an intermediate line, fishing the fly right into the beach. Much of this fishing is blind casting, just covering water. Along most shorelines I like to keep moving, covering as much water as possible unless I find bait.

For the serious night angler, these open, easy-to-wade shorelines are tailor-made. Even on dark nights walking is safe, and often the fish are close. Some places are good on any tide, with incoming being the prime tide in most locations. On calm nights look for swirls or splashes close to shore. There are locations that produce ideal fishing right along the beach, and the angler that wades too aggressively might walk beyond the fish. If fish are feeding close, stay tight to shore; don't walk on their dinner table.

Along any shoreline it's wise to observe the different water levels and wave actions and how they affect and change its characteristics. A seemingly flat beach has small dips and pools that at high water harbor bait, and these give fish holding spots. Mark and memorize these places, for they produce fish. Any small depression will allow both bait and gamefish to sit, not needing to work

Along ocean beaches when the surf is light, fishing and wading can be easy.

as hard to hold along a beach, particularly when there is wave action or moving water. Just think of the small pockets in which trout lie.

Tides affect beaches in different ways, depending upon the beach's configuration, steepness, water flow, and wave action. If there is wave action, ocean beaches do not need a tide to create water flow, but a tide will fill the holes, giving more water depth. This brings in bait and gamefish, making many open beaches best for fishing during the last two hours of the incoming and the first two hours of the outgoing tide. Gentle-sloping beaches can be good on low incoming tides, when the angler can wade out and fish moving water as it floods the shallows, bringing bait and gamefish activity with it. A tidal change can trigger feeding action along some beaches, turning fish on as the tide starts to rise or drop. Tide creates water flow, moving not only bait but gamefish as well—and this movement generates feeding activity.

3

Small Creeks

Pocket-size sections of water are usually easy to fish. Often a mid-distance cast will cover the entire creek, and many small outflows are productive only at the mouth. Most large systems harbor a number of different water types. Flats, points, rock piles, and small creeks and streams within the major system offer a variety of fishing opportunities, and the largest require time to explore. All large estuaries have tiny creeks spilling into them, but many small pieces of water also exist along bays, sounds, and shorelines. These streams, though not large in size, offer impressive angling.

Fishing Small Creeks

Water flowing from a sheltered location is a potential fish-producing area, for it flushes food and creates motion in the area into which it empties. Some water flows are so small that they go unnoticed. I remember fishing Shelter Island in New York with one of the locals who showed me a creek that ran into Hay Beach. When I asked him where the outlet was, he said, "You just walked over it." It was so small that I missed it in the darkness. Yet this little flow attracted fish during a short period of the tide because it forced bait into the open water. Although not a major hot spot by any stretch of the imagination, this little creek demonstrates the importance of water flow, no matter how insignificant. Most good outflows release enough water to make fishing interesting, with the stronger or larger ones the most desirable to fish. The creek systems I discuss in this chapter are the small ones: Most of the creeks do not have enough water depth to hold feeding fish during a tide. However, there are also small outflows that feed ponds where fish might swim up the creek on a big tide to access the pond.

Most small creeks and backwater outflows are only good on falling tides, when they empty their rich volume of food into a larger body of water. There are two basic kinds of creek systems: One is a small opening that drains a larger backwater bay or tidal pond; the other is a network of streams looking like forked lightning running through a marsh. Either system spills through a small opening into a bay, sound, or ocean.

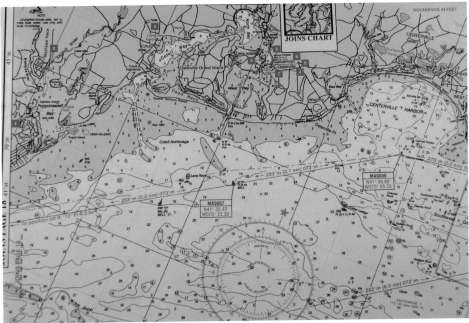

This photo shows how a creek or outflow will appear on a chart. Note the number of creeks and flows there are in just 10 miles of shoreline.

On a nautical chart ponds appear in blue, located near the shore, often showing a cut to open water. Some are marked "creek" or "inlet," and the larger ones have breakwaters to protect the openings. Marsh creeks appear as shaded areas with clumps of grass. The larger ones are marked with a blue line, the smaller ones with a black line. There are also ponds on both Martha's Vineyard and Nantucket, opened by the state at given times of the year. These openings bring hot fishing, but only the locals know when this occurs.

Outflows are generally simple to find, but are not always easy to reach. Many are private, in prime residential locations, and others are unreachable due to tricky wading. Certain creeks sport soft mud and steep drop-offs, offering little backcasting room. However, in some areas a quiet nighttime approach will open up many good spots to the careful angler. If the area is large enough, a small boat will give access and the ability to cover more water. Sea kayaks are ideal for the wading angler to gain entrance to small water.

The simplest system to fish is a bay emptied by a creek. Wading is usually much better here than in a marsh creek, and the only information needed before fishing is the eddy's cycle. When the outflow will start discharging hinges upon the creek's mouth and the back-bay size. The outward water flow begins at some point after high tide, when the bay's level reaches the height of the outside water, stops filling, and begins to run out. Creeks with small openings frequently run out later in the tide, and continue to run out until well into the incoming tide. If the back bay is small, it will fill and run out soon after high tide. But if the opening is too small, large bays never reach the outside water level. The small mouth does not allow enough water into the bay in a six-hour period to fill it. This causes up to a several-hour lag time between the beginning of the outgoing tide and the creek's outflow.

The mouth of a small creek is best for fishing as the current first starts to flow out, and can be fished right through the tide. Some outflows run into a rip flowing along a beach, enhancing the fishing properties of both. Very small creeks may only be productive right after high tide, because they are too shallow once water levels drop. Larger outflows are good right through the tide, and can be hot on low incoming tides as the outflow continues to pour out while the incoming tide begins to flood.

A typical clear-water small creek. There are vast numbers of small outflows that empty into bigger water.

Smaller creeks with a good-size bay to empty are fast-flowing near the opening but without sufficient volume, and the current dissipates quickly. This makes the area around the mouth most productive, unless the water travels for some distance over shallows with a good rip, making fishing productive along the entire flow. The fast water just before the mouth will probably be void of fish, because they have to work too hard for their food there. But each water flow is different, and a few casts into the fast rip are always worth a try.

Each creek flushing a back bay requires experience to determine when the water starts spilling out. Each system is an individual with its own time schedule, and most have delays from one to two hours. The same holds true for marsh creeks: Their flows vary depending upon the makeup and size of the system. Different-size tides, like moon tides, affect both flows, further complicating the discharge time. **Time on the water** is essential for creek fishing.

Periods of low light are the normal times to fish small outflows, unless they flow into an ocean beach or deep water (but these are generally larger outlets, discussed in chapter 5). Night or dark days are the best times because most creeks spill into fairly shallow water then, making them hit-and-run places for gamefish, especially weakfish, which generally disappear at the first sign of light. However, in early spring clear-water areas might produce feeding fish and good sight fishing in broad daylight.

The major advantage to fishing a small outlet is that fish are concentrated within several hundred feet of the mouth—and sometimes the fish will feed in even a much smaller area. On calm nights a pop or swirl indicates feeding activity, and the fish sometimes hold in the current like trout. One night I heard bass feeding on alewives in a shallow creek in Connecticut. One fish in particular broke upcurrent, making a smack that caused me to jump. The swirl was only 20 feet away uptide, and a short backcast put the fly on the fish, but slack line caused a missed strike. Walking toward shore, I took a position above the fish, allowing the fly to swing to its lie on a tight line. It hit on the first drift: The twenty-pound bass was feeding, holding in one spot in 3 feet of water.

Weakfish feed in the same manner: holding in one position, taking food as it floats by. During springtime the creeks flowing into both the Peconic Bay and Gardiners Bay on Long Island, New York, are famous for this type of fishing. During the good runs of the late 1970s and early 1980s, many creeks throughout the Northeast produced good fishing.

Because it is much like trout fishing, many beginning saltwater fly rodders learn the sport on small marsh creeks. It is the closest fishing salt water has to

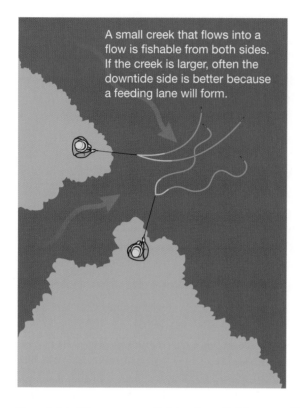

A small creek that flows into a flow is fishable from both sides. If the creek is larger, often the downtide side is better because a feeding lane will form.

nymphing, where the angler, with a short line and light fly rod, just keeps swinging the fly on a dead drift without working it. (This is one of the few places where I would use a 7-footer for a no. 6 line.) And there are times when you need a near-perfect float to make the fish hit.

Working small creeks requires the angler to be quiet, have patience, and learn to develop the touch to hook fish that sip the fly rather than grab it. Blundering into the water with a splash, snapping a false cast on the water, and other such disturbances will disrupt the shallower areas, sometimes ruining them for the night. Never use a light when fishing small creeks. Wade back to shore to change flies unless it's a long distance, then keep your back to the fish and shine the light into your waders, using only the glow to tie knots. A small, flexible gooseneck light is ideal for this purpose.

When checking for bait, walk up inside the backwater, away from the fishing location, to prevent spooking the fish. If shrimp are present, they should appear in the backwater, floating in the current, with their little eyes glowing as they reflect the shining light. Take several minutes to observe them—you will notice that they generally float in a straight position and bend only when moving. I tie most shrimp flies with a straight silhouette, for this is how feeding fish see them.

Shrimp, killies, spearing, sand eels, and spawning sandworms are common baits in a creek system. Depending upon the water's location and the time of year, all these baits are important. This is the reason for checking the backwater, to identify which bait is present. The way fish feed often indicates bait type. A noisy splash generally suggests swimming baitfish, while a steady pop or sip

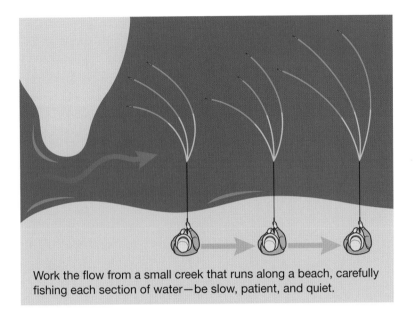

Work the flow from a small creek that runs along a beach, carefully fishing each section of water—be slow, patient, and quiet.

from one position means drifting bait, like shrimp. Sand eels and spearing float with the tide and sometimes bring the same feeding response. In any case, fish the fly on a dead drift, and if one pattern is not working, keep changing until you find the proper fly. In most cases, unless there is a large abundance of one type of bait, a streamer pattern will regularly take fish. There are always small minnow-type baits in backwater areas.

One night Joe Falky was working a fish in one of the town creeks on Shelter Island. After he made repeated casts, I asked, "Joe, why don't you try a shrimp pattern?" Joe's reply was, "If I get the right drift, the fish will take this fly." Sure enough, with persistence the fish finally took his favorite weakfish fly, a single-winged white bucktail streamer. Now, maybe a shrimp pattern would have taken the fish sooner, but in this case proper fly placement was Joe's key to success. Working a stationary fish in a creek is similar to casting to a stream trout taking nymphs. The key is lining up the float: A fish holding, feeding in one location, probably will not move far to take. Some fish demand a precise over-the-nose drift to bring a strike. The float itself need not be drag-free, for most bait is mobile, with some action. A hatch of cinder worms is a good example of how fish will take up a feeding position and hold tight. If the worms are thick, fish easily feed with very little movement.

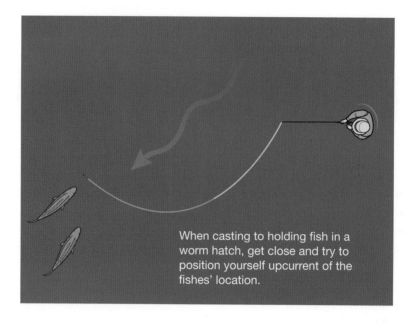

When casting to holding fish in a worm hatch, get close and try to position yourself upcurrent of the fishes' location.

The best fishing position is upstream; make a quartering cast above, then swing or float the fly down to the fish. The fishing technique is similar to working a rip, only try to continually work one spot rather than covering the whole area. Many times a number of casts are needed to find the proper feeding alley, especially if the fish are taking shrimp or worms, which are numerous and float right to them.

Similar to fishing a rip, vary both the distance and position of your casts to get the fly to pass through the fishes' feeding stations. The important thing is to get close to the target. Unless it's flat calm, distance is hard to judge at night. Because most fish are surface feeding, a floating line and a neutrally dense fly is the best setup.

Do not hesitate to try a retrieve if drifting is not working. Proper fly movement can trigger a strike, and on some occasions a pulsating action might be the trick that takes fish. When you encounter groups of fish in a small creek, the fishing can be less sophisticated. Competing for food, the fish are generally not as selective and take much more aggressively. Depending upon the creek, the fish, rather than taking up feeding stations, either work back and forth along the mouth or up and down the current. A long-running current may have fish feeding the entire length, and a creek that spills into deeper water and dissipates might have fish feeding along the front, moving in and out of the current. Pops, swirls, and splashes will help locate fish. Either way, work the flow, covering the water like a rip, casting to different locations on the water. You need to find the correct drift or fly action needed to take fish, using the shortest possible cast for better line and fly control.

There are times when no surface action is evident, yet fish are feeding, especially in the deeper locations. The fish may be taking food near or under the surface without making detectable top-water commotion, or the activity goes unnoticed because of choppy surface conditions. In either case, work the water carefully. No matter how small the section is, it will require time to cover adequately under these conditions. Few patterns are necessary, and a floating line covers most situations. Fish the fly in every section of water, using varying line lengths, floats, drifts, and retrieves to cover the water. Picture this section of water as a condensed rip needing every ripple investigated. As a rule the fish are not competing here, and with abundant food, feeding is easier than in other locations.

I prefer fishing small creeks with a short line, wading down or along the current. Move slowly, a few steps at time, working each section while watching or listening for the slightest indication of feeding fish.

For most small outlets, wading is the most effective way to cover the water. Some creeks do lend themselves to boat fishing if the angler is careful. Apply the quiet approach, using the same procedures called for in flats fishing, but in some cases with more awareness. One mistake could spook the creek for the night, while the same mistake would disrupt only a section of a flat. The silent approach of a canoe or kayak is useful in locations not accessible to the wading angler. Even a float tube could be used in some places with light current or a large section of uneven, non-wadable bottom. Keep away from faster water where current could pull you offshore, for float tubes are not the most maneuverable of craft.

A boat's major benefit in a creek is the ability to follow fish if they move out of casting distance. The disadvantage is the risk of spooking water when approaching, for some sections must be sacrificed to position the boat. When fishing from a boat, work the water in the same manner as you would when wading, try each parcel carefully, and fish the fly right to the boat before casting again.

4

Rips and Moving Water

The outgoing tide flowing over Sugar Reef off Watch Hill Point, Rhode Island, was ideal for fly fishing. There was just a small ocean swell, about a 10-knot southwest wind, and only one other boat. The conditions were right to drift, and once I found the fish, I planned to break out the anchor. About halfway down the rip, a small pod of stripers started feeding. We hooked up one, and by the time it was landed, the boat had dropped below the best water. On the next drift we saw several fish follow the fly above the first location, so out came the anchor. There seemed to be several slots where the fish kept coming to the surface, but they didn't stay long and were not feeding aggressively.

After anchoring I noticed several small pods of butterfish floating in the rip, and as I watched they drifted into the slot and fish rose to feed on them. The bait was small and this was why the fish were picky and not feeding normally—usually in rips fish feed with a vengeance. This was an ideal scenario for fishing a small fly and an intermediate line with little action to the fly. The key was getting the fly around the bait and giving it just enough action to mimic a small baitfish looking to rejoin the school. That day the fishing was tough because the bait was small and not very mobile. But we still took enough fish to have a good day, and the fishing was very technical, which made it special for rip fishing.

In bigger rips when the water is rolling hard, the fishing is often down and dirty, with fast-sinking lines, bigger flies, and a fast retrieve. But when conditions are right, there are many different techniques required to take fish in moving water.

Flowing water needs special attention and requires practice to fish correctly. Give moving water major concentration when fishing the salt, for this flow generates action for many fly rodders. Fish feed in this movement. Whether it's a wild, turbulent, windblown rip or a long, slow-moving section of shallow water, it is *the* place to cast your fly.

What Is a Rip?

Most types of water will form rips. Rips take shape as the tide rises and falls, moving water over bars, in and out of inlets, around points, and over flats.

When water is forced or constricted, a rip or tide line appears, creating a faster than normal water flow. Wind also creates movement by causing wave action along a beach, which in turn forms rips along the shore or in the cuts between bars. Either or both actions together bring gamesters inshore or up top, searching for food and within reach of the fly rodder. A rip need not be strong or large or long-lasting, but need only flow in a given period, moving bait and fish to the angler and giving the fly action.

Certain rips appear as a dark, choppy line that forms below where a bar, reef, or structure ends and the deeper water begins. This section of choppy water is a prime place to cast, but just above and below it are also productive locations. Some rip lines are narrow, running only a short distance before flowing into deep water. Others run for long distances, with holding water throughout. Certain rips are slow, and announce their presence through pressure against your waders, a pull on the anchor line, or the feel of the fly line as it sweeps the fly to one side. Rips can be very strong and are not always associated with big tides—Nantucket's Great Point rip could sweep an Olympic swimmer backward on a tide that fluctuates less than 4 feet.

Rips serve much the same function as does the flowing of a river or stream, bringing food to and making feeding easier for gamefish. However, unlike a river's current, which is consistent for extended periods, rips in salt water can change direction every six hours, and within that time vary considerably in speed. Although this sounds confusing, it's really simple. The tide is high every twelve hours, low in between, and in some locations is predictable to the minute with a tide chart. Other spots, especially backwater locations, require local knowledge, and these areas I will discuss when mentioning different

Big, shallow locations might have fish holding for hundreds of yards. Large flats, banks along river mouths, and big bays will have many acres of shallow rips.

waters. Additionally, wind and the moon phase can affect tide. After learning an area, you can predict water flows and depths and fish them with confidence.

Fishing a Rip

It's important to fish a water flow systematically. Let's wade out into a shallow rip flowing around a sandy point and fish it. If it's dark or in low light, walk slowly, feeling for drop-offs. Before wading too far, try a few casts. Fish feed near shore and your approach will spook them—I have taken fish while standing on dry ground, casting to knee-deep water. To establish the rip's speed and flow, watch the water's surface. Movement and speed of top-water debris, "foam," or bubbles help determine the best way to fish a section of water—it's similar to using bubbles to check a river's flow when fishing a dry fly. This technique is useful on all but the darkest nights.

Dead-Drifting the Fly

Standing in thigh- to waist-deep water, make several casts across-current, letting the fly drift; swing downtide and tighten up at the end of the drift. Try giving the fly action as it dead-drifts, swings, and starts to turn upcurrent. Bump

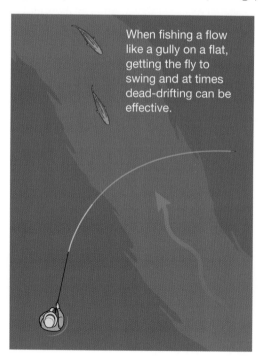

When fishing a flow like a gully on a flat, getting the fly to swing and at times dead-drifting can be effective.

the rod tip or pull without retrieving with the stripping hand, making the fly pulsate. Here is where the two-handed retrieve is very effective because it offers a variety of ways to impart action to the fly (see chapter 14). This simple float, swing, and turn can be so successful that it should be the first choice of fly action when a rip is strong enough to move the line and fly briskly.

Dead-drifting is useful in all but the slowest currents, is best suited to faster flows, and is mandatory with swift tides. The flow needs to carry the fly in the manner of a struggling baitfish fighting to reach sheltered water. The only drawback to this method is excess line; long casts in fast water can create slack line, and strikes can go unnoticed. Shorter casts (40 to 60 feet) give the angler better line control and should be used in the stronger rips if possible.

Adding a stripping action might also provoke a strike. Depending on the rip's speed, vary the retrieve to keep the fly moving. Use a steady retrieve in slow current; swift rips necessitate a slow retrieve or dead-drifting to make the fly appear lifelike. At the drift's end retrieve the fly, using different stripping speeds. Get the fly to swim upcurrent in a struggling manner, or allow it to hold in one position while you apply pulsating rod action. Although unnatural-looking in a fast rip, this last retrieve can be effective and work well in strong water flows if fish are holding below a drop-off.

Covering Each Section

When fishing flowing currents, cast to different positions and vary the casting distances both up- and downtide to get various swings, depths, and actions from the fly. Fish a rip by covering sections, like standing in the middle of a series of bowling alleys. Attempt to work the fly through each section, fishing the fly from above, through the center, and below the faster water. The secret to fishing a rip adequately is thoroughly covering each piece of water. Some anglers get into a rut casting to one point on the water, limiting themselves

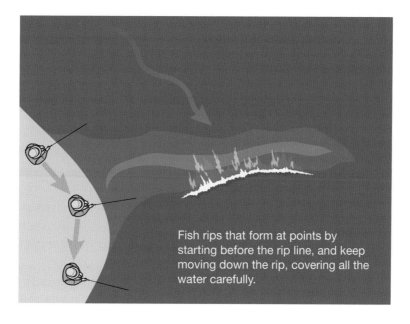

Fish rips that form at points by starting before the rip line, and keep moving down the rip, covering all the water carefully.

to one swing pattern and only a small section of fishing area. Like fishing the sections of a stream, moving up and down the shoreline puts the fly into different locations. Oftentimes moving just several steps positions the angler into the right fly-presenting spot. Fast-flowing, short-running rips generally concentrate fish along a thin band, making a small area of that kind of rip best to target. Position becomes essential, so work such water one step at a time.

After working a location with an intermediate or floater line, try switching to a sinking line and work the water again. Fishing deeper, faster water may demand more penetration (getting the fly down). Offshore rips often require Hi-D lines to reach deep-feeding fish.

There are miles of flowing water open to the long rodder who is willing to work hard. Some of this fishing is pounding the bottom. Even though much of the water is 10 to 20 feet deep, reaching the feeding zone is not always easy. However, with the right bait type and tidal flow, at certain times during the season, fish might be located well up in the water column.

Offshore Rips

Water boiled heavily over the bright sand, rushing with a force we could hear. Our first two attempts to anchor were futile: Hard sand, combined with the fast rips, made it tough to hold bottom. But the boat finally held above the rip line in easy casting distance of the hole below. As we watched, an albacore cleared the water, feeding among the slower bluefish. Bait drifting over the bar was easy prey for the feeding fish, and shadows or swirls indicated their presence. We hoped our offerings would bring the same responses.

One cast answered our questions, as bluefish swarmed upon our lures like mosquitoes on exposed flesh. They were hitting anything that moved—the four- to six-pound blues competed to get hooked. That day I saw bluefish, albacore, bonito, and a nice striper up on a bar. We took numerous bluefish and managed one bonito. The usually selective bonito surprised us by taking a 7-inch swimming plug. It was my first introduction to clear-water offshore rips, and even though we used spinning gear, I knew I wanted to fish these locations with fly tackle.

Only on an offshore rip is this kind of action possible. In September and early October some rips host a variety of gamefish, with action all day long. The larger areas at times have such numbers of diving birds and breaking fish that it's impossible to decide where to fish first.

Offshore rips occur all along the Northeast coast. One large area of shoal waters includes the numerous rips in Nantucket Sound. This is the biggest

Offshore rips can produce big fish all season long. The author took this nice striper with Captain Bob Luce while fishing rips between Monomoy and Nantucket off Cape Cod.

area of open shoal water I am familiar with, and it ranges from the south shore of Cape Cod to outside Nantucket. It runs west over to and including the waters around Martha's Vineyard, with a large portion open to the sea. Similar, smaller areas exist throughout the Northeast and mid-Atlantic, and all are fished in the same manner.

On days of light wind, some of these rips look like a good section of river for rainbows, but so much bigger. Some sections have a number of rips, one after the other. Don't let the size or numbers bother you—think of each rip as one piece of water, and fish them one at a time.

The rips that occur in these bodies of water are awesome. Sandbars rise up from 40 feet in some cases to just below the water's surface. Many areas have shoals in the middle of nowhere, with surrounding water only several feet deep. Wind, waves, and tide all combine to give such locations some of the best fishing and worst boating of any waters in our region. During periods of brisk wind, or in ocean swells, only the most experienced sailor with a seaworthy craft should attempt fishing these waters. Even on calm days, boats of under 20 feet need to run home at the first sign of a breeze. Winds, at certain times of the year, can come up fast, turning the rips into death traps. Night fishing is for pros only.

Larger ocean shoals, banks, and rips are marked as such on nautical charts, showing up as irregular meandering blue sections over the deeper water, marked white. Some appear marked with a buoy. Those far away from a channel may not be featured on a chart, except as low numbers surrounded by a dotted line indicating the water depth at mean low tide. Always expect some changes from the chart in the larger areas, because wind, waves, and tide constantly move the sand. Other locations, because of continuously shifting bars, are not diagrammed. They will appear on the chart only to alert seamen of hazardous navigation.

Characteristics of Offshore Rips

The deeper rips change little from high to low water, unless the rip is on the north side of Cape Cod or above. Large tides make low water the best time for fly fishing, if all tides are good. Fish the shallower banks on incoming to high tide. Stay to the edges on falling water to prevent being trapped. My wife and I and a 23-foot Mako spent several hours stranded on the backside of Tucker-nuck Island off Nantucket because I stayed too long on the bank. She slept—I looked for clams.

Many offshore locations have moving water with good currents on rising and dropping tides. But the rip's direction is important. Look for areas with a flow from or over the shallows that dumps into deeper water. This makes one side of a bar superior to the other, and the tide that brings this flow is best. Isolated rips with one bar and decent-flowing current on both the coming and falling water might be good on all tides. Such locations require patience, because you must wait out the tide. Yet these areas are generally easier to fish. They're small and need less specialized knowledge in order to be fished.

Larger locations, with multiple bars and numerous fishing spots, force the angler to know the area well. Thoroughly covering the water is necessary because the productive places change, sometimes with each tide. When an area has much good water, try to fish and learn several places well, rather than hopping all over and never covering the water adequately. Usually the downtide area, below the rip, is the most productive, and some rips are superior to others because of bait presence, wind, better holding water, or the direction of water flow. There are times when slack or slow tidal flows can be hot, particularly in the morning when the fish are up in low water, grubbing sand eels at first light. (Stripers especially like to feed in this manner, for the bait is at their mercy.) But certain rips go slack for only a short time, and much depends on tide size and wind direction. **Time on the water** is the only way to learn how various conditions affect the water.

Do not disregard open-water areas below the rips, especially during the spring and fall, when top-water bait is present. Watch for breaking fish or working birds in the larger green-water areas. Then approach either from uptide or upwind, drifting into the fish with as little commotion as possible. Get to them quickly, because they will generally not stay up for long. I have taken bluefish and bass in this manner. Bonito and albacore move too swiftly, and chasing them in a boat is difficult.

Flying in a plane over this clear, tropical-looking water, seeing the drop-offs, bars, and rips while spotting schools of fish in the shallows, should excite any fisherman. I remember one experience like this a number of years ago, when I was fishing the shoals off Tuckernuck Bank, near Nantucket. Lack of wind allowed me to work outside bars in a small boat. Bluefish were cruising in 2 to 4 feet of calm, clear water. The action resembled southern flats fishing, with groups of fish swimming from the hole up into the low water, feeding on sand eels. A well-placed popper brought an immediate response. And the entire sequence, from the fish turning, then approaching, and finally striking, was as if displayed on a Hollywood set. It was ideal fly fishing.

However, setups as perfect as this are few. Sometimes the rips are unkind, rolling, wind-chopped, and angry, requiring on the more difficult occasions fast-sinking lines to reach the lies. While the wind conditions can bring great fishing, casting from a tossing, wave-battered boat is hard work, and the fly rodder must hustle to earn each fish.

Squid are an important bait that appear in the spring and, with luck, stay late into the season. These fast-swimming baits hold well up in the water column and pull the fish out of the holes and onto the bars. They are far and away the best friends of fly anglers. If conditions are right, there might be stripers holding along the bars several feet below the surface, looking for squid that roam the bars also in search of food.

Many large areas that are not ideal pleasure-boating sites have surface feeding all day throughout the season. Bass favor both the early and latter parts of the season, and bluefish occur throughout. The ocean species show up in late summer, staying until the autumn storms chase them offshore.

Work the water as you would a large rip, swimming the fly from the bars into the holes. A lot depends upon current speed, water depth, time of day, and types

Strong rips in big tide locations might require a sinking line to fish properly.

of fish present. Without top-water action, work the drop-offs below the rip, flowing over the bars with a fast-sinking line. Cast the fly onto the bar, above the rip line, then fish the fly so it drops on the swing into the hole. Casting above the hole gets the line deeper, so it will drop into the hole's slower water and avoid the swifter surface current. A good trick is to cast well uptide and let the line and fly drift. This allows the fly to descend well below the surface. As the line swings down the flow, use a fast retrieve with long, hard pulls. Try different angles to the current to find the best flow and swing. **Keep trying different techniques** to find the best way to reach the fish.

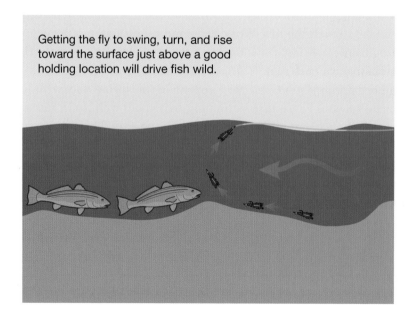

Getting the fly to swing, turn, and rise toward the surface just above a good holding location will drive fish wild.

A sinking line might be necessary when fishing deeper bars (over 10 feet), even if the fish are on the edges. A heavy tide would never let a top-water line get the fly to the fish. With an ample supply of bait on the bar, it's unnecessary for the fish to rise to the fly. Sometimes reaching the feeding level of the fish is the only way to catch them. In very fast, deep locations, use the deepest-running line you have, as there are places where reaching the fish can be difficult. A lead-core shooting head is the best choice to fish very heavy rips. It requires a special setup and is tough to cast, but lead-core is the most effective line to obtain deep penetration. Deep, fast waters in some locations might be unfishable with fly tackle.

When bonito and albacore are present, they both produce a deep surface boil that makes a chugging sound, or they show by greyhounding along the water's surface. Fish for them with an intermediate or fast-sinking line, trying different retrieves to bring a strike. Fly speed and action seem to be the key with either fish, but at times fly size and color is important, too. Both fish are fickle, and hard-and-fast rules don't apply, so experimentation will be necessary on each outing. Anchoring and holding in one spot is a good way to work these fish, if drifting does not work.

Fish with top-water lines during low-light times, when the fish should be up feeding with the changing light. It is very exciting to watch a big fish bust a top-water bug in a rip. Dusk and dawn are prime fishing times, but if fish are feeding in bright sun, it's even better. Remember, baitfish do not adjust well as the light varies, and gamefish have easy feeding then; good surface and subsurface action is possible. Work your fly along the bar's edges with a slow retrieve, casting at different angles to the rip. If the rip is not too swift, fish might be feeding on the bars, picking sand eels as they rise from their beds. A slim pattern worked over the bar should get any fish's attention.

In daylight in clear water, bars show up brown, and dark green indicates a hole below the shallows. Fast-sinking lines are a must if fish are holding in the deeper water well below the drop-off. In the deepest sections, heavy current may prevent the fly from getting down. I would concentrate on the shallower areas unless fish are showing.

With adequate light, fish are visible. Look for them cruising over the bars. Even if they are not surface feeding, they frequently will take a properly fished top-water offering. As with other places, unless the water is too deep, top-water flies and poppers pull fish up, particularly in clear water. They work well even in strong sunlight. Depths of 2 to 6 feet are ideal both for spotting and bringing fish up. Remember, the faster the current, the harder it is to fish deeper waters.

Working Offshore Rips

There are three basic ways to work offshore rips. The first two are free-drifting to cover as much water as possible while floating downtide, and anchoring to fish a rip from a stationary position. Both methods are discussed in chapter 7, on fishing a reef. As in a rip over a reef, fish use the current over a bar to feed and hold. Some of the drop-offs on offshore bars are akin to those of a reef, except that the bars lack structure. Use either of these techniques in moderate sea conditions only, when the rips are not too turbulent. As with reefs, once you find gamefish it's better to fish for them from a holding position. Fly action, line control, and covering the water adequately is better from a stationary position.

The third approach is to hold above and along the rip, using the motor to keep the boat in position. This allows the angler not only to fish from a stationary position, but also to slide along the rip line to work the entire length of the bar. In this way, locations and water conditions that are difficult to fish any other way can be met effectively.

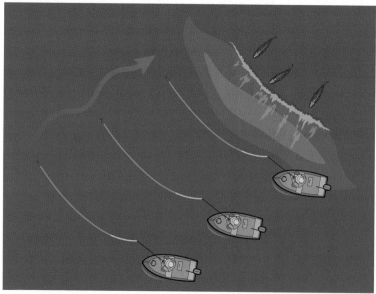

When drifting down a flow above a rip line in a boat, cast across the flow and let the line sink. Just at the rip line, start your retrieve using long, sharp pulls.

Anchoring can be difficult and dangerous in the deeper, faster rips, for a slipped anchor may put the boat below the rip, into turbulent water. One person needs to concentrate on running the boat, facing the bow into the rip and applying enough power to keep the craft from being pushed over the bar. Slide along the bar, angling the bow slightly to one side using motor and rudder, maintaining a slow glide along and just above the rip. Wind can make the maneuver more precarious; a novice should never attempt this in dangerous waters. This practice works as well in heavy rips over reefs, where anchoring may be hazardous. Most charter boats fish rips in this manner. In locations with structure just below the surface, this is the only safe way to fish. (Remember, hooking a fish with the motor in gear disqualifies it as an IGFA record.)

As the boat slips lengthwise to the current, keep casting along the rip's edge, working the fly to resemble a baitfish fighting the tide. Cast at different angles to the rip, both retrieving and letting the fly hold in one position by imparting a fluttering action with the rod tip. Without any sign of fish, work with a sinking line, trying to get the fly into the hole. But keep watching, because fish can show at any time and must be dealt with quickly. Fish do hold in the holes, sometimes staying for long periods, but don't count on this.

Fishing Conditions in Offshore Rips

With the congregations of gamefish that invade during late summer and then build to a fall climax, be prepared for a variety of fish types and fishing situations. Without local knowledge, the help of a friend, or the use of a good boat, most anglers will be at a loss in these places. Many good guides are available, and some specialize in fly fishing. A good guide service can help the novice not only find fish, but also learn how to fish these areas. Experienced anglers fishing new locations or different water might want the assistance of an expert as well. But before making this choice, be sure the guide understands fly fishing and that you both realize what to expect from each other. Ask the guide's advice as to tackle needs. When tackling big rips, my advice is to go heavy, for most rips are strong, and lifting fish from deep water is difficult. Expect windy conditions, with the necessity of a sinking line a good possibility.

Bigger tackle will generally work in most situations, but the opposite is not true. Fishing a rip off Martha's Vineyard, and too lazy to change rods, I used a no. 12 line for bonito. Most top bonito anglers believe light lines and leaders are a must, yet I tried the heavy outfit anyway and did better than my partner, who was using a no. 9. Incidentally, he is a much more experienced bonito fisherman than I am.

Some offshore fishing environments do not lend themselves to fly tackle, so the angler or guide needs to choose one that does. Unfavorable conditions will always be a factor in offshore rip fishing, making fly fishing there a challenge, even with the best game plan. Weather is a major consideration, particularly in locations open to the sea, where ocean swells or high winds could make fly fishing difficult. It doesn't hurt to have some spinning tackle along, and a good captain will.

Bass and bluefish are the major visitors to these waters, frequenting the rips throughout the season, with the ocean speedsters invading in midsummer if the location suits them.

Because of the ideal surroundings, sand eels are the major baitfish inhabiting sandbars throughout the season. In some cases their dominance is so strong that you could fish one fly with confidence all season long. In some of the bigger offshore rips there can be smaller inshore sand eels 3 to 5 inches long and big offshore sand eels 7 to 10 inches long. Small, sparse yellow or green-and-white sand eel patterns work well, but also have some 8-inch-long eel patterns in yellow or black and yellow. Another good pattern is a white Deceiver. Schooling baits of the herring, bunker, or mackerel groups, along with squid, appear on the deeper rips, and some spearing hold in rips closer to shore. But the sand eel is king in the fall, and when no other bait activity is evident, stick to long, thin patterns. In the spring and summer, squid might be the dominant bait, and this is the ideal food source to bring the fish closer to the surface.

Offshore rips need top-water bait to make them fishable. The deeper holes do retain fish, but these are beyond the reach of the fly rodder. Bird activity—not just the funneling over feeding fish, but terns picking or diving along a rip or over the bars—is a vital positive sign. Birds feeding indicates ample small-bait supplies to draw fish up within range of fly tackle. Surface bait is the key to fly fishing fast-running rips.

5

Estuaries

A flow or current running into any larger body of water creates ideal feeding conditions for most species of fish around the world. The jungle rivers of Central America pouring into the Caribbean, a cut emptying a Bahamas flat into open water, a stream into a river and a river into a lake, sound, or sea are all locations where water flow enhances the fishing. In the waters of the Northeast, this kind of flow is even more significant because many of these currents come from estuaries, and their waters are rich with food. Their discharge in spring and late fall is warmer than is the cooling water of a sound or open ocean.

Estuary-marsh systems have several distinct characteristics. They are located inside the protection of a land mass and are connected to open water by at least one creek or river outflow, though some might have several sources of water that fill and empty the major body of water. They all provide a spawning and nursery area for gamefish, baitfish, and crustaceans. Quite simply, they are the major reason why sea life exists close to shore in salt water. For gamefish, estuaries are a food-producing machine.

One of the major differences from one system to the next is the amount of freshwater that enters the main body. There are systems that are almost pure salt water, like Pleasant Bay on Cape Cod; mixed systems, like Chesapeake Bay; and big river-marsh systems, like the Kennebec in Maine. Some estuaries are river systems that run for miles, while others are small ponds that have a small single opening. The elaborate nature of each marsh type would fill a book in itself. My objective here is merely to give enough information to allow the fly rodder to fish each of these types of water successfully.

Two special events occur in many backwaters: the invasion of big baits like blueback herring, menhaden, and alewives; and the worm hatch. The spring runs of big baits can offer fishing for big stripers. After spawning, the baits move back into the open waters of estuaries, where the fish are waiting. When conditions are right, this is a great opportunity for big fish on fly tackle. Unfortunately, overfishing has devastated some of these good runs, and only time will tell if they come back. Later in the season menhaden show up, and there can be good runs right into fall.

The worm hatch or cinder worm—actually the spawning cycle of the *Nereis* worm (also called clam worms or sandworms)—falls right into what a long rodder is looking for. With this small bait that is easily matched with a 3- to 4-inch fly, the only gear needed is a light to midsize fly rod and a floating line. Often the casts are short, and at times locations are packed with fish—and some are big. The worm transforms, swarms, spawns, and dies, often in about six hours. The big worms grow to 2 to 4 inches long, and swim through the water in a spiraling flow. They often leave a small surface wake. In some locations they hatch on new and full moon tides, while other places have spawns that last up to a month. Each hatch is different, and there can be completely different scenarios from one location to another. Some hatches only occur at night, but other locations can have hatches in the morning or afternoon. Weather is a factor, and cold fronts with wind will disrupt the hatch—hot, still weather is best. In places with night hatches, the ideal tide is high outgoing after nine o'clock. The falling tide triggers the hatches, and the serious worm-hatch anglers fish through the tide, looking for activity. It's easy to recognize these anglers—they develop dark circles under their eyes, looking like raccoons.

Fishing a Worm Hatch

Spawning worms occur in many locations, but usually they are associated with areas in or around estuaries. A full-blown worm hatch is an event that anglers never forget. Fish bust all over, and often they are difficult to take. One problem is that one day the fish are cooperating, but the next day everything changes. Usually too much food in the water is the problem. Orange, red, or black fly patterns 3 or 4 inches long that have active materials and leave a surface wake work well. A small pattern with a spun deer-hair head and a marabou wing is a good choice. Use a floating line, and try to keep casting to feeding fish. In a location with current, fish will take up feeding stations and hold like trout. Take a position above a feeding fish and try to keep swinging the fly by the fish's nose. If the hatch is heavy, fish will not move very far to feed—they don't have to. Get upcurrent of the fish, using a straight or quartering downcurrent drift, and get the fly close. At night try to get close to the fish's position, within 25 to 40 feet.

Don't get rattled! When fish start busting all over, try to concentrate on one fish. If there is no pattern and the fish are scattered, keep a tight line and keep casting lengths to less than 50 feet if possible. Remember, these fish are feeding on a slow-moving target that is not trying to escape. Too much slack or a big bow in the line is poison. Often the fish are just sipping the fly and gliding forward, so the take is light. At night any slight pull or tap is usually a fish. With enough light, don't be afraid to make a strip-strike if there is a surface disturbance close to your fly's location.

I have had limited success fishing during a hatch with an intermediate line and a 6- to 7-inch-long olive or orange Snake Fly. If nothing else is working, try fishing below the surface using a medium-fast retrieve with long pulls. This can also work when the hatch is slowing down. I think that as the worms start to disappear, some fish will cruise around, looking for any leftover food.

Mixed Fresh- and Saltwater Systems

Backwaters, bays, estuaries, river systems, and small creek systems are basically marsh areas with mud-peat-type banks that have tall grass or reeds growing in them. Grassy mud banks are a sure sign of an estuary. Depending on the location, these waters have bottoms of mud, sand, gravel, rocks, or a combination of these. The marsh's size or location determines what types of water are in the system. Small marshes might be fishable only at the mouth; the big systems usually harbor all types of fishing water except surf. Excellent fishing opportunities exist where each system empties into open water, and beaches, jetties, flats, and structure near these openings are very productive.

With the exception of larger rivers and bays, many backwaters empty out much of their water twice a day. This flushing chases bait to different areas within the system or moves it out into open water. This outflow is important, for it creates the two key ingredients necessary to good fishing: breeding ground for bait and moving water. When scouting new fishing locations in estuary systems, look for outflow areas—they are the best places to start.

Water outflows appear in all sizes and shapes, from tiny step-over creeks to the Hudson River. The Hudson is really a system in itself, providing a major spawning area and a nursery system for a number of species, including the striped bass. The results manifest themselves miles from shore, in the great blue-water fishing in the Hudson canyon.

My longtime friend John Posh showed me this when he ran his small boat upcurrent, looking for an opening in the marsh grass where a creek spilled out into the main river. Seeing the cut, he dropped power, eased the craft over a bar at the creek's entrance, then entered the backwater. I watched in amazement as the depth recorder's numbers started to rise, reaching 17 feet before we anchored alongside a grassy bank. When I quizzed John about whether the motor would spook fish, he assured me that because of the depth and the constant movement of the fish, there would be action before long.

The hole was unique: There were two creeks flowing in and feeding the pool, and one emptying it. The largest flowed in at a right angle to the pool, undercutting the bank. The meeting of the currents created a strong whirlpool, and a perfect fish-feeding environment. As we readied our tackle and allowed the water to settle down, several fish began feeding in the pool's quiet water to the left of the small creek. I started to work this section located off the bow as John fished the faster water below the stern. I had several 5-inch-long orange Deceivers to try. Judging by the swirls, the fish were small, leaving only minute rings as they fed against the bank. I hoped the fly was not too long. My fourth cast brought a solid take. To my shock the water erupted as a good fish exploded, running from the sheltered water to the protection of the cut bank. The fish's size caught me off guard. However, the line cleared the stripping basket, and once on the reel, I applied pressure to roll the fish from the swirling current.

The boat's position, which permitted easy fishing, now made landing the fish difficult. It required pulling the fish up and across stream to reach the eddy behind the boat. The fish fought in midstream, finally swimming across the current and back into the pocket where it had been feeding. From here I could bring it back across and down the slower current, and swing it into the quiet water behind the boat. John quickly netted the fish, and as rapidly as possible we tagged and measured the bass. We revived the striper and set it free: 30 inches—a prize in such sheltered waters.

Feeding lanes form where creeks and rivers flow into the main body of an estuary. If possible, fish the downtide side of a big flow and the uptide side of a small flow.

Any time you find two flows merging, whether it's a small flow into a larger one or two flows of the same size, fish it like a small trout creek flowing into a big river. A feeding lane will form where the flows meet, and just like the feeding lane of a trout stream, it will hold fish. Stripers like to hold and feed in these locations. Often such places hold bait or have bait flowing into them. Whether you are fishing from a boat or from shore, keep fishing the fly across or along the feeding lane. Try both dead-drifting to make the fly swing into the lane or casting into the lane and retrieving the fly through the holding water.

Some tidal estuaries are the arms of the sea where fresh and salt water meet. These backwater locations are formed when a river system, large tidal creek with freshwater, or a combination of both blends with the sea. This union creates a protected zone linking fresh and salt water, connecting the mingled flow to the ocean. Most large rivers, like the Connecticut or the Piscataqua in New Hampshire, and the entire Chesapeake Bay system have a complex tidal network of bays and creeks that offer exceptional fishing. Some of the deeper waters hold trophy fish.

The Chesapeake Bay, an enormous expanse of water, offers hundreds of miles of back-bay fishing. It encompasses two states and includes five large river systems and numerous streams, bays, and coves, all with countless fishing opportunities. (As of this writing there are restrictions to fishing for striped bass in the Chesapeake; check the state game laws before fishing.) Many other locations have similar layouts, perhaps not as large but with the same common denominator: a mixture of fresh and salt water, rich with food, which acts as a breeding place, nursery, feeding ground, and home for many sea creatures. The food chain from the marsh to the sea is critical, making these areas important fishing locations. Like the Chesapeake, other areas have systems within a system that provide numerous fishing opportunities in each small section.

Most estuaries appear on nautical charts as a green or horizontally lined grassy section, marked as a marsh, with a blue-colored river or large creek running through it. Large complex systems show sizable sections of either rivers or backwater bays, and there are individual charts to aid in navigation. These helpful maps give water depth and bar, creek, and bay locations. They are well worth purchasing.

Tide sizes greatly affect the appearance of a backwater. In most cases a larger tide gives a stronger current flow, making the northern estuaries—Cape Cod and north—faster-flowing and more changeable. However, small tides can produce strong currents, and the large volume of water exiting a marsh gives certain sections incredible force. Those who have visited the Chappaquiddick Bridge on Martha's Vineyard can attest to the force a 3-foot tide can develop.

Drainage Outflows

Many tidal systems are large and spread out, with miles of creeks, and contain cut banks, holes, bars, and drop-offs. Each flow is a potential fish-holder. Many drainage cuts appear in marshy areas, either dug during the 1930s by WPA workers or occurring naturally. The man-made cuts run in straight lines, while the natural flows meander like dark snakes across the estuary. At low tide the cuts are obvious. But covered with water and concealed by grass, they are a hazard for waders at night. These holes can be deep, with sharp drop-offs.

Drainage gullies run into small tidal creeks, creating a flow into a flow and concentrating fish in certain places along the creek banks. When a marsh begins to empty, these little ditches are the first places to have water movement and discharge into the deeper, larger water. Fish feed at these locations, working the outflow, taking bait as it is swept into the main creek. These areas are also productive when the main creek begins to flow, causing back eddies along the banks below each discharge. Such small outflows, although not major fishing spots, can be productive and are good places to try at higher tides. Listen for feeding fish holding below the outflow. Fish these areas in the same way you would work a small creek. When wading, be careful not to create ground vibrations. If fish stop feeding upon your approach, wait several minutes until they start up again. Work the areas with current flowing into deeper water. If the water is shallow, don't wade too close: Fish from 30 feet away, casting into and across the flow. Use floating or intermediate lines, and let the current swing your fly on a drift into the backwater, then retrieve the fly up along the bank.

The boating angler can fish from the middle of the creek, casting to each bank and working the outflows while moving downcurrent. Casting straight into the bank allows a longer drift than casting from shore. From a boat it's possible to cast and then mend the line downcurrent, making the fly swim along the bank for greater distance.

Larger Creeks and Deeper Areas

Falling tides are best for most systems. The dropping tide seems to trigger feeding: The fish have either entered the system with the coming tide or have been waiting for the falling tide to begin to feed in the outflowing water. The uppermost, shallower sections are best just after a high tide because the fish start here first and then work into the deeper water, feeding on the way. Many spots are hard for the wader to reach and a boat will only spook the fish, although accessible areas are worth fishing just after the tide starts to move. Fish the reachable upper areas first, then move back with the tide and find the deep sections with creeks flowing into them. These areas might collect and hold fish, allowing concentrated fishing as the tide drops. If you find such a place, try sitting there for a given time as the tide goes out: Waiting in these locations is unique because you hear the fish coming, working their way into casting range.

Fish take up feeding stations along creek edges, darting from sheltered spots into the faster water, using these rips to find food. This is mostly top-water or subsurface fishing, except in early spring when the fish are sluggish or in the daytime when the fish hold in deeper spots. A floating or intermediate line covers most fishing situations. Use a sinking line only during the day or when there is no apparent surface activity. In the larger, deeper locations, fish might hold in the holes and drop-offs, providing hot action for the angler willing to probe with a fast-sinking line. Fish such an area like an offshore or deep rip by casting to different places in the hole, swimming the fly through the water.

Location and position are important to a boating angler. A sinking line needs time to penetrate the flowing water to reach deeper sections. This may mean anchoring farther away from the drop-off to give the line and fly time to sink. Place some casts well above the hole so the line catches the current along the edge and then tumbles into the hole. If you are fishing pocket-size sections, positioning is more important. Changing anchor length or moving a few feet up- or downcurrent could help you place the fly in just the right spot.

More open areas, those of the main sections of the river or bay, should be fished according to the water there. Large rivers and bay systems will have every type of water condition except surf action. It's important that the angler analyze the type of water found and apply the proper fishing technique. The back bay's protection is ideal for a stormy, harsh atmosphere when many other locations are blown out. But the open, large sections pose a threat to small boats, chopping up quickly on a tidal change, as wind combining with a rip turns the water turbulent. Larger bays can turn rough without tide as the water walls up in the shallows, making some sections fishable only from shore. Heavy wave action at the mouth, or along a bay shoreline, may make the water too dirty, pushing fish to deeper water. Fishing experience is the only way to know where to fish, and when the weather is too rough to fish.

Estuaries do offer shelter during storms. Many times action improves as fish move in for refuge, riding out the rugged open-water conditions while still being able to feed. Smaller waters offer flat conditions in even fairly strong winds, allowing a sheltered location in which to fly fish. While many other locations are unfishable with a fly during bad weather, most backwaters allow some protected fishing—and at times the action can be hot.

Cut Banks

The one fishing situation unique to a marsh is the cut bank. Any stream trout fisherman can verify that overhanging banks hold fish, and getting a fly to the fish in such places is tricky. Because of the soft nature of a marsh's ground material, the banks change more frequently than freshwater riverbanks do. Avoid walking on the edges of banks; they can cave in underfoot, toppling large chunks of sod into the main flow. The best approach is to walk above the bank, casting straight across or quartering downcurrent, allowing the line and fly to swing into the overhang. Concentrate the drift and retrieve mainly on the cut bank, but fish the backwater, too. Retrieve upcurrent slowly after the drift, fishing the fly carefully along the bank. If the flow is strong enough, hold the fly in different spots, causing it to pulsate while suspended in place.

Most bends along an estuary creek form pools much like those in a trout stream. Fish may be found in the slow water's back eddy. If possible, fish these holes from head to tail, but keep back from the cut areas of the bank. Fish several different patterns and use a sinking line if the hole is deep. To cover the

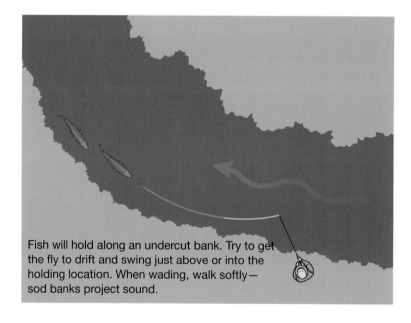

Fish will hold along an undercut bank. Try to get the fly to drift and swing just above or into the holding location. When wading, walk softly— sod banks project sound.

water completely, work the area thoroughly with one setup, then walk back up and fish the entire hole again with a different setup.

The boating angler can fish these banks in the same way, using as little motor as possible in the smaller water. Casting from a boat will allow a better drift, making the fly more lifelike.

Unlike cut banks in a trout stream, which provide feeding stations as well as homes, marsh banks are dining-only. This is true even for very large holes, even though fish might stay in these places a little longer. This means that not every likely looking bank will hold fish.

Working an Estuary System

The bait types present influence how to fish a section of water. Estuaries offer a larger selection of food than any other type of water. This makes bait identification significant, not only for pattern choice but also for pattern action. Check the bait near where you want to fish but be careful at night, when a light might shut down the action in your fishing spot. Large hatches of worms and shrimp will occur throughout a marsh, but specific baits will differ from one place to another, necessitating a light check. One night, after you've finished fishing, shine a light on the water to see the different kinds of life present. The numbers and types of baitfish, crabs, shrimp, worms, eels, and other creatures

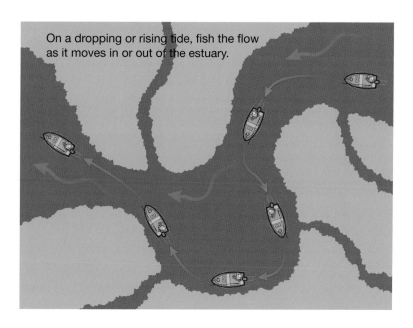

On a dropping or rising tide, fish the flow as it moves in or out of the estuary.

are amazing. When one food source doesn't seem to dominate an area, try a spearing pattern or a Snake Fly.

The better holes in a system retain fish for some time, offering, in some cases, several hours of fishing. If the fish are moving quickly, using a boat is the best way to follow them: Even if they travel only several hundred feet, a marsh's broken shoreline might prevent the wading angler from following. The vast amount of shoreline in larger systems is unreachable to the wading angler, and a boat is required. Without the mobility of a boat, the wader must be content to fish accessible water, working it hard and hoping the fish will be there.

Work the falling tide, starting from the smaller, shallower water and continually backing down with the fish until you reach the estuary's main body. Here the fish should continue to feed, moving into the deeper holes or flowing out to open water with the tide. Upon reaching a large bay or river system, the fish begin to work back up the tide, feeding as they go. Larger systems are fishable at all tides—reaching the fish is the only problem.

Because of their size, the larger systems demand more research than any other type of water. They have numerous water flows, cuts, holes, bars, and rips that continually alter with changing water levels and current direction. In addition, these areas can become discolored with larger amounts of freshwater, making the water hard to read. Again, the boater has an advantage: With a depth finder an angler can poke along at high tide, find the holes, cut banks, and drop-offs, and cover large amounts of water with less time and effort. Northern bays and rivers demand special care from a boater. Many sections harbor rocky ledges that rise to the surface and can "bite" the prop or lower unit. The rocky contoured coasts of Maine and New Hampshire, combined with large tides, require more research than the soft-bottom areas that make up most estuaries. Since any section can contain hard structure, learn the water before moving about at high speed.

With almost continuously moving water except during a slack high tide, there is always potential for feeding activity somewhere in an estuary system. Fish these rips as you would any moving water, with the larger, faster sections requiring the same techniques as for a large ocean rip.

Larger estuaries stretch out for miles, extending from the upper grass shallows all the way to the sea. Some anglers spend lifetimes fishing these systems and continually unlock previously unknown treasures. Changes occur constantly because of weather conditions that modify the delicate balances within the system: New and different fishing spots form each year, and new types of food and gamefish are brought to different locations.

Fishing can begin early if a location is extensive enough to hold wintered-over striped bass. Some larger areas have their own striper breeding populations. Bob Pond, inventor of the Atom plug—a man who has accomplished much to help conserve the striper—tells me there is a brood stock as far north as Nova Scotia, with separate breeding areas located along the coast to Virginia. The rivers of the Chesapeake Bay system and the Hudson River are the major striped bass spawning areas.

Shallow bays, exposing their mud bottoms at low water, attract fish on incoming to high tide. Bait moves into these protected waters to feed, followed by the gamefish. In spring the sun's rays bake the mud, making shallow bays warmer. Many times fish are surface feeding along the shoreline, chasing bait. Poppers or top-water flies are ideal for this fishing. Weakfish show soon after the bass, feeding at night in the small creeks, along banks, or on the flats, usually retreating to deeper water at first light. Bluefish are the last to arrive, appearing first at the mouths of many systems. Depending on the season's rainfall, they may not venture into a main system like the Chesapeake; they might wait at the mouth for freshwater levels to fall, or they might move north, missing the area altogether. (Unlike bass, which breed in brackish water, the chopper's tolerance for freshwater is low.)

Once they enter an estuary, bluefish feed virtually all the time, depending upon bait activity. The best periods for the wading angler to fish for blues are evenings and early in the morning. In larger areas boating anglers can have nonstop top-water bluefish action all day.

Weakfish feed actively in spring and early summer, working the night tides. They prefer the small bait-filled creeks. Weakfish leave all but the largest systems in mid- to late summer. Bass, though notorious for night feeding, can be active in the daytime during the spring. In some large systems they will feed erratically in the daytime throughout the summer. Fall brings the hottest bass feeding time. Large amounts of bait near the mouths of estuaries attract schools of gamefish as they pass by, making water around an opening a hot spot during the fall run. Some outlets attract migrating fish that move up into sheltered waters for several days to feed before moving on. Not only does the abundant food draw the gamefish in spring and fall, but warm water spilling from the system will hold the fish, too.

Saltwater Estuaries

It was after first light and the jetty at the mouth of Menemsha Harbor was still vacant, even on a Saturday during the derby, with a good incoming tide. Walking the beach to the stones, I could hardly believe my fortune. After an unsuccessful predawn outing for stripers, and a first-light crack at bonito or albacore along the beach, I was trying to salvage a fishless night. I hoped I could take an ocean speedster from the jetty.

My luck ran out, however, as several other anglers arrived while I was climbing the rocks. One of them, Dave Foley, had fished Lobsterville blow with me the night before, and he had worked hard after my departure, without a touch. We took places along the rocks, giving the spin fishermen the end so as not to tie up the tip where four or five anglers could fish in our two places. There is a nice rip that forms along the jetty on incoming tide. The current runs down the beach, hits the rock wall, flows around the tip, and rushes past the harbor and into the back bay. The flow moves bait to the jetty, then into the estuary, giving the fish easy pickings, creating a feeding line about 40 feet out. This line was the focus of my fishing as I kept working a small white Deceiver through the shearing water.

With an early ferry back to the mainland, time was limited, and as my departure time neared, the line tightened at the same time a flash appeared where my fly had been. Fly line flew from the stripping basket, indicating an ocean speedster, and the run was hot, with backing whistling through the guides as the fish ran off. The spin fisherman to my right yelled "Stop casting!" and to my surprise everyone did. The fish was now swimming parallel to the shoreline, and I walked quickly to shore, telling everyone to continue casting and just watch my line. Reaching shore, I was able to land the fish, a nice seven- to eight-pound bonito, without difficulty. I saw now that the fish had started to feed regularly, but the ferry would not wait. I waved to Dave and headed home, knowing that, with my limited time and the crowded conditions, I'd been fortunate to make that catch.

Marshes are not always associated with river systems. Many such areas contain all salt water with only small feeders of freshwater running into them. These places tend to be very clear. Cape Cod and Long Island lack freshwater rivers, and most of their back bays are saltwater estuaries. Rhode Island does have several small rivers, yet it still has a number of saltwater ponds that flow gin clear with breachways, harbors, or river mouths connecting them to the sea.

Pure saltwater estuaries are my favorite areas to fish, for they offer the chance to work good fish-holding water with less effort than other locations require. Some locations offer good sight fishing either at the mouth or up inside. There are creeks in Maine that begin to flow in about two hours into the tide. The fish start to flow in when the water level at the mouth is several feet deep. On the ebb, look for fish to begin spilling out at the beginning of the outflow. If the creek has holding water, some fish might stay in the deeper sections right through the tide. These bodies of water provide the possibility of taking many species, always with the likelihood of big bass that frequently venture into such locations to feed. The number of large fish in back-bay areas is surprising, and because the water is clear, these bays are easier and safer to fish.

Most saltwater estuaries on a map or nautical chart show a narrow opening running into a large pond or back bay. Some systems include a harbor holding large boats, like Pleasant Bay in Cape Cod or Great South Bay on Long Island. These systems are large and need to be broken in small sections for fishing, as we have done with other waters. Smaller areas, like Cape Poge Gut or the Ponds on the Vineyard, and the breachways and ponds of Rhode Island, provide great fishing at their openings, and for the adventurous angler great fishing within the system. But like tidal river estuaries, they take time and experience to master.

Nantucket and Martha's Vineyard have unique estuaries, attracting such inshore and offshore gamefish as bass, blues, weaks, bonito, and albacore. I

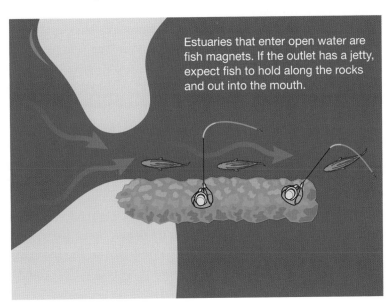

Estuaries that enter open water are fish magnets. If the outlet has a jetty, expect fish to hold along the rocks and out into the mouth.

witnessed a run of bonito and albacore in Edgartown harbor on a Saturday during the derby that was unbelievable. Although not ideal for fly rodding because of the mob, without the crowd it would be fishable. Across the island, Menemsha Bight and the blow to the southwest is a haven for fly rodders. Both shore and boat anglers gather there when bonito and albacore are running. First light on an incoming high tide puts fish right along the beach. With the rising sun the fish move, gathering into the rips in front of each jetty. The entire Lobsterville Beach is ideal fly rodding, with the outlet adding another dimension.

Characteristics of the Saltwater Estuary

Most pure saltwater estuary systems have the same general appearance as a tidal estuary, with large areas of marsh grass, a network of creeks, and sizable expanses of water throughout. But unlike river marshes, which tend to have soft bottoms, saltwater estuaries have mostly hard bottoms, which makes them easier to wade. The systems with strong tides have footing that can be like concrete, but shifting sand bottoms still occur throughout the system, sometimes after each tide. The bottom sections close to a system's mouth are least stable, and in areas where the sand never settles, the ground can be mushy underfoot. The footing is most stable near cuts protected by a break wall, which keeps the mouth open and stabilizes the bottom. Only the back areas within the system have dark, muddy, clam-flat bottoms.

Many systems have small openings with extensive backwaters, similar to the creeks we discussed in chapter 3. A lag time in the tide occurs here, but because these systems are larger than small-creek systems, the water flow can be much more forceful. (Several spots on Cape Cod have rips resulting from large tides that are frightening, cutting sand from beneath the angler's feet with the force of a high-pressure hose.)

Tide movement is not terribly significant in these systems, because there is always moving water and feeding fish somewhere. (Learning the particular patterns of specific areas within a system is important for fishing success; the angler must find out where and how fish move.) At most outlets the beginning of the outward flow is best. Some can be hot right to the ebb, and the lower water can make things easier for the fly fisher. Some locations (such as in Pleasant Bay on Cape Cod) are best at the first part of the incoming tide as the bay water rips out, flowing over the rising incoming water. Unfortunately, most anglers leave before this tide begins.

Larger openings, say 100 feet wide, are good as water starts flowing into the bay, moving fish through or bringing them from the bay to the rip. Incoming tides put fish at ease, allowing them to roam without risk of being trapped. Falling tides take fish to the deeper sections, concentrating them there as the water level recedes. The openings around these deeper sections serve as fish funnels when the water rises again, unless the deep section is large enough to hold them at all tides.

Moving water is the key to fishing these systems. Rips form over bars, around points, across flats, in narrow channels—any place constricted flow will develop good current. Even larger sections will have adequate flow due to the enormous amounts of water passing through the system. Many places in a saltwater estuary are similar to a flat or shallow rip and should be worked in the same manner.

Larger systems are similar to river systems, with much the same kinds of water, which can be fished in similar ways. Most saltwater estuaries are void of structure, with sand or gravel bottoms and deep cuts, holes, cut banks, large flats, and ripping water throughout. Use the basic fishing techniques for these kinds of water. It's not necessary to get fancy; use what works and what feels good to you.

For most situations, I prefer an intermediate line, unless the section is very deep or very fast. It's best to try a top-water line first, then to go back, after thoroughly covering the area, with a deep-running line. When fish are feeding, they'll usually come up for a fly. But there are times when the angler must reach the feeding level to take fish. In these situations, getting the fly down is the only way to interest them.

Although boats are more effective for fishing estuaries, wading can be very productive, and in some locations the quiet approach might be better.

Eelgrass, a long, narrow, ribbon-shaped nuisance, can make fishing marshes a chore, and at times impossible. Moon tides, wind, storms, and commercial shellfishing are some of the factors contributing to large amounts of grass in the water. A weedless, cone-shaped fly will allow fly fishing in all but the worst eelgrass-infested areas. Sometimes the weed will be thick only near shore, allowing a fishable retrieve throughout most of a drift.

As with big tidal estuaries, the boater can cover more ground in a saltwater marsh than can the wader. But because the water is so clear, a boat can spook fish easily, and those locations reachable from the shore should probably be fished by wading. This is especially true in areas with narrow openings, where an outboard motor will alarm fish. The places that spill into open ocean have wave action that makes boating dangerous.

Fishing Fast Water

Areas with deep, fast water require special attention in a saltwater estuary. Dealing with heavy rips within the system or at the mouth may pose a problem: They can create bows in the line, preventing the fly from appearing lifelike and not allowing the fly to work naturally under the surface. The best way to obtain line control and proper fly action in these situations is to fish a short line. Cover the water by moving around it rather than by casting a long line: Casts of 30 to 50 feet are ideal.

Work as you would if you were nymphing, covering each parcel of water thoroughly. Once you learn the feel of a dead drift, try this technique, which works in rips of all speeds but is especially useful in strong currents: After casting, feed another 10 feet of line out through the rod tip, keeping the tip high. As the current takes the line, drop the tip and fish the fly through the swing. Even in a fast current, the fly will get some penetration during the free float, swinging not only across the current but also toward the surface. The fly will look like a baitfish coming up to the surface—an inviting target. **Keep trying different techniques.**

This technique is also effective with sinking line and can be used with various mends. Toss the fly across-current and roll-cast additional line downstream, then either dead-drift or retrieve. This gives the fly the look of an erratic, fluttering baitfish traveling downcurrent, then suddenly turning and trying to escape upstream. For additional float and depth, allow more line to slip after the roll cast. This is also a deadly technique in freshwater rivers and streams.

Fishing Conditions in a Saltwater Estuary

Pure saltwater systems are ideal locations for the marine fly rodder. Clear, protected, fishable, easy-to-reach water combines the look of the tropics with the flowing currents of a trout or salmon river. Some waters hold all major game-fish; the possibility of hooking and landing a big fish exists on every outing.

Unlike river systems that may have both winter-over and spawning activity from stripers, salt marshes have only scattered off-season populations. They need migratory movement to bring gamefish. Bass and weakfish arrive first, starting to show in early to mid-April, working up the coast in a northerly flow. Some groups of fish appear at almost the same times in scattered locations along the shore. This indicates that there is an offshore flow of fish that travel the open ocean, cutting in ahead of the inshore migration. This is especially true of bluefish, which arrive in Martha's Vineyard at nearly the same time they move into the Chesapeake Bay in Maryland.

The best period to fish a saltwater system depends upon the time of year, species of gamefish sought, size of the fishing location, and the amount of human traffic within the area. Most active daytime feeding happens in the fall as gamefish cast caution to the winds, feeding heavily for their move south. The gin-clear water makes striper fishing primarily a low-light game, except for the less-traveled places or the mouth areas, where wave action plus deeper open water could hold daytime-feeding fish. Offshore species, bonito and albacore, are daytime feeders and are not bothered by boat traffic; in deep water they will chase a boat to strike a lure, but constant harassment will drive them from shallow locations. Blues are more skittish, but in a feeding spray or during the fall, they will feed all day long. Weakfish are spooky in the clear water, feeding entirely at night.

Dark rainy days, especially in the fall, bring action from blues and bass, and depending on the location, bonito and albacore could mix in. Small areas, with the exception of openings, have mostly night, dusk, and dawn fishing. The larger, deeper places may have action throughout the day if boat activity is not too intense.

Locations with large holding waters have resident fish all season, providing there is ample food. Bass are prone to settle in a convenient place and return there each year, with some fish spending much of their active lives in one area. Weakfish locate and stay in large mixed-water bays like the Delaware or Chesapeake. But most pure saltwater estuaries are not big enough to retain weakfish for extended periods. They move into the bays, on night tides, in the spring and fall to feed. Bluefish are rovers, constantly in search of food. They, like weakfish, generally hold only in large areas, but feed even in the daytime inside small shallow areas if there is enough bait to attract them. Such locations are good right until the bluefish leave in the fall. Bonito arrive from offshore in mid- to late summer, feeding in and around the bays, mixing in with the later-arriving albacore. Both stay until the heavy October weather pushes them to deeper water.

An outlet does not need rolling surf to provide action: The outrushing tide generates enough activity to allow feeding. Wave action always enhances a location, though, confusing the already bewildered baitfish even more. If this action is too strong, it can sand up the water, moving the fish offshore. However, tidal outlets, even when water along the beach is cloudy, remain relatively clean and hold fish when other parts of the beach are unfishable. This condition may concentrate the fish at the mouth, or bring the fish up inside the bay to avoid the riled-up water.

Tidal flow direction influences bait and gamefish activity, making the down- or below-tide side superior on an outgoing tide. The current forces a majority of the outlet's water to one side—current flowing from the left makes the outlet's right side more productive. Wave and wind action might alter this, but ordinarily the lower side is better. This principle holds true for any outlet, creek, breachway, river, or harbor that empties into a larger body of water with tidal movement. On incoming tide the side with the strongest flow is generally best.

Waves rolling into a bay outlet create great fishing, but produce some of the worst boating conditions possible. The swells plow into the outrushing current, breaking unevenly like small volcanic eruptions over the ever-shifting shoals. Small boats have no place in these conditions, and even a good-size craft is at the mercy of the sea. I prefer fishing ocean outlets from the shore, for even on calm days the water around them is tricky. Nighttime boat fishing here is out of the question.

Outlets that spill into sheltered waters allow the use of all types of craft. The sea kayak was made for poking around smaller estuaries, but use caution when crossing large sections of water in bigger locations. Menemsha on the Vineyard hosts a flotilla of canoes, prams, and small boats, all crowding the inlet on incoming tide when the bonito run is on. There, if a wind kicks up, only a short paddle is necessary to reach shore. Incoming tide should make most openings flat calm, but watch the outgoing. I once witnessed two anglers in a canoe trying to cross the Menemsha mouth on an outgoing tide after staying too long in a wind. Fortunately both were good seamen, for it took all their skills to keep the craft from tipping; wind against tide is a dreadful foe.

Kayaks are great tools for fishing estuaries. Jimbo Meador is poling a grass edge looking for fish. He developed the Native Ultimate with a tunnel hull in which you can stand up and pole to cover water much more efficiently.

Wind, other than producing rolling water at the mouth, will not alter fishing in smaller bays. It does move food to a shoreline, but with the baitfish comes the weed. In most estuary systems, strong currents have far more effect than wind. Only in the bigger bodies of water is the wind a factor to influence bait movement. Like river marshes, most bays are fishable in all but the nastiest weather, making them ideal when most other places are blown out. Wind, however, can alter the tide, changing both the height and the time at which current begins to flow; **time on the water** is the only way to master the specifics of a particular location.

Saltwater bays are a haven for baitfish, with shallow protected areas for sand eels, shiners, shrimp, and crabs. Most of the larger locations offer enough deep water for bunker, herring, mackerel, and a host of other baits. Although these areas are not as rich as a river marsh, they do contain an abundance of food.

Look for the schools of bunker and herring to ripple the surface as they move about in the deeper water, while the shiners and sand eels hold in the quieter locations near the rips. The smaller baits—shrimp, crabs, and worms—appear

Captain Dan Marini and Peter Alves team up to take a nice fish from Pleasant Bay. This fish was chasing early-season herring.

at night in the sheltered upper locations of the bay, but show throughout the bay when spawning or mating.

The best fly patterns to use are similar to those used for a river system; most types of bait appear in both locations. Other than during the times when worms, crabs, or shrimp swarm, a spearing or sand eel fly is the good choice. These are dominant baitfish throughout the season, and only if bunker or herring are present, which arouse the bigger fish, will I fish larger patterns. Lefty's Deceivers and Snake Flies, in white, hot green, or black, cover many situations because the fast-moving water creates aggressive feeders. Only bonito and albacore require special flies, yet at times even they will strike properly fished attractors.

6

Jetties

Some fishermen associate jetty fishing with large rods, heavy lures, and big baits, perhaps because that's the kind of tackle they see other fishermen use on jetties. No doubt jetties do, at times, demand rugged tackle and techniques to extract fish from the harsh surroundings. The fly rod seems out of place here. But those same surroundings, though unkind, help the fly fisherman by bringing fish close or concentrating them for intense feeding. Some anglers feel the long rod is unsuited for tough fishing. This is nonsense, because if fished properly, the fly rod will outperform all other angling methods. The critical matter is this: The fly must be fished in a manner that will make its advantages work.

Some years ago my brother, Paul, and I tried fishing a jetty sticking out into Cape Cod Bay. Not following my usual practice of checking the place beforehand, we stumbled our way out, trying to determine how to fish this beast. A cold northwest wind blew at 25 miles per hour, with higher gusts seemingly trying to knock us from the rocks. Luckily, the jetty was fairly flat for most of its length, permitting us to use our lights sparingly, for both our batteries were low, the beams fading to only knot-tying brightness. (Actually, the poor lights saved us, because we were ready to go somewhere else but didn't want to navigate the rocks without lights.)

Good-size waves rolled into the jetty, making its end unfishable and too dangerous even to think of venturing near. The wind-driven spray was like a slap in the face, forcing us to keep our backs to its chill. But the water in front of me looked fishable. Finding good footing, I stripped line from my reel and prepared to cast a large herring pattern into the white water rolling along the rocks. The waves swept across a sunken bar and spilled into what appeared to be a good hole next to the structure.

Although there was little light, I could feel the fly working perfectly as it swam with the white water, turning, then coming to rest in the hole next to the jetty. I cast to the left, making the fly swing through another spot, when a fish bumped the fly and I saw a boil in the slowly gathering light. Several casts later the fly suddenly stopped, and a large fish exploded only a rod length away, dangerously close to sharp rocks. Yelling to Paul, "I'm into a good fish," I relieved

Jetties give access to deep water and can hold big fish.

some tension at once, hoping the fish would run, but instead it wallowed several times before swimming off along the jetty. As the fish headed out to sea, I cleared the loose fly line from the stripping basket to the reel, but I could feel it rubbing along the jetty's rocks. I hung on, holding my rod high, and, luckily, the line came free. Paul asked, "Have you still got him?" I answered, "Yes, but I don't have a prayer."

Well, I was wrong, for the bass then turned and ran down along the beach, away from the jetty, giving me the fighting angle I needed to land it. As I walked toward shore, the strong wind helped by giving my line a bow and forcing the fish onto the beach. Reaching the shoreline, I scrambled down the slippery rocks, then walked up the beach to distance myself from the jetty, hoping to keep the fish away from its snags. The tired striper had regained some strength and fought well by using a rip that swung along the shore and then ran out along the jetty. Not knowing the condition of my leader, I used only moderate force. More was not needed, because the waves and rod pressure sapped the fish of its last strength, and I guided the big bass, using the white water, onto the sand.

On the beach lay my second surf-caught fly-rod bass over forty pounds, and I had a new appreciation for jetties. In the following days even my brother, who would never think of fly fishing, tried the long rod because of my ongoing success with it. Fly tackle fishes a jetty as well or better than spinning gear because a fly can work right up to the rocks, and will continue to perform even after stopping because it breathes and pulsates while suspended in the moving water.

Anatomy of a Jetty

Scattered along the shores of the Northeast coast are many rock and wooden structures that have been built to protect beaches from erosion or to keep harbors or river mouths from filling. These are jetties, and their dimensions and construction depend upon water depth, tide fluctuation, location, and exposure to open water. A jetty can range from a small set of wooden pilings just wide enough to walk across to huge barriers, 20 feet high, built of neatly placed stones. Some jetties extend hundreds of feet into the sea.

Jetties are sometimes called breakwaters on nautical charts. Not all jetties are marked on these charts, but when they are they appear as solid lines guarding a harbor and protruding from a shoreline. Jetties are easily recognizable—the fisherman should have no trouble locating one.

Some jetties are fishable from a boat, but it's really best to work one by fishing close to it. This way, retrieving toward the jetty is possible, which will make the fly more lifelike, as if it's a baitfish seeking shelter. Never attempt to fish an ocean jetty from a boat when there is wave action—motor failure in this situation could spell disaster. And older jetties need special attention and gear, for they could have holes and gaps along their entire lengths, especially nearest the ends of the jetties. Gruesome tales of anglers slipping into these traps, becoming lodged and unable to free themselves, should be all the warning anyone needs to treat them carefully. Broken-down jetties are best fished with a partner, and each angler should use aluminum-studded wading sandals and have a headlamp with fresh batteries, a surf belt over a rain jacket, and even a small flare gun in case of an emergency. Any type of studs on the bottoms of footwear is a necessity when fishing from rocky structure. Another valuable piece of equipment is a stripping basket. Fish a big jetty without one, and it won't be long before you lose a fly line. The line will find its way into a hole between the rocks, and the wave action will tangle it into the structure, well out of your reach.

Even though some anglers consider jetty fishing strictly a nighttime game for bass, many jetties, especially those in deep water, offer good fishing all day long. Because of the special construction of these man-made structures, large amounts of bait live inside the numerous holes and crevices among the rocks or pilings. These holes provide a home for cunners, small blackfish, and eels, as well as a refuge for schooling bait. Even when schooling bait are not present, gamefish will still forage among the rocks; some jetties host every type of gamefish, and in the fall, big bass will show in broad daylight.

Most jetties are fishable on all tides, and different sections become more or less productive as water levels change. Rock structures at the entrances to harbor and river mouths should be best on an outgoing tide, when bait is being

In the fall albies and bonito provide exciting fishing for many anglers.

flushed from protected water. When there are two jetties, the jetty on the down-tide side or downcurrent will usually be best because the crossing current will push both bait and gamefish to that side, concentrating both along the jetty wall. The same pattern will hold true for a single jetty, making the side below the tide best on a downtide; for instance, when the tide is running left to right, fish the right side of the jetty.

Depending on their location, most jetties have rips flowing around the ends or along one side. Rips form at the end of beach jetties as the water flowing along the shore is forced around the structure. This situation means that certain tides will increase a jetty's productivity. The wave action creates flows along the jetty's lee side. Water from the surf builds up on the inside bars, then exits along the jetty's side. River mouths, harbors, and breachways are classic examples of good water flow on an outgoing tide. Rips form along the rocks facing the channel, flow the entire length of the channel, then spill out into the bay, sound, or open ocean.

Wind and wave activity tend to improve larger deep-water jetties by bringing bait and creating action around the structure. White water and rips will

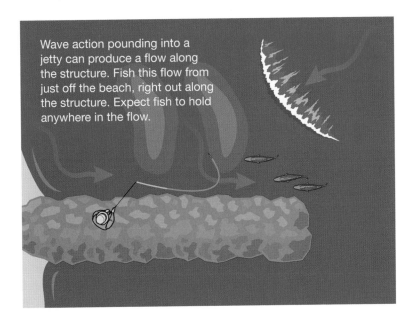

Wave action pounding into a jetty can produce a flow along the structure. Fish this flow from just off the beach, right out along the structure. Expect fish to hold anywhere in the flow.

make the bars near the jetty productive, as they do in any surf-fishing situation. Shallow-water areas may become too dirty and wild as strong winds or large waves make fishing impossible. In this situation, the lee side might by the only fishable location.

Fishing a Jetty

Large jetties appear overpowering, standing tall with waves crashing against their sides. The beginner viewing this monster for the first time wonders how he can even hook a fish, let alone attempt to land it. The first thing the novice needs to do is to look the area over and find a safe perch along the jetty's side. This spot should be near enough to the water to eliminate slack line and missed strikes. Once this spot is found, and before starting to cast, the angler needs to plan how to land a fish. Only then is the angler ready to begin fishing.

Jetty fishing suits the long rodder to a T because many times, particularly at night, the fish are at the angler's feet, permitting close casting. Even daytime jetty fishing can be close, although with more light the angler can cast and control more line to cover more water. However, day and night fishing techniques are similar on a jetty, and only the fly patterns and leader types need be changed to suit the species sought, since bonito and albacore require longer, lighter leaders, without shock tippet.

With the exception of live bait, a fly is probably the best tool to use for the many conditions encountered on a jetty. Patterns tied with materials that breathe—marabou, long bucktail, saddle hackle, Crystal Hair—move and create action merely by sitting in the water. This ability of a fly to appear lifelike while suspended is the key to jetty-fishing success. On a jetty, as in any situation where the strike zone is limited, leave the fly suspended in the zone for as long as possible.

The jetty angler's main concern should be to work the rips along the jetty or the white rolling water that is either behind the bars or along the rocks surrounding it. Long jetties might have many sandbars; usually these bars will stop short of the jetty, leaving a cut in the space between. Because the water working along a jetty is usually rolling to one side or quartering in, the fly should be drifted with the wave action, in the same manner as for fishing a rip. Actually, there is often a rip running along the jetty's side in the opposite direction of the wave flow. This turbulence makes line control a major problem, especially at night. Short casts of 20 to 40 feet will help maintain contact with the fly. Make longer casts only when the presence of significant light permits control.

Cast at different angles to the jetty, starting at one side and working around as if placing the fly at different positions on a clock face. Begin at 9:30 and move around to 2:30. Fish as if you were working a streamer for early spring trout. Try to determine what locations give the best controlled drift or retrieve. Casting straight out or straight to either side should give you the best line control, because the current will then drift the fly seaward.

Fish any cuts between sandbars and the jetty. The ends of the bars and, if it's reachable, the hole behind a sandbar are ideal spots to cast to. The white water rolling over the bars or around their ends should be fished as you would fish waves rolling into a beach. But this will require less effort because the waves will be sliding past, not directly into, you. Cast into the tumbling water on the bar, swimming the fly with the flow, into the hole behind it. A dark section should appear below the white water; this is the deeper water that the waves spill into. Work this section with different-length casts, using a short line. Get the fly to flow first into the hole, then swim around the bar and back the other way with the rip. Contact with the fly should be your foremost concern. If several casts give you better line control, then use them instead of attempting this with just one cast.

Water within 3 feet of the jetty, right up against its sides, needs attention. Always fish the fly right to the rocks. Several years ago I took a forty-six-pound bass with little more than the leader outside of the rod tip. Picking up to cast, I felt tension, as if I had snagged the rocks. Feeling movement, I struck and the large fish exploded at my feet. Without fishing tight to the structure, I might never have known the fish was there. It pays, therefore, to make several casts along the jetty and to fish each cast out. At the end of the swing, the fly will come to rest against the jetty; allow it to sit as if it is a baitfish holding, and allow it to move with the waves. Work the fly in a similar manner several yards out, using waves flowing off the structure to keep the fly swimming parallel to it.

It's better to fish a jetty's entire length before making a change of fly pattern or line type, unless the jetty is very large, because it's too time-consuming to keep changing while you're trying to cover the area. This method is also preferred when fishing a rip, beach section, or ocean hole; work a section, then go back over the same water with a different fly pattern or line of a different density. If there is any indication of fish activity, stay and work the area hard, trying different patterns and lines there. Keep covering the water, working carefully to reach as much water as possible, and keep a sharp eye out for feeding activity within casting range. Covering the water around the jetty well is important.

At times a constant retrieve, while pointing the rod tip at the fly, is necessary to maintain contact. On dark nights, *feel* is frequently the only way to tell the fly's location, but there are other indicators. White foam should dot the water's surface. This foam is visible on most nights, giving you a clue to current flow and speed. Like trout fishermen do when drifting a dry fly, use visual aids when possible. Determining fly location with a short cast is not too difficult, even at night. Pick a spot on the water and keep following that point with the rod. Fishing in daylight simplifies this and is the best time to learn a piece of water.

With a well-designed fly, fancy retrieves are usually unnecessary. A short, slow, pulsating action, retrieving only enough line to feel the fly, is best: Slow movement will keep the fly in the water longer and make it an easier target for the gamefish. Flowing water requires less retrieving: Apply most action with short pulls or flicks of the rod tip. Although I still prefer to fish with the rod under my arm, anglers who like to hold the rod might have an advantage because it gives a longer reach and allows the rod tip to help create fly action.

When there is enough water depth near the jetty, a Hi-D sinking line is an excellent wind-cutter when fishing subsurface. Combined with a floating fly, it can be used to fish below the surface without dragging the fly along the bottom. Work the fly in the same manner as you would with an intermediate line, but retrieve faster so there is more tension on the line. Keep the fly moving unless there is a swift-enough current to swing the line in a steady sideways motion. I prefer to fish with an intermediate line unless the water is too deep. I use the sinker only after working the neutral-density line first.

Poppers and top-water sliders are good daytime jetty lures. Fish them through the white water and along the bar's edges, using a medium to fast retrieve. Work them right up to the rocks, let them pause there for several seconds, and give them a twitching action. Sliders are good nighttime flies as well.

If standing room is at a minimum on a hot jetty, pick a spot with good active water and hang in, working hard for a given time. Gamefish will work along the jetty, swimming in a circular pattern, feeding in the current or wave flow. Hang tight, let the fish find you, and your patience will be rewarded. Fish each small section; apply different retrieves, floats, and drifts; and change fly patterns or line types to completely cover the water. Heavy wave action, with rolling white water, is good for bass, concentrating them close to the structure, but it would be unfavorable for bonito, driving them to deeper, cleaner water. Less-active water can be productive for all species, depending upon the jetty's location, water movement, bait activity, and time of year.

Fishing Quiet Water around a Jetty

Still or less-active water requires different fishing techniques, and the angler must explore more water because the fish are spread out. Quiet water opens many locations along a jetty, including the end, which generally is not safe to fish during wave activity. Calm times can be excellent in shallow locations, making casting easier. Such places are best at incoming to high tide, either in the morning, evening, or all night, when bass, blues, or weaks cruise. Flat water is ideal for bonito and albacore on jetties in deep-water locations.

Poppers and surface sliders provide action in calm water, pulling fish in search of a meal from great distances. There are times when a large, slowly worked top-water bug will lure fish from nowhere. I favor working still water with an intermediate line, covering as much water as possible because fish could be anywhere, not just near the structure. With the exception of small top-water bugs, intermediate line fishes the surface lures well. Some intermediate lines will work a popper, but a floating line is still the best choice when fishing small bugs.

Flat water gives some gamefish too much time to research the fly. These fish require faster, more enticing retrieves and more lifelike fly patterns. This is especially true with the sharp-eyed bonito, who will swim up, examine the fly, and speed away in one motion. But identification is critical at these times.

Not that flies needs to be exact imitations, but they should resemble the bait in size and shape. Precise imitations might be better yet.

A jetty's height allows an excellent view for spotting fish. In daylight, polarizing sunglasses help one see subsurface activity. While fishing, keep watching the water for feeding fish or bait activity. Fish sections along the rocks, making long casts to cover as much water as possible. Use flies, poppers, or sliders, working them to get a lively action. Make the lure jump in a short pulsating movement, alternating speeds, or in long gliding motions of different speeds. But keep the fly moving, and work it right to the jetty edge.

Some jetties and breakwaters have good sight fishing. This is often not classic flats sight fishing because the water might be 5 to 10 feet deep, but if fish are cruising near the surface, looking for bait, it can be fun. Other than the height advantage, mobility without making noise is on the angler's side. With good overhead sun, fish will show up well, and unless bonito or albies are running the jetty, you often have plenty of time to position yourself for a cast. If possible, move down the side of the structure or kneel down to eliminate some of your silhouette when presenting the fly. There is one advantage if the water is deeper: The fish will take the fly more aggressively. A clear intermediate line will get the fly down enough to entice cruising fish unless they are running the bottom, in which case a fast sinker is the best choice.

Jetties that have a strong flow along the structure are more difficult to fish. Fish can hold along the structure, at times well down in the water column. A flow can be created by wave action where water builds up on the inside bars and rushes out along the gully between the structure and the bar. A jetty at the mouth of a harbor or inlet will have strong flows if the opening is small and the backwater is large. The breachways along the coast of Rhode Island and the outlets along the Long Island and New Jersey shoreline are prime examples of heavy flows. Some jetties, especially the big ones, are too difficult to fly fish, but if the location is fishable, a fast-sinking line is often the only answer. The technique is to cast upcurrent, let the line sink, and fish the swing as the fly and line flow below your position. Keep the cast fairly short, 20 to 30 feet.

Stripers will often hold right along the structure, waiting to ambush bait as it flows in or out of the inlet. Fly tackle is not really suited for this fishing because the fly is not in the strike zone for very long. But the patient angler can get enough good drifts and swings to make a fish hit. If you have enough light, keep watching the line as it flows past your position. If the line stops, try lifting the rod. A fish might take the fly as it dead-drifts before you begin the

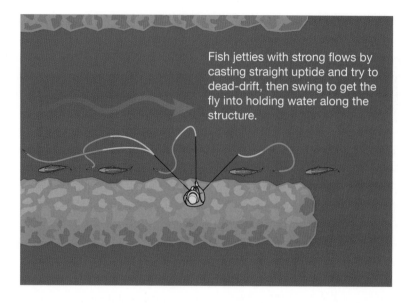

Fish jetties with strong flows by casting straight uptide and try to dead-drift, then swing to get the fly into holding water along the structure.

swing and retrieve. Hooking fish on the dead drift can be tough; often there is too much slack unless the fish holds the fly for a long time. Try casting at different angles, from straight up the flow to across the flow. In a heavy flow only the straight upcurrent cast will work. If you have the room, try a longer cast but retrieve some of the loose line as it drifts down, then fish the swing. This will get the fly a little deeper and give a little longer swing. In inlets with heavy flows, fish at the beginning or end of the tide when there is less current. I like to start fishing just when the flow begins. This gives about half an hour of prime conditions where the fly will stay in the strike zone for much of the drift and swing. **Keep trying different techniques.**

Landing Fish

Big jetties present major difficulties when landing a big fish. The big fish that I have landed from jetties were in locations that were walkable. I hooked the fish from the jetty and walked onto the beach. This is the best and safest way to land fish that are too big to slip up onto the rocks. Planning is the key to landing that special fish, and it starts with moving quickly as soon as the fish starts running. After the fish clears the line from the basket, keep the rod high and climb up to the level part of the structure. Only if the fish runs along the structure should you hold your position or move with the fish. Mostly they run away from the jetty, however, and if this is the case, start moving toward shore.

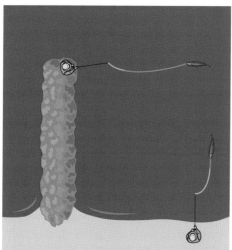

When hooking a big fish from a large jetty, start walking in while the fish is running. Once on the beach, gain as much ground away from the structure as possible.

Don't run—put the rod butt into your side, keep the rod level with the water, and walk toward shore in a normal manner, not backwards. Forget about the fish—just look down and step from stone to stone.

You are going to lose line as you walk, even when the fish stops running. Fishing big jetties requires big tackle and at least 200 yards of backing. At this point in the battle, you will know if your tackle is up to par. Walk far enough to reach the waterline and then carefully slip down the side of the structure. Once you reach the beach, walk quickly along the shore, away from the jetty, and try to keep gaining line. The more ground you make away from the structure, the better—at least 100 yards, but I prefer 200. The fish will eventually head back toward the jetty; however, they often don't have a lot in the tank after the first run. What really beats these fish is all the drag from the line in the water. At this point you are in control, unless the hook pulls out or you make a mistake.

Unless you have a partner who will climb down the rocks and attempt to corral a big fish along a slippery, wave-washed wall, walking in is the only choice. Jetties that run for many hundreds of yards, where walking in is out of the question, require team fishing even when landing a halfway-decent-size fish. I feel that a fish is not worth having a friend risk possible harm, but for those who want to roll the dice—have fun. If I can't walk off the jetty and land it myself, I don't fish the location.

Jetties provide access to deep water with only a short cast, and they are a casting platform that gives the angler elevation. During bad weather they are a place to hide and a good fishing location. Jetties located at the mouth of an outflow benefit from the rich source of food inside the protected waters. A jetty need not be large or long or even very high to be a productive fishing spot. Over the years they have provided me with a wealth of fishing opportunities, and most of my big stripers.

7

Reefs and Rocky Points

My first introduction to reefs came at an early age, when I fished a hometown spot called Frost Point. This rocky area protrudes out into Long Island Sound in Westport, Connecticut, looking like a point at high water, then exposing its offshore rocks as the tide drops. (Many reefs at high water resemble rocky points, and require the same fishing technique.) Several rocks are wadable on a high outgoing tide, allowing easy fly casting to good holding water before the rip. As with many shallow reefs, the point and structure are good on any tide, and the outer rocks hold fish for the boat angler on higher tides. At low water there is a large sand flat, scattered with rocks, that is wadable, and the rest of the reef is fishable to the careful boat fisherman.

Penfield Reef, in Fairfield, Connecticut, is another local area that I fished in my midteens. This location is a classic fishing reef, reaching out over a mile into Long Island Sound. The main body, 50 yards wide in places, consists of a raised gravel and mussel bed running to a section of rocks, with the edges gradually tapering off to sand flats on both sides. Only the end is unreachable to the wading angler. Rocks dot the last section of Penfield, which is guarded by a major lighthouse, plus a marker to the east highlighting another section of large rocks. The entire location offers good fishing, with the flat inside areas ideal for wading on most tides, while the outside rocks attract boat fishermen. To the east, this structure has claimed both boats and lives because that area is some distance from the main reef, and is overlooked by those not familiar with the area. Because of its size and scattered structure, a reef and its surrounding waters demand attention.

The word "reef" strikes fear in the heart of every seaman who has ever sailed a craft, and so it should, for the large numbers of vessels these structures have claimed over the centuries. Modern boats, even with the best equipment, still fall victim to the jagged reefs. Though cursed by the pleasure boater, reefs attract fishermen as open trash attracts raccoons. Those rocks that can crush a boat's hull provide sanctuary for gamefish, with holding water next to none.

The main reef resident is the striped bass; it loves structure, and the meaner the reef the better the bass like it. Not only do these rock piles provide

Big points like Watch Hill, Rhode Island, are ideal fish-holding locations.

holding water for stripers, they also are good feeding places for other gamefish. Bonito and bluefish feed on or near the surface, working the rips to prey on confused baitfish. Weakfish prefer to work deeper sections, although at times it is hard to predict where these fish will be, especially on larger reefs that contain many types of water.

It should be obvious that reefs come in a variety of sizes and shapes, and no two are alike. The surrounding water gives each section of this structure a different look, and it takes time and experience to learn the best fishing locations and tides for each reef.

Most sizable reefs appear on nautical charts as a reef or ledge. However, many good fishing locations identical to reefs appear on charts as rocks or islands with scattered structure around them, with some structure covered at all tides. Small asterisks with dots circling them indicate rocks that are hazardous to navigation, with many, but not all, showing a mean low-water level. These asterisks also indicate the locations of good fishing structure. Offshore shoals can be hard and rocky, but may not be marked with the asterisk because their structure is generally not harmful to boats. Reefs differ from shoals because reefs are more dangerous to navigation. But both locations produce fish, and either can be fished in the same way—consider them the same kind of fishing water.

Reef Types

There are two basic kinds of reef: shallow and sunken. Most shallow reefs will show at low tide, exposing large boulders, mussel beds, and hard rocky areas. Take the opportunity at low tide to study these areas, not only for fishing places, but also to note the locations of large rocks if you plan to boat around the reef. Shallow reefs are ideal for the fly rodder because there is less water to cover and the fishing is easier than on the deeper offshore reefs.

During a falling tide is the safest time to wade a shallow reef. Like flats fishing, some deeper sections may trap the angler during rising tides, or strong rips may sweep him or her off the reef.

Boating anglers will find that rising water on a shallow reef, although poison to the wader, is the best time to fish. This is especially true on unfamiliar water, where a falling tide can trap a boat. In calm waters the best-size boat for shallow-reef fishing is 17 feet or less, which will allow better mobility with less motor use. (Bass hounds who regularly fish rocky reefs wear out a prop a season, even when using the motor sparingly.)

Some sunken reefs are unfishable with a fly unless the fish are on top, feeding near the surface. Sunken reefs are prime when the water is flowing, bringing bait to the waiting fish or moving fish up into the ripping water to feed. Large reefs have both resident and migratory fish, needing either wind, wave action, bait, large tides, or a certain time of year to start periods of heavy feeding. But, as with other water types, two factors generate feeding: the rushing tide combined with an influx of bait. The best tides during which to fish a sunken reef are generally the first part of the outgoing or the beginning of the incoming. It's better to fish deeper reefs on low tides because then there is less water to cover.

In the deeper locations, unless there is surface feeding, use a fast-sinking line to reach the fish. The accepted way to fish such locations is to troll with wire line or to deep-jig. The fly fisher can do neither. The only solution is to drift with a fast-sinking line, using a countdown system. Cast out, then count off the seconds needed for the fly to reach a given depth, starting with a count to ten for deep water. Drift with the current and work the deeper locations, using the sinking line to reach a given depth before retrieving. Each section of water is different, so investigation will be necessary. Sinking lines have "sink rates" (check the chart on this in chapter 16 on tackle)—the number of inches per second they settle. Wind will alter a line's sink rate by causing the boat to move at a different speed from the tide. Cast to different locations around the boat, testing various angles and different sink rates until you find the casting angle that reaches the fish.

If conditions are right and you can get a straight drift down the flow, set the boat up to drift in slower water just off the reef's edge. Then try casting upcurrent, letting the line and fly flow just below the boat's position. As the line swings past the boat, use a fast retrieve with long, hard pulls. This technique gives the fly a long, fast, sweeping action that can excite fish. You will sacrifice some depth, but the added action might be worth it. The ideal setup is to get the fly to swing and rise right at the reef's edge near the downtide side of the drop. **Keep trying different techniques.** This is also effective if there is wind blowing against the flow. But if the wind is over 15 knots, you will be limited on the depth that the line and fly will penetrate below the surface.

When working a sinking line, especially from a high-sided boat, be sure to keep the rod tip low, pointing it toward the line. This position will allow better hooking power and a more positive retrieve.

When fish are holding in hard-ripping water 25 feet or deeper, conditions need to be ideal for any chance of success. A strong wind will sweep the craft

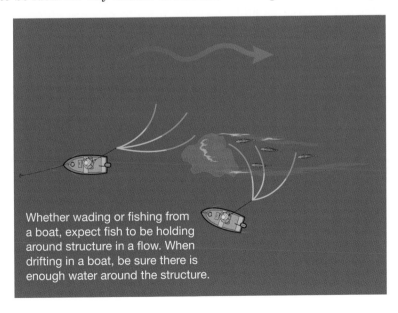

Whether wading or fishing from a boat, expect fish to be holding around structure in a flow. When drifting in a boat, be sure there is enough water around the structure.

briskly along the surface, making deep penetration nearly impossible. Even if fish are holding in shallower water, the boat will either overrun the line or drag it away before it can sink. This fishing is frustrating and requires practice to master, although it *can* be mastered.

My belief is that the long rodder should leave the deeper waters to the big boys and concentrate effort on places better suited to fly tackle. Areas from 10 to 20 feet deep are more suitable for fly rodding. This water is easier to cover without constantly fighting to get the fly, for maybe only a brief period, into the strike zone.

When weakfish moved into Long Island Sound in the late seventies, taking up residence on reefs and offshore bars, jelly-worm fishing became popular. The approach was not what a largemouth bass fisherman would use, but something new, not requiring the skill needed to worm fish. This was simple fishing: Just cast, using a light spinning outfit and a white or purple jelly worm on a small, single hook. Then set the rod in a holder and wait for the action to begin. Time and location were important, of course, but once the word got out, the fishing was hot and easy.

Now, if these fish would take a dead-drifting rubber worm, why wouldn't they hit a long, thin, deep-running fly? It all sounded like ideal fly-rodding conditions, so I made plans to try both night and daytime fishing. Several other anglers said they fished flies, with no success, but under the right conditions I believed weakfish would take a fly as readily as any other artificial—perhaps even better.

My first success came on a night boat trip. John Posh and I tried fishing an outside rip after several hours of chasing bass. The tide was near ebb, but John felt there would be ample current to bring action. While I rigged a sinking fly line, John hooked a plastic worm to a light spinning rod, fishing it in the manner previously described, to act as fish finder. Before I even started to fly cast, a fish picked up and dropped the worm. Although action was slow, the worm had several more takes, and John landed one fish before I finally felt the slow, deliberate take of a weakfish. The fish hit on a very slow retrieve, inhaling the fly deep inside its mouth, and after a short head-shaking battle, John netted and brought it aboard. Although the tide was spent, John also managed to take a fish on a fly, and we missed several others.

In the weeks to come, fishing was excellent, with daytime action as good or better than night tides. One sunny, calm afternoon, with John and Captain Pete Kriewald, I had great success; once I had perfected the drift and countdown, the fly outfished all three anglers using worms. With the sinking line I could cover more water, and the fly's movement and action were superior to the worm on that particular day.

This angling is akin to fishing a deep, slow pool or pond with sinking line, where you try to fish a nymph or streamer to find the feeding level and the holding location of the fish. The moving boat adds another dimension, however, but this will not be a problem once you get the right drift and casting angle. And a drifting boat is beneficial for finding fish in large areas.

Fishing a Shallow Reef

If you plan to wade a reef, start to work your way out as soon as the tide permits. Long reefs tend to lure anglers to their ends—to the pot of gold. But don't be tempted into charging forward without working the entire length. Fish feed all along a reef, and sometimes the middle portion is better than the end. Fish all the water slowly and carefully. Wading allows a slow, quiet, thorough approach.

Reefs that lend themselves to shore fishing are good bets in a rolling surf, providing the fly rodder can reach fishable water. Usually there will be a protected corner that is tranquil enough to fish; many times bait is driven to a pocket on the reef's lee side, providing easy feeding for the gamesters and ideal conditions for daytime bass fishing. Fish this water the same way you would fish an ocean beach, because the fish will feed right up in the white water. To prevent hang-ups, use weedless flies or buoyant patterns; even with a topwater line, the waves will roll the fly into the rocks.

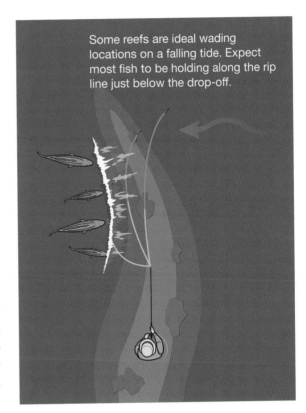

Some reefs are ideal wading locations on a falling tide. Expect most fish to be holding along the rip line just below the drop-off.

Nighttime will find bass, blues, and weakfish feeding in the shallows over a reef. Fish by casting well above the drop-offs, in the flat water, and allow the fly to drift into the drop-off. Direct some casts straight out from the reef, downtide or quartering, working the fly on the swing, and retrieve uptide. Expect fish to be everywhere. Fish feeding in the low water will announce their presence, so keep a sharp eye and ear out. Daylight tides can be productive, too, and first and last light are my favorite times to fish this kind of water.

Use a top-water line to fish places less than 10 feet deep. But if the fish are bottom-grubbing, bounce the bottom. As with any rocky structure, weedless flies combined with deep-water lines will keep the hang-ups to a minimum. Another good trick to keep the fly just off the bottom is to fish a long leader with a buoyant fly. This is also a useful setup in the surf to keep the fly from drawing through the sand, dulling the hook.

Shallow reefs see top-water action all season long, with daytime feeding of bass and blues in the spring and fall. Weakfish are primarily nocturnal feeders, surface feeding all night all season long, and with some good mid-depth day-time activity in the spring and summer. The offshore species will not usually frequent shallower spots, but they can appear in unexpected places.

All rocky areas will have resident bait—cunners, blackfish, crabs, and eels. But the real catalyst bringing gamefish to a reef are the bunker, herring, mackerel, squid, and other large deep-water baits that can set an offshore reef on fire. Sand eels and shiners are vital to low-water reefs, and sand eels, the big offshore species, are a major deep-water bait as well.

Fishing a Point

Most shallow inshore reefs create points at high tide. Rips form around points because the points restrict water flow. A high incoming and high outgoing tide will produce the best water flow at a point until the reef starts to work with the falling water. On a high incoming tide, fish from the reef will usually move into shore to feed.

Not all visible points are connected to reefs. But those points that are, or are near rocky structure, are the best fishing locations. Small points might have only a few prime standing spots from which to reach good fishing water. Fishing such areas takes patience, for the angler must constantly work the same piece of water, hoping the fish move in to feed.

Covering this water is similar to fishing a rip. Cast above and below the rip line, varying both direction and distance to cover the whole point. Standing on a rock will help casting distance and fly control, and most areas have scattered stones. If the point is large or has several casting locations, work around it, fishing each parcel of water.

When fishing a point from shore, be sure to cover all the water, not just the rip line.

Most areas require a certain retrieve, or a drift-and-retrieve combination. Sometimes the water right at the point is fast enough to allow a long drift; if so, let the fly swing with the current from the fast water into the slower water below the rip. Mix up retrieves until you find the one that works. Usually, a slow to medium speed is best, combined with a pulsating movement added to the fly.

Surface and shallow-running flies are best unless cold water has the fish bottom feeding—use a bottom-bouncing line and pattern then. Top-water lines, intermediates or floaters, are popular and easy to use. Some locations are unfishable from shore with fast-sinking line, even with weedless flies.

Fish points from a boat by anchoring and casting to the shore so that the cast reaches the shallower water. If you're fishing a popular wading spot, respect the shore fishermen by staying beyond their casting range. Position your boat above the rip line to reach both the reef's edge and the drop-off. Use the fishing techniques recommended for the shore. Approach all locations cautiously, and use the motor sparingly, drifting into as many spots as possible.

Fishing Deep Reefs

Large rocks positioned along a reef provide ideal holding water for saltwater gamefish, as they do for fish in a stream. Stones that are submerged at high tide appear in the rip as flat spots with rolling water trailing from those spots. Depending upon rip speed and the water depth over the structure, the rocks are located from 1 to 3 feet uptide from the flat spots. Deeper structure is not so well defined. The entire rip is potential fish habitat, and the rocks offer better holding water. Fish the current formed by the structure as you would a rip, by casting above the faster water using casts of varying length and position.

Put special emphasis on any large chunks of structure; try to paint the rock with the fly, both on the sides and the top. Most fish hold along the edges, in the drop-off, using the structure to break the rip's pull. This method is ideal for shallow reefs, which offer similar water. Fish this exactly as you would cover a submerged midstream rock in your favorite trout water. Keep making the fly swim past or behind the rock. Remember, saltwater fish hold as trout do, maybe not for as long or as frequently, but during feeding there are many similarities.

Drifting in a boat over a reef's deeper waters allows better fishing coverage. Cast into rips while floating by, working as much water as possible during the float and concentrating on structure. Although somewhat harder for a fly rodder, this type of fishing is common practice with spinning tackle. Once you've located the fish, anchor and cast from a holding spot. When drifting, place the cast so it keeps tension on the line so that the boat will not overtake the fly. A cast quartering downcurrent into the wind is the best possible angle.

Big boulders are good spots to fish. Many reefs are dotted with this type of structure, which provides holding pockets for fish.

The worst is downwind. Try casting in different directions until you find an angle that keeps the line tight but allows the fly to get down—if you're using a sinking line.

When holding in one place, fish the swirling water by casting above the structure, letting the fly swing by or over the rocks, covering the water as you would a rip. Try a technique I call "slipping." This allows you to work the section just below your position by swimming the fly along the rip's edge and into the drop-off. Cast quartering downstream to a spot along the rip or the boiling water caused by the reef's structure. Pulsate the fly with the rod tip, making it slide along the rip's edge, as a baitfish would when being swept across the reef. Do not retrieve until the fly comes to rest below the boat, and then only after letting it flutter in the current. This is a very effective way to work a drop-off where fish either hold or cruise along the edge, looking for food. Slipping the fly across the rip, rather than retrieving, gives it a natural appearance. Along with standard flies, try poppers, sliders, or big top-water deer-hair flies. Apply this method to offshore rips, outflows, or anywhere a heavy current exists, when retrieving upstream would make the fly look unnatural.

Deeper water requires the use of sinking line if fish are not showing and not responding to top or subsurface flies. Work this water as you would a deep rip, casting to different locations. Let the line sink at different rates to get the fly to various depths. When fishing with a partner, one needs to work deep while the other tries the top water to find where and how the fish are holding. When anchored near a heavy rip, especially one with structure, always use a release anchor.

Wave action over structure usually enhances productivity, unless that action is too violent. Reefs become dangerous in rolling water, making navigation around them tricky. Most boaters should steer clear of rocky places during periods of heavy surf or wind-driven waves. For good seamen, some locations are fishable, but keep below any overpowering forces that could propel the boat into turbulent water. Either run up to or anchor along the edge of structure, fishing the downside of the reef, but never place the craft in a situation where wind, tide, or waves can push you into rough, rolling water or structure.

Strong winds create unfishable conditions on some reefs, turning the water into a broken chop and making boating a risky business. Avoid wind against a rip, especially with wave action, where a change in tide can bring unsafe conditions before the boater is prepared to deal with it. Moderate winds that do not create heavy seas tend to enhance the rip over a reef by picking the rip up.

Wind also moves bait along or over a location. Onshore wind pockets the bait and moves the fish inshore, particularly during fall runs. Places like Montauk, at the tip of Long Island, turn on when late-season winds put the fish onto the reefs and along the beaches.

Large offshore reefs are fishable at all times, but if they are more than 20 feet below the surface, they may not be suited for the fly rodder. The only time that any of the deeper rips are fishable with fly tackle is when the fish are up in the water column or when they are busting bait on the surface. Bass begin to inhabit reefs in the spring as they move into their seasonal feeding locations, with bluefish not far behind. Choppers might appear on top in the spring and summer, but depending on bait type, most feeding takes place in deeper water, many times below the reach of fly tackle. Bass prefer night tides, and like the bluefish much of this action occurs in water too deep to fly fish. Fall brings fish up, with all-day action not uncommon as different gamefish begin their seasonal feasts.

Boats equipped with depth finders and recorders not only can detect depth and bottom configuration, but can also mark gamefish and bait present. These instruments give clues to fishing depth and style. Bait or fish holding in 5 to 15 feet of water are reachable with a fly. The same at 40 feet would probably mean finding another spot. Along with high-tech gear, look for the obvious signs of feeding activity, such as bird movement, working fish, or boat activity. When large baits are being fed upon, the bigger seabirds, herring gulls, and black-backed gulls flock to the area, trying to snatch the pieces. Big birds are a sure sign of big bait, for terns will generally not bother working over food they cannot pick up. When the larger birds get excited, it's a sure sign of fish.

Unlike ocean beaches, flats, or creeks, reefs—like trout streams—always have resident fish around their structure. Like river occupants, reef fish need something to trigger their feeding. When fish move into a creek, or onto a flat, they are looking for groceries—so fish found in these locations are often hungry. But fish encountered on a reef are not always feeding; the reef's ground cover also provides a protected home where inshore species can hold for the entire season.

8

Flats

Fishing with overhead sun in clear, shallow water is perhaps the most reward-ing, challenging, and difficult way to catch fish. If I could only fish one way, it would be sight casting to fish in 2 to 3 feet of clear water. Watching a fish turn, approach, and take a fly in skinny water is as exciting as it gets.

I had a day I will never forget on Dogfish Bar near Lobsterville Beach on Martha's Vineyard. It was a clear June morning, and I wanted to check out the bar in daylight. I had fished it several times at night with other anglers, but wanted to see the drop-off and thought it might be interesting to do some sight casting for stripers. There was no one in the water, and I had never heard anyone mention they had sight fished at low tide on the bar. I was about one-third of the way along the bar when I spotted a good-size fish cruising in about 2 feet of water. I dropped a small sand-eel pattern about 5 feet in front of the fish. The fish glided to the fly, turned nose-down, and sucked it in. About ten minutes later I had a fish about 34 inches long at my feet. I was using a new pattern and could not believe that the fish took it so aggressively. Many times fish this size are really tough to fool.

My day was already made when several more fish appeared, sliding out of the deeper water and up onto the bar in about 3 feet of water. Again I cast ahead of the lead fish. Two of the three fish descended on the fly, and the big-ger one took. It was about 38 inches—I believe my best sight-caught fish up to that time. I was on cloud nine. But what happened next just shocked me. Two monster stripers came up onto the bar and crossed about 40 feet in front of me, swimming right to left. I dropped a quick cast in their path, and the lead fish lit up—just became bright—as it swam to the fly. Unlike the two previous fish, it turned on its side and ate the fly. It took over twenty minutes, but I finally landed the fish. I used my rod to mark the length and was reviving the fish when a spin angler walked up behind me and whistled. I hadn't noticed his approach because I was engrossed in landing the fish. I said that I thought the fish weighed about thirty-five pounds, so the angler grabbed the fish by the jaw and tail and felt the weight—again he whistled. "Hell," he said, "this fish is close to forty pounds." Well, it probably wasn't forty pounds, but it was 46 inches long—my best fish caught sight fishing—and I have not come close to a fish that size with that technique since.

In one day I had landed three big stripers in very clear, shallow water at midday in June. With that kind of success, I thought I had finally found the secret fly pattern for sight fishing, but the next day I couldn't buy a fish with that fly or any other. I had hit just the right day, when the fish were on and feeding aggressively.

Sight fishing for stripers can just drive anglers nuts. Success depends upon fishing pressure. Finding fish that are fresh from migration will produce good fishing, as will finding a location that has an abundant bait supply with fish on the feed. When fish get too much fishing pressure, catching them is tough. If fish bolt from your fly like they have seen the devil, it means they have been pounded, and you need to get lucky and find some green fish.

Stripers are generally not comfortable in shallow water during the day. They are at home in these locations in low light or at night, but not in bright sunlight. Bonefish are spooky, but they constantly feed in skinny water—it's how they evolved. For stripers to feed in shallow water means that they cannot find enough food in other locations, so they move into the flats. There are more stripers on flats in the daytime today than there were thirty years ago. This is a windfall for fly rodders because fly tackle is ideally suited for shallow-water fishing.

Bluefish also move in to feed in shallow water. The first time I experienced this was off Saugatuck Shores in Westport, Connecticut. Joe Murray and I were looking for fish in my 13-foot whaler when we saw fish pushing bait right on shore. I nosed the boat into the shallows and dropped anchor. Eight- to twelve-pound bluefish were feeding in 2 feet of water. Not having waders, we jumped in, got wet, and started fishing. The fish took poppers, and we could not believe they stayed in such shallow water for so long. At times the fish were feeding in 1 foot of water, with their backs and tails above the surface. We took fish for about an hour—it was my first introduction to daytime shallow-water fishing.

Bluefish are more aggressive than stripers and take poppers at times, but they too can be picky. What makes fishing for bluefish in shallow water exciting is the way they jump. I have watched bluefish give five or six good jumps, cartwheeling like tarpon. They also run and fight better in the shallows than in deeper water, where they tend to turn sideways and bulldog. Shallow-water bluefishing can be some of the best fly rodding ever experienced, but it does not happen as frequently as finding stripers in shallow water.

Fishing Flats

Spotting fish requires some training, but there are a few tricks to improve success. Good sunglasses are essential and will help pick fish out in lower light, on darker flats, and in deeper water. Look for 100 percent IR- and UV-rated glasses in colors like copper, amber, brown, or orange. Try to fish with the sun to your back, and use elevation when possible. Look for shadows, a fin or tail, even an eye. Fish are hard to spot because their reflective scales help them blend with the bottom, and they can change color to match their surroundings. A fish that swims from a dark bottom onto light sand will look like a green torpedo at first, but in a short time will begin to blend with the lighter bottom.

Keep covering the water, looking about two-thirds of the time within 20 to 80 feet and one-third of the time 100 feet plus. Continue looking for fish, but take time to scan the surface for tails, fins, and wakes. Sometimes when concentrating too hard on spotting fish, you miss a surface disturbance that is right in front of your nose. Even in places that have a flow of fish from one location, keep looking around. I don't know how many times fish have slipped up on me from behind—never stop looking back. When you see fish at a distance, keep looking ahead of them. Many times there will be a school of small fish and in front of them a group of bigger fish. The only time I will not take my eye off a target is if it's a single or small group and the sight conditions are difficult.

When wading, use the surroundings. Getting in the proper position will make spotting fish easier. Part of finding fish is picking a spot that allows you to detect their movement. Move less, move slowly, and cover a location well. In a boat it's easy to cover large sections of water, but wading is a game of patience. The advantage of wading is a quiet, low approach that lets the angler get closer to the fish without spooking them. The ideal places for wading have natural flows that funnel fish through slots. A depression that drains or fills a flat, a series of bars that channel fish along a shoreline, or a point on a big flat are all places that let the angler set up and ambush fish. I always try to post-off and let fish come to me because they are usually coming from one direction, and they are moving and I'm not. Spotting fish is much easier from a stationary position, which is why spotting from a moving boat can be more difficult even though you are higher up.

Other good places to post-off are along the edges of drop-offs. Stay back about 40 feet if it is a slight drop-off; along deeper channels you will have better visibility by moving to a slightly closer position. Fish will either run the edge or nose up onto the flat. Anglers that post too close to the edge will spook fish and

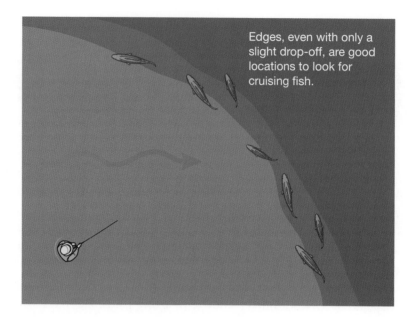

Edges, even with only a slight drop-off, are good locations to look for cruising fish.

often do not have enough time to make a cast. Posting-off is also effective along a bank, from a breakwater or jetty, or on an ocean beach with light surf. These locations will give you more elevation for spotting fish, but keep low when presenting the fly because the fish can also see you better.

Grass flats will have fish, at times in water depths of 18 inches. I once hooked a fish in knee-deep water that might have been close to twenty pounds. I spotted just the tip of a tail about 30 feet away and dropped a fly to what I thought was the head—I guessed right. The fish took, and it seemed like the world exploded. The fish ran off the flat and well into the backing before it pulled off. I could not believe a fish that size would be in such skinny water in broad daylight. Fishing over such dark-colored flats requires ideal light conditions to actually spot a fish—mostly you are looking for a fin, a tail, or any surface movement. Fishing in patches of mixed grass and sand really improves your ability to spot fish because as they move from the different-colored bottoms, they will stand out. A slow-sinking fly works well over grass flats—it helps prevent hanging up on the bottom.

Getting the Fly to the Fish

The key to successful sight fishing is getting the fish to see the fly. Unless the fish are hot, attacking the fly as soon as it hits the water, you need to calculate

Locations that have mixed grass flats can be good sight fishing.

the speed of the fish, the speed of the flow, and the fly's sink rate to get the fly in front of the fish. It's better to be 10 feet ahead of a fish than 1 foot behind. If you cast too far in front of a cruising fish, let the fly settle to the bottom, and as the fish approaches, give the fly a short pull so it hops in front of the fish. This is an effective technique that works well on hard-to-take fish. Try to just use one pull because if the fly moves too much, it might spook a wary fish.

If the fly is behind the fish, the fish might not ever see it. Most fish are looking down, and I have had any number of fish swim right under my fly and never see it. I've even spooked some fish when they hit the leader. This is

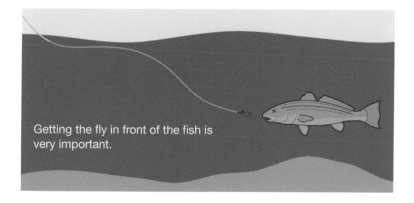

Getting the fly in front of the fish is very important.

seldom a problem with fish up in the water column, however, and often these fish will take more aggressively. A good trick, in locations with a flow, is to pick a spot on the bottom and see how far you need to cast above the spot to get the fly on the bottom. Then you only need to estimate the fish's speed.

A fish swimming straight at an angler gives the best casting angle. Just place the fly in the fish's path, and if it keeps swimming in the same direction, it will see the fly. A crossing angle requires more lead, and you need to judge the distance to cast the fly. If the cast is too long, quickly adjust the fly's position to intercept the fish. If you wait too long and the fly moves toward the fish at a close range, it will usually blow the fish off the flat. A small bait does not swim at a gamefish in shallow water, and this is why casting to a fish that is swimming away usually ends up spooking the fish. Only if casting to a school of fish where the fish in the middle of the group might make a mistake and take the fly would I try casting to a fleeing fish. Often the lead fish in a school will spook, but the fish in the middle might still take. Large groups and schools of fish are usually easier to take because there is competition for food. Remember, none of this matters if the fish are hot and feeding wildly. But don't think that is the norm: Most sight fishing is tough—that's why it's so much fun.

Boating the Flats

Boat anglers can fish flats during most tides providing there is sufficient water depth to float the craft and allow maneuvering without spooking fish. Small

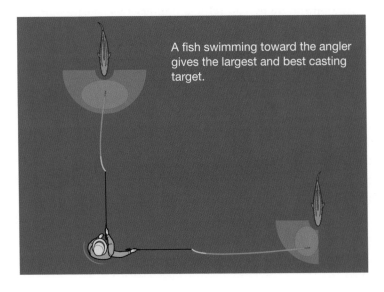

A fish swimming toward the angler gives the largest and best casting target.

boats are best for this fishing, allowing the angler to pole or paddle quietly or to anchor and then wade. Some areas are too shallow and limited for boats. Larger-boat owners are wise to fish flats of 4 feet or deeper, working the rising tide to avoid being trapped, which would require a long wait for the flood to free the craft again.

The boat fisherman needs to proceed cautiously on the flats and try to move in such a way that he covers water without running the engine. Set the anchor and periodically let out line to slowly keep fishing one small section at a time. Drop the anchor as if you were setting an anvil on a glass table. The fishing strategy is identical to that of the wading angler, but avoid clunking around in the boat because water transmits every vibration. (Outdoor carpeting on the bottom of a noisy boat will help dampen most noise.)

The use of an electric motor is ideal for any situation requiring a quiet approach; more anglers are using them in saltwater fishing. It may not be powerful enough to run up a strong rip, but it will work well for moving across and downstream. Under many fishing conditions the electric motor will increase angling success.

Bright lights, like loud sounds, are poison in low water—both boating and wading anglers should avoid them. Avoid light in any low-light or dark situation: Except for a constant light source, the continued flicking on and off of a headlamp will spook gamefish. Bright lights shining over or into the water can ruin a given area for some time. For certain types of fishing, I use a neck light to find my way and a small penlight to change flies, turning my back to the fishing when using them.

Anglers who own a flats skiff designed for poling in shallow water can basically use the same techniques as the wading angler for daytime sight fishing. Boats with poling platforms put the poling angler 4 to 5 feet above the water, with the fishing angler about a foot to 18 inches above the surface. The major advantages when fishing from a boat are height for visibility and the ability to cover more and different water. Depending on the type of skiff, you can still fish some skinny water, and it's easier to explore places that are tough to walk, like soft flats and uneven areas. And you can fish longer into the tide on big flats with big tides.

Longer casts are often required from boats because of the height of the angler above the water and the effect of hull pressure. Stripers are very sensitive to vibrations that many boat hulls produce. Depending on wind chop and how well the boat poles, fish might spook at a fair distance. And there is

Boats designed for shallow water fishing pole easier, make less noise, and help to cover more water.

another factor—how well the angler can pole the boat. It takes some practice, and if there is wind and a flow, it can make for a long day. Those who have a good skiff and can use a pole are lucky, but don't think that buying a flats boat will make you a guide.

Fish move into shallow water to feed. They might hold at times just along the edge or in the depressions inside the first bar, but usually these fish are waiting for the tide to begin feeding. In the daytime, if you happen to run into a large group or school of fish that are milling around, back off and wait for the coming tide. On many occasions I have found fish that were just holding in one area. If I tried casting to these fish, it usually disrupted them and the opportunity was lost.

Low-Light Fishing

Flats offer ideal fly-fishing conditions for many types of angling. It's the perfect location for early-morning popper and slider fishing. Top-water fishing is a little like sight casting because you see the fish take. Fred Jeans and I had a great morning at the mouth of the Housatonic River in Connecticut. There was just enough light to see any activity breaking the water's calm surface as we waded onto a shallow flat paralleling the river's outflow. Tide was near ebb as the river continued to flow out, and it would do so for some time even after the tide started filling the shallows.

I had little hope for action at first light, figuring most fish had dropped into deeper water while waiting for the flood tide to start before moving onto the flat to feed. Splashing noisily through knee-deep water, we were pleasantly surprised when a fish to our left spooked, leaving a wake while it ran to deep water. We needed no further encouragement to prepare our tackle and start fishing.

One hundred yards away a wake appeared, cutting a path toward us before disappearing just beyond casting range. To my left a tail appeared, dimpling the water as it cruised slowly 70 feet away. Casting a dozen feet beyond the wake, I started to retrieve, using short, steady strips as a fish approached the fly. The fish turned, tracked, and struck in one motion, taking the fly more gently than I expected from a bluefish. For the next three hours Fred and I enjoyed great action with both bass and blues, taking some fish in 1 foot of water. Using both flies and poppers, we hooked and landed a number of gamesters. Fred, experiencing this fishing for the first time, turned to me at one point and said, "People spend thousands of dollars and travel great distances to get fishing this good." He was right, for shallow-water angling is a delightful fishing experience.

On a calm morning, watching a big swirl appear behind a surface lure will remove the sleep from any angler's eyes. In low light or at night, fish that are in shallow water are looking for food. Both an intermediate and a floating line will work well. When blind casting while covering shallow water, I like to wade slowly, casting across or quartering downcurrent. My first choice is to fish the surface when that works, but often fishing subsurface is more effective. An intermediate line and a 5-inch Snake Fly are my go-to system. However, if there are 3-inch-long sand eels, tiny bunker, or hatching worms, then matching the food type is essential. Other than sight fishing, most flats fishing is blind casting unless there are surface-feeding fish. This can be great fun and much like casting to sighted fish below the surface. The big difference is that these fish should readily take a fly.

There are times when thick concentrations of bait can be a problem. Fish feeding in thick schools of small sand eels can be tough to take. When there is too much bait, your fly gets lost in the shuffle. If fish are feeding wildly and not taking, try getting the fly down deep. On a really shallow flat, find a drop-off or gully where you can get the fly below the bait's level. Here there is a chance that a fish will notice the fly and take it. Otherwise, it can be a long morning.

Deeper Flats

Boat anglers have the advantage of being able to cover large sections of water and fishing flats that are too deep for wading. Many back bays have vast areas of water 4 to 6 feet deep that are ideal for boats to drift, and some places offer shallow sections that are not reachable from shore. Long Island's south shore, most of the inner coastal area of New Jersey, and, of course, the huge shallow sections of the Chesapeake are prime examples of flats for boaters. Most of this fishing is covering water, casting blind while drifting with the flow. Intermediate and fast-sinking lines are both effective. I like fishing a 7- or 8-weight with a sink-tip line of about 200 grains. A light rod is less tiring and more fun to fish because often you are making hundreds of casts.

Cast at an angle to the flow, and try mixing up the retrieve with short and long pulls. On some casts let the line and fly dead-drift, then use a fast retrieve as the fly swings below the boat. When two anglers are fishing, it's wise for one angler to cover the water by swinging across and down the flow while the other angler works the fly angling downcurrent.

Big Tide Locations

In big tide locations the last two hours of outgoing and the first several hours of incoming are often the best tides. On big flats like those along shorelines of Cape Cod Bay, you need to watch the tide. In some places anglers fish nearly a mile from shore—you don't want to be wading back to shore that far in waist-deep, flowing water. And be sure to know the bottom, because many locations have bars with depressions that can be 18 inches deep.

One night while fishing the flats at the mouth of the Housatonic in Connecticut, several anglers and I were into fish on an outside bar. Although it was time to leave, a brisk offshore wind held back the water, giving us some bonus fishing. However, the wind finally turned onshore, raising the water faster than we realized and requiring us to dry our waders before the next night's fishing.

On smaller flats, move with the tide. Some places are good starting at the drop, and you can wade right out down to low. This is true in small tide areas where the locations might be wadable during most of the tide. Many river systems have flats along and out in front of the river's mouth. But, again, in big tide locations watch the tide because the flow will still be pushing out, sometimes for several hours, when the water starts to rise. Often the outflowing water will flow over the incoming tide—you will know the strong incoming push has started when you feel your lower legs getting cold. Boat anglers need to watch big flats on falling tide. I often anchor the boat, lift the motor, and wade the shallows while I keep moving the boat into deeper water. If I'm planning to fish the incoming tide, I just let the boat go dry.

Night Fishing

Nighttime on a flat is just as exciting, when the fish smack or pop as they feed. On calm nights it's possible to locate fish by sound, and the careful angler can stalk to within casting distance.

Calm-Water Flats

Fish flats that have no current or only a slight flow by covering as much water as possible. At night try to locate fish by sound or smell. Surface-feeding fish make pops, slurps, or splashes. These sounds carry for some distance on still water on a quiet night. Still conditions tend to scatter the fish, forcing the angler to track them down; the fish's feeding sounds help locate their presence.

When hunting calm flats, the wading angler has a distinct advantage over the boat fisherman for several reasons. Obviously, the greater ease of a quiet approach is one; the ability to feel the subtle current is another. The major reason, however, is the ability to feel the bottom, to know when a bar is being approached and that deeper water is on the other side. When approaching a bar, stop and begin casting at the first sensation of walking upgrade—do not wait until reaching the top of the bar. If the bar is only 20 feet wide and there are fish lying on the edge of the opposite side, after reaching the bar's top you may be too close and will alarm the fish.

Wading at night on a flat seems much easier because the area is just one big fishing location. However, on a dark night a big flat can become spooky. How close is the drop-off? Did I plan the tide properly? And what is that dark object moving toward me? One night while fishing with several friends, I spotted a big fin sliding through the water not far from our location. My fishing partners thought I was kidding until I walked back to the boat and trained a light on the fin. For the rest of the night we fished close to the boat.

Never fish a flat, or actually most locations, without checking it first in daylight—not just for safety purposes, but also to get a lay of the land (see chapter

12). A floating line works best in calm conditions with slow-moving water; an intermediate line is my choice for fast-water flats. Night fishing entails thoroughly covering water, often using a slow retrieve. I have covered fishing in the dark in other sections of the book, so to avoid redundancy I will just say that when working a flat, expect the fish to take at any time during the retrieve. Rod-tip strikes are common, and with every step there is a possibility of spooking fish. You can be careless walking along a beach, but not when moving on a flat. I have even caught fish while walking or standing with the fly trailing from the rod tip. If the fly is in the water, be ready for action.

Fast-Water Flats

Rips and currents vary on different flats depending upon the flat's location much more than upon the tide size, unless you are planning to fish upper Maine or the Maritimes, where the tidal bore is extreme. The strongest rips occur at river mouths, bay mouths, or tidal inlets with small openings, where sizable amounts of water are forced to fill a large backwater. Points and reefs can also create nice rips by forcing extra water to flow over shallows. Fish this moving water as described in chapter 4, using the drift-and-swing technique in faster rips.

Some currents appear broken, with jagged lines formed by the water ripping over rugged hard sand. The bottom at low water looks like a washboard; this water is similar in appearance to the waters rainbow trout like to hold in. Fish hold just below these rips, suspended in depressions that slow the current, feeding as a trout would in fast water, by letting the water flow bring dinner.

Casting from shore or boat, work each jagged line, presenting the fly so it swings above, through, and below each ripple. Be sure to reach each small section, because the fish may not move far to strike. Keep watching for movement indicating a follow or missed strike. Fish hold in certain sections and may not see the fly until it's too late, causing a short strike. Keep watching the fly's general location, because a follow will be visible on all but the darkest nights. If a fish misses, give it time to settle back in before casting again, and let the fish grab the fly. Hook-setting too quickly will take the fly away, causing another miss and probably spooking the fish.

An intermediate line is my choice even for fast current, unless the flat borders a drop-off. After working with an intermediate line, fish the deep fast sections with high-speed sinking line, swinging the fly to different locations in the hole. In most cases the fish are looking to the surface to feed on what is floating or swimming by and will rise to take.

When long rips form over a bar, walk along fishing the entire length, with emphasis on the ends where water is ripping around the bar. Keep covering the water while also working the deeper water down from the bar that may hold fish. Use both floating and neutral-density flies to match baitfish in the area. Precise imitations are usually unnecessary unless fish are keying on one bait. Attractors fished slowly on or near the surface cover most fast-water flats situations.

Ocean Flats

Many shallow locations exist next to ocean holes. Some are only reachable during low tide when wave action is slight. Ocean flats near holes are fishable because they keep relatively clean unless there is a heavy swell. Low tide on an ocean beach exposes large dry-sand areas near the deeper holes. You can fish along the edges of the holes by using the shallow bars for walking to fishable water. Although ignored by many anglers, these pockets hold nice fish; usually bass move in at dark to feed. Also, on an incoming tide the dips between the bars might have fish moving in to feed.

In the right conditions some locations might offer good daytime sight fishing, usually by working the edges looking for cruising fish. This can be a good bet in the spring when stripers first arrive along the outer beaches. In late

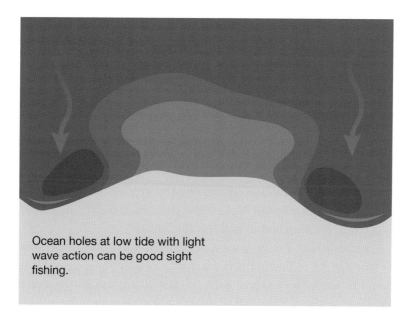

Ocean holes at low tide with light wave action can be good sight fishing.

A nice striper took a small baitfish pattern in knee-deep water.

spring and into summer, look for stripers to feed on sand eels at first light. At times you can see fish nosing in the sand with their tails above the surface of the water. Walking outer beaches with light surf can be productive fishing.

On nights of light surf, when wading is permissible, the shallows between ocean holes are worth trying, with more effort applied to the hole's edges. Fish them as you normally would work an ocean hole, using an intermediate line with neutral-density or buoyant flies. In current, drift the fly on a slow swing, supplying some action with the rod tip and using a slow or fast retrieve. Current, if there is wave action, should come off the bar, flowing from the shallows into the hole. Fish will work the edges along the drop-off, feeding in the moving water or along the white water. Make most casts across-current, fishing the fly so it swims from the deep water into the shallows.

White water, even if only knee-deep, might have fish. Fish this rolling water, getting the fly to flow with the wave or retrieving it through the white water. Stand to work the retrieve over the flat along the fringe, not just fishing the deepest sections. Then, after working the perimeter, keep walking out to fish as much water as possible. Move cautiously, for fish are spooky in calm water, and continually use your senses for spotting or smelling fish. On calm nights the odor of fish will be evident if they are feeding in the hole.

Several other places similar to ocean flats appear in backwaters, such as in Pleasant Bay in Chatham, Massachusetts. Large flat areas hold water. When the water recedes, strong rips form where it spills from the drop-off into deeper cuts. Here the angler can walk the flats, staying back from the rip line and drifting a fly from the shallows into the drop-off on the other side of the rip. Approach such drop-offs carefully to keep from spooking fish, or taking a quick swim. Work this water like a rip, using an intermediate line, swinging the fly into the hole, then retrieving it from the deeper water back to the shelf. Fish along the edge first before venturing near the drop-off to work the deeper water. When fish are present they will generally rise to take the fly, making a fast-sinking line unnecessary. Deep drop-offs that retain fish during the day at all tides can be fished with a deep-running line both day and night. Some locations with deep-holding fish are unreachable with fly tackle because of the current speed and depth; fish the deepest holes at the bottom of low tide.

General Tips for Flats Fishing

Flats need not be large—some are banks or shoulders along a river mouth, a beach at low tide, or a small creek that fills an estuary. Not all flats are sand: Mussel bars, gravel banks, and mud banks are areas of shallow water that hold fish. Be aware that areas of mud can be soft, and in some locations they can be dangerous to wade. Pay special attention to areas marked as mud on a chart. Shallows that are subject to wave action can be entirely different after a storm—a place with a good wadable bottom might change—so check your location before walking out on a dark night.

Lower phases of the tide—the last two hours of the falling tide and the first two hours of the incoming tide—are better for wading, and these tides tend to concentrate fish in big tide locations. Any depression or a gully that forms a creek at both a dropping or coming tide will collect fish.

Flats are fishable all season long, and large concentrations of bait make them more productive. Juvenile baitfish and crustaceans use flats to feed and develop, making them fish magnets at different times of the year depending upon the bait type. This is why a flat might be hot one spring and not be productive again until the summer of the following year.

Warm weather can make flats fishing a special experience.

Shallow-water fishing is ideal during calm conditions, which allow the angler to wade comfortably while seeing and hearing fish. A hard wind chop will make the fishing more difficult. A moderate wind on some flats may be helpful by concentrating bait or gamefish along a shoreline, against a bar, or into a cove. Wind also influences tide, either by holding it back or speeding it up.

The signs of feeding activity in shallow water should be obvious, especially during the day. Yet I've seen action go unnoticed, perhaps because the angler does not expect to find fish in these locations and does not know what to look for. Getting back to Angus's belief—expecting to catch fish—also expect to *see* fish and you will spot them. Not just in shallow water, but in every type of water, look in any and all locations for the slightest sign of activity.

Actually spotting fish in shallow water can be more difficult because the signs, like a fin or tail dimpling the surface or a wake or bulge cutting the calm water, can be subtle. Gamefish can feed quietly, especially in an environment like the flats, which turn the generally aggressive bluefish into a more cautious predator. Of course, there are times when a blitz occurs, leaving little doubt that fish are feeding, but even then approach cautiously, for they still spook easily.

Bonito and albacore are less likely to go into the shallows, but on several occasions, while fishing for other fish, I have watched them move over flats to feed. Although bonito seldom stray far from deep water, weakfish, blues, and stripers are frequent visitors to the shallows, with bluefish the most aggressive daylight feeders there. Weaks are almost exclusively nighttime users of the flats, and rarely have I taken one in broad daylight.

When preparing to fish a flat, determine the bait present and match it with a fly pattern and fly action. Weakfish and bass can be very selective if feeding on shrimp, worms, and baitfish, requiring a close imitation and proper presentation. When weakfish are sipping shrimp, the combination of a floating line and a shrimp fly, fished on a free float, could be the only method that will take fish. Get as close to the fish as possible, keeping casts short and above the target, making a dead drift much easier to obtain. Use this technique for bass taking shrimp as well.

Never presume that a piece of water is too shallow to hold fish, particularly in low light, when fish can be anywhere. Apply this thinking to all locations when encountering low water, to expand your fishing possibilities and success.

9

Ocean Beaches

I crossed a narrow sand spit separating the bay from the open sea. The wind-blown surf gave the steep beach an uninviting look that made you realize the fishing was going to be hard. The broken surf seemed to be coming from two directions, which made sense because the wind had changed during the night from straight onshore to quartering. Stripping 70 feet of line from my reel, I stretched the no. 10 weight-forward intermediate line, carefully coiling it into the stripping basket. Then I started working downtide, letting the rip swing my fly on a dead drift, adding a pulsating action as the fly flowed into the rolling water along the beach. Occasionally there was a strong smell of bait or fish, but my fly went undisturbed. Several times I felt weight on the line, but there was no grass.

The flow down the beach was heavier than I liked, but that's October on Cape Cod. Trying different casting angles to the waves running off the beach, I found that a quartering angle into the wind worked best to keep the fly in fishable water. But casting too long a line created too much slack, and I was missing takes. I started making short casts to give a better drift and let the fly stay in the feeding lane longer. As I worked up the beach, the line tightened as a midsize striper inhaled the fly. Another short cast produced another fish. It was not hot and heavy fishing, but by working just the water close to the beach, I picked up half a dozen fish in what appeared to be unfishable water for fly tackle. Perhaps switching to a sinking line would have been the best choice because they track better, but with a short cast I was able to fish productively. Using a short line in heavy water conditions gives more control and the ability to stay in touch with the fly.

In a perfect world we could fish light rods, floating lines, and small flies, and catch fish right on the surface. And given the choice, that would be the way I would want to fish—watching fish take top-water flies. All too often, however, the roll along an ocean beach requires getting the fly down and getting it to hold in the flow. When fishing a shallow beach with 1- to 2-foot surf, a floating line can work but an intermediate line is a better choice. On steeper beaches with 3- to 5-foot surf, sinking lines track better, get the fly down, and are less

Barb is working on a nice bluefish silhouetted in the wave.

affected by the flow. Sinking lines also cast better into the wind and handle bigger flies more efficiently.

Learning to fish a beach properly is important, for there are hundreds of miles of shoreline stretching from Maine to the Carolinas, all teeming with fish. The entire East Coast has various types of sandy beaches ranging from small isolated pockets to huge expanses like Cape Cod. These beaches offer a variety of water depths, rips, surf conditions, and fishing opportunities for all skill levels of marine fly fishermen.

A sand beach is a section of shoreline made up of sand, gravel, or in some cases softball-size stones mixed into the sand. Some beaches have large smooth boulders scattered along the shore. Beaches vary in depth, the steepness of the slopes indicating how much water is out front. A very steep beach will have good water depth close to shore. Depending upon their location and the composition of the bottom, some beaches change from year to year, or even after a heavy storm, while others remain constant for generations.

In some locations shifting sands along beaches form large holes along the shore. Called ocean holes, these sections appear as darker water flanked by sandbars. Occurring in numerous sizes and shapes, their shifting nature causes them to change constantly. These holes make a beach interesting and offer an ideal environment for bait and fish. I once witnessed Cape Point at Hatteras on the Outer Banks in North Carolina shift about 300 yards in four days—ten D-9 bulldozers couldn't move that much sand in a week. At low tide you could walk out and fish, but the sand was unstable and it took several days after the wind shifted before the point stabilized. Be aware that sand locations can change overnight. After a storm, check the beach before wading in low light.

Beaches appear on nautical charts as any section of open shoreline, and some have large sections of rocky structure, large stones, or rock outcroppings. The most popular beaches are named for navigational purposes. Water depth on charts is listed in feet at mean low water. On some beaches, like Nauset on Cape Cod, ocean holes are not marked because of their ever-changing characteristics. A good beach generally drops off rapidly, showing deep water near the shore, although some shallow beaches can be productive. A shoreline with a large expanse of shallows, indicated as a green section on nautical charts, is called a "flat" and is the subject of chapter 8.

A sustained wind may bring weed onto some beaches, making them unfishable. Ocean holes along Cape Cod fill with a fine clinging weed on east or northeast winds. The locals call it mung, and the name fits, because the weed will coat a line so badly that fishing is impossible. When encountering this weed, try moving to different locations along the beach because one section might be cleaner than

A heavy weed called mung can make fishing impossible along some beaches.

another. If it's not too thick, fishing is possible, but make casts short. When fighting a fish, keep shaking the line with the rod tip to keep the line free. If it's not cleared, the weed buildup can prevent line from passing through the tip. Such a weed can clog a spinning outfit—and mono is smoother than fly line or backing.

Bait along any shore eventually lures fish to it, but it's not always easy to determine when this occurs. Summer months generally mean fishing during dark or low-light periods because some species, particularly stripers, are sluggish, feeding less when the water temperature is higher. A good combination for any shore is an incoming tide in the morning or evening; the changing light plus the moving water can trigger fish to feed. Morning tides are ideal for bonito or albacore, which are not nighttime feeders.

Spring and fall (especially October to November) can be an excellent time to fish beaches, with nonstop action all day long as the gamefish feed heavily to replenish weight lost during the spring trip north, or to store fat for the year-end migration or hibernation. These migrations make the open-ocean shores from Maine to the Carolinas very popular when mixed schools of gamefish are blitzing the beaches. Fall, from September to December, is the best time for large concentrations of fish, which start early in Maine and spread southward as the water cools. Spring spreads out the fish, but fishing can be hot if conditions are right. Spring action begins in the southern areas around mid-March and moves northward as the water warms.

When fish are this concentrated, it should be easy to find them; however, many beaches have feeding fish during midday without visible clues. Casting along deep beaches is the best way to locate fish at these times; work the shoreline, try flies of different densities, and use both fast-sinking and surface lines. (Remember that the intermediate line is the foundation for most fishing situations.)

On windy or noisy nights, the only way to find fish is to keep casting and searching for active fish or their scent. When gamefish feed on baitfish, it can generate an odor, but even large concentrations of baitfish will produce a scent. The aroma can vary from a strong fishy smell to a scent similar to cucumber or melon. When detecting foreign fish scent, try to locate the source by calculating the wind direction. Keep walking upwind until you lose the scent, then start casting, working back to the starting point. Particularly at night, "nosing" out fish is an effective means of finding them on beaches.

Beaches with rips running a great distance along the shore require the angler to keep moving, to fish the entire shoreline rather than hit only a few spots. Saltwater fish either take up feeding stations, as trout do along lengthy stretches of water, or cruise such sections searching for bait. The fly rodder who remains stationary may miss this action. If fish are found along such a section and then depart, keep moving, usually downstream, until they are relocated. Very large beaches are easier to fish when several anglers cover more water and keep pace with the roaming pods of fish searching for food. (The help of a spin fisherman is valuable when you're covering a large section of water.)

All species of fish actively feed along beaches, but each reacts differently to the same conditions. Stripers are the most tolerant of any condition, and will go almost anywhere in pursuit of food. Blues can be nearly as aggressive, but they prefer deeper water.

The primary advantage of beach fishing is the ability to park a car and then fish without a boat or other special equipment. Actually, many outer beaches with surf action are unfishable with boats because it's too dangerous to work a craft inside the surf line. It's best to fish most ocean beaches from shore because the fish tend to be close, right along the surf line. Cautious wading is necessary when the surf is rolling.

Sand walls like this often form along the beach where a good, deep hole is located.

Reading an Ocean Beach

Fishing open beaches with rolling surf can be pleasing and rewarding, but it can also be frustrating. The sight of breaking surf makes it hard to imagine how a fish can survive in what appears to be a mass of turbulent water. Yet this large volume of wild suds is the ideal feeding ground for stripers and blues.

Let's sit on a sand dune and learn to read and fish this type of water, for it can, if conditions are right, be perfect for fly fishing. Start by watching the waves as they roll toward the shore: See when and how they break, how long they roll, and where the white water begins and ends. Patterns should begin to develop if you are on an ocean beach with holes, such as Nantucket, Cape Cod, or Hatteras, North Carolina, and other similar areas. Dark areas should appear where the white water stops rolling, indicating a hole or drop-off on the backside of a bar.

Sandbars build up along beaches, running either parallel to or angling toward the shore. These bars break the waves before they reach the beach. They also form deep areas along the shore as currents from the waves carve the sand. Bars that angle into shore are highlighted by a wave that starts to break some distance out and angles toward the shore. Watch this water as it rolls to see if it's spilling into a drop-off. When a wave breaks, rolls for a short distance, then disappears, there is a drop-off right where the white water ends and spills into the hole. Fish feed under or on the edge of the white foam, depending upon how much water is rolling over the bar.

The angler must get a fly to swim through the white water, then into the hole. The fly must look like a baitfish being swept by the waves, or as if it were trying to escape. (The trout fisherman might compare this to fishing under or around a waterfall.) If the surf is sweeping your line too quickly, not allowing the fly to work properly, try casting at different angles or timing the cast to fall between waves so the fly will swing more slowly through the water.

Heavy surf requires sinking lines to get the fly down to the fish. But never use weighted flies in combination with a sinking line, for the too-heavy fly will be dragged through the sand by the surf action, dulling the hook point. Instead, use a high-density sinking line with a buoyant fly to get penetration without bottom-dragging. (Most sinking lines used in the surf are actually sink-tip/ sink-head-style lines that are designed after the Jim Teeny line, a floating or intermediate running line with a 25- to 30-foot sinking head.) Work the fly through the deep or fast water, letting it drift in the faster current or retrieving with various speeds if slower current permits. Make sure the fly swims at a natural rate of speed—don't rush it through the water like Superminnow. The properly swimming fly is one that flows with the water, moving along normally as if it belongs there.

Poppers and sliders are deadly when worked right in the surface foam. Plan to cast right after the wave sweeps over the bar, landing the fly in the white water and working it like a struggling baitfish. Work surface patterns in this manner as long as the fly is not being dragged too swiftly across the surface. As with a rip, cast to different points on the water to get different swings. An intermediate line works well for surface patterns, sometimes enhancing the action by dragging the fly below the surface after each pull of the retrieve. This works best for most light to moderate surf applications; use a fast-sinking line to get deeper.

Fishing the backsides of bars, the locations closest to the shore, is just one way to find fish along a surf line. Bars also shield and form large holes along a beach; some have a football shape and can be over half a mile long. These areas are obvious during wave action: The offshore sheltering bars roll white, forming a protective wall around the hole. Offshore bars range from a castable distance to over a quarter mile from the shore.

Several cuts, sometimes more, appear along bars to bleed off the surplus water caused by wave action. If they are reachable, fish the cuts—the deeper water between bars or between a bar and shore—as you would a rip, for they, like the deep water of the hole, are good places to drop a fly. Gamefish lie in ambush at the edges of these cuts for bait to flush from the hole. Some cuts are deep and fast, requiring a sinking line unless the fish are surface feeding.

Big ocean holes can be unfishable for the fly rodder if the surf is very large. The surf will roll too hard for an angler to control the line, requiring casts beyond fly-tackle capability. In the event the water in a hole is rolling too hard at high tide, check it during a lower tide, when the bars may break the strong wave action enough to permit fly fishing.

Normal surf can make an ocean hole a hot spot, providing productive fishing for the angler willing to work hard and precisely cover all the water. The wrong strategy is to drive from spot to spot, making several casts in each place and trying to hit as much water as possible at the best tide. I've watched anglers run down the beach, make several casts, then leave, rushing to the next spot as I was landing a fish, and not even looking for the obvious indications of action. Working the rolling surf well takes time. Fish fly patterns of different densities, sizes, and colors. Vary retrieves from slow to fast, getting the fly to

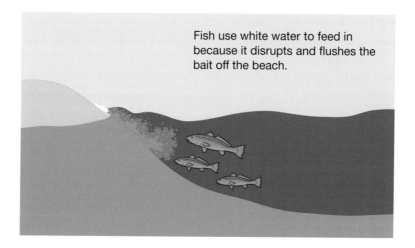

Fish use white water to feed in because it disrupts and flushes the bait off the beach.

flow through the water at different speeds. Some locations need a dead drift, as in fishing a rip, to make the fly appear lifelike, and too rapid a movement will look unnatural. Change fly line in heavy water, where a full sinking line will be necessary to reach the fish.

What Is the Wash?

One area where wave action creates a feeding zone is the trough along the edge of the beach. This section of white water is also called the wash or slough and forms along ocean beaches when a wave flows back down the beach. It is located near shore where the wave action occurs and causes turbulent water and easy feeding for some gamefish. Wave size determines wash size. The wash is wadable in small surf, but unreachable during big swells. This section of water is tumbling, like the steep base of a river rapids or waterfall, but it is not stationary: It moves up and down the beach with each wave, rising and falling with the tide.

A wave breaks and its force drives it up the steep beach. The wave actually rolls uphill, rising well above the water line, then washes back down the beach, plunging into the hole. This creates a rolling action as the wave washes down the beach and mixes with another incoming wave or spills into slower-moving water along the shore. Some locations along a hole have ripping water running along the shore and a wash pouring into the rip. The actual wash is the point where the receding wave meets the sea. Look for the rolling turbulent water along the shore, where the broken waves roll from the beach back into the oncoming waves.

Fishing the Flow or Wash

When water along a beach gets rough, line control is the key to success. Several factors that influence fishing conditions are wave size and speed, steepness of the beach's slope, and the angle the waves break onto the beach. Waves over 4 feet high create heavy water movement, and on steep beaches with fast-moving waves, the force can double. With waves 2 to 4 feet high, I often use an intermediate line unless the surf is fast. When I begin to lose line control, it's time to fish a 300- to 450-grain fast sink-tip line. I prefer intermediate running lines with a fast-sinking section that is about 30 feet long. The color difference between the fast-sinking section and the running line is helpful in determining the fly's location.

In bigger surf, line control can be difficult when fishing the trough along the edge of the beach. There are two variables that can influence the line and cause loss of fly control: the flow up and down the beach, and the flow that runs along the beach. In smaller surf the flow along a beach is fishable, but when bigger waves are rolling onto a beach, it's better to just work the trough next to the beach. Casting too much line, or casting when the wave is running up the beach, oftentimes creates slack in the line that causes loss of contact with the

At times fish will feed close along a beach.

fly. Try to time the waves flowing down the beach, and cast as the last wave of a set begins to flow off the beach. A good trick is to feed some line after making the cast, letting the fly and line move with the wave down the beach. As the flow begins to dissipate, start retrieving with quick, long pulls. Also try casting at an angle to the flow, and as the flow slows down, hold tight, letting the line and fly swing into the trough. It's important to keep in touch with the fly and keep the line as straight as possible. You will need to try different-length casts to find the best distance to allow the fly to work through the trough without losing line control.

Waves that break at an angle to the beach create a sweeping flow that adds another element to an already complex fishing condition. If you cast straight off the beach, the line will sweep in the direction the wave is flowing; waves breaking from the left will carry the line to the right quickly, allowing the fly less time in the strike zone. To combat this, try casting straight into the direction the wave is flowing up the beach. Time the cast just as the wave starts down the beach, and begin retrieving when the wave flows into the trough. The line should swing from left to right, making the fly swing through the trough, and the retrieve should end with the fly to your right with a left-to-right flow. Also try letting the line and fly swing without retrieving to see if you can get a different presentation and stay in the strike zone longer.

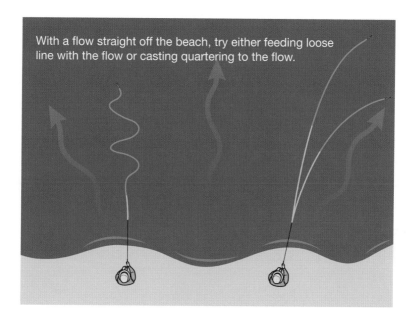

With a flow straight off the beach, try either feeding loose line with the flow or casting quartering to the flow.

Earlier I mentioned the flow along the beach. This flow often occurs when the surf hits the shoreline at an angle. A good trick for fishing this effectively is to cast out and walk with the flow while retrieving. This keeps the line and fly straight off the beach and prevents the waves from catching the line during most of the retrieve. Depending upon the wave size and speed of the flow, you can fish a good section of beach on each cast. To judge the flow's speed, watch the surface foam and walk at the same pace. I like to walk back and work the same section of beach several times, moving with the flow in order to fish the entire hole.

"White water," another surf term, is the point where a wave breaks and rolls over a bar, reef, jetty, or large rock, then spills into deeper water. Along ocean beaches there can be many different white-water combinations as wave size and direction, wind, and water levels alter the wash. This water offers superb fly rodding because it is, on all but the roughest days, within fly-casting distance. The rolling water brings even big fish within fly-rod range, making it possible to take a large fish without a large effort.

The white water that forms behind bars after a wave breaks is an easy feeding area for many gamefish. If you can wade onto the bar, cast along the face of the waves parallel to the bar, letting the fly and line swing with the white water from the shallow bar into the drop-off just behind the bar. This water is

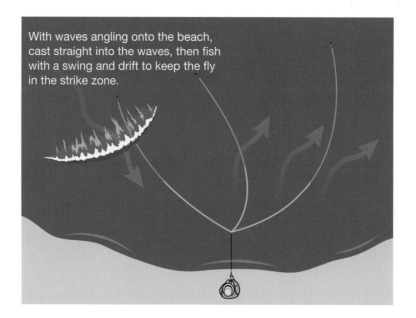

With waves angling onto the beach, cast straight into the waves, then fish with a swing and drift to keep the fly in the strike zone.

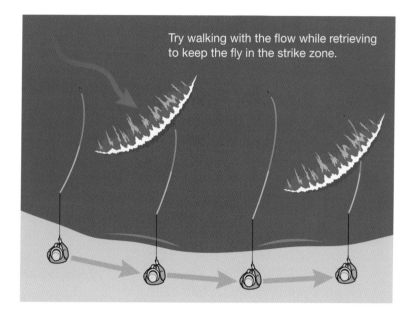

Try walking with the flow while retrieving to keep the fly in the strike zone.

often deep and is an ideal feeding location. Exposed bars neutralize the wave's fury and often produce a slow flow along the inside edge of the hole. This is an ideal fly-fishing location because it concentrates fish into small sections of bubbling, rolling water where fish need to strike quickly and feed aggressively. This is generally called fishing the white water. Remember, in big surf, wading out onto bars or turning your back to the surf can be dangerous, but there can be hot fishing in small to midsize waves—pick your days carefully.

The deep water, or hole, that forms inside an outer bar is an ideal place to fish when there is heavier surf. Look for locations with bars that break most of the wave's power, and fish the flow that sweeps from the hole out to open water. This water can be a mixture of foam and bubbles or just a flow formed by wave action. This flow along a beach is different because there is usually less wave action at your feet—most of the wave's power is spent after hitting the outer bar. If you can cast to the bar, work the flow from the shallow bar into the deeper section, swinging the fly across the flow. As the fly swings away from the bar, either let it flow on a dead drift or add action with long, sharp pulls. Mix up the casts using different retrieves while casting at different angles to the flow. If the hole is working well, don't rush through this water. **Keep trying different techniques,** because all this water can hold fish. This is often an easy location to fish and is productive even when you cannot reach the bar.

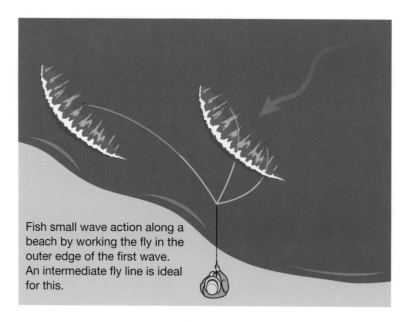

Fish small wave action along a beach by working the fly in the outer edge of the first wave. An intermediate fly line is ideal for this.

Because of their openness, beaches do not usually form strong rips from tidal flow unless they are near a large opening, at a point, or part of a land-mass that constricts water flow. Ocean beaches can be dull-looking without wave action, although this is the easiest time to fly fish the surf. I prefer *some* surf because it enhances fly performance, creates rips, makes fish feed more aggressively, and details the holes. White water breaking over bars highlights them as it contrasts with the dark water of the holes. Wave activity on shallow beaches, or heavy surf, can make fly fishing impossible, driving the fish beyond fly-casting distance.

Surf comes either from offshore weather fronts or onshore wind. Wind, though a thorn in the fly rodder's side, creates excellent fishing along beaches with favorable wave action; it drives in both bait and gamefish and can cause a feeding spree right at the angler's feet. Wind can also alert the angler to bait or gamefish activity by bringing you the fishes' scent. If possible, fish landmasses with multiple wind exposures, with the onshore wind driving fish onto the beach. If the winds are too strong, find a quiet pocket in the lee. The marine fly rodder must use a moderate wind as a friend to help enhance fishing. Shorelines with a quartering onshore wind, blowing to the fisherman's noncasting shoulder, help the caster reach productive waters and fish them properly.

Flat Water

Ocean beaches can offer good fishing during calm periods, when the tide provides just enough movement along the bars and shoreline to keep things interesting. This tranquil setting is ideal for fly tackle, and a fly will look more lifelike than spin or conventional lures. Fish the shoreline the same as you would a steep beach. Make some casts parallel to or quartering along the shore while working the fly to swing in the rip for maximum action. Use a retrieve when there is no wave or water movement to give the fly action. I prefer a pulsating action for this fishing. An intermediate line is ideal in these conditions; however, a sinking line might be useful for fishing the deeper areas.

When water is flat, the holes will have no definition and must be located either by finding them during daylight with overhead sun (the holes will show up as dark blue in contrast to the lighter bars) or by learning to read the beach. The sandy shoreline will suggest the way the bottom is shaped—flat beach, shallow water; steep beach, deep water. Sand will pile up along the shore, forming a sharp drop-off at the water's edge at high tide, resembling a tapering wall in front of the deep-water sections. The highest part will indicate the deepest section of the hole. Some drop-offs can be shoulder high and should be approached carefully at night on foot or when driving a beach buggy.

A large sand point formed by wave action is a great location to fish on any tide.

Sandbars, or points, build up on either side of ocean holes, dividing the deeper sections of the beach. In contrast to the holes, the shoreline at a point has a much more gradually sloping beach, indicating shallower water. Rips form over and around these shallow sections, bringing food into the drop-off. Fish lie along the edges, feeding just below the rip or on the edge of the white water if there is surf. Points at a distance appear defined, but need to be located by using an inshore landmark. Surf helps to outline and locate a point, but once you reach it, it will all but melt away.

When there is enough wave action, points have both heavy rolling white water washing into them and a rip pouring across and spilling into the adjoining hole. This rolling water holds fish, but it may be too rough for line control, and it's best to apply effort to the white water on the hole's edge. Cast into this white water, allowing the fly to swing from the shallow water and drop into the hole. Here, white water and wave action combine with the rip; try to fish between the waves for better line control, as the force of all three will sweep the fly out of control. Just upcurrent from the drop-off is the best position. Fish this water as you would a short rip, by making the fly swim with the white water into the hole. Vary the casting length to different spots until you find the right drift. If varied casting does not work, move until the fly works into the drop-off. Strong surf may require using a fast-sinking line combined with a buoyant fly to penetrate the swift current formed by the waves rolling over shallows.

Rocky Areas

Beaches located near rocky structure, or with this structure distributed along the shoreline, are more likely to hold fish for longer periods than will a pure-sand beach. Large rocks, sections of ledges, and mussel and kelp beds all provide cover and protection, just as deep water does, for many marine fish. This same cover, however, makes fishing and fish-landing more difficult. At night or during low light, snags are hard to detect, making sinking lines or sinking flies hard to use because even-keel or weedless flies hang up in some types of structure. Landing fish can be murder, for even small fish are able to tie you up in rock formations, kelp, weed beds, or other structure scattered along the bottom. Check the tippet after fighting a fish, after every hang-up, and periodically throughout the fishing session for wear. Barnacles and sharp structure can fray and weaken tippets with the slightest scrape.

Fish shorelines dotted with sand-polished boulders in the same manner you would a sand beach, concentrating on the water around the rocks: This is

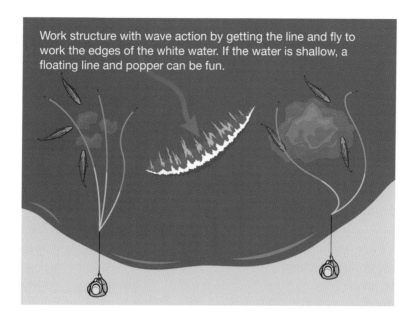

Work structure with wave action by getting the line and fly to work the edges of the white water. If the water is shallow, a floating line and popper can be fun.

true even with surf action. Stripers especially like to feed around rocky structure, in the rolling water created by wave action. Smooth rocks will cause few hang-ups; an angler can cast right next to them. Then, either retrieve the fly or drift it in the same manner as for fishing the wash or white water. If fishing a field of rocks that are below the surface, use a buoyant fly to fish the moving water, casting as the wave flows over the rocks.

If conditions allow, such places are productive on calm nights: Work a popper along or among the rocks. When fishing around big rocks, try to get the popper to push lots of water and make a good splash. A two-handed retrieve can be very effective with sharp, quick pulls. In less than calm water, if the popper does not produce a good splash, it might go unnoticed. And even in flat water, a noisy popper will pull fish from a greater distance.

Fishing near any hard structure necessitates regular and ongoing inspection of the hook point for damage. Rugged structure, however, is another story, requiring weedless flies or a buoyant weedless combo to keep from snagging bottom if fishing deep is necessary. Use a heavily dressed deer-hair-headed fly, weedless, with intermediate line to get the fly down with few hang-ups. Floating or intermediate lines also work well with surface and subsurface flies over rugged structure to pull the fish up from their lies.

Getting below the Bait

Both rocky and sand areas will have surface action, with fish feeding on the edges or under the white water when there is wave action, and on calm days attacking bait as it swims from the shallows into deeper water. When encountering surface action in deeper water along a shoreline, cast first to the breaking fish, using shallow-working flies or poppers. If action does not come with several pattern changes, try fishing under or to the side of the breaking fish. Concentrate on the fish that are feeding on the edges or below the breaking fish, picking up the dead and wounded bait as it sinks. When baitfish are too thick, the gamefish will swim through the schools grabbing mouthfuls, not singling out individual baits.

As the surface action continues, some fish will feed beneath the schools. These fish are feeding on individual bait pieces and are more readily taken. This event occurs frequently when stripers feed on tightly packed schools of sand eels, small herring, and peanut bunker. At times these conditions will drive anglers crazy with wild surface action but few strikes. Here the long rodder can shine, working a small pattern under the schools, either letting the fly dead-drift like a lifeless baitfish or retrieving it slowly, allowing the fly to flutter up and down as if crippled. I have even just let the fly lie on the bottom, and fish still pick it up. Fly rodders fishing below feeding fish can frustrate spin anglers who only use surface lures—getting below the feeding frenzy is important. Lightly weighted sinking flies are ideal, used with an intermediate line if the water is not too deep, or a sinking line if the drop-off is too great.

Working the edges, away from the feeding fish, is also productive. Here your fly is not competing with other baitfish, but looks like a loner separated from the school's protection. Try both applications, getting below or working the edges of feeding (but not striking) fish in many different types of water. Always try the edges when fish are not cooperating. In shallow locations without room to get below thickly packed bait, fish can be very tough to take, and the only method here is to fish the fringes.

Working rock-studded shorelines and structure from a boat offers great fishing, particularly in the fall as schools of migrating fish move down the coast. Many times, feeding fish work just beyond casting range, and while the boat angler is into constant action, the surf fisherman watches with envy. Areas like Buzzards Bay, Martha's Vineyard, and Nantucket Sound in Massachusetts; the Rhode Island coast; Montauk; and the entire south shore of Long Island to New Jersey are ideal for boat fishing, provided you keep a watchful weather eye.

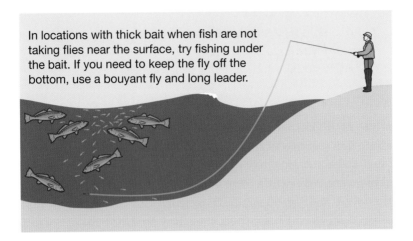

In locations with thick bait when fish are not taking flies near the surface, try fishing under the bait. If you need to keep the fly off the bottom, use a bouyant fly and long leader.

Maintain a safe distance from the surf line, especially on shores with structure, for a power loss here combined with an onshore wind can put boaters in danger. Many areas, particularly along rough ocean shorelines, require special safety equipment: extra line in 100-foot coils with snap hooks for fast connection, or a second anchor and line, could save lives. Long anchor chains, 6 to 10 feet, are best for holding bottom. An extra mounted motor is ideal, but make sure it starts quickly and runs well. The buddy system, another boat close by, is safe and reassuring in big water, and assistance is only minutes away. I can remember several occasions when the assurance of another boat allowed me to fish waters like Cuttyhunk, Block Island, and the shores of Rhode Island, which would have been unthinkable had I been alone in my 13-foot Boston Whaler.

Many small craft are safe in open water, providing the operator's and the boat's limitations are known, and sheltered water is fairly close at hand. The small-boat (craft of under 20 feet) operator should never press on when conditions begin to look bad. Always find refuge at the first sign of bad weather.

10

Cliff Fishing

The coastline of Rhode Island, like the coastlines of other states bordering ocean waters, has sections of rock formation jutting into the ocean. In periods of heavy surf, these sections may appear unfishable to the novice fly fisher. But to several pioneers, rocky cliffs have proved to be a new fishing frontier.

Fortunately, I had the opportunity to learn this fishing from the two men who discovered it. Herb Chase first, then Ray Smith, both of them from the Newport, Rhode Island, area, pioneered this frontier—and learned to catch fish from seemingly unfishable water. Herb was an expert saltwater fly rodder who had fished all over the world; he had taken three permit on a fly before this was a popular fishery. Ray mostly fished locally but was on the water all the time, fishing his favorite spots along the cliffs. I can still see both anglers perched on high rocks, working the white water flowing off the rocks. Herb and Ray are now fishing better waters, but I have good memories and feel gifted to have known and fished with these friends.

Fishing with Ray was a learning experience. As we walked in the morning light to one of his fishing spots, Ray pointed out different plants and flowers living on this apparent wasteland of rocks. A thick fog cast an eerie light onto the dark rocks, which contrasted with the white water swirling around the heavy structure. Standing on a high perch near the shoreline, Ray pointed to the area I should fish, commenting that the water looked excellent. Heavy surf with good white water is best for fishing cliffs. I had never fished this particular spot before and marveled at the number of holes and holding areas it possessed. When I'd reached the spot that Ray suggested, I stood back and watched the rolling water for a good ten minutes to make sure it was safe. The location was dry, indicating no waves had reached it, but I expected to be chased before the morning was out. Sneakers and light, quick-drying pants, rather than waders, allow more mobility; wearing such an outfit is the safest way to fish cliffs in the summer. Colder weather requires waders and rain gear to prevent freezing from constant spray.

To work the rolling surf, I kept casting and then swinging my fly with the white water into a deeper section located just beyond the rocky drop-off. A large bowl would form after a set of waves rolled against the rocks, then the water buildup would boil outward into the ocean, its foaming white a sharp contrast to the dark sea. This churning water was my focus, for it is here that fish, mainly bass or blues, feed. Lying in the holes under this foam, they feast on bait as it's swept into the deeper water. Twice I spotted a fish's fin or tail as it fed in the rolling white water, taking advantage of the confusion caused by the turbulent surf.

Timing my cast, I caught a perfect surge that carried the dark fly down with the boiling water, like a baitfish being swept from its rocky shelter to open sea. The bass, unlike a fish in calm water, struck hard, with no hesitation, pulling line from my hands as it used the flow and raced to open water. Clearing the loose line easily, I let the fish run, hoping it would clear the rocks. Once in open water, where it would not have all the advantages, I could fight the fish on better terms. Even though the fish was not large, it swam easily in the rolling white water; the rocks were its domain.

There was a good landing area to my right, and I started to shuffle toward it, taking a few steps, then stopping to see where the fish was swimming. Luckily the bass stayed on top, keeping away from the ledges and kelp 30 feet below. All the while I wondered how much skill and luck it would take to land a large

A fish is hooked in the hole off the rocks.

Once the fish is under control, the angler works the fish to the first pocket and then the second pocket.

In the second pocket it's safe for the angler to land the fish.

fish. The striper was now tiring, finning 40 feet from the rocks, close to the landing pool. I waited for a larger wave and kept the fish off the rocks. Then, as a heavy swell surged against the structure, I pumped the rod several times, reeled quickly, and made several steps backward. This action brought the fish with the water's force up the rocky wall and into a pool, where I could hold it until the wave receded. With the fish in this lower pool, I needed only to wait for another wave, which would sweep the fish higher up, to a safer perch—a place from which I could handle it without fear of being swept from the rocks.

I held up the ten-pound bass to show Ray, who gave the thumbs-up sign, delighted that I had taken the first fish. Then I released it in a quiet cove to my right.

Ray landed two fish that day; neither was large, but hooking, fighting, and landing them under these conditions makes any fish exciting. Through the years, Ray took several fish in the twenty-pound class from rocky cliffs, but lost many larger fish to this harsh environment.

Rocky cliff structures exist along the coastline in Rhode Island (mainly in the Jamestown-Newport area), in Massachusetts (both north and south of Boston), and along the coast from New Hampshire to northern Maine. This fishing also exists on the West Coast, in Canada, and throughout the tropics. Though not normally regarded as ideal fly-fishing areas, these huge rock formations that jut into the ocean (and that hold off the heavy seas as no man-made structure could) can produce excellent fishing; the holes and pockets located at their bases are ideal gamefish feeding grounds. Any high rocky formation exposed to the open sea that will permit safe standing and access to fishable water is a worthwhile fishing spot.

Nautical charts mark some cliffs, but the best indication is deep water shown right next to shore. On a chart, short lines drawn perpendicular to the shoreline illustrate cliff walls. A cliff seen from a distance is unmistakable because its dark massiveness contrasts strongly with the rolling white waves. In heavy seas the water thunders against the walls, cascading into the air. In areas with small tides, changing water levels may have little effect on fishing around cliffs, although angling strategy may vary. In some spots, lower tides can be unfishable because they would require an angler to move below the tide mark on slippery black rocks; this situation is too dangerous to attempt. The large tides of upper Massachusetts and Maine make fishing at low water treacherous, tempting the angler to venture out on slime-covered rocks where secure footing is impossible, but the knowledgeable angler with the proper footwear can fish at lower tides. Ledges with jagged surfaces and locations with barnacles covering the rocks offer better footing at low tides; however, incoming and high tides are the best times to fish rocky cliffs because the angler can stay high and dry. If wave conditions permit, it might be possible to fish any tide in some areas.

Finding Safe Fishable Water

Cliff fishing depends on sea conditions: the size and direction of the swells, the force of the waves and the distance between them, and what kinds of waves are present. Wind-driven waves occur close together, breaking one on top of another, with little shape. Waves created by an offshore low-pressure weather system have shape, with space between the swells. These spaced swells offer better fishing. Wave action and white water are what bring the fish into a cliff to search for food. Schools of bait become trapped against the cliffs, making easy feeding for gamefish. Like jetties, rocky cliffs hold resident food—crabs, small blackfish—that live close to the rocks; the wave action makes them vulnerable to gamefish. Fall migrations bring the hottest fishing, but white water is an important factor because it brings the fish within casting range.

When surf is light, most locations are safe to fish, but walking can be difficult.

Finding good-looking holes around cliffs is easy; finding the holes that are fishable with a fly takes a little more doing. From high ground, look for mushrooming clouds of white water along the rocks, water that rushes out and spills into darker, deeper water. There should be a contrasting line between the two. If the waves break before hitting the wall, there must be a shelf or shallow area in front of the cliff, which will make swinging the fly into deeper water difficult. The prime fishing locations are where white water rolls back from the rocks directly into a hole, and where there's a high perch nearby to allow safe, easy casting and a place nearby to land the fish. Such spots are usually good in all wave conditions and fishable on most tides. Just remember that when a large sea is running, only the highest, safest perches are usable.

After finding suitable, safe fishing water, you need to pick a spot on the cliff that is high and has a landing area close to the fishing hole. Places that require climbing down the face of a rock, even 4 or 5 feet, put you in danger. When changing a fly or working on the tippet, move back from the water's edge. Never turn your back to the ocean. Keep watching the horizon for possible rogue waves if the surf is big. If an outside swell looks threatening, move back. When swells reach 8 feet, only the highest dry locations are safe; if you constantly need to keep watching the waves, the fun is gone.

Always think safety first—this fishing is only dangerous if you do something foolish; otherwise, driving to the fishing spot is more hazardous. Most of this advice is not so important in small surf, but with waves over 4 feet, any miscue can be deadly. If you become careless and are caught by a big sea, quickly find a wall to duck behind. I did this once when I walked out on a long ledge in what appeared to be 4- to 6-foot surf until a set of 12-footers walled up. In my case, I had a 4-foot-high section of ledge large enough to get behind that blocked the wave's force. Luckily only white water rolled over my position, but even if the wave was bigger, the wall would have deflected most of its force. It's better, however, not to get in this position in the first place.

Although rolling surf brings the best action from the rocks, good fishing is possible during flat, calm periods. Work the area as you would a beach with structure, fishing from hole to hole, covering as much water as possible. Bonito and albacore feed along Rhode Island in calm times. However, there will be times when the inability to make long casts will frustrate the fly rodder, for the fast-moving gamesters tease even the long-range spin fisherman, staying beyond everyone's reach.

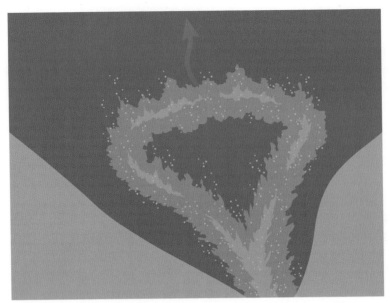

Look for locations along the structure that create a mushroom-like plume of white water that flows out to sea.

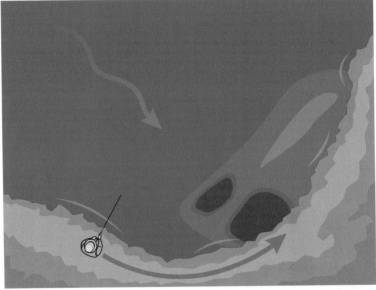

Safe landing pockets that the angler can work a fish into make landing easier.

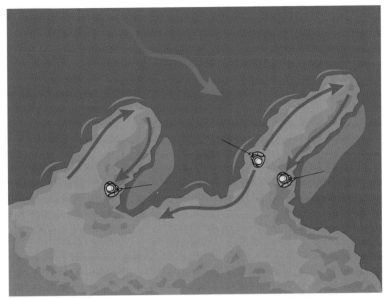

The lee side of a point is another good location to land fish.

How to Fish from a Rocky Cliff

The rushing water that rolls off the cliff into a hole is so strong that a lure will appear unnatural swimming upstream against it. As with a strong rip, flies should be worked naturally, flowing with the current like live baitfish. But the difficulty in fishing this rip is that it flows *away* from the angler, sometimes heading into an onrushing sea, and this makes line control difficult. The key is to time casts with the waves so that the rushing white water will carry the fly in a natural manner out into the deeper water. Casting too soon will allow the wave to push the line inward, toward the cliff. Casting too late will cause the line to miss the flow or be caught by the next inward wave, and the fly will never reach fishable water.

The water around holes develops a rhythm. Offshore swells often move shoreward in sets of three or eight, with the largest waves usually arriving last. When waves break like this, water builds up against the base of the cliff, then pours out after the last wave, causing boiling water to flow into the hole. Casting into the rolling water just when the last wave of a set hits places the fly in a perfect position to ride the white water out. When you cast, try to imagine you're throwing a bottle that, if it lands at the proper time and place, will be carried out to sea without breaking. Predicting wave timing takes observation to see how the sets form several hundred yards from shore. When a wave walls up, look beyond to see if a set is building behind it. Wave sets will appear as a series of large rolling mounds, building in height as they approach shore. If the wave is a single, treat it as if it were the last wave in a set, and cast as it breaks.

Without structured wave sets, watch the water level against the rocks and try to estimate when the buildup of water will spill back out to sea. The water level will climb along the rocks and hold against the wall, acting like a soap dish of water tipped upon its edge. The dish holds the water because of the force of the oncoming waves. When overfilled, the dish empties as the wave's force subsides, rushing out into deeper water regardless of the waves continuing to break.

Since broken windblown surf has little shape or pattern, fly anglers must continuously experiment to achieve the proper drift that will swing the fly into the hole. If an irregularly breaking surf keeps catching the line before it can swing into the hole, try slipping extra line on the flowing wave to give the drift more distance. If the line and fly are being pushed back and forth, hold tight and then allow the fly to work in the wave action like a struggling baitfish, letting the surging water work it back toward the hole. The only way to fish broken water is to keep casting until you develop a feel for the particular area. False casting is a necessity here to develop proper rhythm: Wait, holding your line in the air, for the proper time to drop the fly on the water. Keep fishing; only practice and experience will teach you how to fish this water. Each small piece of water differs to some degree, so there are no hard and fast rules as to when and where to cast. **Keep trying different techniques** until one works. There is no other way to learn except through practical experience—and I know of no freshwater fishing conditions that resemble these, although I have never fished below Niagara Falls.

Fish activity can help you determine the proper time to cast, because fish feeding in a hole at the base of a cliff may develop a rhythm. When the fish show themselves during the outflowing surge, keep casting to them. Try to get the fly to the fish just before they show—like getting a dry fly to a trout just before it rises. Keep watching adjoining holes for tails, fins, surface splashes, or spraying bait. Above all, keep casting. Water will roll off the rocks in different ways, depending upon wave size and direction, and the number of waves in a set. Even though the section you are fishing may be small, many casts must be made to discover the correct combinations of drift direction, line, and fly types. The most important thing is to achieve the right swing so the fly will reach the hole.

The trick is *not to retrieve*. "Do not retrieve the fly; let it work in the white water," Ray used to explain in his lesson to all newcomers, swinging his hand in a pendulum-like gesture. This is sound advice. The rushing water is so strong that a baitfish looks unnatural swimming upstream. Once you can get your line to flow out with the breaking wave, let the fly dead-drift, swinging with the flowing water, and feed extra line to get a longer, deeper drift. Little fly action is necessary other than a pulsating motion on the swing or a slow retrieve after the water stops rolling. (Unlike most strong rips, this water flow diminishes after running only a short distance into deep water.) Don't worry about losing touch with the fly at times, because the fish in these areas usually take with authority (they need to, for their food passes by so quickly). Try to work the fly in as much water as possible, making it swing to various sections of the hole. This is similar to fishing the rolling water from a sandy beach and can be approached in the same manner. Along a sand beach, mushrooming clouds will also develop, with white water boiling straight out to sea, yet it occurs less frequently, without the rhythm that develops along a cliff. But fish it in the same manner; in each case, work the fly in as much water as possible, fishing patiently, trying to make the fly swing to various sections of the hole.

Losing flies can be a problem. Learn to use the water flow to keep your flies from hanging up, and also to free them. If the area in front dries up, don't retrieve but let the line sit for the next wave to raise the water level, then strip in quickly with the flowing water. If your fly becomes stranded on bare rock, let the next wave pick it up and carry it free, then strip in quickly as the fly comes back toward the rocks. Free lodged flies by creating a bow in the fly line so the back-rushing water will pull the fly loose. Be careful not to leave too much slack, for then the line itself can become tangled in the rocks and you could lose an entire fly line. Flies hooked in kelp usually pull free before the tippet will break. Most anglers use twenty-pound-test tippets when fishing rocky cliffs; however, this raises the chances of losing a fly line—be sure to have good knots connecting the backing to the line. (See the knot section in chapter 17.) In any event, *never* try to climb down a cliff to retrieve a hung-up fly—break it off. A friend once tried to retrieve a favorite popper embedded along a Rhode Island rock wall. Even though the surf was mild, he got caught, and his 270-pound frame looked like King Kong clinging to the Empire State Building, as the surf showed him what strength was.

Depending upon wave size and the location of the cliff, sinking line—either intermediate or Hi-D—is the best choice for this fishing. Heavy water with a swift flow requires a fast sinker for adequate penetration. In windy conditions fast-sinking lines cast better, giving more line speed; in calmer conditions or slower-working holes, an intermediate line is best. Carry an extra spool for a line change in case there are varying conditions. First look at the wave size, and then take either a spare floater or fast sinker. I usually fish with an intermediate or fast-sinking line, but if the surf is mild, it's important to have a floating line with poppers or surface sliders for when fish are feeding on the surface. Blues and especially bass feed right in the white foam, hitting surface flies worked along the top. Fish top-water flies by swinging them down with the flowing water and popping them with rod action. Or cast the surface fly across the white water, fishing it in the flow or working it so it fishes the end of the flow, then bring it through the boiling backwash after the water has lost some of its power. Fishing at the end of the rushing water is a useful technique if the angler can cast beyond the boiling water, bringing the fly back through the foam after it has lost some of its force. Use surface sliders and flies or noisy poppers, trying different retrieves and fly movements, though the swing method with no retrieve should be the procedure used most often.

To sum up this kind of fishing: You are water watching. Learning wave behavior from **time on the water** breeds success. The actual fishing is trial and error, for once the fly reaches the right position—bang! The fish is on. Fish feeding in this turbulent water need only to see the fly. It may take a hundred casts, but with persistence they are catchable. There are no subtleties here— fish take like a freight train.

Fancy fly patterns: Keep them in the box. In this rolling water, fish strike at shadows. Flies need to have action, and they need to be dark, weedless, and durable. That's what makes this fishing fun. It's simple. I have had very good success with flies made from active materials like marabou, saddle hackle, or ostrich herl. These materials look alive just sitting in the bubbling water, even after the flow stops. But a big, black, single-wing bucktail fly will catch fish as well. The only times I would switch to a lighter-colored pattern, like a Snake Fly, are during periods of low surf or on calm days.

As long as there is rolling white water, enjoy cliff angling even on bright summer days. After dark, these waters are out of bounds to all but the most experienced anglers; even calm nights can be dangerous because the rocks are extremely slick. These waters are also taboo to the boat fisherman on all but the calmest days; even then, only the skilled mariner who knows the water well should venture into such areas.

11

Chasing Fish in Open Water

Open water is just what the name implies: an area of deeper water, not reachable from the shore. This water ranges from just beyond casting distance of the land-based angler to all the way out to the blue water. This open-water zone acts as a link connecting rips, shorelines, and shallows to offshore waters. Areas of open water exist throughout the Eastern Seaboard, including large bays and sounds. Some of these areas contain no structure or defined rips, but some do have moving water that depends on tide and water depth. Places like Delaware Bay, Long Island Sound, and Narragansett Bay are examples of contained open water that is moving and extensive.

Some open-water fishing is unsuited for the average boater; a veteran may be needed when fishing certain waters. But many open-water areas have feeding or cruising fish out in the middle of nowhere. With this in mind, I headed out one August morning in search of top-water bluefin. I met two good friends, Captain Curt Jessup and Captain Roger Swiderski, at the Point Judith boat ramp in Rhode Island. There was a run of ideal fly-rod-size bluefin along the coast from south of Martha's Vineyard down to Block Island, ranging from 1 mile to 10 miles out.

Our trip did not have a favorable start. Pea-soup fog with visibility less than 100 feet forced us to pick our way out with radar and GPS—having two captains along was a big plus. Once outside the breakwater and away from the congested harbor entrance, we headed east to a 100-foot-deep area where I had found fish before. A radar beacon buoy marked the location, so it was easy to find in the fog.

Getting close to the location, we found birds on the water, and several times during the trip, there appeared to be surface-feeding fish. The visibility was so bad, however, that getting to the fish in time was impossible. We kept shutting down and trying to locate the fish by sound, and we came close several times. It was frustrating because we knew there were feeding fish, but getting to them was proving to be difficult. Fishing open water often means chasing surface-feeding fish, and even in clear conditions it can be tough if the fish are not holding very long on top.

As the morning wore on, my companions became antsy about calling it quits, but I knew that the fog often clears in this location around ten o'clock, so we kept hoping for a break. Just as we started back, the fog broke, and we saw that we were close to two schools of feeding fish. I approached the closest school, running just ahead of the splashes, and slid the boat within casting range. After shutting off the motor, I cut the wheel hard left to make the boat glide alongside the school, not into it. Curt was already casting, but I told Roger to wait until the boat's forward momentum had slowed. As the boat's drift diminished, I yelled for him to cast. A fish took about 30 feet from the boat, hitting on the run, and bolted under the boat.

I watched in horror as Roger stood against the gunwale and just held on, the rod bending under the boat. I screamed to let the fish run, but a second later the fish broke off with a pop. I thought the rod—a 10-weight XX Albright that I was testing—had exploded, but fortunately it was still in one piece. Turns out the fly line had wrapped around the reel. Roger did all he could—he was handcuffed, but kept the rod from hitting the gunwale. The tippet was thirty-pound test, and the knot from the fly line to the heavy mono section had parted. It was a bad break but a good strength test for the rod, though not one I had planned.

Captain Roger Swiderski shows off an ideal-size fly-rod bluefin.

Barb caught this nice oceanic bonito just south of Block Island.

The rest of the day went better. Roger took two fish, and in both cases he was patient and waited for the boat to stop drifting. I discovered this trick accidentally while running the boat when other anglers were fishing the bow. The bow angler would cast much sooner than I could, but often I would hook up quicker, and many times the fish would sound before the bow angler could make another cast. I realized that casting too soon, when the boat was still drifting toward the fish, created slack in the line, and sometimes the fly never moved because the boat floated into the line. Turning the boat eliminated some of the problem, but just waiting several seconds before casting gives better contact with the fly. **Keep trying different techniques.**

Bluefin tuna, bonito, false albacore, and oceanic bonito are favorite targets of boating anglers from midsummer until bad fall weather chases the fish beyond the range of the small to midsize boater. Bluefin and oceanic bonito are classic open-water fish that usually feed some distance from shore. There are times when they flirt with long-distance surf spinning gear, but usually they range about 1 mile out to blue water. Bonito and false albacore are targeted by shore anglers, but the best fishing is in water at least 10 feet deep. They will feed in big rips, mixing with stripers and bluefish. If big bluefin mix with other gamefish, the bluefin will try to eat them.

Called hardtails, these ocean speedsters create a feeding frenzy with fly anglers that actually makes some of them crazed. And bluefin are the worst! I have friends who drop everything at the first mention of tuna. Anglers who chase bluefin know that it's usually day-to-day action with miles of boat travel. The fish do at times lock into one location, and that makes for great fishing, but mostly it's hard work. Anglers that fish every day will sometimes keep up with the fishes' movement, but weekend warriors that fish one or two days a week can burn a lot of gas and time with few results. Successful tuna guides are popular in late summer and fall, and there is a good reason why: They know how to find fish.

All hardtail fishing is unpredictable—one day the fish will eat well, and the next day they'll be picky. It's what makes this fishing rewarding when it works. Perhaps the most predictable albacore fishing is in North Carolina. In the fall, Harkers Island draws anglers in droves to some of the best fly rodding for albacore there is, and the fish are big.

Throughout the season there is good open-water fishing for other species. One event that offers unique fishing is the finning of bluefish in the spring. I have found this in the deeper waters of mid–Long Island Sound and in other open-ocean water throughout the bluefish's range. On calm days the blues appear finning on the surface, swimming around in what I always assumed to be a spawning ritual. But biologists believe they do not spawn till mid-August, although the bluefish's sex life is still very much a mystery. This fishing runs hot and cold because the fish are both spooky and finicky. On good days the action is exciting, and small-boaters are able to drift, casting to cruising fish. Many days a long cast is needed, but with the help of a spin fisherman casting a hookless plug to bring the fish closer, a fly rodder can still have action.

There are many fly-fishing opportunities that small-, medium-, and long-range boaters can enjoy. Probably every species we fish for spends some time living and feeding away from the shoreline, and many fish use open water to migrate.

Tide does not affect many open-water locations, except to move water. Yet some tides are better for fishing and, along with wind, demand an angler's attention. Wind either pockets or concentrates bait to improve fishing; bait is necessary to attract and hold gamefish. Unless the gamefish are using the area to spawn or are migrating, the presence of bait will always improve fishing.

Most open water along the Northeast coast is best in fall, when fish movement is at its peak as surface-feeding schools of fish work their way south. Fish on the move sometimes feed all day, mostly beyond the shore fisherman's reach. Without wind to drive them in, or bait to attract them, the fish are content to stay in deeper, safer waters.

For years I fished the Rhode Island coast with a group from Connecticut, taking a few days in October to hit the fall run. Weather permitting, we ran the breachways in small boats, then roamed the waters outside the surf fisherman's scope. When there was no visible activity, the reefs, rips, and offshore rocks were the best fishing locations, for they held fish. When we found feeding fish in open water, the action was fast; depending upon the time of year, we caught a mixed bag of bass, blues, bonito, and albacore.

Open-Water Techniques

There was a time when I thought that running down the fish quickly and getting the fly immediately to the fish was critical. At times this might be true, but often a planned approach is best. Too many anglers run feeding fish down and ruin the fishing for everyone.

Captain Dan Marini holds a big albi taken off Rhode Island.

Try to determine what type of fish are feeding, how they are feeding, if there is any flow or wind that can help position the boat, and how long the fish are on the surface. If the fish are holding in one spot and staying on the surface for several minutes, slowly move toward the fish—gliding into them with as little commotion as possible is the best plan.

The most exciting feature of open-water fishing is the hunt. You first see the birds, then spot the feeding fish showering spray into the air, as you anxiously run the boat, trying to intercept them before they disappear. The fly rodder is at a real disadvantage if the fish are popping up and down quickly, not giving the angler time to cast into the school. However, the navigator must maneuver the boat properly, allowing the fly rodder to use both wind and boat motion for casting and retrieving. Downwind casts are easy, but retrieving is difficult. My choice is a crossing pattern, approaching the fish downwind, then turning the boat to quarter into the wind. This allows the angler to make a quartering downwind cast as the boat slides by the fish. It uses the boat's motion to keep a tight line for retrieving while giving the angler a good casting angle. Equally important is having the wind on the angler's noncasting shoulder. The sight of feeding fish can cause you to forget the menace of line drift caused by wind blowing into your casting hand's ear.

Chasing fish in this manner requires planning, good boat handling, and a careful approach. All participants in the craft must be ready when the captain speeds off after feeding fish. The acceleration of a high-powered boat can send gear and people flying, sometimes overboard, and serious damage or injury can result from a hasty departure. Keep all unsecured gear in a safe, out-of-the-way place. Loose hooks and gaffs not only get in the way, but can also cause harm. Either sit down or have a good handhold as the boat runs, especially in choppy seas. Standing is better for the spine because the legs will absorb most of the hard jolts.

The captain needs to plan the fastest and best route to the fish. Arrive at a point upwind or uptide, leaving room to ease into the fish without disrupting their feeding and to reach them with a fly cast. Running over the fish generally puts them down, causing not only you to miss the action, but others in the area as well. Don't be the unpopular boat that fouls up everyone's fishing.

Once upwind of the fish, try to anticipate what direction they are moving, and ease the boat into their path. Use the least amount of motor possible, cutting power once your position is correct. Easing into the feeding fish may permit many casts before they sound. A wild approach gives perhaps one shot,

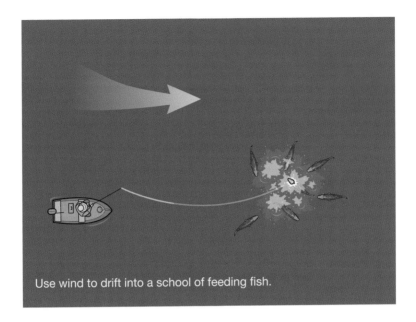

Use wind to drift into a school of feeding fish.

decreasing the chances for a strike. But even after the fish stop breaking, keep casting. There may be fish below the surface ready to jump on the next moving object, and if they're not badly spooked, they might come up again.

Large schools of surface-feeding fish are similar to an iceberg, where only the small tip is visible to the eye. But the rest are there, around and below the top-water action. Anglers using depth recorders have charted heavy fish activity some distance away from surface-feeding fish, indicating that although the fish are spread out over a large area, surface feeding occurs only in certain spots.

Work spooky, fast-moving fish by sitting in a central location and letting the fish come to you. This is particularly true with bonito and albacore, which can be like ghosts. For these ocean speedsters, anchoring in a rip where fish are feeding is more effective than chasing them. The ocean speedsters, particularly albacore, are very fussy, and when feeding on certain bait may not even respond to trolling lures. If one school of fish gives you fits, move to another location, where the fish might cooperate better.

While approaching breaking fish, keep watching the terns, for they will stay above or ahead of the fish, and the birds' sudden departure indicates another feeding school of fish in the immediate vicinity. The birds will leave, flying low, and head directly to the feeding schools. Following their flight helps

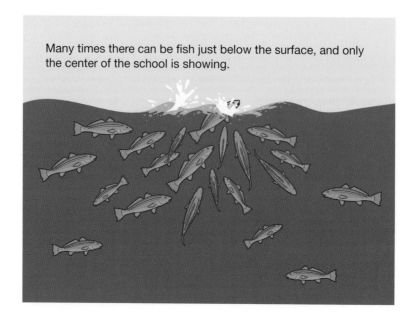

Many times there can be fish just below the surface, and only the center of the school is showing.

to spot other surface actions. Also keep watching the high-flying terns, which will drop down, making a beeline to the first signs of feeding activity.

Observing other fishermen's movements is another way to locate fish activity. Groups of boats, or boats that keep racing and stopping, are sure signs of fish feeding on top. Large numbers of boats competing for surface-feeding fish only spook them, making fishing unpleasant and particularly difficult for the fly rodder. I have been in situations where anglers would crowd in, trying to reach the action, casting over my boat to reach the fish, crossing lines, and making fly fishing impossible. When rivalry reaches this stage, leave the pack and look for fish on your own. There are always other schools, and the smart angler usually finds good fishing away from the mob.

Bluefish feeding in a frenzy are generally hot to bite, hitting the first thing that flashes within their reach—even terns are careful not to dive near the snapping jaws. Getting a fly or popper into the feeding fish should produce an instant take, but on certain occasions it may not be so easy, and you might be doing several things wrong. I have witnessed times when a fly popper retrieved through busting fish brought little response, while a spinning popper brought immediate action. With heavy surface action plus a wind chop, the small fly popper may go unnoticed for several reasons, such as not enough splash or not enough speed. The good fly angler who is able to make a long, quick cast and start an immediate fast retrieve has a better chance of pulling fish to the popper. But the novice might be easily frustrated, because there is all this action, yet fish are not jumping on the line. Speed and splash combined are the key, for the surface lure must excite the fish to trigger a strike. (See chapter 14 for how to work a popper properly.)

If the fish are difficult to take with top-water gear, sinking flies or lines are a better solution to combat loss of speed. Getting below the surface commotion allows the angler to work on fish that are not frantically feeding, looking for the excited, escaping bait. Fish working below the surface feed deliberately, taking the food one piece at a time, sometimes eating the dead bait as it sinks. These fish bite better and are easier to catch, allowing the fly rodder more time to present and retrieve the fly while covering a section of water unreachable with surface lures.

With heavy concentrations of feeding fish, this angling should not be tricky—requiring only a basic retrieve—or demand fancy fly patterns. A pulsating retrieve with fast short pulls, which makes the fly appear "wounded," would be my first choice. If this is nonproductive, use several different actions until finding the right retrieve.

Normally, white bucktail tied on a 2/0 or 3/0 hook, with a single 4- to 5-inch wing, using some flash, is a good, simple-to-tie bluefish fly. Only when encountering sand eels or bay anchovies would the angler need to select patterns to match the bait. Under most conditions easy-to-tie flies work fine, and the way the choppers destroy them, anything better would go to waste. When using poppers, pick a large white one that pushes plenty of water—the more splash the better. A coat of epoxy will keep it functional longer.

Stripers also feed this way, primarily in the fall as they fatten up for their migration. This can be ideal daytime angling because the fish hammer flies and poppers cast into them as they feed. The technique is basically the same as for fishing bluefish; many times the two species dine together, with the bass normally feeding deeper than the blues. Yet often enough they might both be on the surface. Bass are easily alarmed, and must be approached more carefully than blues. They also strike more positively than the slashing bluefish, missing less when attacking poppers.

Bass are ideal top-water fish when conditions are right. Opportunities exist to take large bass, for many times there are bigger fish mixed in the schools, and the next cast could bring a prize. The old saying is "big plug, big fish," and in the fall I prefer to use larger flies and poppers, hoping for a better fish. Unless they are feeding on small baits, try the bigger offering first before matching the bait size.

Weakfish are unlikely surface-feeders in open water, although several anglers have told me of witnessing such events. I never have. Yet weakfish are catchable as they feed under surface-feeding bluefish, picking up the dead and crippled bait. The only problem is getting the fly past the bluefish, and this can be difficult even for the spin fisherman with fast-sinking jigs. The fastest-sinking line with a small fly fished behind or to one side of the surface action is the only chance. Then expect to take mostly bluefish, which is not such a bad concession. Stripers also might be feeding under the bluefish, but frequently mix and feed with them, too. Bluefish in many locations arouse other species and create excitement and competition, triggering feeding sprees.

Bluefish are the most common visitors to open water, starting with spring spawning and in some cases feeding right through the season. On good days top-water feeding can drive the inexperienced angler nuts. It's best to fish for them using previously described methods.

Night tides could bring spring and early-summer striper action to some locations, but this would be mostly charter boat fishing, requiring local knowledge. The best open-water bass fishing occurs in the fall, beginning at dawn and going all day until fading light chases the angler to port. My favorite time is first light, and overcast days produce the best fishing.

The Atlantic mackerel, a smaller, slimmer version of the bonito, spawns in open water during the early spring into summer. They are an ideal light fly-rod fish when found near the surface, and they are fishable down to 20 feet. Usually a sinking line works better to reach the fish, even when they are right near the top. The best way to find mackerel is with a Scotty jig: a multiple-hooked rig attached to a shiny weighted jig and fished with a light spinning rod. Lower the rig to a given depth and jig it, trying different depths until finding fish. Unless the mackerel are thick or near the surface, fly rodding might be tough, but when they are, small bright flies, 1 to 2 inches long and worked in a jerky, erratic manner, are deadly. Although small, mackerel are a fast, hard-fighting fish. It's unfortunate that these fun baitfish/gamefish have been decimated by overfishing, and many popular locations are now devoid of fish.

In many areas, you must navigate a breachway or river mouth to reach open-water fishing grounds, making weather an important consideration. Wind

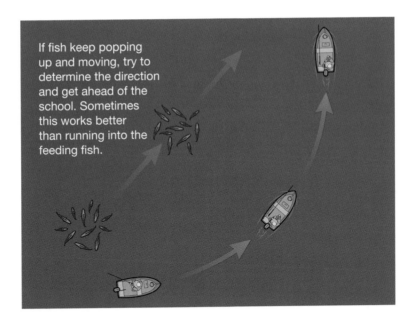

If fish keep popping up and moving, try to determine the direction and get ahead of the school. Sometimes this works better than running into the feeding fish.

and ocean swells can turn these places into gauntlets, making it unnerving and occasionally risky to scamper through. Be aware of the conditions before heading out, and do not roll the dice if they are threatening.

This particular fishing demands smart boat handling and alert fish- and bird-watching to put yourself within casting range of fish. Once you're there, it's typically easy fishing when circumstances are right. The angling skill involved in open water is getting the offering to the fish quickly. Line control is important. Keep the fly moving to excite the fish. If casting to the side of the fish gives a straighter, more positive retrieve, do it. Sometimes the center of the action is too hard to fish with fly tackle, and working the edges can then be more productive. Getting near the fish helps, but keep the fly moving!

Employ the techniques used in open water to any situation—reefs, offshore rips, or river mouths—anywhere surface feeding occurs, providing there is enough water depth to prevent spooking the fish and water conditions allow a free drift. Although this fishing is feasible alone, a good team is preferable, and will certainly be more fun. Top-water feeding is the ultimate in fly fishing, and when it occurs in midday, it's even more enjoyable—open water offers this possibility.

Blue Water

Most of the fishing I've discussed so far has been from the shallows to mid-depths—waters in sight of land. The other extreme is blue water—the deeper, warmer ocean waters associated with the Gulf Stream. Compared to fishing other water types, blue water is a different world.

Many fly rodders go blue-water fishing but never think to bring their fly gear, feeling it's out of place or in the way. However, opportunities can always pop up, offering a lifetime chance to make an unusual catch. Seth Cook, a good friend and fly rodder from Worcester, Massachusetts, caught a white marlin with a Mickey Finn while offshore fishing with another angler. They ran into marlin balling bait on the surface, 30 miles off Martha's Vineyard. After landing several fish, Seth asked for a shot with fly tackle. Casting into the feeding fish, he took his first billfish on a fly. If he hadn't brought fly gear along, he would have lost this opportunity.

I have heard many tales of blue-water anglers who cursed themselves for not having fly tackle, and I've listened to offshore anglers say, "If only a fly fisherman had been aboard." There are times, of course, when fly fishing is out of the question, due to the size and power of the offshore species sought. Though periods do exist when fly fishing is not feasible because of rough conditions, the fly rod may offer a blue-water angler another fishing dimension, especially when fish are feeding on small baits.

Anglers wanting to fly fish blue water should do so with an open mind, planning to enjoy fishing with offshore tackle while hoping to have a chance to use fly tackle. Going offshore with intentions to fish only fly greatly reduces your chances of fishing success, and may also limit your fly-fishing opportunities. Many times, finding fish with more conventional methods can help to put fish into fly-fishing range.

Blue-Water Tactics

Trolling is a favorite angling method for numerous situations. Some offshore fishermen use this technique as their primary fish-producer, to cover huge expanses of water, and as a means of fishing and searching while traveling. Trolling is not considered fly fishing and disqualifies a world record caught in this fashion. However, some anglers still troll with fly gear just for the fun of catching fish. It can be an effective way to see how fly tackle handles big ocean fish.

If you want to fly fish in a conventional way, there is an approach that can be used even while trolling that accomplishes this. Captain Pete Kriewald, a dear departed friend who helped me understand most of what I know about blue water, and I fooled with a fly-fishing system that worked well with bonito. If conditions are right it will work for any of the smaller offshore species, such as false albacore and skipjack tuna. Set up and troll several lures, working a number of rods to find the best lure and wake position. Then, after finding fish, plan to use only two trolling outfits. Once you've located fish, drop a fly back in the wake. Hold the fly rod and 15 feet of fly line, and get ready to cast. Be sure to troll the fly inside, between the lures; otherwise, fish might hit the fly first. Select a fly—Lefty's Deceivers, Blondes, and Snake Flies are all good patterns—that resembles the trolling lures both in size and color.

When a fish takes a lure—usually the one farthest back in the wake is hit first—throw the motor out of gear. Then make a backcast and drop the fly back into the wake. Schooling fish hit in succession, many times fighting for food. When several aroused fish are looking for a meal, and the struggling hooked fish is causing excitement, one might take the fly.

Getting the fly back into the wake quickly increases the chances for a hookup. This is the reason for trolling only two rods, to give the fly rodder more room for backcasting and to avoid cluttering the wake with lines. Use whatever fly line you cast and handle best. Sinking lines shoot better, but they require a quicker backcast before they sink. I use an intermediate, and it works well.

Larger fish are a possibility with good teamwork. With a big fly-hooked fish, break off the other fish, because prompt chasing will be necessary. This technique attracts any number and size of species, so use larger tackle—14- to 16-weights if the fish are over fifty pounds.

Another means of employing fly tackle when trolling is to stand ready to cast from the boat's stern as a fish is being landed with conventional tackle. Heavy, stand-up gear is best to overpower a fish quickly, for there is a better chance of fish following if the hooked fish is landed quickly. Sometimes a curious fish—several are better—will shadow the hooked fish, looking for dinner. The trailing fish, believing the hooked fish has a meal, will usually strike anything dropped near it. Using a sinking line, cast a sinking fly—near in color and size to the trolling lure—close to the hooked fish. Either twitch the fly or let it sink like a piece of food spilling from the hooked fish's mouth. While the fly remains near the fish do not retrieve, unless you feel action might bring a strike—only the people watching can judge that. One problem is being too close to the fish, making both casting and retrieving awkward. Without enough line to load the rod, accuracy requires practice, and should be perfected beforehand.

In such tight quarters, just flop a short cast next to the craft, aiming at the hooked fish. Place the fly behind the line attached to the hooked fish. The fly in front of the fish will only cause a tangle. Only limited shooting line is needed—more will just get in the way. Having less excess line will allow smooth line clearance to the reel. Hooked offshore fish give the angler little time, and if a tangle occurs, the leader will break like a rifle shot.

Serious offshore anglers are a breed in themselves, generally not wanting to do any other type of fishing. This kind of angling takes substantial finances if you want to do it properly, along with knowledge and patience. Trolling or chumming for hours on end without action can be like watching a swimming pool fill. But that's what it takes to find blue-water fish. However, when it's alive, the ocean is an exciting place, not just for fishing, but for the opportunity to view the other creatures that roam its openness.

The impatient angler (I am one) can do several things to keep sane. One is the trolling method I just outlined. The other is to set up a chum line and blind-cast with a sinking line. Let's say your group is fishing for sharks. Not only sharks, but other fish might enter the chum line. With large baits, smaller gamefish could go unnoticed, but a fly might show their presence. If you're just fly fishing without bait lines out, keep casting. Maintain a constant vigil behind and around the boat while watching the slick some distance back. Polarizing sunglasses are a must for eye protection and to break the surface glare.

Blue-Water Fishing Conditions

Offshore fishing contrasts with all the other types of angling we have discussed. The main difference is water depth: Most blue-water action occurs in deep water—from 70 feet to beyond the continental drop-off, over 1,000 feet deep. What water depth is best for fishing depends on the time of year, water temperature, types of fish present, and fish movement. The three-weekends-a-year blue-water angler needs professional advice for most of these categories.

Finding offshore grounds is easy; it's only a matter of running in an approximate southern direction until reaching deeper water. On calm days look for top-water action while trolling, searching for fish on the trip out. In rough water, along with trolling, watching bird activity is the best way to cover large areas. Even one working bird is a good sign, and an area with numbers of soaring and diving birds means bait and possibly fish.

Unlike a flat, creek, or river mouth, where tide is important, offshore tides have little bearing other than on water movement, allowing the angler to fish as long as time permits. Undoubtedly the best time for the fly rodder is first light, but blue-water fish can explode at any moment. However, rips do form in ocean currents. They are more of a steady flow than a fast current spilling into deeper water, although shallower spots, like a hump surrounded by deep water, may have better concentrations of bait and fish.

One type of rip that does form is a temperature fissure: a fingerlike current of warmth that penetrates into the colder surrounding water, creating movement along the edge. It's much like a stream running into a pond, but in the ocean the finger keeps moving. Bait holds in the tepid water, propelled to and confused by the edges, where gamefish looking for an easy meal might be cruising. Fissures can be small surges running several hundred yards wide to large flows over a mile across. Any border of temperature fluctuation is a potential feeding area. Fish these areas carefully by working in and out or along the fringes.

One element that holds fish as structure does is a floating object. Fish of all types, sometimes schools of them, congregate to feed around and under debris. Weed lines offer the same attraction, harboring bait and gamefish. Some deep-water buoys are notorious for holding fish. These opportunities can be ideal setups, giving the fly rodder holding fish to cast to.

A lack of wind creates relaxed fly fishing. A light chop is fine, but a heavy roll will make standing, let alone trying to fight a fish on light tackle, difficult.

Fish will hold and feed along a weed line because most weed lines hold bait.

This is another plus for morning, because wind usually kicks up by afternoon. Sloppy days, although they're fishable, will frustrate the marine fly rodder.

Chunky and chum flies are two essential patterns used in blue-water fly fishing. For other patterns, look at small offshore trolling lures, matching their sizes and colors with flies tied on #4 to 1/0 hooks for smaller fish, 2/0 to 4/0 for the heavyweights. The meager-size lures used for big fish surprise anglers unfamiliar with this fishing. Now, big billfish teasers are a different game, but lures for the tuna family are small, 4 to 6 inches long, and easily duplicated by a fly. The best colors are white, yellow, green, or a combination of two or all three, plus black-and-white, which is a popular tuna color. Add flash to any pattern.

The distance a blue-water fisherman is willing to travel, plus his boat range, to some degree determines how long the season will last. Deeper, warmer water becomes active early and remains active later in the season than do areas closer to shore. Depending upon your home port, you could travel anywhere from 10 to 100 miles offshore. From Montauk, the canyon and edges of the continental shelf are 68 to 75 miles from shore. But at times the fish are much

A school of feeding albies in Nantucket Sound on Cape Cod.

closer, and fall brings fish near shore. The mid-Atlantic offshore fishery is much closer (10 to 20 miles) and begins earlier, in April. The season for most New England offshore anglers starts around Memorial Day as bluefin, yellowfin, and albacore come in from the warmer waters of the Gulf Stream. This early fishing generally occurs well offshore. Fish begin to move closer to shore as the water warms, with water temperatures from sixty-two to sixty-eight degrees optimal. The early run can be ideal for fly fishing because the fish are generally feeding on smaller baits and there are large numbers of small fish—under one hundred pounds—present.

Summer draws the gamefish near shore, but water temperature, bait and fish activity, and weather conditions are all factors that influence offshore fishing from year to year. Bonito, false albacore, and skipjack show in late summer, bringing light-tackle action to inshore and offshore anglers. Fall brings hot action within reach of even the small-boat angler and, like most late-season fishing, can be superb. However, autumn's often-unfavorable weather makes blue-water fly fishing a challenge, for the fish are closer but might be unfishable because they're unreachable.

The Northeast and mid-Atlantic coast blue-water fishery has become much more popular in the last ten years. Some of it is due to the good runs of bluefin that appeared close to shore in the late 1990s, giving anglers shots at them even with small boats. In recent years fly fishing for bluefin has become a trend with both guides and sport anglers who are patient, have the right tackle, and are willing to burn some gas to find fish. And there are other fish, too: White marlin and dolphin, though less plentiful, offer exciting possibilities. So do both blue and mako sharks, with the blue shark both abundant and ready to take flies. But for the blue-water long rodder, bluefin are still head and shoulders above all other species.

12

Night Fishing

Fishing in darkness must seem strange to the newcomer. Why would someone fish at night? The answer is because some fish feed best in the dark or in low light, particularly during the summer. In recent years I have fished less at night, and rarely catch a late tide. If I plan to fish several hours of darkness, it will always be in the early morning. Knowing the right places, the waters with less fishing pressure, or the places that have daytime feeding fish allows me to fish during the day. Yet I know that by fishing at night I'll catch more fish. Bonito and albacore feed from first light to last—they are gentlemen fish; saltwater fly fishing can be, and is, enjoyed without night fishing. However, the fly rodder who disregards night fishing not only misses a prime angling opportunity, but also misses big excitement. One of the great angling thrills is having a big fish on a flat-calm pitch-dark night come up and slam a fly right at the rod tip. Whether the fish takes the fly or misses, you will never forget it.

Fishing at night is not hard; actually, in some locations it might be easier than daytime angling. Fish are usually closer at night, are not as shy, and tend to strike better. The main concern is to keep in touch with the fly. If this means fishing only 40 feet of line, do so. Anglers generally get in trouble by casting too far or wading out too far. Move slowly at night and take more time to do things. Without seeing well, you must visualize what the fly and line are doing, but what's more important is knowing the right "feel"—to fish without sight you *must* develop it. You use the same senses when fishing a sinking line in a discolored trout stream. Yes, you can see the cast, but the feel of the drift, swing, and strike are the same. Anglers who have bottom-fished or free-drifted a worm on a small hook know this feeling. Yet for some reason many anglers lose their senses when plunged into darkness. Darkness should *enhance* the senses.

Casting is the number-one problem for some nighttime anglers. The first and most important rule when fishing at night is to cast safely. When casting in low light, a good trick to remember is to watch your backcast or watch the rod tip—even if you can't see it. Watching the rod tip prevents any serious eye or face injuries because your face is looking away from the fly as it passes your body. The second rule is to keep the cast straight, which gives instant feel and proper fly action. This is when good casting technique makes fishing easier. Tight loops are important, but casting a straight line is the key to line control. Often a slower, smoother cast produces better results. Anglers who add too much power when trying for extra distance often end up with a pile of slack line at the end of the cast. At night use less power, slow the casting stroke, and shorten the cast. Remember, a 50-foot straight cast is much more effective than casting 70 feet of line that lands in a pile at 50 feet.

When casting across flowing water, a pile of line at the end of the cast might ruin the whole drift. A cast with too much slack line often causes loss of touch with the fly and is perhaps the major reason anglers miss strikes. Pileups also cause knots and tangles, which take time to sort out: Continually check the tippet for overhand knots, because they weaken line strength. If casting straight up or quartering upcurrent, start your retrieve immediately after the fly lands to maintain line control. Casting across or quartering downcurrent allows better feel. Long casts across fast currents make control difficult, and they're not for the night-fishing beginner.

A safe way to fish at night is to watch your backcast. You will never hook yourself in the face.

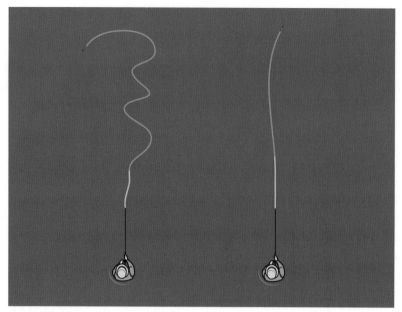

For line control, a shorter, straight cast is better than a long, sloppy one.

Slower retrieves work best after dark. I generally work the fly about half-speed at night. In flat water on a calm night, try fishing a buoyant pattern like a Snake Fly with a big head. Move the fly slowly, and when you start thinking it is too slow, cut the speed in half and go even slower. There are nights when a fly leaving a wake and slowly creeping along the surface can be deadly. But this takes patience and is a difficult technique to maintain for extended periods. If a slow-moving fly is not producing action, try a medium speed, and don't be afraid to employ a faster speed as well. **Keep trying different techniques.**

When retrieving at night, be sure to maintain feel—a slow retrieve downcurrent might allow the line to slacken. While retrieving, keep watching in the direction of the fly. On a bright night, swirls might be visible on a calm surface, and the ones in your line's direction could be fish hitting the fly. Slack line, or too large a line bow, will prevent you from feeling strikes. A quicker retrieve may not always move the fly faster, but it may just keep the line tighter. If you are missing strikes, either retrieve faster or change the casting direction to downcurrent, which will keep the line straighter.

If you make a good cast and maintain contact with the fly, hooking fish is usually easier at night. Generally, you are feeling for the strike and seldom see the fish until after the take, or miss. In many locations, particularly rolling surf, fish never show. Fish will feed more deliberately in darkness, and a slower retrieve offers them an easier target. In low or no light, fish see only silhouettes and use their lateral lines and hearing to sense and locate the fly. This is the reason a surface slider, or a fly struggling along the surface, is so deadly—it sends out the right vibes.

After hooking the fish, the techniques used in clearing the line and fighting the fish are similar to the techniques used in daylight. A problem will occur if you must follow a fish, either by walking or chasing in a boat. Walking an open beach without obstacles is easy, but navigating one littered with slippery stones and debris may take some doing. Whenever possible, head for high ground—avoid wading in the water. Stumbling through waist-deep, rock-infested water at night is dangerous, even with a light. Remember, the fish is not going to run forever; it's better to be cautious and move slowly to avoid a fall. Likewise, the boater must not move into dangerous waters to follow a fish. Boats do, however,

Remember, bluefish feed at night, so take care when grabbing fish.

allow a better means of following fish at night. Using a release anchor, the angler can drift after the fish, staying in perfect position for landing. But when using a release anchor, be sure you know the location well—finding a small float in the dark can be difficult.

At night, consider every fish a bluefish until making a positive identification. When wading near shore, back the fish onto the beach and use a light to remove the hook. Try to avoid lights on the flats or in creek areas, but use them rather than getting hurt. Weakfish and bass are easier than bluefish to handle without a light. Once you become experienced, you will be able to handle bluefish like bass or weakfish. Just keep telling yourself to move slowly and carefully.

Reading water at night is difficult, and not recommended. If possible, check the water at the tide you plan to fish in daylight. Fishing new water at night is for the pros, and in some locations it's for fools. Knowing a place makes fishing it easier. Flats without steep drop-offs, open beaches, and small creeks are easier to read at night. Check jetties, steep beaches, reefs, and rocky locations in daylight. Never attempt new waters at night in a boat; first learn the location in good light. Even in places you know, move slowly.

Use a light to tie on flies, even if it means walking back to shore. A small, dim light shined into the waders is ideal for putting on a fly, but use a bright light for walking about. Remember that lights spook fish. Use them only when walking from place to place. I normally use a light to approach a location, then I sit down and let my eyes adjust to the darkness. It only takes a few minutes for most of my night vision to return. Once my sight improves, wading is possible without lights; however, I make small shuffling steps in rocky areas. A wading staff helps the balance and acts as a probe to feel the bottom.

Boaters should know their fishing spots well enough to approach them without lights. A light is useful to find markers and buoys, but a bright searchlight flashing across the water will send fish scurrying. Plan your approach, using the tide to position the boat. Then either paddle or use an electric motor. A slow, careful approach lets you find the right area and position the boat in the best spot. I prefer shutting down the running lights when nearing the fishing location. Light is a distraction, taking away your ability to see in darkness. Shining a light while someone is running a boat can blind the operator; this is dangerous, particularly at higher speeds. (The old captains of Cuttyhunk frowned on anglers even lighting a cigarette. The dull red cabin light was the only light they allowed.)

Sound travels great distances on a calm night. Pops, smacks, slurps, and splashes announce a fish's presence—use these sounds to find fish. Darkness heightens the other senses—use your nose as well as your ears. On all but the blackest nights, even your sight, though limited, is a useful sense. Surface-feeding fish show in smooth water, as do rips, rock piles, and other anglers. Only on the blackest nights does it seem as if you are locked in a dark closet. The moon, stars, and distant lights illuminate the surroundings. Choose brighter nights when learning; they help the beginner ease into angling at night.

Night fishing might disillusion some beginners. The tangles, the cold, the stumbling around in the dark, and the miscued casting are frustrating, and while you go fishless, other anglers' reels sing with excitement. Night fishing takes experience to master. I keep stressing the importance of **time on the water,** for as in many types of angling, one must suffer to learn. We all have. But once you get the hang of it, fishing without light will become second nature, and will make you a better all-around angler in both fresh- and salt water.

PART TWO

The Important Techniques
for Catching Fish

13

Saltwater Fly Casting

The importance of long casts in saltwater fly fishing varies with the location being fished, the weather, and the water conditions. Fly rodders should not shun ocean fishing because they don't feel they can make long-enough casts. A short cast, despite its obvious limitations, will catch fish in the ocean. Actually, some excellent fishing that requires casts of only 30 to 40 feet is available to the fly fisher. Creek fishing is one example of how productive short casts can be. Many times along a beach with rolling surf, a 30- to 40-foot cast will give better fly control than a longer cast, and often the fish are right in the first roll. Jetty fishing is another example of a location where short casts are effective. Let me relate a story that I have told many times before, but still merits repeating.

One dark morning I was fishing a jetty with several friends, giving them what I thought were the prime places farther out on the jetty while I fished just out from the beach, where a little backwash was created by the wave action. Farther out on the jetty, a good flow formed from the inside bar that paralleled the beach, stopping about 20 feet from the jetty. Breaking waves built up inside the bar and flowed out along the jetty, creating a good feeding zone where my friends were fishing. The backwash I was fishing was small, requiring short casts and plenty of patience. I would rather have been in the better flow farther out, but my friends only had a few days to fish, and I wanted them to have the best shot.

I was getting bored when I felt what seemed to be a slight bump, just a nudge, about halfway through a retrieve. I waited several minutes and made another cast just a little shorter and more across-current so the fly would swing next to the jetty below my feet. As the fly came to rest against the structure, I let it pause before lifting it to make another cast. I felt what seemed to be something holding the fly as if I were hung up on the structure. But something seemed different, so I lifted with a quick pull of the rod, and the water at my feet exploded. Even in the dark I could see white water erupting into the air, and then the run started. Being close to shore, it was an easy walk in, and in no time I was on the beach, following the fish down the shoreline. I knew the fish was big because it just kept running at a steady pace. It was a good twenty-minute fight before I beached the forty-six-pound striper. Thinking back, I believe that my cast was less than 30 feet, and I hooked the fish with only a few feet of fly line out the tip. I feel that in this case, making a shorter cast gave me more line control, and was probably the reason I hooked this fish.

When fish are close, you need only short-cast to catch them, and *some* circumstances *do* bring fish right to the angler's feet. But an inability to make longer casts when they are called for will limit your fishing success. There is an old husbands' tale that says most fish are caught within 50 feet. This statement is true for two reasons: one is because many people can't cast beyond 50 feet, and the other is because, particularly on the Northeast coast, fish will track a fly before striking. So when the fish takes only 30 feet away, you exclaim, "Boy, the fish are close!" But this isn't so; the fish that strikes at 30 feet may have tracked the fly from a long distance. Many gamefish follow a fly until it approaches the shoreline, at which point the fish thinks its target is getting away so it attacks. Thus, without a long cast, the gamefish might not see the fly in the first place. Much ocean fishing involves covering water, casting blind, hunting for fish the way a bird dog works a cover. When you can cast far, you'll cover more water, and show your fly to many more fish.

There are also times when a casting distance of 40 or 50 feet will require the equivalent of a 75-foot cast. Stiff winds, large flies, or casting from the surf or while standing waist-deep in the water require more casting effort. At times fishing rolling surf requires longer casts because, even though the fish may be near shore, you won't be able to stand too close to the waves surging up the beach. Thus, fish only 20 feet out may demand a 60-foot cast.

Don't be discouraged if you are not a distance caster, for long casts are something you can learn. Striving to cast 70 feet is not unreasonable. With the wealth of fine casting aids available today, casting well comes easily. There are many instructional aids, such as classes, books, and videos, available today, and along with improved tackle, they can make learning to cast simple. Because complete casting instruction is beyond the scope of this book, I am not going to spend precious pages preaching casting. However, I will go through a basic cast to emphasize the important points as they pertain to saltwater fly fishing, and I'll also touch upon the aspects of casting that warrant special consideration in ocean fishing.

First, let me emphasize that if you are working too hard, you are casting incorrectly. Fly casting need not cause arm pain even with heavy lines and large flies. When a cast is made properly, the tackle should do most of the work.

After years of teaching thousands of anglers to cast, I found that most casters work too hard, putting far more effort into the cast than needed. Lefty Kreh gave me the best advice when I was seventeen years old. He said, "Lou, you are an excellent fly caster, but you're working too hard." It took some time, but I started to slow down my casting stroke and get more production from the rod. My body was doing more work than the rod was. It was Lefty's pitch: Why are you paying hundreds of dollars for a fly rod and not getting the benefit of a good casting tool? It's what I tell my students: The rod will almost cast by itself—all you need to do is direct it. With this thought in mind, let's look at a basic casting stroke.

Basic Saltwater Casting

Fly casting is actually line casting—you are casting the *line's* weight, not the fly's. Larger, heavier flies are harder to cast because they require larger lines to carry their weight. It's how you propel the line with the rod that gets the fly to the target, or not. Let's analyze a basic fly cast by going over the steps quickly, and then discussing each step in detail.

You begin the cast by raising the rod and pulling it back to throw the line behind you, directing the loop about 8 feet above the water. This is the backcast. The rod should be positioned behind your ear when stopping the backcast. Just before the loop opens, begin to push the rod forward, driving the rod tip toward an imaginary target about 10 feet above the water. The rod should stop in the ten o'clock position. This is the forward cast. To load the rod properly, most anglers should start with about 25 to 30 feet of line beyond the rod tip. This length depends upon the caster's skill level, but it needs to feel right and put a bend in the rod, and the caster must be able to feel the line on the rod tip. Faster, stiffer rods might need more line out the tip to load the rod, or one fly-line size heavier to load the rod. A beginner with a fast rod would be wise to overload the rod with a heavier line. This is not politically correct, but it works.

Making a Good Fly Cast

These instructions are for the right-handed caster. If you are a left-handed caster, reverse the direction.

Begin by gripping the rod with your casting hand, placing your thumb on top or just slightly to the right of the handle. I like to grip the rod near the top of the handle, but this is a personal preference. Hold the rod firmly but not with a death grip, as this can cause tendon problems. Stand at about a 45-degree

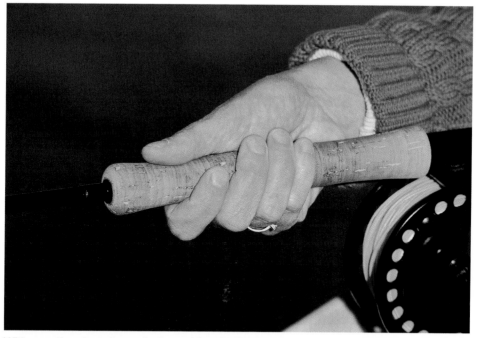

With your thumb on top, grip the rod handle firmly, but not with a death grip.

angle to the direction you plan to cast, with your left foot in front. Plan to use not only your arm and shoulder, but also your torso and legs.

The first requirement in casting is to break the water's grip on the line by moving the line and fly. So rather than attempting to lift the entire line up off the water when hauling a backcast, you must first move the line. With the rod low to the water, slowly raise the rod up just beyond parallel. This does two things: It breaks the water's grip on the line, and it begins to load the rod. Although sinking lines are less affected by the water's grip, slowly raising the rod sets up the cast and produces a smooth transition from the water to the air.

Loading the rod, or putting a bend in the rod, is critical to making a good cast. Loading makes the rod do most of the work. Some casters work too hard because they do not put a bend in the rod before making a casting stroke. One way to detect this problem is to listen to the sound the rod makes as it moves through the casting stroke. If the rod makes noise, a loud whoosh, it's not loaded—a good casting stroke should be almost silent. One of the key techniques in fly casting is loading the rod and keeping the line on the rod tip

Raise the rod slowly and start to bring the rod back to make the backcast, keeping the rod tip on a level plane during the casting stroke.

through the casting stroke. A good tennis player keeps the ball on the racket when hitting a forehand to improve ball control. Just as in tennis, holding the line on the rod tip is an important ingredient of a fly-casting stroke.

After raising the rod, to both lift the line and load the rod, start to bring the rod back, using your forearm and shoulder while transferring your body weight from your front foot to your back foot. The shifting of weight should be coordinated with the moving of your arm and shoulder, and your torso should rotate to the right. As the rod moves back, it should have a good bend, and the tip should travel on a straight plane. At this point in the backcast, the arm and shoulder are doing all the work, and the wrist should be firm. To keep the tip on a level plane, the rod butt must also move back on a level plane. This will help keep the loop tight. The casting hand should move back to a position at least even with your ear—I prefer stopping the rod past my head. The longer the casting stroke, the more time you have to adjust your timing. A long casting stroke also puts less pressure and stress on your body. Remember, try to hold the line on the rod tip as long as you can.

As your casting hand comes to a stop, use your wrist to add the final punch to make the backcast. With a loaded rod, this last step should be just a slight kick of the wrist. The rod should stop cleanly at about a 45-degree angle to the water, though this angle can vary depending on wind, backcasting room, and casting style. If the rod tip travels in an arch, the loop will be larger. Think of the rod painting a garage ceiling, not the ceiling of an igloo. Large loops are usually caused by breaking the wrist at the end of the cast or using only the wrist to make the cast. The wrist should only bend—not break. The rod butt should never exceed a 45-degree angle from the wrist, and the wrist should only be used at the cast's end—not to make the cast. Now, some anglers can throw tight loops while breaking the wrist, but keeping a firm wrist helps develop good casting skills. If you continually throw big loops, try this trick: Tuck the rod butt into the cuff of a long-sleeve shirt or jacket. This is only a temporary fix and should not be used for long, but it will stop you from breaking your wrist.

Once the rod stops on the backcast, begin to prepare for the forward cast. Several important steps set up the forward cast. First, the rod must stay right where it ended on the backcast. As the line travels behind you, watch the loop.

The rod should stop at about a 45-degree angle behind the caster, with the casting hand past the angler's head.

Just before the loop opens on the backcast, begin pushing the rod forward. It's very important that the tip travels on a straight plane. This part of the casting stroke is all shoulder and arm—no wrist.

Just before it opens, begin to push the rod forward, using your arm and shoulder. Keep your wrist firm, and leave it in the same position as when the backcast ended, at a 45-degree angle. You should also feel the rod load as the loop flows back and opens. Anglers that do not look at their backcast must learn to feel when the rod loads to begin the forward cast. This is what anglers do when sight casting to fish, when they do not want to look back and lose sight of the fish.

A good backcast sets up the forward cast because it loads the rod and keeps everything tight. If you make a good backcast, the wrist should still be at a 45-degree angle. Like the backcast, as you move the rod forward, shift your weight from your back foot to your front foot. Rotate your torso to the left, and keep pushing the rod forward. To form a good, tight forward loop, keep the tip moving on a level plane. End the cast using a slight kick of the wrist to turn the tip over, bringing the rod butt close to the wrist. Executed properly, the stroke is like throwing a dart off the rod tip. Pick a spot about 8 to 10 feet above the water, and shoot the cast to that location.

The three major faults, though there are certainly more, that can affect the forward cast are poor timing, slipping the rod forward, and tipping the rod forward. Timing, the transition from the backcast to forward cast, is a crucial part of fly casting. If you use a longer casting stroke, pinpoint timing is not necessary, but good timing is still important. Only with a short, hard, western-style casting stroke is near-perfect timing important. Again, remember to watch your loop, and just before it opens, or straightens out, begin the forward cast. The loop should begin to open and the line will straighten as

the rod moves forward. If you wait too long, the line will begin to fall, losing its energy. Starting your forward cast too soon will cause a snap as the line actually breaks the sound barrier. Early jet aircraft had trouble surviving this phenomenon; your fly will not.

Another way to think of the forward cast: It should develop with your arm and shoulder pushing the rod forward, much like a boxer throwing a punch. If you want to add speed to the forward cast, start the cast slowly then accelerate quickly. Trying to add more power or speed too quickly will prevent proper

Keep pushing the rod forward with the shoulder and arm to gain speed and add distance to the cast. And be sure to keep the tip moving forward, traveling on a straight line. Holding the line on the rod tip for a long time gives more line control and makes timing easier.

Stop the forward casting stroke at the ten o'clock position. The final part of the casting stroke should be a slight bend of the wrist. This tips the rod tip forward and helps form a tight loop.

Here the angler is using a backcast to present the fly. In tight quarters or when the wind is wrong, this is effective technique.

rod loading unless your timing is perfect. One of the casters I know who can do this is Steve Rajeff.

"You're a creeper." That's what I tell students when they slip or slide the rod forward before beginning their backcast. It's a common problem and robs power from the casting stroke. Some casters slide forward and tip the rod forward at the same time. Both faults shorten the casting stroke and can cause the caster to shock the rod or throw tailing loops because the rod is difficult to load. A bad creep also leads to casting too low on the forward cast. Casters that creep often use too much wrist, producing a larger loop. The creep is caused by the caster's anticipation of making the forward cast. A good trick is to watch your casting hand and see if it moves forward before you begin the forward casting stroke.

Using the Backcast to Fish

A good, strong backcast not only makes the forward cast easier, it adds to casting speed and reduces the number of false casts. It can also serve as a fishing tool to present the fly. When attempting to fish with a wind from the casting-hand side, the wind will keep driving the line and fly into the caster. Also, if two anglers are working a shoreline from a boat, one angler must backcast to present the fly. In both cases the backcast becomes the forward (or distance) part of the cast. The key is learning to shoot line using the backcast as you would when making a regular forward cast. The main difference when making a distance backcast is the extension of your arm to shoot more line.

Use the same mechanics as when making a forward cast; force the rod backward and stop the rod cleanly. Once this is learned, most casters can shoot large lengths of line on a backcast—and developing a stronger backcast will greatly improve your forward cast. The key is a tight back loop. This is also a good practice along beaches where people are walking or watching. Most bystanders are not aware of the distance that a fly rodder's backcast extends behind the angler.

Casting Large Flies and Poppers

Big wind-resistant flies cast better with *less* line speed. In the forward cast, allow the line to unfold slowly and drag a big fly to its target, rather than shooting it there. High line speed will cause the forward loop to open quickly, achieving good distance with small flies; however, a big bug will slow down once the loop opens, preventing the cast from shooting. I prefer to hold more line in the air with air-resistant flies; this provides more weight to carry the fly and affords a longer period before the loop opens.

To reduce casting speed, make a longer, slower forward stroke to give the cast more power and time to develop. This is why some anglers have problems throwing large flies with sink-tip/sink-head lines. These lines have short, compacted front sections with short rear tapers that develop high speeds in the air. The line's head is fast-sinking material, and the thinner running line is either floating or intermediate-sinking material. Because of the line's construction, if too much speed is developed from the casting stroke, the line outruns the fly, loses power, and falls in a heap, or just cartwheels into a heap. Let's look at the proper technique to cast a fast-sinking line.

Casting Sink-Tip/Sink-Head Lines

Sink-tip/sink-head lines have replaced the once-popular shooting heads. Shooting heads are still used by some anglers, but these new lines cast and fish like shooting heads but without the annoying bumping of the knot through the guide from the splice that connects the head to the running line. (See chapter 16 for more information on sink-tip lines.) Casting a sink tip is different than casting a floater, and the techniques are similar to casting a shooting head.

Once the larger, heavier section is outside the rod tip, make the cast. If the line has a short rear taper, extend the head (the dark section) about 3 feet beyond rod tip—lines with long tapers allow for more extension. Most casters can extend the head about 10 feet, but too much line out the tip can cause the loop to collapse. Each manufacturer's line has a sweet spot, an ideal length to extend beyond the tip. This sweet spot, along with casting style and skill, will vary—find your best distance to extend the head beyond the tip and stay with it.

Casting a sink tip requires some adjustment. Many anglers use too much power and speed when first casting these lines. Sinking lines are thinner in diameter, so they shoot through the air with less resistance compared to a floating or intermediate line, and their density develops more speed than a floater. Using too fast a casting stroke can create too much line speed. A couple things happen when the loop moves too quickly. First, because of the speed, the loop will open prematurely, without carrying enough running line to make a long cast. The other problem is the loop piling up or tumbling at the end of the cast. Both problems cause loss of distance, and a cast that lands in a pile will either tangle or cause you to lose contact with the fly until the line straightens out.

Because a sinking line generates so much speed, a slightly larger loop, along with a much slower casting stroke, will produce a better cast. A slight rolling of the tip on the forward cast and backcast will open up the loop just enough. I try to throw about a 3- to 4-foot loop when casting a sinking line. My casting stroke, which is slow to begin with, moves even slower depending on the wind, fly size, and line type I'm casting. Try adjusting both loop size and casting speed until the loop shoots out and turns over smoothly at a desired distance. One trick to try if the loop looks like it might collapse is to pull the rod back at the end of the cast. This will kick the loop over and straighten the leader. Some distance will be lost, but the line and leader will land straight. This is only a fix for a bad cast, however—a good caster seldom needs to employ this technique.

Although some anglers will argue this, I feel that sinking lines cast easier if you let them work for you. They are less affected by the wind and are a better choice for casting big flies. And for speed casting to surface-feeding fish, a sink tip will get the fly to the target quicker. The ability to shoot more line on the backcast allows the angler to, at times, make a long cast with only one backcast. When running up with a boat on breaking fish, just lob the loose line out the tip onto the water in front of you and make a smooth backcast, letting as much line as possible shoot out before making the forward cast. With some practice, you will be amazed at the speed and distance that a sink tip can deliver a fly.

Handling Too Much Line

Put excess fly line or running line back onto the reel when it's not in use, unless you're alternating casting distances. Extra line knots up and prevents the caster from straightening the cast with a tight line. When only one cast in ten pulls out all the line, reel in enough to get at least half the casts to slap the rod. Certain locations and conditions—jetties, creeks, or cliffs—might require only short casts, and more line only complicates matters. When casting to a fish near a boat, either in a chum slick or to a fish following another hooked fish, surplus line could tangle, causing a broken tippet.

Take time to practice casting with a very short line. Shorter line won't have sufficient weight to load the rod, particularly with large flies, so casting will be ungraceful. Long rod strokes are best, to toss the fly much like a kid casting a bobber with a cane pole. Rather than a cast, this is more an overhand lob that uses the fly's weight as much as the line's. Keep rod motion smooth and rotate the arm out, tilting it 30 degrees away from the body. Unlike a normal cast where the loop is controlled and rolls over the rod, this loop is sloppy. Tipping the rod out will help eliminate tangles.

Keeping a High Backcast

Most anglers envision marine fly fishing occurring on wide-open water, with ample casting room. This is true when flats fishing or fishing from a boat, but many locations, such as steep beaches, rocky cliffs, and jetties, or areas with tall sawgrass and high dunes, demand elevated backcasts. Even on flat rock-covered places I prefer a high backcast to prevent broken hook points and parted leaders.

A low loop might occasionally drop when a caster tires or gets sloppy. Casting for long periods drains strength, making the wrist and arm wander. This begins to open the loops, affecting line speed and causing the fly to hit on the back and forward casts. Fishing in low light and darkness is a time to consciously keep back loops higher, because it's easy to let down in the darkness and begin to allow the line to drop.

Very few situations call for a classic high backcast—one that shoots upward at the one o'clock position—but for those that do, a shorter forward cast is the compromise. A higher backcast diminishes some loading power because it prohibits the longer drift of a low backcast. And the cast is not being made on a straight plane, lessening the power even further. When throwing a high backcast, I prefer to stop with the rod higher on the backcast. I keep the back drift shorter to prevent the line from dropping. This allows ample room for loading the rod, but doesn't permit the cast to fall.

Casting a Switch or Two-Handed Rod

Casting a switch or two-handed rod requires different techniques. My experience is limited, so I will offer my insight but advise anyone who wants to learn how to cast a very long rod to get a good video or, better yet, attend a casting class.

With a two-handed rod, the basic casting stroke that I use is similar to casting a surf spinning rod, but the timing is much more critical. With the forward cast, you are pushing forward with the casting hand and pulling backward with the retrieving hand. With the backcast, you are pulling backward with the casting hand while pushing forward with the retrieving hand. The timing is similar to the western-style casting stroke, which is much shorter. I tend to use a longer stroke, which is probably not the right technique but it works for me.

Trying to carry too much line during the casting stroke can affect the cast. Work the line's head just out the tip and make the cast. Like a standard fly cast, line control is very important. Using a longer rod gives more distance, but keeping the line straight is essential for maintaining fly control. A straight 100-foot cast is far preferable to a sloppy 120-foot cast. I am sure that using proper spey casting techniques is more effective, and in the right conditions being able to make a long roll cast would be useful.

I did get a chance to cast and fish an 11-foot, 9-weight switch rod from Orvis, and found that casting the rod required different techniques with the switch line. The casting stroke required really good timing, and the stroke itself was a long push rather than the punch you give 9-foot rods that cast off the tip. Switch rods seem to cast with the top 25 percent of the rod, not just the tip. Actually, if I hit the tip too hard, the loop would coil and at times pile up. Casting into a good wind was tough, because the fat-diameter line just stopped at times. Also the design of the line created a funny loop that sagged. The front section of the loop was small and well formed, but as it shot forward, the back section of the loop dropped, creating a banana shape that caught wind like a sail. Again, I want to emphasize that I'm not skilled with all the proper switch-rod techniques, so it could have been my problem. But if a good caster finds these rods are a chore to cast, it is wise to get help and learn from someone who is skilled with this tackle.

After I put a standard 12-weight intermediate line on the switch rod, it felt more normal. It performed well, casting like a shorter rod with less adjustment to the casting stroke. I did need to change the stroke to compensate for the rod's length, but other than that, it was a smooth-casting rod. Using a standard line that matches the rod might be easier for most anglers to cast and fish. The extra rod length was an advantage for clearance on the backcast, for roll casting, and for eliminating much false casting. And the rod performed well casting with either one or two hands. When casting with one hand, hold the rod farther up the grip than normal. Work your hand up the grip until it feels balanced.

Casting at Night

It requires practice, **time on the water,** to get the feel of night casting. Try fishing first during the daytime while closing your eyes to experience what night fishing is like, checking every few casts to see if the line is straight. A bright moon and low-light periods at dawn and dusk are excellent opportunities to familiarize yourself with night fishing. Without visual aids, you must develop timing and feel; it places the angler in a blind person's position: relying solely on touch.

The newcomer to night fishing should fish a shorter line, using a longer arm drift and stroke. Overloading the rod with a larger-weight fly line (a 9-weight line on an 8-weight rod) will improve feel. Focus mainly on keeping the line under control, maintaining feel at each point of the cast, and concentrate on keeping the line straight after the cast. Short, controlled casts are preferable to long, sloppy ones. And as I mentioned in chapter 12, watch the rod to prevent serious injuries. Remember to watch your backcast, even though it may be too dark to see the line; this will eliminate the possibility of a hook in the face—barbless flies slip easily off the scalp, causing no lasting damage, but a hook in the eye is permanent.

Try fishing with fewer false casts to reduce the time the line is in the air. Most anglers make too many false casts: Only two or three, at most, are required. One is better, especially when fishing a shorter line. Too many backcasts are tiring and will affect your timing. This is also true when making a long backcast. Making numerous long false casts, holding 50 feet of line in the air, is tiring. Two are ideal, but if you can make the cast with only one false cast without losing distance, all the better. Long backcasts give the forward cast more power and add to distance. When making longer backcasts, use a longer stroke and more arm motion. Remember that additional line in the air means a longer pause between casts.

The Importance of Roll Casting

Roll casting, in combination with standard casts or by itself, is an integral component of saltwater fishing. The roll cast has many uses: Picking up sinking lines or large wind-resistant flies is time-consuming and nearly impossible with a standard cast; and roll casting brings even lead-core lines up to the surface to allow effortless lifting of the line. Roll casts also keep an angler from retrieving a fly too close, which would necessitate bringing the leader into the tip top. Using a roll cast with 10 to 20 feet of fly line outside the rod tip will cut down on the number of false casts needed to begin the next cast.

The line length and use of this application varies, depending upon conditions; jetties and rocky structure, for instance, may require a full retrieve if the angler is too far from the water. A roll cast might slap the hook against the rocks, dulling or breaking the hook point. Some surf situations also prevent its use because the fly continually drags through the sand, grinding down the hook after only several casts. If a fish strikes with the rod upright, make the intended roll cast; the line motion and speed will be sufficient to drive the hook home. Sharp hooks are a necessity.

Three basic steps are required to make a roll cast. First, raise the rod to the one o'clock position and allow the line to stop. Not allowing the line to stop makes roll casting difficult. Next, force the rod forward as if driving a nail to a point 6 feet above the water in front of you. (Choosing an imaginary spot above the water to drive a nail into will help you punch the line out and add more power to your cast.) Then bring the rod to an abrupt halt, which will roll the line out and onto the surface, making pickups simple.

Sometimes several roll casts in rapid succession are needed to lift fast-sinking lines or flies to the top. To lift large flies and popping bugs, begin the backcast while the fly is in the air. This will keep you from having to pick the water-resistant lure from the water.

Hauling will add distance to a roll cast, giving the long rodder a new casting tool when a backcast is impractical due to crowds, wind, or simple lack of room. During the roll cast, haul with the line-holding hand at the same time you apply the power stroke. With the right conditions, 60-foot roll casts are possible. This technique works best when making crosswind or downwind casts with flies of modest size.

14

Retrieving

Retrieving is sometimes a forgotten part of fly fishing. Anglers might talk about speed or strip length, but mostly they dwell on fly types, line types, casting, and rod action. There are times when the retrieve is not a factor when casting into aggressively feeding fish, but when the fishing gets tough, the proper retrieve can make a big difference.

Choosing a retrieve type, or style, is the first decision. Some anglers prefer to retrieve holding the rod with the casting hand and moving the line with the noncasting hand. Although this is a popular retrieve, I feel that retrieving with both hands is more effective. I retrieve with the rod under my arm, using both hands to manipulate the line. This works well with a fast retrieve, a steady retrieve, and a retrieve that requires long, sharp pulls. It is ideal for poppers and other surface flies where a continuously flowing fly action is effective.

The rod-under-the-arm retrieve is also very effective for hooking fish. When the fish takes the fly, you just keep bringing in line until you feel the fish, then a firm pull is all that's needed to drive the hook home. It works well on all types of fish, including tarpon. Recently while on the phone with Steve Huff, the legendary Florida skiff guide, he mentioned that anglers are now using this retrieve when tarpon are feeding on worms. He calls it the Tabory Retrieve.

The Two-Handed Retrieve

I learned about the two-handed retrieve while reading one of Joe Brooks's fly-fishing books, where he mentioned using both hands to improve fly speed. Once I started fishing with this retrieve, it seemed so natural—adding a flow, a rhythm to the fly's movement—that I soon became addicted to it. It was not long before I fished almost exclusively with a two-handed retrieve. It became my trademark.

When I first started recommending this technique, I ran into a number of doubters. There were anglers who actually believed that you would drop the rod after hooking the fish and that fly action was limited. But what always loomed large was hooking fish: How could you hook a fish without using the rod? Well, the rod should never be used to hook a fish unless the angler is fishing small hooks and using a very light tippet. Trout anglers use the rod to set the hook because the rod tip bends and absorbs most of the shock. When fishing in salt water, however, the ability to penetrate a fish's tough jaw with a big hook is the major issue. Anglers who lift the rod to hook a fish lose some of the positive pull required to drive the hook home. I tell my students that you use the rod to present the fly and fight the fish, but you use your hands to work the fly and hook the fish.

Let's take a look at some of the benefits of this style of retrieving, which has become popular for many types of fly fishing.

Getting Started

After making the cast, use the noncasting hand to slip the rod under your casting arm, putting the handle in your armpit. The reel should be just behind your triceps muscle. Be sure to hold only the rod's handle, not the reel. If you feel your arm going numb, you're probably pinching the reel handle into your upper arm muscle. Use just enough pressure to keep the rod in place. Some anglers use their noncasting arm to hold the rod, but I prefer using the casting arm, as it's a much easier motion to transfer the rod from the casting arm into the casting hand. I find that when sight casting, it seems to be much quicker with less motion. Once you use this system, the movement of the rod from arm to hand and back again becomes second nature. I never think about it—if I need to make a quick cast the rod is there, ready for action.

A fast retrieve is just one advantage with this system. Using both hands, the combination of different retrieves is endless, depending on how skilled the angler is. After making the cast,

Using a versatile two-handed retrieve gives many options.

fly fishing in salt water is manipulating the fly line, whether you are fishing blind or sight casting.

A continuous retrieve keeps the fly moving in a steady flow. Depending on the speed needed, this can be simply a hand-over-hand retrieve. When using short pulls, the fly's action will be slightly erratic; for a steady flow, use long pulls and try to start the next pull before finishing the current strip. This is a good retrieve when fishing for stripers feeding on *Nereis* worms.

A good retrieve for fishing deep rips and faster currents is long strips using a hard, sharp pull. This retrieve is often ideal when using a fast-sinking line to swing the fly across and downcurrent. It is also perhaps the most difficult two-handed retrieve to learn. Start with your hands together and grip the line with your noncasting hand. With your casting hand, cup the line loosely and lightly pinch it with your thumb and forefinger. The line should lie across the palm of the casting hand. Now pull down with the hand that is gripping the line, and rise up with the hand that is letting the line slip. This will give a long strip, and with some practice you can get a fast retrieve that really gives great action to the fly.

Hooking Fish

Hooking fish with the rod under the arm does two things: It creates a straight line between the angler and the fish, putting maximum pressure on the hook set; and it keeps the fly in the fish's range if the strike is missed. Striking with the rod will often move the fly many feet from the fish, but hooking with both hands keeps the fly close. Many times when hooking fish you just continue retrieving until the line tightens. Often there is no need to set the hook because the routine of stripping sets the hook automatically.

There are many other advantages as well. Fish that take a fly swimming toward the angler create slack in the line, in which case it's easier to recover line with two hands and adjust to the way a fish is moving. Some anglers like to set the hook using a long, hard pull, which can pop a leader if the fish strikes hard and quickly turns. By using a two-handed retrieve, you can adjust line tension depending on how a fish takes the fly. If there is slack in the line, a steady recovery of line is more effective.

Another benefit of the two-handed retrieve is having two hands to control the line when the fish runs. I use one hand to apply pressure to the line and the other to keep the line from tangling—and I must admit, the way fly line can tangle, there have been times when I wished I had three hands. After hooking

One advantage with a two-handed retrieve is having two hands to control the line when a fish runs.

the fish, let it run all the loose line out, and then grab the rod once the fish is on the reel.

Benefits of the Two-Handed Retrieve

Retrieving with two hands also lets the casting arm rest after each cast. Constantly holding the rod in your hand when fishing for hours can lead to a variety of debilitating conditions. Breaking up the continuous motion of casting and holding the rod during the retrieve can prevent problems like tennis elbow.

A popper needs to produce a big splash and a hard pop to be effective in broken water. Although not really a two-handed retrieve, with the following popper technique you are fishing with the rod under your arm. Actually, your casting hand will be positioned near the first stripping guide, and the line will slip through that hand. With the noncasting hand, make sharp pulls while the casting hand quickly lifts the rod about 1 foot. This makes the popper jump forward with a strong, hard pull so it pushes lots of water. The popper's face will drive slightly into the water's surface rather than skip along the top, producing more splash and noise. In a wind chop a popper needs to make a good deal of commotion to be effective.

When fishing for any of the ocean speedsters—tuna, false albacore, or bonito—a quick take-up is an advantage when hooking fish. A continuous, fast recovery of loose fly line allows the angler to feel the strike and set the hook. I'm sure this is true with other binge-feeding gamefish as well. I use this retrieve a lot—not just for a long pull, but also with a slower retrieve with shorter pulls. I like it because either hand can quickly grip the line when a fish takes. This retrieve also works well when dead-drifting the fly. I like to keep pulsating the fly as it drifts without taking in line. Keep making sharp pulls with the noncasting hand, but don't take in any line. You can also try pinching the line with the casting hand as it feeds out. This will give the fly a fluttering action, making it look like injured bait.

Altering the strip length when using a steady, flowing retrieve is a good way to fool fish that are tasting the fly. Stripers will track a fly but might not take. At times they will kiss the fly between strips as it pauses. On a number of occasions I have watched stripers follow the fly and appear to just nip it after each pause. Try mixing up your pulls, using a variety of strip patterns—for instance, three short pulls and then one long quick pull—to see if you can catch the fish off guard. Even if you can't see the fish, if you feel slight bumps or are hooking fish short that quickly pull off, they are probably striking short. Breaking the steady retrieve pattern might be the trick that proves successful. It is also a good retrieve to use when covering water because it looks like a crippled baitfish. Sometimes I don't even keep track of altering the retrieve—I just keep mixing different pull lengths and how long I pause between strips.

When fishing at night, short pulls with a slow, flowing retrieve is an ideal fly action. Anglers who are very patient do well crawling a fly slowly across the surface, creating a wake. On calm summer nights, a fly that leaves a wake might be the only effective fly action. (When using this retrieve in low light, however, be aware that when casting across-current, a large bow will form in the line.) This also works well for bonefish—at times a slow, steady action will bring a strike. If a fish keeps following and will not take, try one longer strip and then let the fly sit.

There are times when casting blind and fishing at night will require a survival retrieve, one that works when you are half asleep. When fishing is slow but you don't want to quit, this hand-over-hand system allows the angler to fish without working hard. When anglers get punchy, the first thing to go

Retrieving with one hand is still popular with some anglers.

is concentration, and just when you let your guard down, a fish hits. A two-handed retrieve gives you a better chance of hooking a fish because both hands are holding the line.

Some anglers might feel that holding the rod allows them to use it to add action to the fly. But using the rod too much might sacrifice solid contact with the fly. Keeping in touch with the fly by forming a straight line with the rod and fly line is essential for hooking fish. If the rod is not in line with the fly line, you have slack and a less positive hook set. A basic rule when retrieving is to keep the rod pointed toward the fly line, and keep the rod tip down. When wading, the rod tip should be touching the water; when fishing from a boat, get as close to the water as you can without touching the gunwales.

I'm not saying that the two-handed retrieve is for everyone or that it should be the only retrieve to use. Some anglers might be so in tune with a single-handed retrieve that trying to use a two-handed retrieve would be difficult, even impossible. However, there are conditions and circumstances where this system is extremely effective. The next time you are on the water, try putting the rod under your arm and start retrieving. You might discover a new way to retrieve that will help you catch more fish.

Retrieves for Different Conditions

Whatever retrieve you choose, here are some thoughts on how to produce effective fly action. The retrieve is what makes the fly look alive, and thus needs to fit the water type, bait type, and fly type. It also allows the fly line to flow, which makes the fly work properly. Generally speaking, in slow water a faster retrieve is more effective, and in faster water a slow-moving fly works well. However, try different techniques—trial and error is the best way to determine the best technique for different water. Learning to retrieve in good visibility will help improve technique. By watching the fly move, you can learn what retrieve is best in different situations and what retrieve is best for different fly patterns. Some fly patterns work better with certain retrieves in different waters.

Flowing Water

I believe the best retrieve in moving water involves getting the fly to swing across the water column while flowing toward the surface. In currents that are mid- to fast speed, a fast-sinking line works best because you get more rise in the fly. Try casting at different angles across the current, letting the line and fly drift before retrieving. As the fly drifts, make sharp pulls with the line but don't take any of it in. This will make the fly dart as it swings. In a slower flow, use soft pulls and let the fly dead-drift longer. An intermediate line will often be more effective in a slower flow, but a fast sinker will still work.

As the fly swings farther downcurrent, begin retrieving, using long pulls and a fast retrieve. Try alternating short, medium, and long pulls with different speeds of retrieve. This will work well in water depths to about 10 feet if fishing from an anchored boat or standing on shore. In a drifting boat, letting the line and fly drift longer will give more penetration, but in very fast flows, the fly will not remain in the strike zone for very long.

I like flies with active materials that breathe well in the water. A good example is the Snake Fly, which gives good action and has a buoyant head that makes the fly dart toward the surface. Another advantage of using flies with active materials is that the fly still looks alive when letting it flow without adding action, or dead-drifting. Without adding action, the fly looks like a natural bait as it flows with the tide, or a crippled baitfish struggling in the current or settling to the bottom.

When fishing on the surface with a popper or slider, use a stop-and-go retrieve. Another good technique is to let the lure dead-drift and give it small twitches, like a crippled baitfish. When fish are feeding on small, slow, mobile foods like shrimp, crabs, or hatching worms, dead-drifting can be very effective. If fish are cruising, keep working different sections of water to cover as much water as possible. If fish are holding, feeding like trout in a specific location, try casting above and drifting the fly over the fish's feeding station. When wading, get above the fish and cast so the fly makes a short swing over the fish. Unlike with trout fishing, these foods are somewhat mobile, so a drag-free drift is unnecessary.

Up- and Downcurrent

When working different flows, adjust the retrieve depending on the speed and direction of the flow. Casting straight down a fast current might require just holding the fly in the flow to give it action, and using a slow retrieve to bring it back up the flow. When casting downcurrent it's better to cast at a slight angle, letting the fly swing. You are actually walking or slipping the fly without giving forward motion. This can be very effective when working the edge of a drop-off. Casting downcurrent requires less skill because the flow keeps a tight line and a good connection to the fly. Beginning anglers fishing at night can use the flow to keep a tight line—quartering to slightly angling downcurrent will help keep contact with the fly.

Casting up into the current requires fast handwork and a straight cast to stay in touch with the fly. The angler must be ready to retrieve just as the line hits the water. In a fairly fast flow, the retrieve must be fast, and a two-handed retrieve is often necessary. Working a fly downcurrent makes it look alive and appear to be escaping. Fishing down a flow allows the fly and line to work deeper when using a sinking line. When fishing upcurrent in a fast flow, the fly will not get down very well even with a fast-sinking line.

Calm Water/Top Water

Calm water presents a good opportunity to use surface lures to bring fish from a distance. Feeding fish are attracted to noise—this is why a popper or surface slider is often more effective in quiet water than a fly. One effective way to fish at night, or in low light, is to use a slider, a fly that moves along the surface, leaving a wake. I don't know if it's the wake, the sound, or perhaps the vibration that draws fish so effectively to a slider. Try different speeds and move the fly with short to long pulls to find an action that works. Sometimes a very slow action, moving the fly 6 inches every ten seconds, is deadly on dark, hot summer nights. This might drive some anglers nuts, but it works. Jack Gartside's Gurgler is a good cross between a popper and slider—it makes just enough noise to drive fish crazy, and is a good bet on calm mornings. Use 4- to 6-inch-long pulls to create a bubbling action along the surface.

In a wind chop, bigger-splashing poppers are more effective because they make more noise. If casting into surface-feeding fish, a slider or smaller popper is less effective. Unless your offering creates enough commotion, it might go unnoticed. This is often the reason inexperienced anglers have problems catching fish at times—they aren't moving the popper fast enough to create a good splash. In the broken surface of a wind chop, unless the lure makes enough noise and splash, it does not usually attract attention. Fishing below the surface can be more effective if the angler is not hooking up while fish are surface feeding.

Surface-Feeding Fish

Casting to surface-feeding fish is often simple: Get your fly out there and bang! The fish should take. But there are times when surface-feeding fish are hard to take. Too much bait means too much competition, and a seemingly sure opportunity can become difficult fishing. This can happen frequently in schools of sand eels, small menhaden, or small herring. If you make half a dozen casts into surface-feeding fish with no hookups, it's time to fish below the bait. This works best in water over 5 feet, but becomes ineffective in less than 3 feet.

Use a sinking line and cast across or near the feeding fish. Start with a ten-count to let the line and fly sink, and then begin retrieving the fly in short jerks. The action should simulate a crippled or dying baitfish. The trick is to target the fish that are feeding below the surface action on the dead and crippled bait as it falls to the bottom.

One day on the outer beaches of Cape Cod, I fished next to several spin anglers. We were all fishing into surface-busting stripers that were feeding on peanut bunker. The spin anglers were using poppers while I bounced the bottom, fishing a sinking line and a Slab Fly. At one point I hooked up five casts in a row. On several occasions I actually let the fly just sit on the bottom, and the fish picked it up off the sand. The spin anglers never caught on to what I was doing and took only one fish while I kept hooking up. In this case it was not the lure itself but the offering's location that made it effective. If the spin anglers had used bucktails fished along the bottom, they would have caught many fish.

Rolling Surf

Fishing moving water along a beach is different from most fly-fishing situations. There is often a flow along the beach and wave action that pushes into the beach. Maintaining contact with the fly is very important. There are times when you need to feed line after casting but before retrieving. This is often the case when timing the cast after the last wave of a set rolls off the beach. After the cast lands, keep feeding line until the wave's force diminishes, then begin the retrieve using medium to long pulls and a fast retrieve. If the waves are not large, 2 to 3 feet, try a slower retrieve. In bigger surf with more water movement, line control is difficult; a faster retrieve helps to maintain contact with the fly. Also try dead-drifting with a short cast, letting the line and fly slip a few feet, then holding the line and letting the fly hold in the flow. Keep trying different angles with different-speed retrieves to find the right combination. Much of the retrieve in rolling surf is trial and error.

Working a fly off cliffs is very similar. You cast into the waves as they flow off the structure, feed some line into the flow, and then hold tight so the fly sits in the flow as it dissipates.

Retrieves for Different Fish Types

Most of the time the water type or bait type will dictate the type of retrieve to use. I know that many anglers believe that the ocean speedsters—tuna, false albacore, and bonito—require a fast-moving fly. This might be true sometimes, but I have often taken these fish using a slow retrieve. I feel there are times when a fast retrieve is important, not to attract fish and make them take the fly, but to feel the strike. When these fish are swimming toward the angler, the strike can go undetected because the angler never feels the take. I have watched albies take my fly with no hint of a strike, and only by switching to a fast retrieve did I hook the fish. A good example of this is when a boat is drifting down a flow and you must cast to feeding fish that are moving downcurrent toward the boat. A fast retrieve is necessary to feel most strikes unless the fish takes and turns. Many times, however, the fish just sips the fly and glides to the next bait. Fishing with the rod under the arm is a distinct advantage in conditions when fast-flowing fly action is necessary.

Using different retrieves and knowing which ones are most effective in certain waters will make you a better angler. Some anglers get into a rut and use one type of retrieve all the time. This is especially true with anglers who use weighted flies. Learning a number of retrieves and knowing when to use them will help you fish different types of water more effectively. Be flexible and **keep trying different techniques** until one works.

15

Hooking and Fighting Fish

Preparation is the single most important consideration when trying to hook and hold a saltwater fish. Being ready separates the very good saltwater fly rodders from the fair ones. When a fly fisher is not ready, no matter how good an angler he or she is, the fish has the advantage. Saltwater fish are big—by a freshwater fisherman's standards, they are huge—and even a ten-pound schoolie striper will cause problems if you are unprepared.

During one summer in the early 1970s, I encountered some excellent fishing in the Norwalk Islands. Large schools of bass and blues were feeding vigorously in shallow water during the day. Copp McNulty and Frank Smith, two local anglers, took several large fish on fly tackle, twenty-nine and thirty-one pounds, respectively. These were the largest fish any of our club members had taken up to this point. (The Connecticut Salt Water Fly Rodders has an active group of hard fishermen who enjoy chasing fish in Long Island Sound.) These fish were located between Stamford and Westport, Connecticut. Several fly rodders got wind of this hot fishing, and we all went exploring—we knew the approximate location, and all we needed was to sniff out the fish.

Pete Kriewald, an old fishing partner, and I cruised out off the reef that runs from Goose Island to Copps Island in Norwalk. There is a large shallow area of rocky structure there that holds fish, and it was here we found Copp's boat. Both Copp and Frank were fishing, and as we slowly approached, we saw several schools of fish were working throughout the area. The gamefish were chasing baby snapper blues, which move up into such areas to feed on small bait. Like many predators, the small blues now turn into the bigger fishes' dinner.

As we moved slowly up into the area, poling our way along with an oar, a school of fish came up behind the boat. We both had our rods ready and managed to hook and land a few fish. This particular school had smaller fish, but we still had a ball using light 9-foot rods to catch several nice stripers. It was ideal fishing because the five- to ten-pound fish were on top, taking poppers. In this very location several days later, Pete Kriewald took a world-record fish of forty-five pounds, which is described in appendix two.

Several days of hard fishing produced great action, and it was amazing to have such good daytime fishing during the summer. Mornings and afternoons were best: Poppers were the hot lure. Both bass and blues seemed to congregate and feed on the moving tide, keeping the poor little snapper blues running for their lives. In my estimation there is no finer fishing than daytime top-water action, and this was at its best. There were several other anglers also enjoying this action, and some big fish were hooked and lost. Fighting fish in tight quarters can be tough. The area we fished was ideal for hooking fish but very tough for landing. The Norwalk Islands are all rock, kelp, and reef; this particular area was a large shallow with stones and heavy structure. To land a fish among such debris called for strategy and teamwork.

Late one afternoon John Posh, a good fly rodder from our area, had the fun of battling a big fish. There were three boats fishing the location, and by the amount of commotion in the calm water, we all knew John had hooked a good fish. After being hooked, the fish ran off, throwing water like a frightened porpoise. The other angler in John's boat just stood watching—making no attempt to follow the fish. John continued fighting it from a stationary boat, allowing the big bass to get farther out. The fish rolled on the surface several times on its long run—the last splash was over 200 yards from the boat. By not chasing the fish, John was at its mercy. With so much line out, the fish was uncontrollable. And with all the structure in such shallow water, the fish finally dove to the bottom, cleaning his clock. All John did was reel back an empty fly line. He was lucky to get that.

Similar things happen when you have made no advance preparation. Always brief everyone in your party so each angler knows what to expect long before anyone hooks a fish. Be set up, like a rehearsed play, so everyone knows the right procedures to use and no one is left standing dumbfounded when a fish runs and hides. Be prepared for any fish, large or small. Have your tackle, leaders, hooks, lines, and drag systems ready—don't be caught napping when a fish takes. Begin fishing by stretching the fly line to eliminate the coils that form by being packed around the spool. Then during the day make sure the line remains straight; when changing tackle, always stretch the new line to remove the coils—they can cost a fish and destroy your tackle. (The force of a strong fish driving a knotted fly line into the first guide can break the guide off, ruining a day's fishing.)

Let's discuss briefly what takes place when a fish is hooked, fought, and landed. The main concern after hooking a fish is to clear the free line, then fight the fish by applying as much pressure on it as possible. Once the fish is close, be cautious, for this is the second most critical period in fighting a fish; the first is clearing the line. In both cases you are fighting a fish on a short line. With only the slight stretch of the fly line, all the strain is on the tippet. Whether playing a fish from a boat or the surf, have a plan prepared. This is especially important in difficult locations—jetties, rock cliffs, shorelines with structure, or rips with heavy currents—where you must follow the fish in order to land it.

Setting the Hook

Of course, the first step in catching a fish is hooking it. Some fish hook themselves; there you are retrieving, and suddenly the fish is on. However, fish take differently depending on the situation, and how they take will determine your hooking procedure. School bass slam flies, while big striped bass take very subtly, just sipping the fly. The major concern is to allow the fish to bite, to take hold of the fly. *Do not* strike by sight or sound, for sometimes fish come up and break behind the fly or popper, not taking. Striking too soon pulls the fly away from them. Wait for the fish to bite, to grab the lure, before attempting to set the hook. If you are missing strikes when fish are chasing poppers, look away from the action and feel for the hit rather than watching for it.

Bluefish swim behind surface bugs, swirling several times before taking—it's critical to feel for the solid take before setting. Tarpon are huge fish, yet

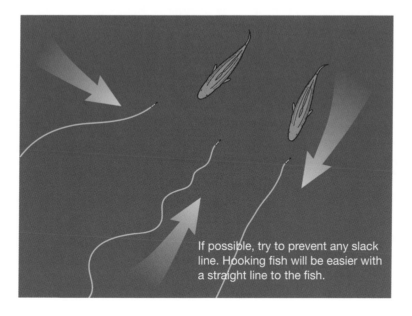

If possible, try to prevent any slack line. Hooking fish will be easier with a straight line to the fish.

they sip a fly very gently; frequently an angler doesn't know when a tarpon has taken the fly. Large striped bass swim up and inhale a fly; all the angler detects is the line slowly tightening, a feeling similar to that of hooking a piece of seaweed. Bluefish chomp, cut, and slash during the day, yet at night they can be very subtle, sometimes taking as softly as a trout. Weakfish usually take a fly like a fish taking a nymph; often you don't even feel the fish strike, just the line tightening. In all these cases, striking at the first touch might mean missing the fish, because the fly will be pulled away before the fish actually has it.

After a firm take is felt, there are many different ways of driving the hook home. As I mentioned earlier, I fish with my rod underneath my arm, hooking fish by pulling the line with my hands. Although it looks unconventional, using this method I can exert more direct pressure with straight pulls of line rather than with the rod. Furthermore, if a fish does not take, all I do is keep retrieving, for the fly has moved only a short distance and is still in the fish's reach. Striking with the rod moves a fly many feet, possibly out of the fish's range.

If you prefer to strike using the rod, hit with one quick pull or a series of short quick pulls. Don't yank back hard, because you can break a leader by applying too much sudden force. When a fish takes close while you are preparing to roll cast, make the intended cast, for there is enough power in a roll cast to set the hook.

Sharp hooks increase hooking percentages. Keen-edged hooks penetrate easily, especially when they are barbless, because the hooking surface is cut in half. I remember my first day in Costa Rica, and going out after lunch to try the river tarpon fishing. Anchoring in a river hole, Jack Frech, an old surf partner, and I started probing the dark river water with lead-core lines and heavily dressed flies. In short order I felt my line tighten. Feeling the fish, I struck hard, then watched an eighty- to one-hundred-pound silver king soar 10 feet into the jungle air and throw the fly. To me it was exciting just to marvel at the distance jungle tarpon can jump. But the guide was not very happy. Retrieving my fly to check its condition, he examined it and threw it disgustedly to the deck, shouting, "This hook no gooood, mon!" The Costa Rican believed a hook needed a barb to land fish. I fished exclusively with barbless hooks then and continue to do so now, regardless of the four-letter Spanish words the guide called me.

In the week that followed, the mood of our young jungle fisherman changed as I hooked and landed enough fish to prove my point. My percentage of fish landed to those jumped and lost was over 50 percent. Considering that I lost some fish to worn leaders, my hooking percentage was excellent. I believe barbs are unnecessary in fly fishing. There are those who will disagree, and each angler should make his or her own choice, but if barbless hooks can handle tarpon—the hardest fish to hook and hold—they will hold anything. Combining sharp hook points with barbless flies is a winning blend for me.

Take time to file all hook points carefully. When bumping the bottom or fishing from the shore, keep checking hook points to make sure they are sound. Several times I have wondered why I missed a fish until I checked the hook point and found it damaged.

Clearing the Line

After hooking the fish, your first challenge appears: getting the loose line onto the reel. Most saltwater fish are large enough to run. If you do catch a small fish, hand-line it in, without the reel, as you would a small trout. Use your retrieving hand to strip in line while locking the line to the rod handle with the forefinger of your casting hand. With larger fish you need to get the loose line clear in order to fight the fish from the reel.

A hooked fish is going to run off or hold in one position, throwing and splashing water. If it runs, coils of loose line on the boat's bottom, the water's surface, or the stripping basket must be controlled and cleared. To do this, hold the line loosely with your noncasting hand, allowing the line to pull through. I prefer to apply light hand pressure on the line, rather than letting it flow freely. Some pressure maintains control and prevents the line from flying about. But be careful—too much pressure causes burned fingers. Keep the coils clear of obstacles, especially your reel. Holding the rod under your arm will keep the reel and rod butt from tangling the line, and two hands manipulating the line will provide better control. In the event the fish wants to run, let it go. Your major concern is to keep the line clear until it tightens onto the reel. Then grab the rod and begin fighting the fish.

If a hooked fish thrashes, holding in one position when you are wading, simply back away from it, providing it is safe to do so. When fishing a safe, sandy beach—those on Cape Cod are an ideal example—back up and clear the line from your stripping basket. This method allows better line control. By backing away from the fish, you can get the line onto the reel before the fish runs. If the fish continues to thrash (big bass often wallow on the surface before running), walk toward the fish quickly, reeling up the extra line. But always keep tension on the fish while retrieving line.

The Run

Once loose line is eliminated and direct contact from the fish to the reel is established, start to apply pressure to fight the fish. If there are obstacles or structure to clear, hold the rod high to allow the fish to run and the line to clear the structure. If there are no obstacles, immediately turn the rod horizontal to the water, applying sideways pressure to the fish. Holding the rod straight up will give the fish an advantage; this is true not just for big saltwater fish, for I also use this method when trout fishing. Applying pressure to a fish's side makes it work harder for every bit of line, and with sideways pressure you can turn and tire a fish more quickly. Photos of rods straight up in the air on the covers of catalogs and magazines look great, but sideways pressure works more efficiently to tire the fish. If you wanted to drag a sled weighing 400 pounds, you would throw the rope over your shoulder to pull it more easily. However, if you held the rope below your shoulder, against the side of one arm, you would tire very quickly—it's the same for the fish.

If you are fishing an area where there is current, try to roll the fish toward slack water by tipping the rod down horizontally to the eddy side of the current. This should lead the fish into the slower water.

When a big fish runs, apply as much heavy pressure as possible as soon as you can. A long run from a good fish is what we all hope for, but it can turn into terror when the fish runs to the end of your spool and pops the tippet. Applying the right kind of pressure at first will slow the fish down more rapidly. Fighting the fish hard and landing it quickly will increase the fish's survival rate after release. This is why I play even trout very hard; I want to land the fish quickly. A fish that swims briskly away from your grasp will usually live. The survival rate is lower when a fish must be revived.

Applying Drag

After clearing the line and getting the fish on the reel, apply pressure with the reel drag and your hand. Most light-tackle fishermen prefer to apply heavy drag with their hands. Set the drag pressure on your reel to no more than three to four pounds. Apply additional drag for twelve- to sixteen-class tippets with your hand, either by palming or fingering the reel spool. Applying pressure to the exposed spool of the reel is easy—just palm the spinning rim. Every modern reel I'm familiar with has an exposed spool. Other reels require you to reach inside and finger the line or the inside of the spool—with fast-running fish, finger the spool to prevent burns. When fingering the spool, do so gently at first, applying more pressure as needed, but refrain from clamping down suddenly because an abrupt jolt could snap the tippet. Fast-running fish demand a softer approach; alternate your fingers to keep from altering your fingerprints. Drag can be increased on direct-drive reels by cupping a hand over the spinning handle, but be careful not to bust your knuckles.

Pointing the rod toward a running fish quickly reduces drag and eliminates the resistance of the guides on the line. When a fish is close and a large portion of the fly line is in the guides, this can be a significant reduction. This is why you should never increase reel drag above four pounds. The drag may feel too light when the backing is going through the guides, but when the fly line is back on the reel, the resistance doubles. If, in the heat of battle, you forget to back your drag off, it could cost you a good fish.

Once the fish is close, apply additional pressure by holding the fly line against the rod with the rod hand. This measure makes it easy to reduce tension merely by releasing your finger. It is best not to use this procedure when a

Use the palm of your hand to apply more drag. Using the palm enables a quick change of the drag pressure.

fish first runs, because the backing will carve grooves in your fingers. If you're wading, the blood may attract sharks.

Proper drag application is what helps land fish. Knowing how to apply pressure can be learned from actual fishing experience or at home on your lawn. Get a youngster to take a run with your fly line and try different ways of applying drag. Breaking off a neighborhood kid or two is not nearly as bad as losing a nice fish.

Pumping the Fish

After stopping your fish, don't allow it to sulk and regain its strength, but apply pressure immediately and start to pump the fish in. Moving the fish promptly prevents it from diving. A big, tired fish may try sounding, looking for refuge at the bottom. Big sandy beaches, like those on Cape Cod, will not present a problem because the bottom is clear. However, places like Rhode Island's rocky shore; Great Bay, New Hampshire; Montauk, New York; or areas of the Chesapeake, where there are fouls and snags, will.

Pump the fish by raising the rod, moving the fish toward you and reeling in extra line while lowering the rod again toward the fish. Use the reel only to recover line, not to bring the fish in. The rod is the lifting and moving tool that allows the reel to collect the line easily. Angus Cameron's favorite Scottish ghillie says it well: "When he pulls you quit pulling, and when he quits pulling you pull."

If fishing from a boat, always try to follow the fish when it is possible and safe. The closer you can stay to the fish—within 100 yards is ideal—the better you can control it. Once the fish gets out beyond several hundred yards, there is so much line stretch that it is hard to apply pressure, which is the plight of the shore angler. Stay comfortably near the fish—not right on its back, but close enough to control and land it quickly. When following a fish by boat, do so slowly to prevent overrunning. Pace the boat speed so the angler can stay even or gain line slowly. Don't create slack and make the angler crank frantically.

After fighting a fish for twenty minutes, your tippet strength remains constant. But once thirty to forty minutes have elapsed, the strain on the tippet starts to break down the monofilament. Fluorocarbon seems to hold up better, but in either case expect to lose strength. After an hour, a tippet may lose considerable strength because the constant stress fatigues it. We have all heard the story of someone fighting a fish for a long period and finally losing it because the leader just lost its strength. The tippet takes all the punishment because it is the weakest link with the most stretch. Pressuring a fish early in the fight discourages the fish quickly, making it possible for you to land it sooner.

Short-Range Fighting

When a hooked fish is close and the fly line is back on the reel is the second most critical time in fighting a fish. The line is shorter, so there is much less stretch, which puts additional pressure on the leader. Even if you fought the fish for only twenty minutes, during that time it could have rubbed the leader, fraying it. And because of the short line, you can't apply the same amount of pressure as you could during the fight. A short line requires less pull to move the fish, and even though the angler should keep fighting the fish hard, do it with measured force—soft hands.

When fishing from shore, allow a hooked fish to tire itself out in deeper water, especially in rocky areas that require leading the fish to where you can land it. However, do not allow the fish just to mill around, possibly diving to a snag; keep pressuring it. You will need luck in rocky locations, because the fish could swim into or over areas difficult or impossible for landing.

Landing in Special Locations

During periods of heavy surf, fishing is very productive off the rocky cliffs of areas like Newport, Rhode Island. When fishing high rocks with white water, be careful when landing fish. Once the fish is close, there are only certain pockets in which to land it without getting too close to the water's edge. The combination of the powerful surf and the slippery rocks requires planning when fighting a good fish. Once the fish is on, it's difficult to start looking for spots to land it; knowing safe places beforehand is the key to handling fish in rough rocky locations. Once the fish begins to tire, move to one of these locations, leading the fish there before it is too close to the rocks and coming into the wave-action's influence. Such places allow the angler to remain above the rolling water, for going down below the surf line to chase a fish is too dangerous. Look for V-shaped places in the rocks, or pools among the rocks where the fish can be led and landed in two stages. (Sometimes the fish must be brought to a holding pool, then worked to higher ground with the help of several waves.) Fishing rocky shores requires patience and good judgment.

Landing fish from a big sandy beach is easier, unless there is a huge swell present. Even then, if you work the swell properly, it can help land the fish.

When fishing beaches with rolling surf, allow the waves to work for you. Move down the beach, just to where you get wet feet, and try to move the fish toward shore. Once the fish gets inside the surf line—the rolling white water of the wash—the surge of the waves will pull it backward. If you can turn the fish out of the trough, the next wave will push it closer. Be prepared to move quickly, backing up the beach to gain line, and then following the fish down the beach's slope to stay close. Attempt to turn the fish by applying sideways pressure to keep it inside the wash. The key is to turn the fish's head so it faces the beach. This helps to punch the fish through the wave. If the fish remains sideways to the beach, it will be difficult to move. When the fish is inside the first wave, the next wave, with the assistance of rod pressure, will throw the fish up on the beach. Always use wave action to your advantage.

Surf beaches with rips, or large rips along shorelines, require the angler to keep close to the fish. Fish will follow the current, many times running along the shore after being hooked, which allows the angler to stay close by walking with the fish. In locations that permit following, always chase the fish. In crowded locations this is a must to prevent other anglers from fouling your line.

Most big jetties require the angler to walk the fish to shore, unless flat places exist along the sides to slide the fish into. If the fish has to be walked in, do so while it is still some distance from the jetty. Once the fish is near the side, every step requires concentrating on walking and keeping the fish away from the rocks. (An onshore or quartering-over-the-shoulder wind will assist by bowing the line and helping to lead the fish ashore. Hold the rod high, letting the line form a belly to guide the fish shoreward without bringing it closer to the jetty.) Start to walk in while the fish is running, unless the fish runs alongside the rocks, straight out from shore. In that case apply light pressure to try to get the fish to swim away from the jetty, walking to shore only after the fish is parallel to the beach. On the trip in, concentrate primarily on walking, pausing occasionally to make sure the fish is still swimming along or toward the beach. Upon reaching the shoreline, slide down the rocks on your tail, using your feet to slow your descent to the sand. Then move quickly up the beach, distancing yourself from the jetty, to land the fish.

A long-handled gaff can be used from a jetty if you plan to kill the fish. However, handling a gaff might be tough when you are fishing alone, and the use of gaffs for striped bass is now illegal in some states. I would suggest not getting involved with gaffs. Land small fish with your hand or by grabbing the line and lifting. When releasing the fish, make sure to keep it clear of the rocks.

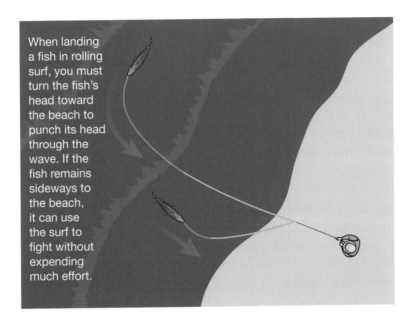

When landing a fish in rolling surf, you must turn the fish's head toward the beach to punch its head through the wave. If the fish remains sideways to the beach, it can use the surf to fight without expending much effort.

Do not attempt to pressure a fish when it is facing away from you. Try instead to turn the fish toward you. Once the fish is facing you, it will be very easy to move. If the fish is visible, you will know when it turns; otherwise, use your sense of touch (when the resistance is less, the fish is facing you). Once the fish turns toward you, apply as much pressure as you can to get the fish in quickly. If the fish turns sideways or away from you, try to roll it back. Bear in mind that a fish is almost impossible to pull backward in the water. You can pull a fish sideways in flat water, without a flow, but not backward, even when it's tired.

A tired fish is still capable of making a good run, so keep your reel drag the same. Apply any additional drag by hand.

Use Enough Tackle

When fishing rocky shores or heavy surf, use larger tackle that is capable of moving heavy fish. No. 10, 11, or 12 rods from 9 to 9½ feet long are ideal for these situations. Even when fishing strong tide rips from a boat, you are better off with larger tackle. Years ago, while fishing Great Bay, New Hampshire, with a no. 8 outfit, I lost several big fish. It's an area of strong current, heavy weeds, and rocky structure. Once, a fish took my fly and began to swim upstream. I said, "Oh boy, I've got this guy," then the fish turned around and headed downcurrent like a freight train. Before we could get the anchor up and follow, the fish sounded, ripping my tackle to pieces along the bottom.

Another time in Great Bay, a good bass hit a popper. We had a release anchor, but before we could get to the line, the fish ran out and popped the eight-pound-test tippet. It is best in strong rips or heavy bottom structure to fish twelve- to twenty-pound tippet with tackle that is capable of holding a good-size fish. You are just fooling yourself if you believe light tackle will handle large fish in rough conditions. Even a ten-pound fish is formidable under the right circumstances.

Fighting and Landing from a Boat

Fishing from a boat has several advantages, such as mobility, range, and the ability to remain close when fighting a fish. One problem when fishing from a boat, especially with some species, is in lifting the fish. Turned sideways, a fish is difficult to raise. I believe it's easier to handle fish from shore because you don't have to lift the fish up; you just slide the fish onto the beach. So when landing fish from a boat, make sure you're clear of all obstacles once the fish is close. If using an outboard, tilt the engine up. When anchored, sometimes it is best to pull the anchor and drift to keep the fish from tangling in the line.

Keep the rod low when the fish is below the boat.

When lifting a fish from below the boat, do not pick the rod too far above the horizon. High sticking will cause rod breakage.

A release anchor will help in this situation: Attach a lobster float to the end of your anchor line; you can disconnect the anchor rope at any time and come right back to the float once the fish is landed. This also eliminates the need to retrieve an entire anchor line during the first run—it's a must for the solitary angler.

Fish always seem to want to swim underneath the boat. When this occurs, stick your rod in the water and keep the tippet from rubbing against the boat's bottom, where barnacles or other snags can cut your tippet. Keep the line clear and don't allow the rod to hit the edge of the boat—rods can break under that kind of stress. Move to either the bow or stern and sweep the rod underneath the boat to clear the line to the opposite side.

Using a Landing Tool

Once a hooked fish is near the boat, be prepared to either net or gaff it. Grab small striped bass with your hand by the lower jaw, then unhook and release them. But have landing equipment ready for larger fish. Trying to land fish from a boat can be a comedy skit. I have seen people use gaffs and nets incorrectly, and this can be funny unless you lose a prize fish—then things get very serious.

If Hollywood were to make a movie on gaffing, it would be somewhere between a horror story and a comedy: Some people are slashers, others have a golf-swing technique, and then there are the stabbers. People who under normal circumstances act civilized can turn into maniacs when a gaff is put in their hands, and this is why fish are lost. Leave the use of a gaff to the professionals, and only for big tuna.

Nets are better landing tools for most people and much safer to use. A net is not a spear with which to stab or chase a fish. Put the net into the water and lead the fish toward it with your rod. A fish can only swim sideways or forward, so once its head is in the net, its body will follow. Allow the fish to swim into the net, then scoop from head to tail and then up, in one motion. Be sure to check your net each season. Some netting materials will rot, leaving you surprised after having a prize fish fall right through the net.

Landing nets are a big help when releasing fish from a boat. The major advantage of a net is in not having to bring a fish into the boat. Once the fish is in the net, hold it by the side of the boat, unhook it, and release it. Make sure when releasing to hold the fish by the tail to be certain it is capable of swimming under its own power before you let it go.

When purchasing a net, choose one large enough to handle big fish. Small fish fit in large nets, but the opposite is not true. Choose a net that is drab in color. Bright white or orange can spook fish, especially in clear water.

Handling Fish

Careful handling of all boated or beached fish is essential. Fish can harm an angler, whether they bite, stab, or try to eat him or her. Saltwater fish can do damage even when lying apparently harmless. After beaching a fish, never kick it ashore with your foot, especially striped bass. Handling a fish in this manner is unethical because it will injure the fish, and it could possibly cause you harm as well. Stripers have spines on their dorsal fins that are like surgical needles and are capable of driving into your foot, in some cases breaking off. I have seen fishermen hospitalized in horrible pain after being impaled by a bass. Striped bass also have spines on their pectoral fins and gill plates that can stab and cut.

Grab hardtails and bluefish by the tail and lift with the other hand. Here Ed Mitchell shows how to land an albi.

Bluefish have an extremely powerful bite accompanied by very sharp teeth; they require proper handling. To give you an example, bluefish were rare visitors to Maine and New Hampshire bays in the early seventies. Many years ago, a school moved up inside Great Bay and eight fish were landed in a short period of time; from these eight fish caught, *five* anglers received bites. The old largemouth bass fisherman's trick of grabbing the fish and putting the thumb inside the mouth and lower lip doesn't work with bluefish. When doing this to a largemouth bass, you have the fish—with a blue, the fish has you. When fishing with youngsters, be careful to keep them away from bluefish. Bluefish are capable of severing fingers; if they can break plugs in half, your flesh offers little defense.

Even weakfish have sharp canine teeth that can stab you. When handling bluefish and weakfish, grasp them behind the head, holding firmly but not squeezing too hard, to remove the hook. With small stripers, grab the lower jaw securely to remove the hook. It is wise to carry a pair of needle-nose pliers or some hook-removing device.

Remember that although some fish may appear dead, they might not be. It's best not to put your hand inside the mouth of a bluefish until it's gutted. Never trust a shark, even when it is gutted; a shark's jaws, triggered by an involuntary reaction, can snap shut like a steel trap even after death. Several people have been seriously injured after fooling with a "dead" shark.

When offshore fishing, let the captain and mate handle all the fish. Sharks need little explanation; consider them all dangerous until proven otherwise. Other offshore species are also big, strong, powerful fish capable of inflicting damage with the flick of a tail. When landing smaller offshore species like bonito and false albacore, handle them by the tail. Their tails provide an ideal handle that is easy to grab. Even fish over twenty pounds are quite manageable using this method—I have landed small bluefin to twenty-five pounds by grabbing their tails. These fish do have teeth, but they are fairly docile to handle compared to a bluefish.

Catch and Release

If you plan to release your fish, handle them gently. Fighting a good-size fish for a long period of time will exhaust it, so don't just drop it back in the water: Be sure the fish is capable of swimming. Place even small fish gently into the water. Handle large fish delicately, for their bodies and skeletal structures will not support them out of the water; handling a fish roughly may affect it internally.

Handle all of the offshore species with care. Quickly getting them back into the water and swimming is essential to their survival. These fish die fast, so use good pressure and land them quickly. I have found that holding them by the tail in the water and moving the tail from side to side revives them in short order. Though the way to revive most fish is by moving them forward and backward to get water flowing through the gills, hardtails seem to respond well to the quick side-to-side motion, and often they will bolt from your hand in several seconds.

Sometimes large striped bass are so tired after a fight that you can lead them right to the side of the boat, grab them by the lower lip, and unhook and release them. Be sure to take any released fish by the tail and work it slowly back and forth to force water through its gills until it can swim away. However long it takes, it is your responsibility to make sure the fish can swim. With bluefish, use pliers to release the fish and be on guard: Bluefish can see just as well out of water as they can in—sharks and piranhas are two other species with this unnerving ability.

A good way to handle a striper is to use a landing device or your hands to grab the lower lip, unhook the fish, and release it without lifting it from the water.

One more note on releasing fish: No matter what the species, be sure the released fish can swim powerfully away from your hands. There is nothing worse than seeing a fish go belly-up out of your reach because you didn't take the time to revive it properly.

Stringing Fish

In some locations, when wading after dark a distance from shore, stringing fish is not advised. On several occasions anglers have run into problems with fish trailing in the water behind them. I talked to one angler who had a very unpleasant experience on a Connecticut reef, when a large shark tried to eat the fish off the end of his stringer. Due to the shark's aggressive behavior, the angler was almost pulled from the reef. Heavy surf conditions can also pose a problem to the angler trying to string fish, especially striped bass. The surf can roll the fish up behind you, either knocking you over or impaling you with the spines of the dorsal fin. I would not advise stringing fish in any areas away from shore. If you plan to keep fish when fishing near shore, keep them on a stringer or put them in a tidal pool. However, small animals and gulls could ruin your catch, and the safest practice is to take killed fish right to the car.

Enjoying the Harvest

If you like seafood, saltwater fish are delicious, so plan to take some home. It is always nice to enjoy a fish meal, but the fish will be tastier if cared for properly. It is wise to have a cooler with ice to place fish in, especially during the summer months, when sun and heat can ruin the flesh. Prompt cleaning improves the flavor of most caught fish, especially bluefish, which can turn strong if allowed to sit too long. If cared for properly, all species will be excellent eating, offering many enjoyable meals from the sea.

Saltwater fly rodding differs from freshwater angling in many ways. Anglers who have never felt the power of a big saltwater fish on a fly rod have missed a wonderful fishing experience. Being able to control this force makes fishing in salt water exciting. But to hook, fight, and land a good-size fish takes more than wishing, hoping, or praying. Preparation is the key to fly rodding for any fish, large or small. Make sure both you and your tackle are ready. Looking back upon fish I have lost, I realize it was poor preparation that cost me the fish. Using inadequate tackle, tying poor knots, and not changing a fatigued leader are some mistakes I've made. I was successful when I was prepared. Whether you hook an eight-pound light-fly-rod weakfish in a small creek or a bluefish in the Montauk surf, be prepared for battle.

PART THREE

Tackle, Flies, and Gear

16

Tackle

The Northeast and mid-Atlantic freshwater angler is not concerned with strength and power when rigging tackle because very few fish will run into the backing. The Great Lakes have large, strong fish, but even these cannot compare with the power of a saltwater fish. Big striped bass are capable of making runs of several hundred yards against heavy spinning tackle. A light fly rod would be insufficient to grapple with a big fish even in calm conditions, let alone the harsh locations where most sizable marine fish roam. A midsize bluefish, eight to ten pounds, has incredible strength, requiring beefy tackle to raise it from a rip or deep hole. I suggest that beginners not undergun—use tackle heavy enough to control saltwater fish.

I fished with well-known editor and fishing editor for *Field & Stream* John Merwin several summers ago, on Cuttyhunk Island off the coast of Massachusetts. I was designated pole-bearer and brought the tackle. John had said, "Don't bring me anything too heavy. A no. 9 is fine." In the morning darkness, we waded cautiously over the slippery rocks along the edge of Canapitsit Channel, leading into the harbor. There was only a small swell running, and the current flowing along the channel was slow, near slack low tide—hardly rough water conditions. But although the water seemed calm enough, there are many other factors that come into play when choosing tackle.

The dawn's first light brought action. Working the mild white water that rolled over the kelp bar, we took several striped bass. The fish were not large, maybe to seven pounds, but their game way of feeding and stubborn fight made the morning a fun experience. The bar was very slippery, with smooth scattered rocks and heavy kelp, so the footing was less than desirable. Chasing a fish was out of the question. Positioned along the channel were large barnacle-covered boulders—some near the channel's mouth were as large as a compact car. As we slipped our way back to dry ground, John said, "You're right, a 9-weight was as light as you would want to fish, and a 10-weight would have been better. I even had problems with these small fish. I don't know what I would have done with a decent-size fish, let alone a large one."

When selecting tackle, decide what areas you plan to fish and consider possible conditions, like ground cover, heavy surf, reefs, jetties, flats, and so on. Then determine what types of fish you will pursue. Weather conditions and time of year are also factors. Spring and summer offer calm, mild conditions, with small bait the predominant food. Fall fishing brings heavy weather, rolling surf, high winds, and large baitfish. A no. 9 outfit will cover most fishing needs if you mostly work sheltered bays, beaches with light turbulence, or open water with no heavy current. However, landing a large fish will take patience and some luck with such an outfit. Even without strong current or heavy wave action, a large fish will hang tough. Without a bigger rod's sufficient lifting power, a Mexican standoff will occur, and the fish are usually the winners in these situations.

The most popular rod length is 9 feet. This length casts well, and for many fishing conditions it's the best choice. Certainly it should be the first choice for a beginner angler, as well as the boat angler. That said, two-handed spey rods and switch rods offer some advantages. They give more clearance when casting from a steep beach or when deep wading. They also improve casting distance and the ability to make a long cast with one backcast, and they roll-cast well. They do, however, require a different casting stroke and some adjustment in timing.

While using two hands to cast makes casting easier, taking some of the workload off the casting arm, the downside when using a longer rod is casting into the wind and fighting fish. Rods 10 feet or longer catch more wind, requiring more force to push a cast into the wind. With good technique the wind is less of a factor, but casting into a 20-knot headwind will always be difficult. When fighting a fish, an 11-foot rod makes the angler work harder to achieve the same force that can be applied with a shorter rod.

Casting 8- to 9-weight switch rods will be tiring if fishing big flies or if casting for long periods. Remember that casting the line for a 9-weight switch rod is like casting a 12- to 13-weight fly line—and you're doing it with a rod that is 11 feet long. And if you need to fish the fly close in, right to your feet, longer rods are more work. Line management also becomes a problem when making casts of over 100 feet. Fishing that much line out of a stripping basket requires a clean, tangle-free line and a controlled retrieve that lays the line smoothly into the basket. Trying to fish without a basket in the surf will test most anglers' patience.

Where longer rods shine is in locations that allow distance pickups. Here the angler can keep the head section of the line out the tip, make a backcast, and throw a long cast with little effort. A good example would be fishing a big ocean hole that has a flow running along the beach. If the outer bar is exposed, most of the wave action is broken, with little wash along the shore. This situation is much like a big salmon river where the angler can lift the head section of the fly line after it swings against the shore and shoot the line back out with one backcast. If there is wave action, the shoreline is a good location to fish, as is the middle of the hole, so fishing the fly right to the beach would be important. But in this case the shallow water along the shore is not the prime holding water, like the deeper water in the center of the hole or the water below the drop-off just inside the bar.

Rods of 11 feet or longer are ideal for certain types of fishing, but they have limitations. They are good second or third rods to use in locations that complement their advantages.

There are places, such as small creeks, tributaries, and tidal areas, where lighter tackle works well. These locations permit fishing with trout outfits, no. 5 to no. 7. Chesapeake Bay harbors many three- to five-pound bass, which are great fun on light tackle. Weakfishing on Long Island's Shelter Island creeks is akin to trout fishing. These small waters need a delicate approach, making lighter tackle ideal. Trout rods do work, but their use is limited to certain waters, and trying to use them for inappropriate locations will frustrate any angler planning to fish the brine seriously.

Light rods are fun, and they *do* catch fish. But they have limitations, and they can kill. Larger fish that are fought and released on light tackle have a much higher mortality rate than do fish landed with heavier gear, because the fight is usually longer. When a fish fights to exhaustion, it may swim away, but the chemical changes caused by the struggle can harm it in the end. Light tackle has its place, but under many conditions it does not allow an angler to fully enjoy the sport or to pursue gamefish in varied habitats. Comparatively speaking, *any* fly rod is light by most saltwater tackle standards.

Bonito fishing requires a soft touch. Most of the top bonito fishermen prefer a no. 8 to no. 9 outfit both for presenting the fly and for fighting this speedy gamester on a light tippet. The bonito's large, keen eye does not generally permit using a heavy tippet, especially in clear waters like those of Martha's Vineyard or Nantucket. Most experienced bonito fishermen believe lighter tackle is the only way to take these fish. Yet a medium-action rod with a no. 10 line has worked fine for me on a number of occasions when I've encountered the ocean speedster.

The improvements in the types of graphite used to make rods and how they are bonded together have been a windfall for fly rodders, especially in salt water. And since there are many sources for graphite, the price of building rods has become more affordable. When you compare the newer rods to those made even fifteen years ago, the improvements are exciting. The newer rods are lighter and have more flex, more power, and better casting ability. And they have good fish-fighting capability, even though they are still fairly light. Now an angler can fish a 9- or 10-weight rod that feels like an 8-weight.

Most Atlantic fly-rodding situations require sturdy tackle to fish properly. There are two choices for covering most conditions in the Northeast. The most popular is a 9-foot rod for a no. 9 line. The other choice for less-demanding locations is the 8-weight. For those planning to fish small bays, tidal areas, or mostly sheltered waters, either of these rods is a good selection. An excellent starting outfit, it will become your bonito, bonefish small fly, and light-tackle outfit. Even in small to midsize surf, a 9-weight outfit works well. I prefer to have 200 yards of backing, just in case I hook that once-in-a-lifetime fish. The flows and riptides can give big fish lots of momentum, making them hard to stop. If you want to go lighter, a well-designed, beefy, 9-foot 7-weight can be fun in the right conditions, and for sight casting to spooky fish in calm water, a good 7-weight is hard to beat.

When you need to go heavy, the best choice is a 9-foot rod for a no. 10, 11, or 12 line. Ten- to 12-weight outfits are best suited for big surf—not so much for presenting the fly, but for fighting fish. If a big fish gets over an outer bar, you need the lifting power of a large rod. The bigger-size rods are also good for small bluefin and big albies and for fishing heavy fast-sinking lines in big rips. Rods bigger than no. 12s are special offshore sticks built for lifting strong, heavy fish. They range in length from just under 8 feet to about 8½ feet long. The shorter length is better for fighting fish. For general fishing these rods are too stiff to cast for long periods. They are designed for ten casts a day and for lifting, and are not suited to the repeated casting of the Atlantic fly-rod angler.

Even some 12-weights are tough to cast for long periods unless they have a softer action. This again is where the construction of better, stronger rods has made our fishing easier. There are some 10- and 11-weight rods that are stronger, lighter, and easier to cast than 12-weights made in the late eighties. I feel confident that a well-designed 10-weight rod will get the job done in most conditions where I used to use a 12-weight.

However, there are problems when tackle is pushed beyond its capabilities. Cooper Gilkes, a good friend and one of the best saltwater fly rodders on Martha's Vineyard, told me of just such an event. He hooked a large striper along Lobsterville Beach that walked him and his no. 9 outfit up and down the shoreline for almost an hour before it pulled free. Coop is a great angler, and had he been using a heavier rod with more lifting power, he may have been able to move the fish. With the lighter rod he was at the fish's mercy and could only hold on. And this particular beach is open, without heavy currents or surf. Had the conditions been rougher, the battle would have ended even more quickly than it did.

The development of high-tech rods is coming along so fast that the type is not yet dry before a more advanced rod is introduced. With the choices and price ranges available today, my advice is to shop around and try before you buy. There are many very good rods available that sell for around $300, and some companies offer rods at an even lower price that work well. The better rods have quality hardware, good rod wrapping, a well-designed ferrule, and an anodized aluminum reel seat. Big hard-chrome, stainless steel, or recoil snake guides with two good titanium stripping guides plus a large tip top allow better line flow and permit line connections or tangles to pass safely through. Guide wrappings need not be fancy, but they should be neat, with sufficient coats of finish to make them strong. An extension butt can help ease wrist strain when

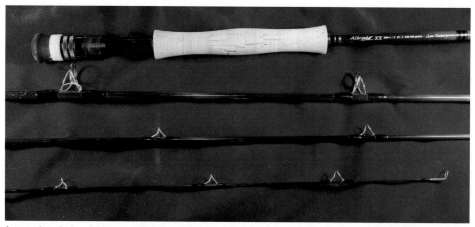

A good rod should have a fighting butt, large stripping guides, large snake guides, and a large tip.

fighting fish—a fat, round butt is most comfortable. Today's rods use either the blank-over-blank ferrule or graphite-plug ferrule. These are just as strong as a one-piece fly rod, and both bend with a smooth arc.

There was a time when three-piece rods were the craze. Eliminating the ferrule in the middle of the rod supposedly made the rod stronger, but in the last ten years the four-piece rods have taken over the market. They are a better size for travel and ideal for folding into two pieces when fitting them into a car.

The major advantage of many new rods is how the different materials are blended to produce rods that are light and yet fairly strong. As companies strive to build lighter and faster rods, however, there are some drawbacks. Rods that are thin-walled and fast might be more fragile. It's not that the rod is weak or poorly built, but only that it is designed for speed. These rods are less forgiving to angler abuse like high sticking and casting very heavy fast-sinking lines, and are less likely to withstand the impact of a hit from a heavily weighted fly. A racecar is not an off-road vehicle.

We must put more emphasis on making a better *fishing* tool: one that performs in the field, not just at the indoor casting tank. There are so many good rods on the market today that the choices are endless. Top anglers and casters make claims that one particular rod is better than another. That's nonsense. Take ten of the best rods sold today and disguise them, then have casters try to determine the maker. It would be fun to see the results.

Many years ago Ted Simroe, the well-known rod designer for the Leonard and Rodon rod companies, gave me some good advice about building rods. Ted said he built his rods for fishing, not casting. He felt that too many rods are built for casting—they perform well in the casting pools at shows, but are not always suited for fishing. Fast-action rods are good for sight casting, but I want a medium- to medium-fast-action rod for most of my fishing. Actually, even for sight fishing, a slightly slower rod will work well because it loads with less line out the tip. I do a lot of wading for stripers and bonefish in shallow water. Some of the opportunities I get at fish are within 30 feet, even less, and if the rod is so stiff that it needs 40 feet of line to load, casting accurately is more difficult. And for continuous casting, stiffer rods are more tiring.

When choosing a rod for Atlantic saltwater angling, consider more than just its ability to throw a rocket loop. You must think of fighting fish, casting for long periods, throwing large flies, and roll casting. And the faster the rod, the better *your* timing must be. If you own a rod that is too stiff or too fast, one way to tone it down is to use a heavier fly-line size. This will overload the rod and soften it slightly. The reason for overloading a rod is to dampen the faster action of modern blanks. Using a heavier fly line, increasing the weight by one size (a 9-weight line on an 8-weight rod, for instance), makes the rod bend more, which helps load the rod better. Rods that don't bend enough make *you* work harder. Overloading will dampen a stiff-action rod.

The Atlantic coast fly rodder, particularly the surf angler, needs a versatile rod. Some beach locations host several fish types. Conditions might dictate casting big flies along heavy structure, requiring a rod with lifting power. Then, farther down the beach, a school of bonito might show, demanding a rod capable of handling a fast-running fish on a light tippet. If you must walk half a mile to the car for a lighter rod, you'll probably miss the bonito action. Yes, the "expert" will boast that, with the proper skills, even a stiff rod will fish a fine tippet—but most anglers are not experts. Keep the odds in your favor by fishing a medium- to medium-fast-action rod, a rod that bends, one that covers multiple waters, conditions, and species of fish. Consider all the variables, then choose a *fishing* rod, not a "pool slinger."

Reels

After choosing a rod and line combination, selecting a reel is easy. There are two basic reel types of importance: direct drive and anti-reverse. At one time there were several anti-reverse reels on the market, but their popularity dwindled and many reel companies stopped making them. The mid- and large-arbor direct-drive reels now own the saltwater market. When you are reeling, the direct drive takes in line on each turn of the handle, without slippage: You always know that the line is being retrieved. Direct drives are the reels of choice for experienced anglers and serious night anglers for that reason. Anti-reverse reels allow the angler to hold the handle while a fish runs. This makes it easier for the novice to handle a large fast-running fish, especially at night. A direct drive's handle spins as the fish runs, cracking your fingers if they are in the way. But the direct-drive reel is simple to use, and is an excellent choice for the economically minded angler.

Another choice is a multiplying reel, but like the anti-reverse, there is little interest among saltwater anglers. Valentine makes the only saltwater multiplying fly reel I'm aware of. It has a 1.5 to 1 retrieve ratio and is anti-reverse. The invention of the mid- and large-arbor single-action direct-drive reel eliminated the need for multiplying reels. Large-arbor reels are very basic, have fewer parts, take in line almost as quickly, and are less expensive to produce.

Fly reels for salt water must have three features: ample line capability, corrosion-resistant parts, and a good drag system. A reel holding 200 yards of thirty-pound Micron or Dacron backing, 100 feet of twenty-five-pound mono, and a fly line is ample for anything that swims in the Northeast except big offshore species. All parts of the reel must resist salt. Every modern saltwater reel I have used was built with sound materials. Using an old salmon or trout reel might pose a problem, because some vintage reels have steel springs. Yet with constant care and maintenance, even such a reel will perform well.

Drags and Drag Systems

A drag system does what your car's brakes do—it slows and stops something. If a car's brakes are faulty or old, the problem may not surface until the time they are really needed, in an emergency stop. The same holds true for your reel. Some anglers get by with a poor drag, until a strong fast-running fish exposes the defect. But then it's too late. The average trout fisherman can get by with a "clicker" to keep the reel from overrunning, but the ocean demands more.

Reels for saltwater are mostly mid- to large arbor. They have exposed spool rims for palming and a smooth, sound drag system, and they should have enough room for ample backing.

Drag systems vary from reel to reel. Some have several washers and springs stacked onto the reel shaft, others use a big washer that rubs against a section of the spool's side, and still others have a gearing system to slow the spool. The type of drag your reel has doesn't matter; what does matter is that the system be sound. A reel's drag should be smooth, strong, consistent, and able to withstand the effects of salt water.

All four qualities are important, but smoothness is to be emphasized, and is the easiest quality to check. String up a rod, and then hook the leader to a car bumper or to someone's (a fast young person is best) hand. Have the car or the person run off line fast enough to simulate a fish. Don't get scientific—just a good hard 50- to 100-yard run will do. If the rod flutters like a willow in the wind, the drag is rough. A smooth, stationary bend in the rod means a smooth drag. (A reel not counterbalanced may appear, in fighting a fast-running fish, to have a rough drag.)

Some drags might need breaking in. This works best with a car or boat. In either case, run off several hundred yards of line at about 30 miles per hour to smooth out the drag. Be sure to use light tippet (four pounds) in case you run out of backing or the driver decides to have some fun.

Perhaps the most important reel quality is resistance to salt water. A well-known fly-fishing tackle company once gave me a saltwater reel to test. On a southern trip for bonefish I used the reel, dunking it every day in salt water. On the fourth day I hooked a bonefish of four to five pounds. The fish streaked off the flats, the reel screaming. I had experienced a little drag roughness the previous day, but nothing like this—the rod was pulsating as if I were casting. My only alternative was to loosen the drag and apply hand pressure. (If it had been a big fish, my fingerprints would have been altered.) Examining the reel that evening, I found an internal steel drag spring had rusted and broken. Upon returning home, I gave the reel back to the manufacturer with my report. The designer went nuts, blasting me for treating the reel incorrectly. It was as if I had mistreated his kid. Based in Minnesota, the designer probably never fished in salt water, and he assumed everyone treated tackle as a curator cares for museum pieces.

Daily fishing is like dunking a reel constantly under water. Braided backing holds water, and every time you fight a fish that runs into the backing, you soak the reel. And every reel will get drenched with the salt spray from waves or spray from running in a boat, not to mention general handling and use. Sweet-water anglers can go for years without touching a drag system, but

corrosive or faulty drag systems will surface quickly in the brine. Many manufacturers are constructing saltwater reels that last. If I had to use only one reel
for an entire year, I would choose one with a simple drag system—fewer parts
mean fewer problems.

Consistency and strength in a drag system go hand in hand. Drags built
with strong simple parts generally remain reliable and uniform with minimum care. The reels I have used that employ a large cork washer against the
spool have functioned flawlessly. Most metal drag systems work fine, but some
need periodic maintenance. Salt affects even noncorrosive metal by fouling the
working parts.

Setting and Checking the Drag

The proper tension setting of a drag is as controversial a subject as what fly rod
is best. My drag settings are adjusted to between two and three pounds. Some
anglers use a scale to test the tension, and for the beginner, that's smart. I test
by feel and prefer to be on the light side. Lefty Kreh advised me years ago to
use no more than three pounds of pull straight off the reel. As usual, Lefty's
counsel was sound. Three pounds of drag more than doubles with a full bend in

This is a good way to test the drag and adjust if necessary.

the rod and the fat front section of the fly line in the guides. When a fish runs and starts decreasing the amount of line on the spool arbor, the drag begins to increase. The drag tension might triple on a reel holding 300 yards of backing if a fish runs most of the line off the reel.

Some drags need double the tension to move them at first. Hot weather or dirty drag washers can add to initial resistance, and may even freeze the drag. Test the drag by pulling line from the reel at the start of your fishing day. When you leave the line in a stripping basket, or if your reel has free spool levers that allow removal of line without slipping the drag, be sure to slip the drag to test it. I keep testing my reel's drag throughout my fishing day, particularly when I'm fishing rolling surf. Sand can lock a reel, or I might unknowingly hit the drag control. I don't know how many times I've found the line wrapped around the reel or rod handle after casting.

Good reels have drag adjustments that tighten with a certain number of turns or by levers with adjustable positions. A precise setting is possible when there is more play in the drag adjustment, considerably lessening the chances of accidentally overtightening the drag.

Follow the manufacturer's advice for maintaining drag systems. Some drags should not be oiled or may need a certain type of lubricant. Metal parts generally need some coating to protect them, but washers might be adversely affected by oil. I coat springs and working parts with a spray-on protectant. If you want to try this, don't just hose the material over the reel: Drag washers may not function if thus soaked, and the fly line will absorb the spray, adding its scent to your hands or leaving a trail of scent in the water. One product that lubricates well and will not add an offensive scent to your tackle is WD-40. WD-40 has a fish oil scent, and some bait anglers actually spray it on chunk baits when they have soaked too long in the water.

Recommendations

There are a number of good reels on the market with very fair price points. More expensive reels will last a lifetime and keep ticking, but they come with a big price tag, and an extra spool might cost half the price of the reel. I tell students that if you buy an $800 reel, the spool will cost more than many decent reels. But some anglers want the best, and these reels can be passed down to the next generation.

When choosing a reel, think about fly-line size and type—a floating line will require more room on the spool, diminishing the amount of backing. When choosing a reel size, go larger if there is any doubt about not having enough backing for your fishing needs. To see if the reel balances on the rod, put the reel on the rod and hang a new coiled fly line on the handle. Hold the rod lightly in your hand. It should require no pressure to hold the tip up or down. The fly line will add about the same weight as backing. Medium- to large-arbor spools are standard on most, if not all, new reels. A larger-arbor reel takes in backing quicker and prevents jamming of the backing that can occur with a small-arbor reel.

Some reels have quick-change spool systems that are helpful when changing lines. Other reels you must first take apart, removing several pieces (never do this over sand). When you change spools in the field, a stripping basket will double as a perfect parts collector and carrier.

What Line Is Best?

Fly lines have changed and improved dramatically in the last ten years. Unfortunately, there is no single perfect fly line. In fact, there are so many different good lines that picking the best one might be a chore.

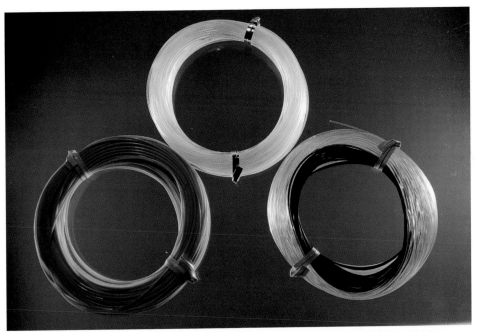

There are many different line types. Floating lines are often light in color. Sink tips have a very dark front section with either clear or colored line for running line. Intermediate lines can be clear, tan, blue, or green.

Fly lines for salt water are designed for distance casting. They have a fat weight-forward section with a thin running line. The heavy front section carries out the lighter running line. Lines vary, but basically they have a front taper, a fat weighted section called a body belly or a triangular-shaped taper, and then a rear taper and running line. They range in length from 80 to 120 feet, and some are even longer. Each feature and design will make the line perform differently, and for each advantage there might be a disadvantage. However, the average angler should not get caught up in the hype of line performance—choose a line that casts well on your rod.

Over the last ten years, I have fished lines from Cortland, Royal Wulff Fly Lines, Scientific Angler, Orvis, Rio, and Albright. What I look for in a good-quality line is shootability and castability. Does the line tangle in a stripping basket? Is the line easy to handle? If the line shoots well and flows freely from the basket, fishing is more fun. Each angler must choose a line that fits his or her fishing and casting needs. Some of the new lines might shoot great but have side effects like causing cuts and burns due to a surface that's been textured to shoot through the guides with little resistance.

The length of the head, the configuration of the front and rear taper, and the size of the running line all affect the line's performance. And the performance of lines will also change depending on the line's density: floating, intermediate, or fast sinking. A fast-sinking line might have a much different taper than a floating line, and there are even differences from one floater to another. For example, a longer front taper on a floating line is ideal for sight casting to spooky fish on calm water because it will land the fly and leader softly. However, that same line will have trouble making a quick cast into the wind and will struggle turning over the leader into a modest wind, not to mention trying to cast a big popping bug.

How to Choose a Line

For general fishing with a floating or intermediate fly line, select one that has a front section, including the back taper, that is about 35 to 40 feet. A longer front section means that you need to carry more line in the air if you want to get the best shooting quality from the line. The front section of the line should extend beyond the rod tip for ideal distance-casting performance. Each line company has different testimonials, but look at the specifications and choose a line that has a shorter front section. Years ago they were called saltwater tapers, and some were really short. A short front section loads the rod more quickly, turns over bigger flies or bugs better, and will cast with less line out the rod tip. This is the best choice for anglers starting out, and it performs well for many situations. Because it makes some noise when landing the fly and leader on the water, it's not ideal for some sight-casting situations, but it will cover most conditions.

What should the first line be—floating, intermediate, or fast sinking? A floating line is an ideal fishing tool for a beginner: It's easy to see, keeps the fly near the surface, is easy to pick up when casting, and will fish many situations. Floaters are the best lines to use when learning casting skills. They are very visible, have less line speed so the caster can watch the cast, and will not hide casting faults like sinking lines. For anglers who plan to fish top water or shallow sheltered water, or do lots of night fishing or shallow-water sight casting, a floater is the best choice. If conditions allow, I would love to fish with just a floating line and watch fish take the fly. However, we fish in a less than perfect world, which is why we need sinking lines.

When buying a line for a long two-handed rod or switch rod, get one that is designed for that rod style. Often these rods need lines that are much heavier to properly load the rod. An 8-weight standard floating line will not load a no. 8 switch rod. To get the best performance from these specialty rods, get a matching line.

Anglers always ask whether it is possible to fish the salt with one fly line, and if so, what line would that be? One line cannot handle the varying conditions encountered along our coast. But there *is* a line that will become your workhorse: an intermediate-density weight-forward line. This line casts better, tangles less, and fishes a variety of situations, from top water to subsurface. It is more versatile than the widely used floating line.

Wind presents problems for floating lines, creating bows that impair hook setting and fly action. An intermediate settles below the surface, evading the wind's effects. In a pinch, an intermediate line can be used for fishing larger, very buoyant popping bugs. This line density will fish from 2 to 6 inches down depending on the current flow—it's ideal for many locations that do not require deep penetration. For most Atlantic fly rodders, an intermediate line should be their first choice because it's easy to use and durable, and it covers many bases. If I was only allowed one fly line to fish the sea, there would be no hesitation— it would be a clear intermediate. I would choose a clear color because it's ideal for clear shallow-water sight fishing.

Most modern fast-sinking lines, also called sink-tip or sink-head lines, are designed after the Teeny lines. These lines had fast-sinking front sections with either a floating or intermediate running line. There are now a number of fast-sinking lines available from most of the major manufacturers. Most have 25- to 30-foot sinking heads. This front section should have a short front taper, which will turn over big flies better and give better penetration. A longer taper will allow the fly to plane up. I like a longer rear taper that is part of the running line. If the entire head or tip (the sinking section) is 28 feet long, the taper should start at the end of the sinking section and extend back 10 to 15 feet into the running portion of the line. This allows the caster to extend the sinking section 8 to 15 feet beyond the rod tip. If the line's head is connected directly to the thinner running line with no taper, it will hinge if extending too much line past the rod tip. A rear taper of at least 10 feet makes casting these lines a pleasure rather than a chore.

An intermediate running line allows for better sinking capability and shoots well with fewer line tangles. The smaller-size lines, 150 to 250 grains, are ideal for fishing 5 to 10 feet of water with 7- to 8-weight outfits. The 300- to 450-grain lines match well with most 9- to 10-weight rods for fishing moderate flows in 5 to 15 feet of water, and they are also effective in 3- to 6-foot rolling surf. For the deeper, faster flows, use a 500- to 600-plus-grain head with 10- to 12-weight rods. There are, however, locations where even these heavy heads are not enough.

If you plan to chase bluefin or other heavyweights, an offshore line is a wise purchase. Anglers not interested in IGFA records often fish tippet weights of thirty to forty pounds. The heavy tippet is more forgiving and will help land bigger fish in less time. This is better for the fish and the angler. Tuna that run over fifty pounds are just tough, and a stronger tippet makes sense. An offshore line is much stronger than a standard fly line that breaks at about thirty pounds. Check with the fly line's manufacturer to be sure that the line is built with a break strength of at least fifty to sixty pounds. And remember that when connecting the backing or front leader section to the fly line, most knots will fail before the line does. Backing for this kind of fishing should be at least fifty-pound Gel-Spun or braided line. (See chapter 17 for knotting information.)

Fly lines come in a variety of colors, but for most saltwater fishing in the Northeast, color doesn't matter unless you're sight fishing, in which case go clear if using an intermediate. Bright lines might look inviting to bluefish, although I have never had a problem with bluefish striking an uncolored line. More likely a bluefish might strike a line when a hooked fish runs sideways across the water, forming a rooster tail with the line, which resembles an escaping baitfish.

To summarize, when choosing a fly line, the intermediate is the go-to line for a good portion of East Coast fishing from shore—it covers all the bases in most situations. A floater is ideal for top-water fishing, skinny-water sight fishing, and to improve casting skills. A fast-sinking sink-tip/sink-head line with intermediate running line is good for deep fast-water fishing, a quick presentation when chasing fish in a boat, for casting big flies, and for casting in tough winds—it might be the best boat-fishing choice.

Shooting Heads

With all the new sinking lines on the market, the once-popular shooting head systems are very seldom used today. I'm sure that some anglers still fish them, but the sink-tip/sink-head lines have all but replaced shooting heads. The only shooting head system I own is a 30-foot section of lead-core spliced to the back section of an Albright sink tip. I cut the sinking section off, leaving the mono-core line's tapered section with full running line. I removed several inches of the lead, leaving the outer coating; threaded in the cut-off section of fly line; used three nail knots over the coating of the lead-core; and coated the knots with superglue to bond the lines. It's a very clean splice. Braided monofilament would also work, but the cut-off fly line has a back taper, which improves the casting quality. This line is just for the deepest rips when nothing else will reach fish. But for all other fishing that requires a fast-sinking line, the one-piece sink tip is hard to beat. For those who still like heads, however, here are some tips that you might find useful.

A shooting head is essentially the front section of a weight-forward (WF) fly line. Manufacturers produce them in lengths from 30 to over 40 feet. You can make your own shooting head by cutting a full-length fly line to the desired length. For years I used a short head made from a no. 12 WF sink tip. Cutting 5 feet off the front, I made the head 25 feet long and used a no. 5 level sinking line for running line. This line worked well at midrange, and I needed few back-casts, even with large flies. And the line flowed tangle-free from the stripping basket—something the older no. 12 floating line would not do. Thank God for modern fly lines.

One double-taper fly line will make several shooting heads. A taper on the head is unnecessary; reversing the original taper makes it cast better. Connect the smaller, tapered end to the running line to make a smaller, neater connection that slides readily through the guides—and the heavy level end turns over with more power. It is wise to reverse all shooting heads in this manner.

Lead-core line is a very fast-sinking line and makes an ideal head for deep fishing. At one time it was the only genuine deep-water line. Some anglers, myself included, still make their own shooting heads from lead-core lines. There are lines on the market that claim to get equal or better sink results than lead-core, but I'll let you be the judge.

Shooting head systems offer many advantages, one being the ability to change line densities without changing reels or spools. Five separate coils of different line densities fit easily in a small ziplock bag. Fasten each coil with a pipe-cleaner tie to keep it from unraveling, and with little bulk you can carry lines to suit any need.

Shooting heads are best for distance casting and for casting requiring fewer backcasts. They are ideal for casting small flies, shooting downwind, and reaching water beyond a weight-forward's range. But shooting heads are more difficult to cast when you are bucking wind with a low-density line—this is particularly true when fishing large, bulky flies and for cross-casting when the wind is blowing into your casting ear, requiring you to backcast into a quartering wind. A fast-sinking sink-tip line handles these situations better than a shooting head can.

The Running or Shooting Line

The running line is the line connecting the head to the backing. It's also called a shooting line. Its small diameter slips through the guides with less effort than does the larger running line of a conventional fly line. Running line comes in different sizes and types and materials—mono, level fly line, and braided mono.

Level fly lines are the easiest to handle, but are prone to knotting when shot from a stripping basket. With large heads—no. 11 to 13—a no. 4 or 5 level sinking line works well with few knotting problems, and the smaller-diameter, harder-surfaced sinking line shoots better. Level fly line comes in 100-foot coils of .025- to .035-inch diameter, in both floating and sinking densities.

Mono, both flat and round, shoots well, and some anglers prefer it for running line. But mono knots coming out of a stripping basket, and does not handle well in cold weather.

Braided mono casts well, is almost tangle-free, and would be my choice for running line if I seriously fished heads. The lighter lines, twenty-five- and thirty-pound test, shoot very well. They are harder to grip and can cut into fingers, but they are still good running lines.

The chart below outlines my recommendations for three tackle outfits that, between them, will handle most of the situations a serious saltwater fly fisherman will face on the northeast Atlantic coast.

Tackle	Applications	Recommended Uses
9- or 9½-foot rod to handle 10- to 14-weight lines, medium to fast action. Reel holding 200 to 300 yards of backing and fly line. Strong construction. For tuna, choose only the best reels.	Large, heavily dressed flies and poppers. Heavy surf. Big structure. Strong offshore or inshore rips. Twelve- to twenty-pound tippet. Large bass and blues or offshore fish. All-season fishing. This outfit will fish lighter tippets and conditions if rod is not too stiff.	Best choice for angler planning to fish a variety of waters. My preference for 50 percent of the inshore fly fishing when encountering heavy conditions where lifting power is needed to fight big fish in heavy water.
9- or 9½-foot rod, medium to fast action for 9-weight lines. Reel holding 200 yards of backing and fly line.	Bay, sound, or flats fishing. Mild surf. Small to midsize flies. Bonito, weakfish, bass, and blues. Eight- to sixteen-pound tippet. This outfit can be used for heavier fishing, but will have limitations.	For angler fishing sheltered waters or mild conditions in bigger waters. This outfit will cover many bases and is the most popular outfit along the coast.
8- to 9-foot rod, medium to fast action for 6- to 8-weight lines. Reel holding 150 yards of backing and fly line.	Small creeks, very protected water, small flies. Spring and summer fishing, light wind. Small fish, five to fifteen pounds. Eight- to twelve-pound tippet. This rod is strictly for light, sheltered-water fishing. Ideal for sight casting to spooky fish on calm days.	For light fishing of school bass, small bluefish, or weakfish; in skilled hands, bonito. In the hands of a good angler, this tackle can handle bigger fish in shallow water with light current.

Other Gear

Stripping Basket

Fly rodders believe they need every piece of equipment but the kitchen sink, and in saltwater fly fishing we even have that: the stripping basket. You can take away all my other extra gear, but leave me my stripping basket. Whether you purchase a fancy one or make your own from a plastic dishpan, learn to use a stripping basket. It will become one of your most important tools, saving you time, effort, and frustration.

A stripping basket is a line-storing device to aid in casting. It also keeps loose shooting line neatly piled and away from the surf, your feet, rocks, weeds, and all the other things that catch fly line. It will hold flies, pliers, and leaders; store your line while you follow a fish down the beach; and bail out your boat in a pinch. Jim Slater, a Milford, Connecticut, fly rodder, glued a fly box to each inside wall of his basket, and easily changes flies in the surf.

The first time I saw a stripping basket was in a photograph in one of Joe Brooks's books. In the picture, Joe was using a cardboard box as a casting aid for freshwater fishing. However, Pete Laszlo, a fine, departed friend and die-hard fly rodder, introduced me to the basket's value. The saltwater fly fisher's effectiveness is greatly increased by the stripping basket. Rough jetties, rolling surf, fast rips, and rocky shorelines are difficult—some are impossible—to fish without a basket. Fishing a sinking line while wading, even an intermediate, is ill advised without one.

Stripping baskets are easy to use, and most beginners catch on to them quickly. A two-handed retrieve is easier with a basket, and with the rod tucked under an arm, there is more room between rod and basket, permitting more effective hand movement. Most retrieves work with a basket; only those needing long or faster strokes are more difficult.

When you first start to use a stripping basket, train yourself to coil the line in a circle around the inside diameter; it will become second nature quickly, and prevents tangles. Keeping your rod centered over the basket, or slightly in the direction of your retrieving hand, will encourage a neater pile.

Unless you're wading in deep water, where the basket should float just below your wader tops, keep your basket low—about waist-high. The higher the basket is positioned, the more difficult retrieving line will be. Deep wading will be difficult if your basket has holes—it will just keep sinking. My stripping basket doesn't have holes, and every now and then I dump out any accumulated

Stripping baskets make fishing easier in such locations as rolling surf, jetties, standing in a strong current, or even a windy day on a boat deck.

water after I've cast. Actually, I often keep some water in the basket when fishing in hot weather to keep the fly line from getting sticky.

Solid baskets work better than the collapsible kind. I made my original basket from a plastic dishpan 12 inches wide, 14 inches long, and 5½ inches deep. There are many kinds of baskets on the market, and most you can customize somewhat.

Wind will affect the soft fold-up baskets by tossing the basket—and line—into the air, causing a tangled mess. This also can happen to soft baskets when fishing the surf. Even solid baskets need something to prevent the wind from tangling the line. There are many ways to customize the dishpan-type plastic baskets, but none will work like the preformed plastic baskets. My advice is to spend the money and buy a preformed basket. The Orvis Company makes the best stripping basket on the market. It has nine cones inside the basket to prevent line tangles, is preformed to fit around your body, and has a groove on each side of the basket to hold your rod when changing flies.

I have used a stripping basket throughout the Atlantic, in the tropics, in Alaska, on big freshwater rivers, and salmon fishing in Nova Scotia. Only the salmon anglers viewed it skeptically—it worked, but it didn't look appropriate.

Miscellaneous Equipment

Other assorted items that make fishing easier include wire-cutting, hook-removing pliers; a hook hone; sunglasses; several fly boxes; a folder to hold leaders and spare tippet material; and insect repellent. One important piece of equipment that every wading angler needs is a compass. Fog can form quickly, and even if wading only several hundred yards onto a flat, being lost in fog on a rising tide can be terrifying. Carry a compass and be sure to know the direction back to dry land. Anglers that wade out on large flats or fish locations with holes and sharp drop-offs should never be without a compass.

Night fishing in various conditions requires two lights: a small-bulbed gooseneck light for fishing protected water and a light with a good beam for wading and walking on structure.

Here is some important equipment to carry. A compass, pliers that will cut wire, forceps, two lights, and a device to sharpen hooks. The new LED lights are less offensive to fish and do not effect night vision as much.

For cold weather, a pair of neoprene gloves with fingers is essential. Exposed skin can become numb and painful on the water in cold weather.

Hip boots or waders are necessary for shore fishing. I prefer waders with a boot foot—stocking-foot waders tend to fill with sand, becoming heavy and uncomfortable. A pair of studded, felt-sole wading sandals is necessary if you plan to fish areas having slippery rocks or jetties.

And you'll need something to carry all the small paraphernalia. I fought using a vest for years, thinking it was too "trouty." Yes, vests work and keep everything in order, but I just can't stop overloading mine. For those anglers able to control their need to carry a huge amount of absorbent gear, a vest is a good way to organize tackle. There are also a number of chest packs that work well—just pick one that you're comfortable with and pack it responsibly. I use a small creel-type bag with several outside pockets and stuff the poor thing till it looks pregnant. Some of us feel we must carry *everything* we think we'll need.

Having the right tackle and setting it up properly is a very important step in becoming a good angler. Learning to use this gear well in different applications is just as significant, for the best tackle money can buy is useless if it's applied incorrectly. Expensive tackle won't make you a better fisherman—only you can do that.

17

Rigging Up

Some anglers spend large sums of money for tackle, guides, and travel but never take the time to learn knot tying. But without a sound knotting system, the big ones usually get away. For years trout fishermen have slid by with poor knots; in salt water this luxury is impossible. Many years ago I lost a nice fish through poor knots. It was my first really large fish hooked on a fly, and at the time may have been a world record, if only I had taken the time to retie a knot. The fishing area was a good-size creek in Southport, Connecticut, that supported a small population of herring that traveled upstream to spawn in the spring. This created a unique situation where large fish would feed at the creek mouth in shallow water. Although the tide was wrong, I knew the fish were working this area.

Frank Schober, my fishing partner, and I fished another spot first, trying a rocky point in Westport called Bedfords. Having moderate success, we took several school-size fish before daybreak. After fishing for an hour, we decided to go to the creek mouth. It was a dark foggy morning and still fishable. However, I had no faith at all—feeling that once it got light, the fish would not stay in shallow water. Only later in my fishing career did I learn to have confidence to fish any time of the day.

We made the short drive to Southport. Walking out, I spotted some bait in the creek. This gave us some hope, but still I did not believe there would be any action. Frank was fishing a large spinning plug, and I had a fly rod. Unfortunately I failed to change the knot used earlier, even looking at it thinking, "The knot seems all right so why bother." What a mistake that would turn out to be! I was still fishing the large fly that was so successful at Bedfords Point, and as we slowly walked out, the heavy fog kept us looking back to keep land in sight. After several casts Frank had a fish come up and bump his plug; he could not even see the fish, but just felt the tap. Then a fish swirled about 30 to 40 feet away from Frank, and having just made a cast, I started retrieving quickly to present my fly to the fish. After only four or five fast strips, a fish suddenly took the fly. I had been looking the other way and really never knew what happened.

The fly just stopped. I hooked the fish with one pull, saw a large swirl and big splash, and felt the fish run.

My hands worked frantically, clearing the stripping basket as the fish slowly headed downtide. Leaning back, I felt its power, realized it was a really big fish, and applied maximum pressure. But the fish kept going. Then, as I pulled back, I felt that sickening feeling as the line went slack. To lose such a large fish was tough enough—for I had never hooked one this size. But to have a bad knot cause the loss was worse. My examination of the tippet revealed the truth: The end had the pigtail shape characteristic of a poor or worn knot. If only I had changed the tippet, I might have landed that fish. With fresh line, my chances of holding the fish would have been much better. Failing to change a knot cost a prize fish.

Saltwater fly rodding requires a larger selection of knots than any other kind of angling. But if you plan carefully, you need to tie only two knots on the water: one to fasten the fly to the tippet, and one to add line to lengthen a tapered leader.

Many anglers buy a line system that is preassembled, and only need to deal with the tippet. This works fine until the system fails and there is no help in sight. But if you learn to build your own line system, you'll develop the confidence and independence to make changes or repairs to it anytime, anyplace. A working knowledge of knots is all you need to achieve this mastery. But don't be intimidated by the great number of knots out there; you can learn them, and once learned, the knowledge will stay with you.

From reel arbor to fly, as many as ten knots are required to set up a line system. Anglers might want to take advantage of a good tackle dealer who can put backing and fly line on the reel. Often this is a wise move because getting the backing on tightly is difficult without using a line winder. However, all these knots are easy to tie, except perhaps for the Bimini twist, though all take some practice to get right. Some of these knots are critical and must give 100 percent strength (the percentage of knot strength is in relation to the line's breaking point); other knots need only be 50 percent or greater strength. But all are important, so learn to tie them carefully.

The finest fishing tackle means nothing if your knots are faulty—they are the single most important link to the fish. Unfortunately, poor knots will announce themselves only under the heavy pressure of a large fish. This is why it is important to test your knots (I'll explain how a little later) and to check your knotting system frequently for wear.

Knots do more than just attach a lure to a tippet. They join unlike materials and materials of varying diameters. My goal for a knotting system is to achieve and maintain 100 percent strength of my tippet. This means that every knot must test over twenty pounds if you're using a twenty-pound-class tippet. The only exception to this is the tippet itself, which would break just under this point if fishing for an IGFA record. All tippet knots should hold to at least 90 percent.

Some connections need more than decent break strength—they must also be streamlined enough to pass through the guides when you are casting or playing a fish. A knot pulled 35 miles an hour by a heavy fish could rip the guides off and will break the tippet if it catches.

The Line System

Let me explain how I analyzed and perfected my line and knotting system. I experimented with different combinations of lines fly fishermen use, and tested all the knots I tried on a sophisticated knot-testing machine devised by the Berkley tackle company. If a low break strength was registered on a given knot, I assigned the knot this low value instead of taking the highest break strength registered or compiling an average. There were some surprises in this testing: Some nail knots broke below tippet strength during the testing, and I found that some knots failed when tied on certain materials but worked quite well when tied on other materials.

As you read through the system, follow it closely. If you use the materials I suggest and tie the knots properly, you will achieve good knotting strength for the entire line. Specific tying instructions for each knot follow in the latter portion of this chapter. If you feel unsure of any knot, take the time to retie it. Even the most difficult knot mentioned will take under five minutes to tie. Saving five minutes is not worth losing a good fish and possibly the fly line.

Putting the System Together

Beginning with attaching the backing to the reel arbor, we are going to build a line and knot system for saltwater fly fishing. We won't use backing of only mono, because it has a lot of stretch and can break or warp a reel spool if a heavy fish exerts pressure while you're winding line back onto the spool. Because we will be using different materials to build the line, sound knot connections are essential—in salt water even small fish run into the backing.

I recommend thirty-pound Dacron or Micron for the backing. Thirty-pound Dacron has been the workhorse for backing for many years. A twenty-pound

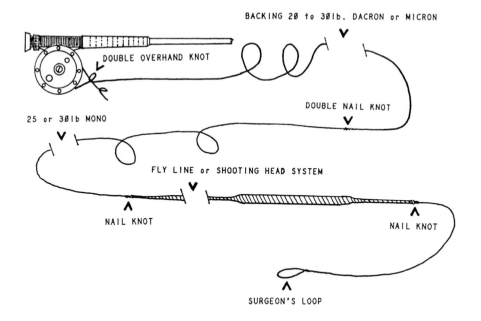

The line system, from reel to leader butt section

Dacron or Micron nail-knot connection could break well below a twenty-pound-class tippet, causing a lost fly line and possibly a fish that will die struggling with the unconnected line. Twenty-pound backing is too light unless you plan to fish a tippet of twelve pounds or less. If more backing is needed, Gel-Spun has a smaller diameter and is a good choice in either forty-five- or fifty-pound test. This will give about 25 percent more line capacity to some reels. I would not use thirty-five-pound-test Gel-Spun because it can cause bad cuts, or worse. Because the diameter is so thin and the material's texture is like a saw, if the backing touches flesh with a fast-running fish, there can be problems. Only if rigging for tuna would there be a need for backing of fifty pounds or more.

Attach the backing to the spool by tying it firmly to the spool arbor with a positive knot, rather than just wrapping it (see page 252). Reel the line on evenly, and every few yards angle the line about 30 degrees. This will prevent a heavy-running fish from driving the backing down deeply into the spool, jamming the line and possibly breaking the tippet.

I advise tying in mono on all saltwater backing setups. Use a 100- to 150-foot-long section of twenty-five- to thirty-pound monofilament line, either Berkley Big Game or Maxima. Double-nail-knot the Dacron to the monofilament, then nail-knot the monofilament to the fly line. The double nail knot is a clean, streamlined knot. However, a double uni-knot may be used; it is faster to tie and requires no tools. This gives a higher break strength than knotting the backing directly to the fly line, and it also provides a buffer—a section of line with greater stretch—to make it difficult for a strong fish to snap the tippet at a distance. The mono is also more durable than most backings.

Dan Blanton, an excellent West Coast saltwater fly rodder, passed this along to me years ago. He felt he needed such a buffer when tarpon fishing in the Costa Rican jungle, to combat the leader strain from a fish jumping a long distance away, where bowing the rod would be ineffective. At such distances the section of mono would stretch, taking much of the pressure off the tippet. I think this system is useful, too, when a large fish turns sideways in the water. The fly line's fat diameter, as it is pulled through the water, creates high resistance against the current, and there is additional strain if weed accumulates on the line. The stretch of the mono section can prevent the tippet from breaking under this strain, and it makes the fish work harder as it pulls against the stretch of the mono. Berkley Big Game and Maxima are excellent lines for this application because they have good stretching qualities and high knot strength.

Next, connect the fly line to the mono or the backing, depending on the setup you want. Some fly lines, especially those with thin coatings, such as sinking lines, will not nail-knot well. After testing, I found in *McClane's New Standard Fishing Encyclopedia* that the offset nail knot works well for connecting fly line to backing, holding to over twenty pounds, while other nail knots broke at sixteen pounds. Use this knot to connect the line to the mono. If you are tying Dacron or Micron backing directly to the fly line, use the offset nail knot splice.

Another fly-line-to-backing knot is the loop splice. You can tie it with the fly line's coating on, or you can strip the coating from the line and splice a loop in the core. Some fly lines have removable skins, and splicing with the core will produce a neater connection; however, a connection with the skin left on is more durable. Knot the backing to the splice with a clinch knot or, better yet, from a Bimini twist in the backing. Make a surgeon's loop from the double line of the Bimini twist and interlock the loops. This loop-to-loop connection will allow you to change the line without cutting.

What sold me on the effectiveness of using Bimini twists was fishing for tuna with Al Conti (see the bluefin tuna section in chapter 19). That day certainly opened my eyes to having good leaders, and how long, constant pulling on a fish affected the mono leader system. Both leaders that landed fish lost five pounds, or 25 percent, of their original strength. The leaders that broke parted between the Biminis—there was no knot failure. And everything that I had heard and read about the Bimini twist was right. Not only are Biminis a 100 percent knot, they also add a shock absorber to the system. A properly tied Bimini should have a tight twist in the double line. These twists uncoil under pressure and, along with stretch in the knot, give the leader system a buffer. This buffer can prevent break-offs when shock or impact occurs while fighting a fish. About five years ago while pulling on a Bimini to show students how effective it was, I realized it acted like a spring. It took me years to see that—boy, am I stupid!

Two Leader Systems

A sound and simple leader system can be built using a Bimini twist with a surgeon's loop tied in the double line, then interlocking the loop to the loop on your fly line and tying on the fly. (A spider hitch can be substituted for a Bimini, but it is not as consistent.) This works well for any of the offshore (hardtail) species in the four- to fifteen-pound range. Tie leaders 4 to 5 feet long, using ten- to twenty-pound test, depending on how line-shy the fish are. With heavier tippets, this system also works for big fish. Many anglers chasing big bluefin use thirty- to forty-pound tippet—some even use fifty-pound. Anglers who fish tippets over twenty-pound test need to use backing at least fifteen pounds heavier than the tippet, along with fly lines designed for offshore fishing. Rio Line Company makes a line called Leviathan with a seventy-pound core. Both Bluewater Express and Mastery Billfish lines made by Scientific Angler have break strengths of sixty pounds.

Sound knots in the fly-line system are essential. Nail knots will work if they are tied precisely, but there is a better system. Form a Bimini with fifty- to sixty-five-pound Gel-Spun using an Albright knot to connect the double line of the Bimini to the fly line. Other systems work, but are not as consistent. And even when the knots failed, they didn't break until over thirty-five pounds, and some went to fifty pounds. After testing, I'm confident that there is no problem when using thirty-pound tippet, and using forty-pound is possible if you take the time to tie the knots well and test them. It's very important to coat both the Bimini and the knot to the fly line with non-water-soluble superglue. Even with a Bimini, Gel-Spun can slip unless the knot is locked with glue; I've even had some Biminis break at thirty-five pounds with fifty-pound Gel-Spun.

To tie in a front loop to the fly line, make an overhand knot in the line, and run a section of sixty- to eighty-pound mono through the knot. Form a nail knot over the fly line, tighten both knots, and pull them together so they jam. Do this in several stages, but be sure the knots are tight, then coat with superglue. This bears repeating: Be sure to tie all knots well—pull them very tight, then add the glue. Remember, the glue helps prevent slippage under very heavy pressure, but it will not prevent a poor knot from breaking.

The heavy-leader concept became popular with the influx of fifty- to one-hundred-pound-plus bluefin in the range of small boats. And for anglers who release fish, a heavier tippet will help land the fish faster. When using forty- to fifty-pound tippet, you can tie the fly straight to the leader. If using thirty-pound, tie in a shock section of forty-pound. Tie a Bimini on both ends of a section of tippet, and make the leader like an IGFA system (see below)—this gives the best knot strength. I tested other knots, but the double Bimini was very consistent. The thirty-pound system is the best choice for most anglers because if you make a mistake, it puts much less strain on the tackle compared to forty-pound. I do not recommend using a fifty-pound tippet.

When fishing for world records for species like bluefin tuna, a double Bimini system is essential. The basic IGFA leader system requires a class tippet at least 15 inches long; if using a shock tippet, it must be less than 12 inches long from the eye of the hook to the single strand of the tippet. But be sure to read the IGFA regulations—not only the leader setup, but also the other rules of engagement. The best way to build a leader is to tie a Bimini on both ends of a section of class tippet material, leaving 18 to 20 inches of line between the Bimini knots. Make a surgeon's loop on one of the double sections of line, and leave the twisted section as long as possible to give more stretch. To the other double section of line, tie in a piece of shock leader using a three-turn surgeon's. A system that works well is using two to two and a half times the size of the tippet section for the shock leader—twenty pounds to forty or fifty pounds.

To tie on a fly, use a non-slip loop or a four-turn improved clinch, and be sure to use gloves and pliers to tighten. Other knots will also work, but be sure to tighten them hard and test them first.

Line System Components

What type of leader material works best—monofilament or fluorocarbon? Fluorocarbon is more durable, less visible, and has less stretch than monofilament. It also does not lose strength in the water because it does not absorb water like monofilament. Because monofilament has more stretch, it gives additional impact resistance, making it more forgiving. Forming knots in monofilament is easier, and after testing, I found I got better knot strength with mono. Fluorocarbon is a better leader material in clear water for line-shy fish. However, on several occasions I have had trouble with impact breakage, and I've talked to other anglers who had the same experience. One day I lost five big bluefin on twenty-pound fluorocarbon. In each case it was the first run, and I was not applying very heavy pressure yet. When the fish ran straight away, the fluorocarbon leader parted when the fish's tail started hitting the leader. After that experience I went to a heavier tippet, and this season I will fish thirty-pound

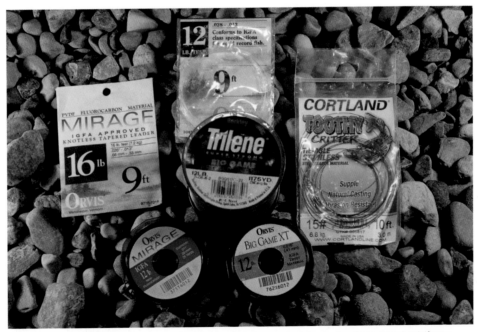

Both fluorocarbon and mono are important leader materials, but unless you test them properly they should not be knotted together in a leader system. And be sure to always carry spare tapered leaders, spools of tippet material, and wire bite guard material. For making large numbers of leaders, a 100-yard-plus spool of mono or fluorocarbon like the spool in the center saves money.

tippet. If I wanted to try for a world record, however, I would need to do some more research before choosing fluorocarbon over mono.

Any of the offshore species can be elusive, and even in good years bluefin are often hard to get. Every hookup is precious—don't let a poor leader system be the reason for a fishless day.

If you choose a shooting head system, the mono section connected to the backing will serve as a running line, and some anglers prefer mono for this purpose. Tie the mono directly to the shooting head with a clinch knot, or use a loop-to-loop connection. Flat mono, level fly line, or braided mono will all work well as running line, depending upon the angler's needs and preferences. Flat mono may be knotted the same as round mono. Attach level fly line either with a three-and-a-half-turn clinch knot, or splice a loop to the end of the line and interlock with a loop on the backing. Braided mono works well with a glue splice: Slide the backing several inches inside the braided mono, and glue the joint using a shrink-tape sleeve or whip-finish to cover the loose ends. This glued connection is the smoothest through the guides. Be sure, when making any glue connection, to use a glue that is not water-soluble. I prefer free-running Duro superglue: It's strong, easy to work with, and holds 100 percent of the line strength.

Whatever fly-line formula you choose, use a nail knot to attach the front of the fly line to the butt section of the leader. The large diameter of the fly line's front will knot well with heavy mono when any standard nail knot is used. I find that the speed nail knot works better than tying a nail knot through a tube—the speed nail knot forms much tighter loops and holds better. Incidentally, a paper clip is superior to a needle for tying needle nail knots: It won't stab you, and it clips securely to a pocket or vest.

To make the butt section of your leader, use thirty- or forty-pound material. Again I would suggest Berkley Big Game or Maxima because both lines knot well and straighten easily, functioning nicely as running lines, butt sections, and shock leaders. The formula used to calculate fly-line size to butt section is simple: For 8-, 9-, or 10-weight lines, use a butt with a diameter of .022; for 11-, 12-, or 13-weight lines, use .024-diameter material. A heavy level butt section will readily turn over any large castable saltwater fly, but a tapered leader may buckle under the weight of some heavy flies.

Leader length depends upon the type of fly line you fish. Sinking line requires only a short butt section, 1 to 2 feet in length. A shorter leader is preferable with sinking line because monofilament floats and planes up, especially with buoyant flies, defeating the purpose of sinking line. A short leader in this case gets much better depth penetration. For most saltwater fishing, a very long (12 feet) leader is unnecessary. Even the sharp-eyed bonito will hit a fly fished with an 8-foot-long leader. Only in clear water on a calm day will I use a leader over 8 feet. To form a longer leader, use a 4-foot section of butt and tie on a 3-foot piece of .019 mono, using a four-turn surgeon's knot. Form a surgeon's loop on the mono and attach your tippet to it. I have one fly outfit already set up for this particular circumstance, and I carry it with me when I'm fishing for bonito. For most floating or intermediate lines, I use a 3½- to 4-foot butt section.

In either case, tie a surgeon's loop to the end of the leader's butt section for a quick-change system to convert tippets. The surgeon's loop completes the working section of your line system. Only when you change lines, or if damage occurs to the system, will this section need further attention. Just remember to check the knots periodically for wear or damage.

The leader's tippet section attaches to the butt section by interlocking two surgeon's loops. Combined, they work as the connection between fly and fly line. This section of transparent line allows you to present the fly so that the fish doesn't see the large-diameter fly line. The tippet is the weakest link between you and the fish. It varies in length from 2 to 5 feet. Although short, the tippet requires three knots from the loop to the fly, and five knots when using a shock leader.

For tippet material I use Berkley XT or Maxima, but there are many other good lines on the market. Both the XT and Maxima are exceptional knotting lines and hold a high break strength even with wind knots. The overhand knot (wind knot) can occur when casting a fly on windy *or* calm days. If it goes unnoticed, it may weaken your tippet by as much as 50 percent with some monos, but with the XT or Maxima the loss is only about 25 percent.

For a straight tippet without a shock leader, tie a Bimini twist (a spider hitch is a good substitute) to a section of mono and form a surgeon's loop with the double line. Interlock this to the butt loop. Cut the tippet to the desired length and tie on the fly using a twice-through-the-eye clinch.

Construct a tippet with a shock leader by tying a Bimini twist or spider hitch to each end of a section of tippet material. Form a surgeon's loop with one Bimini to interlock to the butt-section loop. Tie the other Bimini to a section of shock material using a surgeon's or Albright knot, depending upon what type of shocker you choose. For monos of twenty- to fifty-pound test, or coated wire

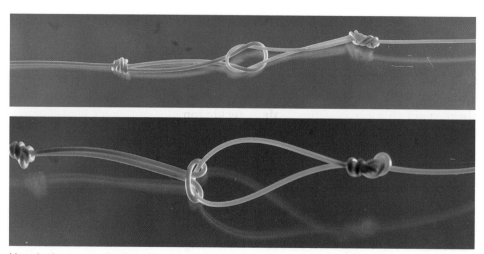

Here is the proper (top) and improper (bottom) way to interlock loops.

of fifteen- to forty-five-pound test, use either a surgeon's knot or Stu Apte's improved blood knot to attach the shocker to the Bimini. Heavier mono of 80- to 120-pound test or solid wire requires an Albright knot from the Bimini's double line to the shock section.

When tying on a fly with braided wire, use a figure-eight knot for a solid connection, or a Homer Rhode loop for free-swing action. The Homer Rhode knot is excellent for use with monos; with a light shocker (twenty-five- to forty-pound test) use the improved Homer Rhode. Solid wire requires a haywire twist to attach the fly.

Unlike the working section of your line, you will constantly alter the tippet during fishing. This is the reason for the interlocking loops—if you break off a fish or ruin the leader, you can change the tippet quickly. In the middle of breaking fish, trying to tie several Biminis and two surgeon's knots could be impossible; however, if your tippets are already tied, it is very simple. Just take off the spent leader and put it in your pocket, unroll a new one, interlock the loops, and tie on a fly. In a little over a minute, you are ready to fish. To tie up a tippet with a shocker properly would take at least five minutes; under the pressure of feeding fish, it could take twice as long. Always have your leaders ready beforehand, then the only knot you must tie on the water is to the fly. If you use a shock leader, this knot only needs to remain secure, not be 100 percent, and it is one simple knot rather than several complex ones. This is one key to saltwater fly-rodding success: When you never have to tie fancy knots on the water, your knotting system will always be 100 percent, and your fish-landing capabilities will increase.

To follow are drawings and knot-tying instructions for the knots previously mentioned. For more information, see *Fishing Knots* by Lefty Kreh. This book is the most complete, comprehensive knot book written. For anglers serious about knots, this is a must-read. Many tackle companies also offer knot-tying-instruction booklets that give helpful information about the particular company's materials.

The Knots and How to Tie Them

With the high quality of today's tippet materials, knot tying is easier than ever before. If you are unfamiliar with knots, it may help if you first learn the knots used to attach fly to tippet. These are the working knots, the ones that are used on each fishing day. Other frequently used knots are those that are used to construct the leader. Learn these knots, too, in case you must build a tippet on the water (it's best, though, to pre-tie your tippets). The knots used to construct a line from reel to butt section will seldom, if ever, be required while you're in the

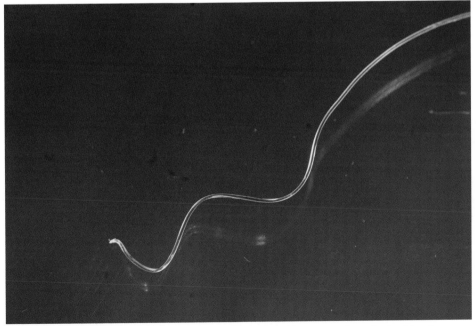

A poor knot can slip. A pigtail at the end of your leader is a sure sign of a bad knot.

A good way to pull up a knot is with pliers. Also some knots will set better if the tier wears gloves.

field, and they may be learned last; I would even go so far as to say you don't need to memorize them, but can construct this section of your line at home, with a knot-instruction text propped open in front of you.

Some of the following knots require four hands to tie. Use your thumb and first finger, and hold your little finger or ring finger against your palm, over the line, to help control the line. This will give you several holding points on each hand and will leave your middle finger free. Don't get discouraged with unraveling and tangling line; like learning to cast, learning to tie knots takes practice.

Wet all knots with saliva and tighten with one smooth and steady pull. Setting the knot in several stages or with jerky motions can weaken it and might overheat the mono, which will reduce its strength. Some knots must be formed before they are pulled tight, but in all cases the final setting of a knot should be in one steady pull. Don't be afraid to pull hard—it's better to have a knot fail in your hands than on a fish. And setting the knot up hard will prevent it from slipping; using pliers to hold the hook will ensure that the knot is set.

For complicated knots, use your thumb and first finger to hold the line, and your little finger or ring finger to hold the loose line against your palm, for more control.

Don't be cheap when tying knots—use enough line to form them correctly. Trim tag ends close, but try not to nick the standing line because the slightest scarring will weaken the mono. And never burn a tag end: The heat will break down the standing line.

I've been experimenting with superglue as a knot binder. Knots that are hard to tighten benefit from the use of glue, which gives a stronger grip and tighter bond. Superglue works well on knots that connect fly line to backing and mono to the front of the fly line. It not only adds strength, but also makes the knot more durable. The knot at the front section of the fly line gets heavy wear, and glue will add life to that connection. Be sure to use non-water-soluble superglue.

It's a good idea to test your knots to be sure they are tight and strong. Here's an easy way to do this at home: Set up your tippet system with a fly or undressed hook. Attach the loop at the butt end to an immovable object (you'll be applying over seventeen pounds of pressure to the line, so make sure it's attached securely to something strong and heavy). Hang an empty five-gallon pail on the bend of the hook, and slowly fill the pail with sand or water (if the pail overturns, sand is easier to clean up than water). Keep filling the pail slowly until the line breaks, then weigh the pail using a bathroom scale. If you've used twelve-pound-class tippet, the line should hold up to 13.22 pounds. If the line breaks before any of your knots do, congratulate yourself—you've tied 100 percent knots.

Test your lines frequently to make sure they are sound. Many substances— gasoline, sunscreen, insect repellents, lubricants—weaken monofilament. Sunlight and heat can break it down quickly, ruining the quality of its knots. Ten-pound-test line weakened by sunlight can break as low as two to three pounds. Some lines are mistreated when they're packaged for sale, or might be faulty fresh from the manufacturer. I test my just-bought leader material by tying an overhand knot in a section of the line. If the line is sound, I can expect a fair to good knot strength, above 50 percent. With poor line, a lower break strength will occur, sometimes as low as 25 percent.

I have done some serious testing on well-known knots and have found that knots that tested poorly often looked funny. If a knot does not form well, retie it. The number of turns will affect the way a knot tightens—heavier-test lines are harder to form and more difficult to set up. With thirty- to fifty-pound-test lines, fewer turns often make a knot stronger. And each angler might tie and pull a knot differently. Find a system that works, and set the knot well using gloves and pliers.

Knots for Attaching Fly to Tippet
Uni-Knot

This is a good knot, and it has many uses. Other than attaching the fly, the uni-knot works well to link lines of unlike material and size.

1. Run the line several inches through the hook eye and fold back, making two parallel lines. Bring the tag end back toward the hook eye and forward again to form a loop.

2. From the hook eye, make six turns around the double line and inside the loop with the tag end. You are forming a clinch knot over the double line, wrapping away from the fly.

3. Hold the double line near the hook eye and pull the tag end just enough to tighten the turns. *Do not* lock too firmly, or heat will build up when the tight knot is drawn down over the mono, weakening the line.

4. Draw the standing line to slide the knot down and lock it against the hook eye. Tighten smoothly in one motion to snug the knot. Trim the tag end.

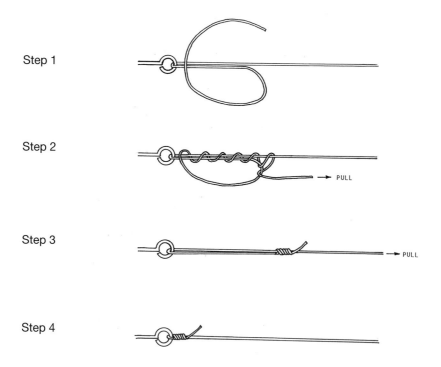

Step 1

Step 2   → PULL

Step 3   → PULL

Step 4

Twice-through-the-Eye Clinch-Trilene Knot

1. Thread the line through the hook eye, leaving a 6- to 8-inch tag end.

2. Run the tag end through the hook eye again from the same direction as the first loop, and form a dime-size loop at the eye. Pinch the hook eye and loop with your thumb and index finger to hold the loop steady.

3. Wrap the tag end around the standing line four to six times, and bring the end up through both loops. Essentially, you are making a clinch knot, but are going through two loops. (Use six turns for lighter tippet—two to six pounds—less with heavier line. I use four turns with sixteen-class.)

4. Pull the end tight, and when snugging the knot, be sure that the two loops lie next to each other evenly and do not cross.

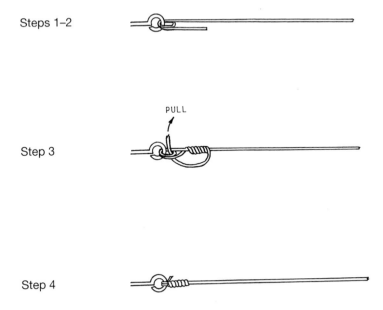

Steps 1–2

Step 3

Step 4

Figure-Eight Knot

A fast knot for tying braided wire to fly.

1. Thread the wire through the hook eye, bringing the tag end over the standing line to form a loop.

2. Wrap the tag end around the standing wire one full turn, then run the tag end through the loop—a figure eight should form. (This is actually a one-turn clinch.)

3. With pliers, pull the tag end at the same time you pull on the standing line. Then pull the standing line while you hold the fly. (Holding the fly and tightening the standing line first will cause the wire near the eye to form a bend.) Trim the tag end, leaving a short tag of about ⅛ inch.

Step 1

Step 2

Step 3

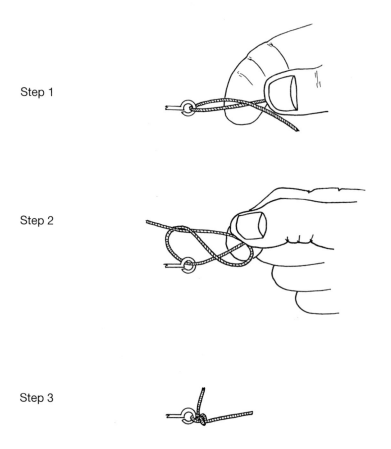

Three-and-a-Half-Turn Clinch Knot

Use to tie on shooting heads or to tie fly to shocker (over thirty-pound test). This is a low-break-strength knot. Do not use it with straight tippet.

1. Run the line through the hook eye and bring a tag end of 6 to 8 inches back along the standing line.

2. Wrap the tag end over the standing line, from the hook eye back, three and a half turns.

3. Bring the tag end forward and thread it through the loop formed at the hook eye.

4. Pull tight and hard, using pliers to hold the hook.

Step 1, 2, 3

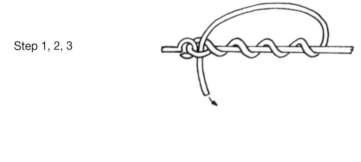

Step 4

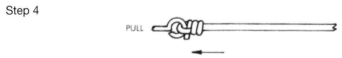

Homer Rhode Loop Knot

This knot is for shock leader only—mono or coated wire—to give a free-swing action to the fly.

1. Tie a loose overhand knot in the leader, leaving a 5-inch tag end.

2. Run the tag end through the hook eye and back through the overhand knot. The tag end must pass through the overhand knot running parallel to, not crossing, the standing line.

3. Snug the overhand knot down onto the standing line—not hard, but firmly. Pull the tag end to bring the overhand knot against the hook.

4. Take the tag end and make a single overhand knot with wire and heavy mono, or a double overhand (surgeon's) knot with the tag end over the standing line. Tighten the knot onto the standing line. (With light shocker—twenty-five to forty pounds—use the double overhand knot for higher break strength.)

5. Pull both the standing line and tag end to bring the overhand knots together. Tighten the knot by pulling both lines at the same time, putting more pressure on the tag end. For heavy lines, pliers are necessary to set the knot hard. Trim the tag end.

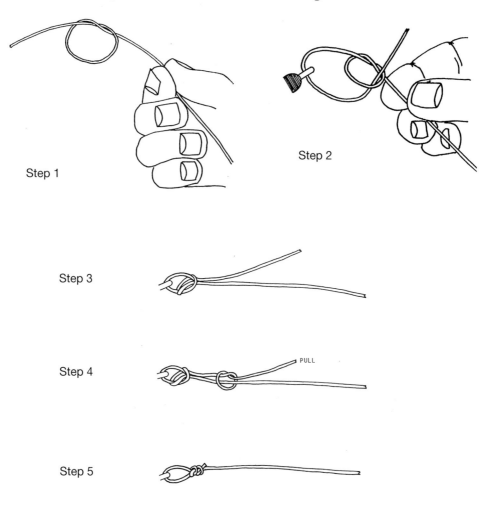

Step 1

Step 2

Step 3

Step 4

PULL

Step 5

Improved Clinch Knot

This is an excellent knot for connecting the fly to fluorocarbon and a very good knot for monofilament as well.

1. Thread the line through the hook eye, leaving a 6- to 8-inch tag end.

2. Wrap the tag end around the standing line four to six times, and bring the tag end back through the loop. Essentially, you are making a clinch knot. (Use six turns for lighter tippet like six-pound test; with heavier line, twelve to sixteen pounds, use four turns.)

3. Before tightening the knot, run the tag end back through the loop you first formed to make a clinch knot. This added step improves the clinch knot, making it stronger.

4. Pull the end tight, and when snugging the knot, be sure that the loops lie next to each other evenly and do not cross, and that the tag end pulls up tightly against the hook eye.

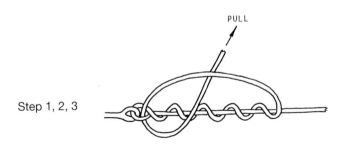

Step 1, 2, 3

Step 4

Loop Knot

For certain patterns, a free-swinging knot like this one gives better fly action. This knot also has very good knot strength.

1. Tie an overhand knot in the tippet 8 inches from the tag end. Feed the line through the hook eye, leaving the loop several inches from the eye.

2. Run the tag end through the overhand knot so the line exits the knot in the same manner as the first line. Do not cross the lines in the overhand knot.

3. Move the knot closer to the eye.

4. Make five to seven wraps over the standing line, and pass the tag end back through the overhand knot. Again, feed the tag end back in the same flow without crossing the lines. For the most strength, feed the tag end through the outer edge of the loop, not through the inside loop.

5. Pull slowly on the tag end to tighten the wraps. To set the knot, pull on the standing line and the fly.

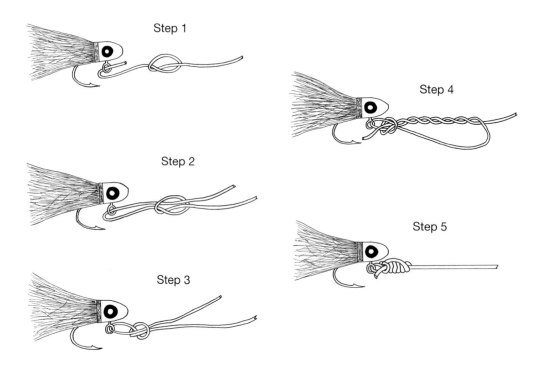

Step 1

Step 2

Step 3

Step 4

Step 5

Knots to Form Double Lines

A double line knots better and has more strength when connecting unlike or different-size materials.

Spider Hitch

The spider hitch forms a double line easier than a Bimini twist does, but it is not as consistent and does not hold up as well under impact.

1. Form a 2-foot-long loop of tippet material. About 20 inches from the loop's end, grab the line between your thumb and first finger. Form a small reverse loop, crossing the double line under the standing line, and pinch the small loop with your thumb.

2. Hold the small loop between your thumb and forefinger, and extend your thumb beyond the forefinger. The loop must extend beyond the end of your thumb.

3. Wrap the double line from the large loop around your thumb and the small loop five to seven times. Thread the remaining line down through the small loop and pull. The loops will peel off your thumb and onto the standing line.

4. Finish the knot by pulling on the end of the large loop and the standing line. Bring the knot up tight and trim the tag end. This knot is actually a multi-turn surgeon's knot.

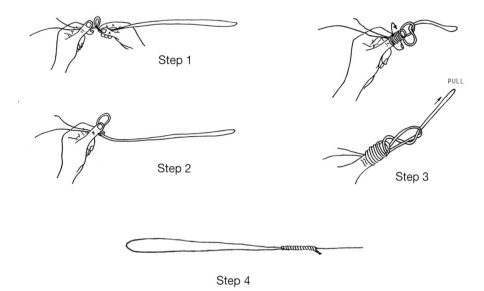

Step 1

Step 2

PULL

Step 3

Step 4

Bimini Twist

This is definitely a multihand knot. Remember to use your thumb, first finger, pinkie, and palm for holding points. Although it's tricky to tie, learning this knot is well worth your effort.

1. Form a loop of line large enough to fit loosely over your knee. Hold the tag and standing ends in one hand, and twist the end of the loop twenty times with the other hand.

2. Spread the twisted loop over your knee, holding the doubled line with one hand. Hold the standing line with one hand and the tag end with your other hand. Pull your hands apart to tighten the twists against your knee.

3. Run the hand holding the standing line down close to the V where the loop splits. Place the first finger in the V, and hold the standing line with your thumbs and middle finger. The standing line and tag end also form a V, and the twisted section lies between both Vs. The upper V forms the knot; the lower V is the locking point.

4. Put pressure on the standing line and roll the tag end over the twisted section. Keep enough pressure on the tag end to maintain the V. Keep feeding line from the tag end to wind over the twisted section while applying pressure to the bottom V with your first finger. The line should be winding down to the lower V, over the twisted section. Be careful not to crisscross the line that is wrapping onto the twisted section.

5. When the two Vs meet, pinch the junction with the thumb and first finger of the standing-line hand. Take the tag end and make a half-hitch over the nearest line of the loop. The half-hitch should tighten into the V; this locks the knot and completes the Bimini, but a clinch is necessary to prevent slippage.

6. Now you must form a clinch knot over the double line that will lock back into the Bimini. Hold the Bimini, take the tag end, and wrap it seven times over the double line—winding back toward the Bimini. This knot must lock back into the Bimini.

7. Pull the tag end and standing line while holding the double line to tighten the knot. Use the thumb and first finger of the other hand to

smooth the knot. While tightening the knot, keep stroking the wraps back toward the loop, pulling away from the knot to prevent tangling. Pull tight and trim the tag end.

Step 1

Step 3

Step 4

Step 2

Step 5

Step 6

Step 7a

Step 7b

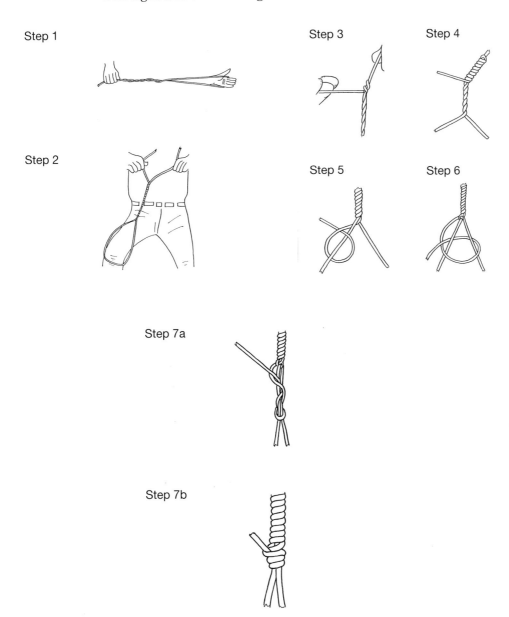

Knots to Tie Line to Line and Line to Leader

Here are three popular knots used to connect lines. The surgeon's works well with all combinations of monos but is not a 100 percent knot. The improved blood knot works best to attach a light shocker (twenty-five to fifty pounds) to a double line. When tied properly, it is a 100 percent knot.

Surgeon's Knot

This knot is easy to tie, and is used primarily to connect tippet to shocker or adding tippet to a leader—either mono or coated wire.

1. Hold the shock leader and tippet parallel for 6 to 8 inches. (Either a single or double strand of tippet will work—double gives better knot strength.)

2. Form a golf-ball-size loop and tie an overhand knot with both lines, pulling the entire leader through the loop, but do not pull it tight.

3. Tie one or two more overhand knots—three would be strongest but might be difficult to tie with some materials. When using leader materials that are close in size, four loops will add strength.

4. Pull from both sides with all lines, snugging the knot together evenly. Cut the tag ends close to prevent snagging seaweed.

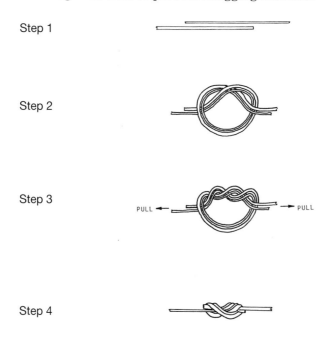

Step 1

Step 2

Step 3

Step 4

Improved Blood Knot

Use for tying a double-line tippet to shock leader—mono to mono.

1. With thumb and first finger, hold a section of double line and a section of shock leader, crossing and pinching them together as they cross.

2. Wrap the double line over the shock leader five times. Then bring the double line back and place it into the V or cross formed by both lines. You have formed a clinch knot with both lines.

3. Pinch this section together and wrap the shock leader over the double line in the opposite direction. Make three and a half turns, and thread the line back through the same opening as the double line. Be sure the shock leader and double line are heading in opposite directions: This will give better knot strength.

4. Pull both lines hard to tighten the knot. Trim the tag ends. (Cinching lines over fifty pounds is difficult—the Albright knot is a better choice for a heavy shocker.)

Step 1

Step 2, 3

Step 4

Albright Knot

This knot is for connecting heavy mono shocker or wire to a tippet. It is best to put a double line (Bimini) on the tippet.

1. Form a 3-inch loop in a heavy section of mono. Pinch the mono at the loop to keep it tight.

2. Insert the double line down through the loop, and grab both the loop and tippet between your thumb and first finger. All four lines should by lying together, with the lighter lines inside. Keep the Bimini or spider hitch close to the loop to give a longer shock tippet for IGFA leader setup. Leave about 1½ inches of loop exposed.

Step 1

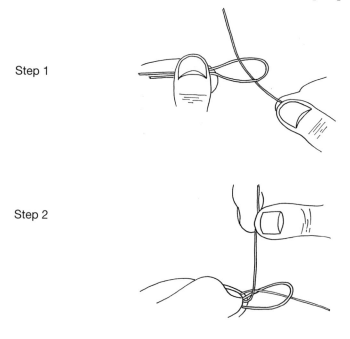

Step 2

3. Begin wrapping the lighter double line over all four lines, winding from the tip of your thumb to the loop's end. Make twelve to fifteen turns with the double line.

4. Thread the double line back through the loop *toward the direction it entered*—this is important.

Steps 3–4

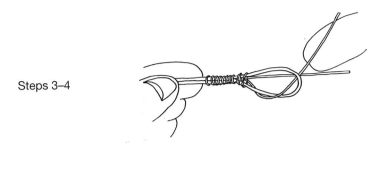

Step 5

5. Pull the standing double line gently to tighten the wraps, and slide
    the coils to the loop's end. Be careful not to tug too hard and pull the
    coils over the loop's end.

6. Keep holding the loop, and pull the tag end of the double line tight
    to prevent the coils from slipping off the loop. To set the knot, pull on
    both the standing line and the tag end. Pull the standing line hard
    while holding the heavy mono for the final set and to test the knot.
    Cut both tag ends close. (The rule of one steady pull to tighten does
    not apply to this knot.)

Step 6a

Step 6b

Making a Loop in Line
Surgeon's Loop

Use this knot to form a loop on the line's butt section and in the double line of a leader. The loops interlock to make the loop-to-loop connection.

1. Form a loop in the butt section's end at the desired length and tie an overhand knot with the loop.

2. Leave the first knot loose and tie another overhand knot, pulling it up—but not tight.

3. Place a strong object in the loop and pull the standing line to tighten the knots. Make the loop several inches long, and pinch the loop ends together to make it tight. A narrow, tight loop is best for interlocking to a tippet. Trim the tag end.

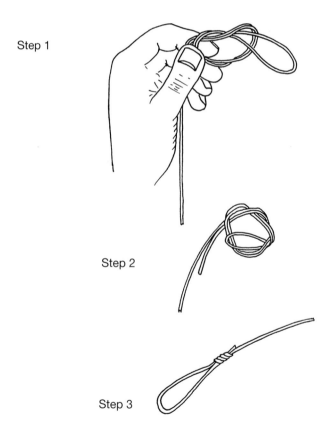

Step 1

Step 2

Step 3

Connecting Leader or Backing to Fly Line
Nail Knot

Mainly used to connect backing or leader to fly line, this knot works well with Dacron or Micron to mono, or mono to mono, for a double nail knot.

Though it's called a nail knot, a hollow tube is easier to work with when tying it. The best tool to use is a fly-tying bobbin. Tie this knot the same way, whether you're attaching backing or a butt section or are connecting two lines. When connecting two lines, lay both lines parallel and tie a nail knot with each line over the other line. Tighten the knots, then draw them together so they butt up against each other.

1. Hold the bobbin handle, fly line, and leader butt section between your thumb and first finger, and allow the main body of the fly line to trail out below your palm. Leave the end of the fly line just outside the bobbin tip.

2. With fly line and leader pinched to the bobbin tube, wrap the leader's tag end back over the tube, fly line, and leader. Make six to nine tight wraps, running from your thumb toward the bobbin tip. Be sure the wraps are neat and not crossed.

Step 1

Step 2

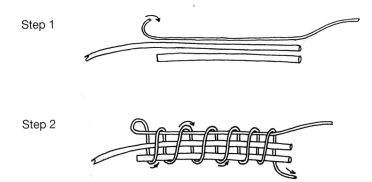

3. Slide your first finger up to pinch the knot to the tube. Pull the leader standing line to tighten the back section of the knot. Keeping the wraps tight is essential.

4. Thread the tag end through the tube's tip and snug up. This will feed the tag end through the core of the knot so it can lock onto itself.

5. Pinch the knot hard and slide it off the tube. Keep pressure on the knot and snug up the leader standing line and tag end. Before locking tight, check the coils to be sure they are together. Pull hard on the standing line and tag end to lock the knot. Trim both tag ends close, then pull the fly line and leader to test the knot. (A drop of superglue before the final locking is extra insurance, but I have never had a nail knot fail.)

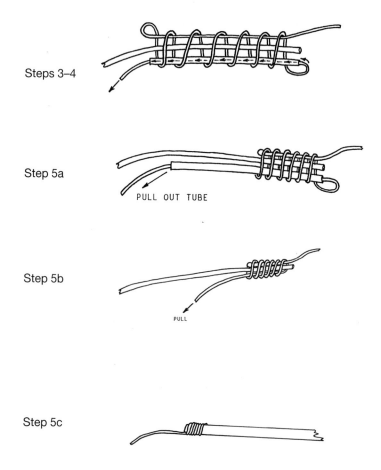

Steps 3–4

Step 5a

PULL OUT TUBE

Step 5b

PULL

Step 5c

Speed Nail Knot

A faster and easier nail knot, this should be used only for attaching leaders to fly lines. It's also called the needle nail knot because a needle is often used to form the knot. I prefer a straightened paper clip.

1. Pinch the paper clip (or needle) and end of the fly line together, leaving about 1 inch of fly line beyond the clip. Place a length of butt-section material against the clip and fly line, with the butt section's tip facing in the same direction as the end of the fly line. Place the other end of the butt section in the opposite direction, facing the palm of your hand, and hold firmly. This forms a large loop of mono hanging below your thumb.

2. Take the section of leader that formed the large loop, closest to the tip of the fly line, and begin wrapping it toward your thumb, making six to nine turns. Keep the wraps tight and close.

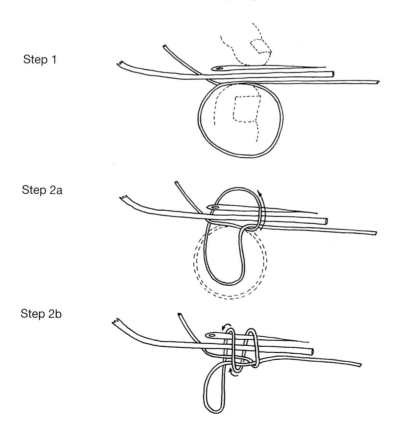

Step 1

Step 2a

Step 2b

3. Slide your first finger up to pinch the knot. Pull the butt section out slowly; you will feel it slipping between your fingers. The large loop will begin to disappear and may start to twist. Keep it untangled, for a knot in the loop will ruin the connection.

4. After the loop disappears, pull both the butt section and the tag end of the leader tight. Pinch the knot again, slide the clip out, and tighten both lines again.

5. If the coils are neat and tight, lock the knot by pulling hard on both ends of the leader. Trim the tag ends close and pull hard to test the knot.

Step 3

Step 4   PULL OUT NEEDLE

Step 5

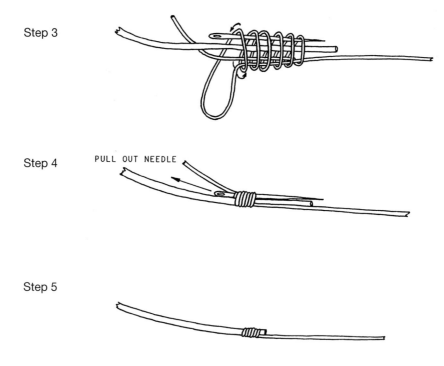

Joining Dacron and Micron to Mono

Use either a double uni-knot or double nail knot.

Double Uni-Knot

See "Knots for Attaching Fly to Tippet" for uni-knot information.

1. Hold the two lines to be joined together; they should point in opposite directions. Form a loop in one line and make a uni-knot over both lines with it.

2. Snug the knot. It should slide freely over the line.

3. Tie a second uni-knot with the other line. Snug firmly, but do not lock tight.

4. Pull each standing line, drawing both uni-knots together. Once the knots touch, hold the line firmly and pull tight. Trim the tag ends.

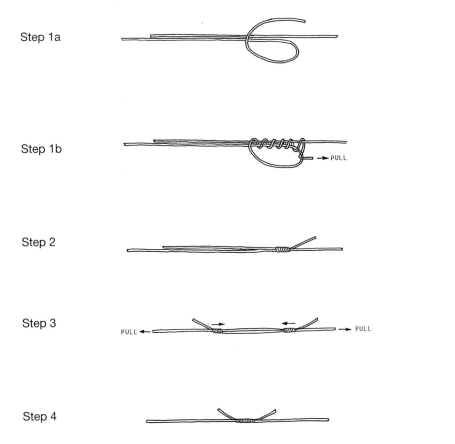

Step 1a

Step 1b

Step 2

Step 3

Step 4

Double Nail Knot

See "Connecting Leader or Backing to Fly Line" for nail knot information.

1. Hold the two lines to be joined together; they should face in opposite directions. Make a nail knot with one line over the other.

2. Snug the knot. It should slide freely over the line.

3. Tie a second nail knot with the other line. Snug firmly, but do not lock tight.

4. Pull each standing line, drawing both nail knots together. Once the knots touch, hold the line firmly and pull tight. Trim the tag ends.

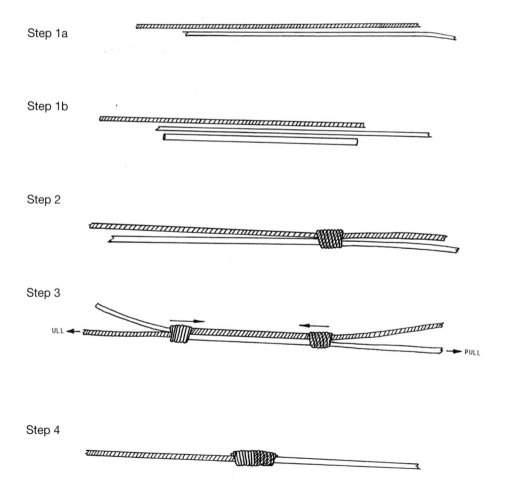

Step 1a

Step 1b

Step 2

Step 3

Step 4

Offset Nail Knot

Use to connect fly line to backing.

1. Tie the same way as you would a double nail knot, but make an overhand knot for the fly line's nail knot.

2. Strip off several inches of coating from the running line's end.

3. Lay both lines together and form a nail knot with the backing over the stripped fly line, then snug down.

4. Make a single or double overhand knot with the stripped fly line over the backing, then snug down.

5. Pull both knots together and tighten—if using a braided backing, superglue will make the knot stronger.

Attaching Backing to Reel

1. Wrap the backing around the spool arbor several times.

2. Tie an overhand knot in the standing line. Tie several more overhand knots in the tag end.

3. Pull the standing line until the knots lock against one another.

4. Reel on the backing.

A knot kit helps keep all your knot tools and materials in one convenient place. A fly bobbin, a needle or paper clip for nail knots, clippers, glue, and sections of lead-core and braided mono fit nicely in a small box.

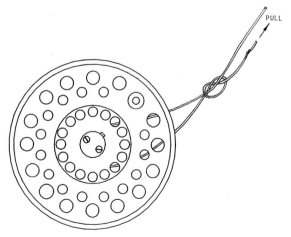

18

Baitfish and Flies

The first patterns for saltwater flies were undoubtedly trout or salmon streamers, such as the Gray Ghost or Mickey Finn. They were used as attractors by the early pioneers looking for new challenges to their growing sport. In *The Complete Book of Fly Fishing,* Joe Brooks mentions that Tom Loving tied flies especially for shad and developed a white striper fly in 1922. Then Harold Gibbs, Bill Gallasch, and Gordon Dean developed saltwater flies in the early 1950s. There were certainly others, many passed on without recognition, but it was Joe Brooks who popularized marine fly rodding with his articles and books. As a boy I read about Joe's accomplishments with envy and started tying flies even before I had the tackle to fish them.

The early saltwater pioneers, like the beginning freshwater anglers, tied *attractors*—flies that suggested, rather than imitated, the fishes' food. They were successful with several colors and sizes without being particular about tying an exact duplication of a baitfish. Even today, several patterns in a few colors and sizes take fish under a number of circumstances.

The modern saltwater fly rodder, however, is becoming more sophisticated, fishing both with attractors and with precise-looking patterns that simulate baitfish to a T. As in freshwater, an exact imitation often outscores the basic attractor-type patterns, although both attractors and lifelike imitations are important and necessary in saltwater fly fishing. I tie some patterns as mixtures to resemble a combination of several baits, offering a multi-look to the gamefish.

Modern materials—there are more than I can keep track of—plus a wide assortment of supplies in a vast selection of colors, afford the fly tyer and fly buyer a much wider variety of patterns. Today's flies not only work better, but they also last longer. Combined with improved materials, fly construction and tying techniques have progressed dramatically in recent years, producing superior flies. The novice saltwater fly rodder need not search widely, as I did only forty years ago, to find the barest essentials. Today good-quality flies in a variety of colors and sizes are available through a number of mail-order catalogs and fly shops, with many stores offering special patterns for local fishing.

Because many saltwater flies are large and simple, they are easy to tie, and most patterns require few, if any, complex tying procedures. A beginning fly tyer can learn by making two attractor patterns: a Clouser and a Lefty's Deceiver. These are simple to tie and are productive. Do not attempt to tie special patterns right away, but learn the basic fundamentals first, then advance to more involved ties after gaining some experience. Basic attractor patterns in three or four colors and several sizes always score in salt water, and some early patterns are still popular today, catching fish as well as they did over fifty years ago.

Many years ago I discovered that foam-headed flies have the buoyancy to act like a minnow-type plug, either slid along the surface or worked with a slow-sinking line to get a bobbing action. I developed these flies out of frustration after fishing next to spin fishermen, who took fish with a slow retrieve while I went fishless because my fly lacked the proper action.

A minnow-type spinning plug's success is not just in its swimming action, but also in the way it dives below the surface, then floats to the top, giving the appearance of a crippled baitfish as it bobs along on the surface, leaving a wake. I needed a fly that worked in this fashion, simulating the bobbing, surface-walking behavior. Flies constructed from foam cast well, are durable if given an epoxy finish, and in suitable conditions have fantastic fish-catching abilities. Single-cell foam used in boat or surfboard repair is ideal for making flies because it does not absorb water.

Jack Frech was the best plug fisherman I have ever fished with. His tough, hard, competitive personality stopped at nothing to find and catch fish, using knowledge and stamina to keep going until he reached his goal. Through Jack, I learned the fishing areas of Nantucket and how to read the rolling surf. One valuable piece of information he gave me was to use barbless hooks, not just for fly fishing, but for all my multi-hooked spinning lures. Barbless hooks are safer, hook better, hold fish just as well as barbed hooks, and make fish release easier.

Jack earned the nickname Professor in Montauk, where he pioneered wetsuit fishing, and was the first to use this technique to work the offshore rocks and bars in the surf. He had a wealth of surf-fishing knowledge—specifically on Nantucket and Montauk. Although he was a human book of information, Jack generally declined to share with others; however, he was somehow willing to reveal his secrets to me.

One night four of us were fishing a haunt of Jack's in the backwaters of Nantucket, working a particular rip. With no surf, it was ideal for fly rodding, but although we could hear fish popping along the rip, there was little action. While the other anglers were fishing different spinning lures, I tried several patterns before finally using a surfboard-foam fly—hoping to find the secret to these lock-jawed fish. Current was working slowly across the point, still coming in, so we killed time with fishing, waiting for the usually more productive outgoing tide. I began taking nice fish with the foam flies—they ranged from twenty to nearly thirty pounds—while the spin fishermen went without a bump. My fly, being smaller than their spinning lures, was ideal to use to duplicate baitfish both in size and action. In a short period I took three fish while the others went fishless. For Jack, this was hard to take, because he believed he could outfish anyone at any time. This shows how effective that fly was, to outfish someone of Jack's ability.

We fished hard through the remainder of the incoming tide, stopping after it went slack. "It must be both the size and the action," I told Jack, and as we sat on the dunes waiting for the falling tide, I tied up a dropper for him, using a foam fly.

Walking back to the point as the tide started out, we continued to work the same corner, and again my success was high—I landed two more fish, losing two others. Jack did take one fish and dropped another, and a third angler also dropped a fish. The effectiveness of my fly, under the right conditions, was obvious. Jack finally saw the importance of fly fishing. Although he had fooled with the long rod for several years, he now wanted to get serious. So the next spring I made Jack a graphite rod, and we planned to get together that fall—but it was not to be. Jack died in a freak boating accident during the summer. It was one of those things that happen to people who appear to be invincible—as Jack did. However, I was fortunate to have fished with him, gaining knowledge from one of the best surf-plug fishermen that ever lived. Many times while I fish the beach, his words of wisdom still inspire me. Jack was a unique man, and a great friend. I miss him.

Baitfish

Being able to imitate a small baitfish will often give the saltwater fly fisherman an advantage over the spin fisherman. Spin fishermen, even when using droppers, have problems duplicating small baits. I have witnessed thirty-pound-plus striped bass gorge themselves on 2- to 3-inch-long sand eels. And even though I took some of these fish on a dropper, with a fly rod I could have presented the offering more effectively. Other times I have witnessed fish feeding selectively on small baits that only a fly rodder could have matched in size and action. It's exciting to think that a fly fisher can cast out a 3-inch offering and quite possibly take fish of thirty pounds or better.

Select fly patterns on the basis of bait type, not fish type. What is a striper fly? A small striper! And "trout flies" are used in salt water. One pattern might catch many species. The major consideration when building or buying flies is that they look like the baitfish the the gamefish are feeding on. Gamefish species and water conditions might, at times, influence fly selection, but the first consideration must be to copy the food the fish are feeding on. Match the bait hatch.

Most areas have both resident bait and migratory bait that move in at different times of the year. Learning these baitfish, knowing where they hold and what their habits are, and determining their sizes and shapes will improve your fishing.

Sand Eels

Sand eels (American sand lance), *Ammodytes americanus,* are the fly rodder's most important bait. When gamefish feed on sand eels, they either will take flies well or will have a horrible case of lockjaw. The presence of thick schools of sand eels will start fish feeding, but at times in such a way as to make the fish difficult to take. When bait is too thick, fish swim through the school, feeding without singling out individual targets. This manner of eating is frustrating for the angler because fish are breaking all over, yet they will not hit. During this type of feeding pattern, fishing below or to the side of the feeding fish is the only way to take them (see chapter 9).

Thick schools appear in bays, off sandy shores, in surf lines, and sometimes back in estuaries. Sand eels have a very interesting behavior: Toward evening or just after dark, they burrow into the sand bottom for protection, and stay there all night long. At first light, they come out from the sand, schooling together for the day. But sometimes they repeat the emergence several times before staying up permanently: They'll come up to the surface, hold for several minutes, then return to the sand. If fish start feeding on them immediately, when the sand eels disappear again, your fly will be the only edible-looking morsel in the water. In some locations sand eels might stay in the sand during the day. When wading in shallow areas, try shuffling your feet along the bottom—if sand eels are there, they will pop out, swim a few yards, and rebury. They can disappear into even hard sand in seconds.

During top-water action, it is important to fish the edges of or beneath the baitfish, where the fly might attract attention. If the sand eels are spread apart in loose formation, gamefish will take flies readily, feeding as they would on any scattered baitfish.

Sand-eel patterns are simple to tie and because of the long, thin, pencil shape, are highly castable. The sand eel, ranging from 2 to nearly 10 inches long, is a favorite food of bass, bluefish, bonito, albacore, and weakfish, as well as many other ocean and deep-water species. They are the single most important bait for the fly rodder in the mid-Atlantic region. Although considered by many to be a shallow-water bait,

Finding baitfish like these sand eels along a beach is a positive sign that fish were feeding before you arrived.

sand eels actually range far out into the ocean, providing one of the major food sources for the Atlantic fishery. These are ocean sand eels, which are much larger and thicker than inshore sand eels.

Silversides

The Atlantic silversides (spearing, white bait, shiners), *Menidia menidia,* is also an important baitfish and is widely distributed throughout the North Atlantic coast. It is a favorite food-fish of all gamesters. Shiners (a local name) live in estuaries, bays, creeks, rivers, shallows, and along many shorelines. Spearing do not usually school up, as do sand eels. At times, thick schools of spearing congregate near estuaries, but in most cases the fish do not hold in tightly packed schools. This baitfish normally spreads out in shallow flat areas or along shorelines, and gamefish single out individual baits.

Spearing are an ideal size for the fly rodder to match: They are thicker in body than the sand eel, and range from 2 to 6 inches long. They are a perfect food for gamefish, which feast on them day and night. Combined, sand eels and silversides offer a mixed bag, creating ideal fly fishing. Both baits have periods where they hold suspended on or near the surface, or move slowly about in one area. Either situation offers easy feeding for gamesters. Other less important baitfish, such as smelt, anchovy, and stickleback, are similar to shiners in size, shape, and color, and spearing patterns will double for these baits. When spearing are splashing on the surface, small poppers can be very effective.

Flat-Sided Baitfish

There are six big flat-sided baits that offer large gamefish a meal: Atlantic menhaden (bunker or pogy), *Brevoortia tyrannus;* alewife, *Alosa pseudoharengus;* herring, both Atlantic, *Clupea harengus harengus,* and blueback, *Alosa aestivalis; and* mullet, both white, *Mugil curema,* and striped, *Mugil cephalus.* Big striped bass and bluefish love to feed on these large baitfish. However, their adult size makes them difficult for the fly fisherman to duplicate. A big bunker might weigh two to three pounds—and trying to cast a bunker-size fly is impossible.

The best action with a fly occurs when fish are feeding on juvenile flat-sided baitfish 3 to 5 inches long. Then herring, bunker, or finger mullet are all good baits to duplicate. When jumbo baits are present, the only possibility is to throw the largest flies in your box and hope to entice a fish that is feeding on food twice the size of your offering. Some excellent fly patterns match these foods well, but size can still be a factor. Dave Skok's Mushmouth and several of Enrico Puglisi's patterns offer large flies that are castable with big outfits. These patterns are made with synthetic materials that shed water better than natural materials. Tied properly, these flies are sparse but still look thick in the water. Under the right circumstance, when the big baits are spread out, fish will take these flies.

In the spring, herring and alewives enter, then exit, freshwater streams to spawn. Big striped bass and bluefish love to feed on them, and will ambush them outside estuaries. I have taken several large fish by duplicating the herring and alewives as they return from spawning, although this is difficult because they are so big and often the real thing will win out.

Bay Anchovies

Another important fall bait is the bay anchovy, *Anchoa mitchilli.* These 2- to 2½-inch-long green- to brown-backed baitfish form large schools in open water, along beaches, and around the mouths of estuaries. They are the favorite food of the hardtails that move inshore. Ranging from Cape Cod south, this small

These baitfish spilled from an albi caught at Harkers Island, North Carolina. They are much larger baitfish than our anchovy up north. PHOTO COURTESY OF CURT JESSUP

bait sometimes appears in ball-shaped schools the size of a truck tire. They move through the water like a blob of oil.

When fish are on this bait they can be picky—there are times when a small, precise pattern is the only way to catch fish. However, in locations along the Carolinas, false albacore feed on bigger anchovies, and I think the fishing success rate is much higher because the bait is larger. In northern locations we seldom see these baits over 2 inches in length, but in locations along the Outer Banks the baits are almost double that size. They are similar in appearance to the bay anchovy, but not as wide-bodied for their length. They might be silver anchovies, *Engraulis eurystole,* or striped anchovies, *Anchoa hepsetus,* which are larger. Regardless of what species of anchovy it is, the anglers in New England wish the bigger bait would move north.

Squid

Squid are an important spring-into-summer bait. They can range in size from 2 to about 10 inches long, and change color depending on their surroundings.

When this bait is abundant, gamefish become aggressive. Squid are the best bait to bring stripers to the surface when the fish are holding in big, deep rips. If stripers are located near the surface in heavy rips, the reason is often the presence of squid.

Other Bait Types

Although the sand eels, silversides, and large flat-sided baitfish dominate the waters from Nova Scotia to the Carolinas, there are special types of food, such as shrimp, worms, crabs, eels, and bottom fish, that are also popular food for gamefish.

Shrimp are plentiful during spring in creeks and on flats, and are very highly regarded as food by some gamesters, particularly weakfish. Usually only smaller fish feed on shrimp in estuaries, but I have taken good-size weaks as they sipped these tasty morsels.

Spawning sandworms, *Nereis* species, are also special baits favored by gamefish. But like the shrimp, they are only present at certain times of the year. Fishing can be great, though, if you find the hatches at the right time. Bass up to twenty pounds feed in small estuaries when the worms are swarming. The best period of the hatch is when there are few worms. Once the main bloom starts, the worms are thick, making your fly one tiny piece in a hundred thousand. Hatches often occur around new and full moons; larger tides seem to trigger the hatch. However, some locations might have a hatch that runs for up to a month. Daytime hatches occur, but they are sporadic and not as predictable as the nighttime hatches. Some locations that produce predictable daylight hatches are Tashmoo Pond on Martha's Vineyard and several of the ponds along the southern Rhode Island coast that have good afternoon and evening hatches. One consistent late-morning worm hatch that I have witnessed occurred in Great Bay, New Hampshire, where fish fed all day long on the worms. Full-size sandworms, not the swarming worms, are a favorite food, particularly for stripers, and are a favorite bait of many bait fishermen.

Crabs are another abundant food. Bass, weakfish, and at times even bluefish dine on crabs when there is nothing else around, or when the crabs spawn in estuaries, offering the gamefish easy pickings. Crabs are numerous along many shorelines, and bottom-feeding gamefish often grub the edges, looking for food. Stripers that roam the shallow flats during the summer are often looking for crabs when baitfish are not present.

Other important bottom baits are cunner, *Tautogolabrus adspersus,* and small blackfish, *Tautoga onitis*, both of which live along rocky shores, around jetties, and in reefs. Many times I have found these small fish in the bellies of bass. One jetty-caught bass of over forty pounds had several 2- to 3-inch-long cunners in its stomach, proving that even big fish grub small baits when hungry.

Eels are also known as a bass bait, and have been used for years by serious striper fishermen. They also attract bluefish; I have had many rigged eels ruined by the chopper's razor jaws. Keep eel patterns sparse to permit easy casting.

Another important offshore bait is the halfbeak, similar to a Balao. Also called ballyhoo, they are generally less than 12 inches in length and have a long snout and tube-shaped body. Being a favorite bluefin tuna food, many guides fish flies that match this bait.

Two guides that provide additional information on baits are my book, *The Orvis Pocket Guide to Saltwater Baits and Their Imitations,* and *A Fly Fisher's Guide to Salt Water Naturals and Their Imitations* by George V. Rogers Jr. Both have good, detailed insights about the types of food that fish eat.

Saltwater Flies

When selecting saltwater flies, five considerations are important: length, shape, action, density, and color.

The first and most important consideration is length, one component of the basic silhouette. Whether you are trying to duplicate full-size or juvenile baitfish, fly length is the single most important aspect of the imitation.

Next is shape, or bulk—whether the fly is fat or thin, round or flat-sided. This form is crucial when considering how the fly's silhouette looks to a fish. Next to the length, shape is the most important component of a fly.

Action is also an important characteristic of a saltwater artificial, for how it works and breathes determines whether the fly has a lifelike appearance. Long bucktail, marabou, saddle hackle, Flashabou, Krystal Flash, and Crystal Hair are some of the materials that create movement even when a fly is floating suspended, without forward motion. The action of these materials makes the fly look alive, or gives it a lifelike struggling appearance when a jerky retrieve is employed. In either case, a pattern with a "breathing" quality appears more natural.

Density is significant in fly construction, making the pattern float, stay at a particular level, or sink at different rates. In conjunction with different-density fly lines, materials of various densities—along with hook size, eyes, and lead wrap—make the fly work at certain levels. When deciding on fly density, consider the type of line you will use and the water conditions you are planning to fish.

Color, though important at times, is probably the least significant factor in the construction of a saltwater fly. There are times, in certain locations or water conditions, where a particular color or combination of colors is most effective. However, black, white, yellow, or olive flies with some flash continually take fish, while fancier flies catch only fishermen. I like to combine color on larger flies, where the changing shades along the sides may suggest movement or give the fly a more lifelike appearance. Epoxy flies tied with a mixture of colors offer a way to blend shades to obtain near-perfect matches. Color becomes more important when fishing in clear water for hardtails or sight fishing for stripers. In clear water, blending several shades of color will make the fly look more lifelike. And dark-colored patterns are often much more effective on dark nights.

Imitating the Sand Eel

Now let's look at the fundamental patterns needed to imitate the three baitfish categories of the Northeast (specific pattern information is in the latter portion of this chapter). The first is a thin fly, duplicating either a sand eel or a needlefish, and tied with only a thin tail and body. The size varies from 2 to 8 inches long, with the average size 3½ to 5 inches long. It is tied on hooks from #4 to 3/0, using either standard or long-shanked hooks, depending on the pattern type. The best colors are all black, all yellow, or white with a light green, purple, or peacock herl top. Add Flashabou or Crystal Hair to some flies, or make an entire fly from these materials for a bright pattern.

I developed a sand eel fly many years ago using brown bucktail for the tail and a dark gray wool body. It was lightweight yet sank quickly and caught many fish, even though it looked ugly. Lefty Kreh described it in *Fly Fishing in Salt Water* as "Unfinished, but having great fish-catching ability."

Another good thin pattern with breathing action is the Snake Fly. Tied in different thicknesses, it imitates slender to medium-bodied bait, and doubles as a worm or eel fly. The Lefty's Deceiver tied sparsely works as well.

A floating sand eel pattern, one that slides along the surface, is useful in calm water when fish are being selective. Eric Peterson, a gifted fly tyer and saltwater fly fisherman from Westport, Connecticut, uses lobster-pot foam to tie up a slender surface sand eel that is deadly on still nights.

Imitating the Mid-Bodied Baits

The second basic pattern is a cigar-shaped fly to imitate shiners, anchovy, spike mackerel, stickleback, and finger mullet. Tie this fly with a wing and tail or a wing only, making the body fatter than for the sand eel. Use hook sizes from #2 to 4/0, and tie some long-shanked for blues and bonito. The fly should be 2 to 6 inches long. The Lefty's Deceiver and Snake Fly are just a couple of examples of fly patterns in this category, but there are many other patterns to choose from.

Probably the best all-around fly is the Lefty's Deceiver. Tied in various lengths and thicknesses, the Deceiver is a good general pattern that casts well, seldom tangles, and looks like a number of baitfish. Lefty Kreh developed this fly in the late 1950s, and its popularity and uses never stop. The Deceiver and the Clouser Minnow are the most widely used flies in salt water.

Smelt patterns are effective because they resemble shiners, and the same fly patterns will copy both bait types. Smelt arrive late in the year or are present early in the spring, when gamefish feed on them. Colors include black, yellow, hot green, and white. Combine either black, red, blue, or green over white, and add some flash to most of these patterns. Peacock herl over white bucktail, tied single-wing fashion, is a good fundamental pattern.

Top-water popping plugs and sliders are excellent patterns. Jack Gartside's Gurgler, a combination of popper and slider, is very effective. Most poppers today have foam heads and tails dressed with materials like bucktail, saddle hackle, or Enrico's Sea Fiber with some flash. If you plan to build your own poppers, preformed heads work well, and there are some good single-cell foams available. Cork, although not as durable as foam, is lighter and is still a good material for poppers. Epoxy the head onto a long-hooked shank, pre-tied with a tail; hook size 1/0 to 3/0, bug length 3 to 6 inches. When building poppers, make sure the hook extends beyond or far below the body to give the bug better hooking qualities.

Make hairbugs by spinning deer hair on a hook shank; they are effective, hook fish well, and are easier than poppers to cast. Hook size and length are the same as for a solid-bodied bug.

Imitating the Flat-Sided Baitfish

The third basic pattern is a big, bulky fly to imitate bunker, alewife, herring, large mullet, or snapper blues (baby bluefish). Make these large flies 4 to 7 inches long, on 2/0 to 5/0 hooks. I use all white, all black, or all yellow, or I layer white, yellow, or pink with a dark top, and add flash in the middle. Along with

Dave Skok's Mushmouth and several of Enrico's Bunker flies, Tabory's Slab Side is an ideal big fly pattern and gives the proper silhouette for any of the large flat-sided baits.

Imitating Other Foods

When exploring creeks, backwaters, or areas that hold stripers and weakfish, a shrimp pattern is necessary. Shrimp flies do not need to be curved. I have photographed shrimp floating straight and bending only when swimming. A basic straight, short bucktail or deer-hair fly tied in a shrimp shape is a fine fly. A deer-hair body coated with silicone sealer makes a nice-looking shrimp, and silicone sealer is also useful when making shiners and sand eel flies, giving them a translucent appearance. Hook sizes range from #8 to 1/0, and the flies are 1 to 2½ inches long. The best colors are pink, white, yellow, or light gray.

You will need other special patterns for uncommon foods, specific water conditions, or locations demanding particular flies. One is a squid pattern tied on a 3/0 or 4/0 hook. The Glow Squid is a very effective lifelike pattern that is easy to tie.

Another pattern is a bulky one for night fishing, to duplicate bottom fish, cunners, or blackfish. Dan Blanton developed this as the Whistler series. A chunky, full-tied fly, the Whistler is ideal for night fishing and is a good pattern to imitate other big baits. Dan uses a variety of colors: The darker ones are better at night. Tie the Whistler on 2/0 to 4/0 hooks, and make it 3 to 6 inches long.

The Snake Fly is excellent for imitating the worm hatch, sandworms, and even small baitfish, because the tail produces a teasing action, suggesting movement while the fly holds suspended in the water. Make this fly on a small hook, #6 to 1/0, with a body 2 to 7 inches long. And make some bigger flies with 8- to 10-inch-long saddle hackle on 2/0 or 3/0 hooks. I prefer black or a green and orange combination when fishing in estuaries, or hot green, white, or a mixture of both in open water. Also try different blends of olive, or blend purple and pink with black. Like the Deceiver, this fly is a workhorse: Tie it in a slight to medium build to match worms, baitfish, eels, and any food that exudes action.

Crab flies are another special offering that is necessary when fish are feeding deep. Tie them on 2/0 or 3/0 hooks, and make them roughly the size of a half-dollar or silver dollar.

A pattern that looks like a piece of chum, or a chunk of fish, is needed when fishing in a chum slick. These should be chunky flies tied in white or light brown: #1 to 1/0 for a chum pattern, 1/0 to 3/0 for a chunk fly.

For bottom bouncing with few hang-ups, the Clouser Deep Water Flies are ideal. I tie them in several colors and eye sizes, making them 3 to 4 inches long.

Saltwater Fly Hooks

Whether I'm tying exact imitations or basic attractor patterns, I build all my flies on stainless steel hooks. I never leave the barbs up, even when I'm fishing for tarpon, which is the most difficult fish to hook and hold. Crush barbs down with vice grips or pliers before tying up your flies. Barbless hooks have a higher rate of hooking success than barbed hooks, are safer to use, and make the release easier.

The development of better, stronger, and sharper stainless steel hooks has made fishing easier. The old standards like the Mustad 34007 and 34011 are great hooks and still take up a good portion of my fly box, but if I need a stronger hook or a hook that will remain sharp under difficult conditions, there are now other good choices. Tiemco, Gamakatsu, and Daiichi are just a few of the quality hooks available today. For a very short-shanked hook, the Eagle Claw 254SS is my favorite. It's strong and dependable. The best hooks need no sharpening, are very strong, and will withstand abuse like being dragged through sand and still remain sharp for much longer than hooks of lesser quality.

Stainless hooks not only last longer, they also won't tarnish the fly and are a safer hook to use. Out of carelessness I constantly poke myself when handling hooks. With stainless I have never had a problem, but with steel hooks, those on spinning plugs, I've often had to cleanse the wounds. Rusty hooks can cause serious infection; although *any* puncture should be taken care of, stainless hooks are less likely to cause serious problems.

There are several common complaints about stainless hooks: One is they will not rust out of a fish. Mouth-hooked fish that break off, so the biologists say, are not hampered by a single hook—and the hook, especially a barbless one, will work itself free in time. A stainless hook is less likely to infect such a fish. A fish snagged in the gills will probably die if it breaks off with either type of hook, but possibly a deeply hooked fish is better off if you use a steel hook because it will decompose. However, most fish are mouth-hooked, and so few fish perish after breaking off that this mortality rate is not really an issue. The other complaints are that they are not as strong and they dull easily. While this was true of the older stainless hooks and the less expensive ones, the best hooks today are equal to steel hooks in strength and might even be stronger.

I seldom lose fish because hooks have pulled straight. In all such cases I was to blame for using an improper or undersize hook. Most hooks straighten when the point does not drive home, which puts all the pressure on the point, a hook's weakest part. After testing a number of hooks from #6 to 3/0 with a vise and scale, I found that even the less expensive hooks would hold a twenty-pound leader if pulled from the bend. This held true even for long-shanked hooks, which tend to bend easier due to leverage; the Mustad 34011, a light-weight hook, held fine to #2 (this hook in small sizes is for special applications only). Hooks of 1/0 and above took the scale to the bottom—thirty pounds—and would be adequate for all inshore species. The best hooks today will never straighten unless the angler uses a hook that is much too small.

One should choose a hook's size and style for more reasons than just fish size. Fly type and action, leader size, fly size, water conditions, and tackle all influence which hook is best for the task. Smaller hooks penetrate better, and once embedded are less likely to shake free. A hook not driving to the bend, but only catching at the point, will straighten faster because leverage, particularly with long-shanked hooks, will pull the hook straight with less pressure. I have landed a number of big fish on small hooks (#2 to 1/0), using them when fly action is critical. Certain fly patterns require larger hooks; a bigger gap improves hooking. Small, light hooks give some flies superior action, allowing them to be nearly weightless. When not tying surface flies, where weight is a major factor, hooks can run larger, though not oversize. I have landed a number of big stripers, from thirty to nearly fifty pounds, on hooks sized #1 to 4/0. Larger hooks might tear a hole in the fish's jaw, becoming loose at the end of the fight; and larger hooks are much harder to drive home in firm flesh.

Flies used in strong rips and heavy surf require more strength because the tackle is usually heavier and the fish are able to exert more pressure on the tackle. (In most rough conditions, fish strike more aggressively). Yet a 1/0 should handle even these tough conditions. In rolling water a heavier hook has less effect on fly action. In open, calmer waters lighter hooks give better fly action and bring more strikes. Longer-shanked hooks work better when fish are striking short, just missing the fly. They are also better for toothy fish, when a wire leader might spook them.

Keeping Your Hooks Sharp

Keen hooks are important to angling success. There are many ways to sharpen a hook, and perhaps the easiest and fastest is triangulating—filing three sides

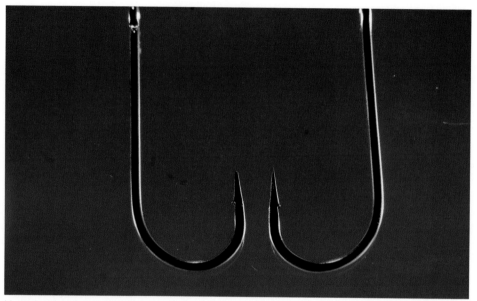

Keep hooks sharp. Note how dull the point is on the hook on the left; the right hook is sharp.

to create a cutting point rather than a round point. Some anglers prefer to file four sides for better penetration.

In *The Scientific Angler,* Paul Johnson mentions an elliptical point, sharpened like a surgical eye suture, with several cutting edges. Paul uses 180-grit Carborundum paper and a jeweler's file to obtain surgically sharp hooks. This degree of sharpness takes time to accomplish, and in some cases is undesirable. A hook with too keen a point might stop against the bone of a fish's jaw, when it should slide off to drive home into the fleshy parts of the mouth. The bony jaw sections of some fish are unhookable, and for these species it is crucial that the hook point glance off the bone and catch the softer mouth tissues. And a longer, thinner point will bend over too easily when fished around rocks or in surf with a gravel bottom.

I prefer a short- to medium-tapered point with three or four cutting edges. A hook need only be sharp enough to catch and stop when drawn across a fingernail (the best way to test the sharpness of your hooks).

Several files are designed specifically for fishermen. A relatively new tool, called the Shur Sharp Sharpener, is the best and fastest sharpening device I've ever used. It consists of two chain-saw files set together, side by side. Several passes with this tool on two sides of a hook's point create a sharp, penetrating, four-sided point. However, a flat mill file, available at any hardware store, will serve adequately as a hook-sharpening tool. This is the ideal file to prepare hook points before getting on the water. Stones and diamond-faced hook-sharpening tools work better in the field—steel files rust too easily.

A Working Saltwater Fly Collection

There are hundreds of basic saltwater patterns, and when you alter color, material length, and dressing bulk, the number of variations rises into the thousands. Though it's easy to do with this wealth of fly choice, don't get caught up in the vanity of having a different fly for each day of the week. I catch 90 percent of my fish on several patterns in four colors, and they're all sized from 3 to 6 inches. If I were forced to use only one pattern for an entire season, that fly would be either a Lefty's Deceiver in white or a white Snake Fly. My second color choice for either would be black. I would have some fishless days with such a fly, but throughout the year, and in most fishing situations, it would be a consistent producer.

Obviously, baitfish in salt water are not as complicated to imitate as are the aquatic insects of the freshwater angler. Even so, saltwater baitfish have characteristics and habits that make them unique. You will increase your fishing success if you learn about the baitfish in your favorite fishing locations and how they behave. In situations where the bait isn't readily visible, watch the local bait fishermen closely. Many bottom anglers are familiar with local baits, and much can be learned from observing what they are using. If you understand your baitfish, you'll be able to use the correct fly and present it properly.

I always prepare a working fly box with fly patterns that match the local bait. When choosing flies, always consider water conditions as well as fish species. I either set up a number of boxes, each depending upon specific needs, or I work from a large storage container from which I prepare a working box. Some flies never leave my box—they are my workhorse patterns. Deceivers, sand eel flies, Snake Flies, slab flies, foam flies, and poppers are consistent fish producers, and although their sizes and colors may change, my working fly box always contains these patterns.

Selected Saltwater Fly Patterns

In this section are patterns for some of the top-producing flies for the North and mid-Atlantic coast. Some were developed for special needs, when a situation arose that demanded a particular fly with specific characteristics. Many of these flies have become all-purpose patterns, and will catch fish in locations that will surprise you. Many more flies are mentioned throughout the text than appear here; to learn more about these patterns and how to tie them, consult the following: *Salt Water Fly Patterns* by Lefty Kreh; *The Book of Fly Patterns* by Eric Leiser; *Saltwater Fly Tying* by Frank Wentink; *Salt Water Flies* by Ken Bay; *Pop Fleyes* by Bob Popovics and Ed Jaworowski; *Saltwater Flies of the Northeast* by Angelo Peluso; *Saltwater Flies* by Deke Meyer; and *Flies for Saltwater* by Dick Stewart and Farrow Allen. Lefty Kreh has also done a tying videotape, *Salt Water Fly Tying,* available through Dark Horse Video.

The following list presents my suggestions for the basic working fly collection of a beginning or traveling saltwater angler. This list is only a starting point and shouldn't be taken as the last word for all situations; each angler must experiment to find the particular flies that will fit all his or her fishing needs. However, I suspect most marine fly rodders will find a number of these flies already in their working boxes, or soon to be added.

Anglers that fish in southern locations that do not have sand eels might carry other fly patterns that match the foods. And in backwater areas, more

---

Saltwater Fly Starter List

10 Deceivers, 4 white, 2 black, 2 yellow, 2 chartreuse; 4 to 6 inches long. Hook size #2 to 2/0.

12 Snake Flies, 3 light olive, 3 black, 2 white, 2 chartreuse, 2 orange and green mix; 4 to 6 inches long. Hook size #2 to 2/0.

6 sand eel patterns, 3 tan over white, 3 purple over white; 3 to 5 inches long. Hook size #1 to 1/0.

3 popping bugs, bright colors, size to match rod and line size. Hook size 1/0 long-shanked.

8 small flies, 2 shrimp, 2 crabs, 2 worm-hatch flies, 2 tiny sand eel flies; 2 to 3 inches long. Hook size #4 to #1.

4 anchovy patterns, 2 tan and white, 2 light green and white; 3 inches long. Hook size #2.

4 big herring flies (Mega Mushy), 2 green and white, 2 tan and white; 8 to 10 inches long. Hook size 3/0 to 4/0.

---

shrimp and crab patterns and smaller baitfish or worm-hatch flies might work better. Areas that have big bait like herring, mullet, or squid might require an entirely different fly setup. The list above is just a selection of basic patterns that work in many locations.

Purchased Flies

Fancy flies will not make you a better angler. Many fly rodders get caught up in the belief that they need something new and ingenious. Stay with the flies that take fish, and use newer and flashier patterns as additions to your arsenal, for special situations. The old standbys are still around for good reason: They work!

Remember that you don't have to tie your flies with the precision of a technical expert; they are not going to the moon. Most anglers take one look at my flies and say, "Boy, they're ugly, but they sure catch fish." And that's what it's all about. I believe that, most of the time, action is more important than good looks. Save the fancy flies for the wall; for fishing success, give me something that breathes in the water.

Professional tyers like Enrico Puglisi, D. L. Goddard, Dave Skok, and Eric Peterson are gifted and can create flies that are works of art—well beyond my skill level. In some cases, depending on the tying skills of the angler, it is better to purchase patterns if you really need quality flies for some fishing conditions, especially if taking a trip that might require special flies. Good flies are like leader material—never skimp, because it can mean the difference between a great day and one that ends in frustration.

Fly care is important, especially if you buy them. Good flies are expensive, but they are worth every penny. Don't just dump them in a box that might crush them or distort their shape. I like hard boxes with foam lining to stick the hook point in. This seems to help me keep the flies somewhat in order. If you have flies that have had their materials crushed, try this trick from D. L. Goddard: Hold the fly with a pair of pliers over a pot of boiling water—the steam will rejuvenate the crumpled fly. I also use this repair for feathers on an arrow. In most cases, it will bring materials like feathers and hair back to life.

Making Your Own Flies

You can increase the durability of your flies by applying epoxy or superglue (the non-water-soluble kind) to the head, and sometimes the body. This also adds weight to patterns that must sink quickly. You can apply epoxy or superglue to your store-bought flies as well. If you want the fly to float high, coat only the head.

Superglue is a good head cement for saltwater flies. It soaks into the wing and tail material, bonding it to the thread and the hook shank. With thin top-water patterns that need extra buoyancy, use the glue sparingly.

Epoxy-bodied flies have a lifelike appearance, and they work well in clear water for fussy fish. But because of their rigid construction, they don't breathe as well in the water, nor do they act as "alive" as some of the standard patterns.

Eyes are important to many patterns, making them look more authentic; this is especially true on large flies, where the eyes are readily apparent. Many companies offer inexpensive clear glass eyes with a black center. It's easy to coat the backsides of these eyes with various shades of bright fingernail polish to come up with just the right effect. To eye a fly without adding weight, paint the eye directly on the pattern's side with nail polish or waterproof paint, using a toothpick as a paintbrush. For sinking flies, use weighted eyes of the appropriate size. Weighted eyes can also add ballast to a bulky buoyant pattern.

I seldom use heavy eyes, only on bigger flies and then nothing over $\frac{3}{16}$ ounce. I would never use heavy eyes on a small fly. I want the fly to hold, suspended in the water column, looking like a live baitfish. Very heavy flies are effective because they add a hopping action to the fly, like a bucktail jig; however, some anglers get into a rut and become one-dimensional, because heavily weighted small patterns dictate how you must retrieve. These anglers cast out and use the same retrieve, never varying the speed of strip length. I prefer neutral-density flies that hold or rise slightly after each pull. Used with a sinking line, these flies move with the flow and look alive even with no retrieve. I like to work a fly with the flow, getting it to swing and then turn up into the current. At times the fly is dead-drifting, and I just add pulls without taking in line. If I'm using a Snake Fly with a bigger head, the fly will nose up after each pull, looking like a crippled baitfish struggling to swim. Gamefish are predators, and predators cannot resist attacking a fleeing or crippled food source.

D. L.'s Crab Fly (D. L. Goddard) Photo page 273

Hook: Mustad 34007 or Tiemco 811S, #4 to #1

Weight: Lead weighted eyes, $\frac{1}{25}$ to $\frac{1}{50}$ oz., tied near the hook eye. The bigger flies need the heavier weight.

Body: Tie sections of tan and light olive sheep fleece onto hook shaft in alternating bands to form the body, and trim to shape.

Crab and shrimp flies. Starting top right going clockwise: Enrico's EP Crab Tan, D. L.'s Gold Bug, D. L.'s Wiggler, Dave Skok's Tan Crab, and D. L.'s Crab Fly.

Eyes: Burn ends of pieces of thirty-pound mono with a butane lighter to form tan balls. Leave eyes plain; they look more natural.

Claws: Olive or tan grizzly feathers cut at quill to form a V-shaped claw, 1 inch long.

Legs: Tips of slender grizzle feathers, 1 inch long.

Antennae: Two black boar bristles or peccary hair, 1 inch long.

Note: Use non-water-soluble superglue or Zap-A-Gap to glue the eyes, claws, legs, and antennae to the body to make the crab's shape come to life.

D. L.'s Gold Bug (D. L. Goddard) Photo page 273

Hook: Mustad 34007 or Tiemco 811S, #4 to 3/0

Tail: Four amber 1¼-inch-long Sili Legs tied at hook's bend.

Weight and Eye: Gold bead-chain eye, $\frac{1}{50}$ or $\frac{1}{80}$ oz., tied in ⅛ inch from hook eye.

Body: Tie in gold Estaz at hook bend and palmer to eye.

Weed Guard: Optional. Two pieces of hard mono tied on top of eyes.

Wing: Thirty to sixty strands of root beer Krystal Flash tied over weed guard, 2 to 3 inches long. The wing should lie over hook point.

Head: Tie off and finish with 5-Minute Epoxy or superglue and color head with red or orange marking pen.

D. L.'s Wiggler (D. L. Goddard) Photo page 273

Hook: Mustad 34007 or Tiemco 811S, #4 to #1

Tail: Four Sili Legs doubled to form eight 1¼-inch-long legs.

Weight and Eye: Gold bead-chain eye, ⅟₅₀ or ⅟₈₀ oz., tied in ⅛ inch from hook eye.

Body: Wrap with Krystal Chenille from hook bend to eyes. Tie in two additional sets of Sili Legs on either side of the eye, again doubled to form eight 1¼-inch-long legs.

Head: Tie off and finish with 5-Minute Epoxy or superglue.

Weed Guard: Optional. Two pieces of hard mono tied on top of eyes.

Tan Crab (Dave Skok) Photo page 273

Hook: Mustad 34007, #4 to #1

Eye and Underwing: Tie in a ⁵⁄₃₂ or ¼ oz. lead eye ¼ inch from the hook eye to bottom of shank so the fly rides inverted. Behind the lead eye, tie in soft tan grizzly hackle fibers, splayed to form a flared wing under and around the hook shaft about ½ inch past the hook bend.

Top Wing: White bucktail with soft brown hackle fibers on top, both splayed over underwing about 1 inch past the hook bend. Tie in the top wing over the lead eye just behind the hook eye. Finish head with 5-Minute Epoxy.

EP Adult Bunker (Enrico Puglisi) Photo page 275

Hook: Gamakatsu SC15, 4/0 to 5/0

Body: Tie in red Silky Fiber at the hook bend, about 1 inch long; this forms the gills and should be at the bottom of the hook shaft. Layer in Ultimate Fiber on both the bottom and top of hook shaft, white on the bottom and either gray, emerald green, sky blue, or yellow on the top, depending on the bait type you want to match and the fishing conditions you expect to encounter. To match a big bunker, make flies about 10 inches long; shorten for smaller baits. Keep layering to the hook eye, and blend in some silver holographic Flashabou to the top section. Add a light section of pink Ultimate Fiber to the fly's midsection on each side from head to tail (this adds that pink highlight to the fly's side that

Large herring and bunker flies. Top to bottom: Enrico's EP Adult Bunker, Dave Skok's Mega Mushy.

most big baitfish have). Trim the front section of the fly to form the head and midsection.

Eyes: Glue on 13.5 mm eyes about ½ inch from the hook eye, and coat head with Zap-A-Gap.

Note: Enrico's Adult Bunker is a tube fly with a tandem hook system, but my tying instructions call for a single hook.

Mega Mushy (Dave Skok) Photo page 275

Hook: Tiemco 600SP or other short-shanked hook, 2/0 to 8/0

Thread: Clear mono, fine

Tail: Pre-tapered white or polar bear Super Hair with Flashabou Mirage on both sides, all tied in mid-shank and coated with Softex or Soft Body glue to just past the hook bend.

Belly and Back: Pre-tapered, blended 12-inch Slinkyfibre and Mega Mushy flash.

Eyes: Size 8 3-D prismatic eyes, held in place with Goop or Zap-A-Dap-A-Goo and finished with 5-Minute Epoxy.

Thick bodied flies. Top to bottom: Tabory's Slab Side, Blanton's Whistler, Blanton's Sar-Mul-Mac.

Tabory's Slab Side Photo page 276

Hook: Mustad 34007, 1/0 to 4/0

Tail: Layered long bucktail or marabou, with some flash mixed in, 3 to 6 inches long. Make the tail wide from the side to suggest a large, flat-sided baitfish.

Eyes: Either glass or lead, but keep the eye near the hook shank, about one-third of the shank length from the hook eye.

Head and Shoulder: Spin deer body hair to form a large, flat-sided head. Hair is trimmed flush to the eye on both sides, leaving the top and bottom tapered longer to the tail. Apply superglue or epoxy to the underside near the eye to balance the fly in water.

Whistler Fly Photo page 276

Hook: Mustad 34007, 2/0 to 4/0

Tail: Thick bucktail and several saddle hackles can be added to the outside of the tail, as can some form of flash. Make the tail 3 to 5 inches long.

Body: Medium to large chenille wrapped between tail and collar.

Collar: Several large neck or saddle hackles palmered to the eyes.

Eyes: Bead chain or lead.

Gurgler (Jack Gartside) Photo page 277

Hook: Mustad 34011, 1/0 to 3/0

Tail: Tie in bucktail and pearl Krystal Flash about one-third of the way from the hook bend so it extends 4 to 6 inches beyond the bend.

Body: Cut a section of segmented closed-cell foam 4 to 6 inches long by ½ to ¾ inch wide, depending on hook size and fly size. Tie in foam at the hook eye, and tie in a saddle hackle matching the tail color—this will form the rib. Secure the foam in four to six places along the hook shaft, stopping at the tail's base about two-thirds down the hook shaft.

Rib: Palmer the saddle hackle along the hook shaft in the same locations as where the foam was tied to the shaft, then tie off at the tail's base.

Shell: Fold foam over shaft to the head and secure just behind the hook eye. The foam should form a collar over the hook eye. Trim foam to leave about ½ inch over the eye. Too large a collar might cause the fly to spin when casting.

Tabory's Pop-Hair Bug Photo page 277

Hook: Mustad 9082S, 1/0 to 3/0

Popper and surface flies. Starting top right going clockwise: Tabory's Surfboard Foam Fly, Tabory's Pop-Hair Bug, Farnsworth's Hard-Bodied Foam Popper, Blados's Crease Fly (tied by Eric Peterson), and Gartside's Gurgler (also tied by Eric Peterson).

Tail: Long bucktail, saddle hackle, or marabou, tied on at least ½ inch from the hook bend. Continue wrapping the hook shank with thread. Make tail 2 to 4 inches long, depending on hook size.

Body: Use either a preformed foam body or cut a perch float in half, make a groove in the bottom, and hollow out the small end so the body will slip over the lump from the tail material. Epoxy the body to the hook shank and paint.

Eye: Paint on, or use stick-on eyes.

Tabory's Surfboard Foam Fly Photo page 277

Hook: Mustad 34011, #1 to 3/0

Tail: Saddle hackle or long bucktail, tied in ½ inch from bend, 3 to 4 inches long.

Body: After tail is fixed to hook, shape surfboard foam to form a body. Many foams are now available for preformed bodies. Cut a groove in the bottom of the body, set it over the hook so the body blends into the tail without leaving a gap, and wrap around the body with tying thread to secure it to the hook shank. Coat the entire body, including the groove, with 5-Minute Epoxy, and paint body after epoxy dries. Apply a second light coat of epoxy after the paint dries. The new single-cell foams do not need epoxy coating.

Eye: Paint on, or use stick-on eyes, before applying the second coat of epoxy.

EP Crab Tan (Enrico Puglisi) Photo page 279

Hook: Gamakatsu SC15, #2

Tail: Tie in several strands of pearl Flashabou Accent, then several small bleached grizzly marabou about 1 inch long to form a flared tail. To the top and bottom of the tail, tie in one orange grizzly marabou about half the size of the first feathers.

Body: Tie in three clear hot orange Sili Legs spaced evenly over the hook shank, then tie sand Fiber 3-D to form the body. The body should be round, with the legs coming out of the body. Just pull the legs aside to trim the body.

Eyes: Tie in $\frac{5}{32}$ oz. lead eyes at the hook eye. Finish with a coat of EP One-Minute Epoxy to keep eyes firm.

Eric's Epoxy Sand Eel (Eric Peterson) Photo page 279

Hook: Mustad 34007 or Tiemco 811S, #4 to 1/0

Body and Tail: Form the main body and tail with pearl Holo Chromosome Flash and white fly fur, with a thin layer of olive Ultimate Fiber mixed with pearl

Polar Flash. This last section should extend about 1 inch beyond the main body and tail. Epoxy the entire body and tail to about ¼ inch past the hook bend.

Eye: Glue on yellow-and-black eye.

Lefty's Deceiver Photo page 279

Hook: Mustad 34007 or 34011, #4 to 3/0

Tail: Six to eight saddle hackles tied at hook bend. Flashabou or Crystal Hair can be added—tie in before the hackles.

Body: Optional on shorter-shanked hooks; longer-shanked hooks need the body—Mylar wrapped over shank, or Mylar tubing slipped over hook shank.

Wing Top and Bottom: Both top and bottom wings are the same. Bucktail, or any hair-type fiber, tied in back of the eye so it extends just beyond the hook bend. Some versions leave the top wing longer.

Eye: Optional. Painted on body.

Note: This fly can be tied in a variety of ways to give different looks.

A good selection of flies. Starting top right going clockwise: Skok's Mushmouth, Lefty's Deceiver, Eric's Epoxy Sand Eel, Soft Foam Popper, Tabory's Snake Fly, EP Crab Tan, and D. L.'s Wiggler for a shrimp pattern.

Mushmouth (Dave Skok) Photo page 279

Hook: Short-shanked hook, #2 to 3/0

Thread: Clear mono, fine

Tail: Pre-tapered white or polar bear Super Hair with metallic Flashabou on both sides, all tied in mid-shank and coated with Softex or Soft Body glue to just past the bend.

Body: Pearl shredded Mylar (such as Angel Hair or Wing N' Flash) for the belly and color of choice of same material for the back, with Softex or Soft Body glue poked into the fibers with a needle.

Eyes: Size 3.5 prismatic, coated with 5-Minute Epoxy.

EP Tuna Killer (Enrico Puglisi) Photo page 281 top

Hook: Gamakatsu SC15, 5/0

Wing and Tail: Layer material to build wing. Start with red Krystal Flash extending just beyond the hook bend. Next, rainbow Flashabou, then a layer each of FisHair starting with polar white, then royal blue, with chartreuse on top. The length of the wing material, except for the red Krystal Flash, should be about 6 to 7 inches long. Tie in a layer of olive Unique Hair over top of wing.

Head and Nose: Slip a section of pearl LA Mylar tubing over the hook from the eye to just past the bend. Tie off the tubing with .004 mono thread at about two-thirds of the shank's length past the eye; let the last third flare, but keep the head tight to form a small nose, like the beak of a halfbeak. Then coat the nose with Zap/CA Thin Formula and 30-Minute Z-Poxy.

Eyes: Stick on 5 mm black-and-white eyes and apply another light coat of epoxy.

Tabory's Glow Squid Photo page 281 top

Hook: Mustad 34007 or Gamakatsu SC15, 2/0 to 3/0

Tail: Layer white, pink, and shrimp Kinkyfiber for tail. Between the pink and shrimp Kinkyfiber, layer pink Comes Alive and hot pink Fluorofibre.

Body: Wrap hook shank with white or tan Dan Bailey's Sapp Body Fur from bend to the hook eye. Tie in six strands of pink or pearl Comes Alive along each side of the body.

Tabory's Snake Fly Photo page 281 bottom

Hook: Mustad 34007 or 34011, #4 to 2/0

Tail: Ostrich herl or saddle hackle, tied near hook bend, 1½ to 4½ inches long.

Squid and offshore flies. Top to bottom: Enrico's EP Tuna Killer, Squid Fly (tier unknown), Tabory's Glow Squid.

Tabory's Snake Flies—a variety of different-style Snake Flies. Using different materials, head sizes, and body thicknesses, you can cover many bait types.

Wing: Two sections of marabou tied about halfway between bend and eye. Leave room for head. Flash can be added, placed between the marabou and the tail. For the best action and for making sparse flies, choose the marabou feathers without webbing.

Head: Spin deer body hair to get good flare. Use fat hairs for best results. Trim head flat on bottom, rounding the top, and leave some hair long for color. Head shape and size will vary depending upon the size and bulk of the fly. The action and density of this fly depends on its head size.

Note: Depending upon the size fly desired, you can make this pattern from 3 to 10 inches long. For making a "worm hatch" fly or tiny baitfish fly, use just marabou for the tail, no wing, with deer body hair for the head. This pattern lends itself to many options.

A small hook size makes this fly very buoyant.

D. L.'s Spearing Fly (D. L. Goddard) Photo page 283
Hook: Mustad 34007 or Tiemco 811S, #2 to 3/0
Body: Wrap with pearlescent thread or pearl body material to form a heavy body.
Wing: Fine white bucktail with a strip of pearl Flashabou on each side. Make wing sparse to extend about two and a half times the hook length.
Head: Mono thread and 5-Minute Epoxy mixed with blue-violet Ultra Glitter.
Eyes: Size 3.5 prismatic, covered in 5-Minute Epoxy.

EP Bay Anchovy, Tan (Enrico Puglisi) Photo page 283
Hook: Gamakatsu SC15, #10
Wing: Several strips of pearl silver EP Sparkle tied just back from the hook's eye. Form the fly's body shape with tan EP-3D Fiber.
Head: Form head with silver Flashabou. Make the head cone-shaped over the tan EP-3D Fiber from the hook eye about halfway down the hook shank.
Eyes: Plastic black-and-white, 4.5 mm. Glue on in the middle of the head.

Eric's Inverted Sand Eel (Eric Peterson) Photo page 283
Hook: Mustad 34011, #2 to 1/0
Body: Mylar tubing slipped over hook and tied in about halfway down the shank and just back from the hook eye.
Wing: Form wing with marabou plumes cut from a feather tied in at the

Small flies—starting top right going clockwise: Enrico's EP Bay Anchovy Tan, D. L.'s Spearing Fly, Tabory's Tiny Baitfish, Small Epoxy Fly (tier unknown), Tabory's Small Streamer (with wire bite guard tied into fly), Eric's Inverted Sand Eel, Eric's Epoxy Sand Eel, and Eric's Small Baitfish Fly.

bottom, then layer in white bucktail, and tan with dark green bucktail on top. Between the first and second layer, add some pearl Polar Flash.

Eric's Small Baitfish Fly (Eric Peterson) Photo page 283

Hook: Mustad 34007 or Tiemco 811S, #4 to 1/0

Body and Tail: Form with ostrich herl, Holo Chromosome Flash, and fly fur. Coat with Softex to form a core that extends about ¼ inch past the hook bend. Blend different colors to match different baits.

Wing: Tie in just past hook eye. Fly fur on top, bottom, and both sides to blend over the core.

Eye: Glue on yellow-and-black eye.

Tabory's Worm-Snake Fly Photo page 284

Hook: Short-shanked hook, #4 to #1

Wing: Tie a section of red, orange, or black marabou, 2 to 3 inches long, to middle of hook shaft.

Worm hatch flies—starting top right going clockwise: Tabory's Worm-Snake Fly (top) is tied with just a marabou tail and (bottom right) is tied with ostrich herl tail; Page Rogers's Worm Fly, Paul Dixon's Worm Hatch Fly.

Collar and Head: Spin a section of elk or deer body hair that matches swing color between wing and hook eye. Leave the hairs that extend back as a collar, and trim the front section to form the head. Trim bottom flat. Finish with 5-Minute Epoxy.

Refer to Eric's Sand Eel as a basic fly recipe for all sand eel patterns. The tail of a sand eel fly can be many different materials, and the body can be a simple wrap of yarn to mono over flash to epoxy. The important feature of the fly is a slim silhouette.

Epoxy Sand Eel Photo page 285

Hook: Mustad 34007 or 34011, #4 to 3/0

Tail: Bucktail, FisHair, thin saddle hackle, Flashabou, Crystal Hair, or a combination of several. Begin tie at hook bend if tying a separate body, or start tie at head and use a clear vinyl wrap or thread over material, securing it to the hook shank for the body.

Sand eel flies—starting top going clockwise: Tabory's Nose Down Sand Eel, Eric's Sand Eel, Tabory's Deceiver Sand Eel (adapted from Lefty Kreh), Tabory's Epoxy Sand Eels in two sizes (the one on the bottom left is about 2 inches long).

Body: When tied separately from tail, use wool or Mylar tubing.

Eye: Painted on body.

Note: When beginning at the head, either make the body epoxy or wrap a vinyl strip over all the body material to hold the body together, then coat with vinyl cement. A dark top, such as peacock herl, can be added. Body and tail should be thin.

The following flies are not pictured.

Clouser Minnow

Hook: Mustad 34007, #4 to 2/0

Eye: Tie on lead eyes ($\frac{5}{32}$ or $\frac{6}{32}$) to the hook top to make the fly ride with the hook point up. Locate the lead eye along the hook shank a quarter to a third of the way back from the hook eye.

First Wing: Tie a hairwing on top of hook shank, laying the hair over the hump made by the eye. Secure the wing to both sides of the lead eye so it extends along the shaft.

Second Wing: Tie in hair to the bottom of the shank, stopping at the eye with the wing laying over the eye and flaring along the bend. Make the fly 2 to 3 inches long. Bucktail is often used for the wing, but marabou works well and gives more action.

Note: Flash can be added between the wings.

Sand Eel Fly, Floating (Eric Peterson)

Hook: Mustad 34007, #6

Body: Round section of single-cell foam, ³⁄₁₆-inch diameter, 1⅜ inches long.

Tail: Split about ½ inch in one end of the foam body. Inside the split, glue a section of hair with superglue to form the tail.

Head: Make another ½-inch split in the other end of the foam body and glue in the hook.

Eyes: Glue on big plastic eyes near the hook bend—the eyes should be one-third the body width.

Note: The fly should be slim, but able to float high.

Shrimp Fly

Hook: Mustad 34007, #8 to #4

Tail: Bucktail or calf tail, 1½ inches long.

Body: Spin light gray deer body hair on hook shank. Trim to a shrimp shape, leaving short side wings for better buoyancy, but leave the fly shape straight.

PART FOUR

Gamefish, Their Habits, and How to Release Them

19

Popular Gamefish and Their Habits

A fish's habits not only affect how you fish for it, but also affect *your* habits, sometimes changing your lifestyle for short periods, or for life. So engrossed are bass hounds with wee-hour tides that they become obsessed, fishing all night long. Families, jobs, and other interests fall by the wayside. And in recent years, bluefin tuna have turned anglers into psychopaths.

I have a friend who will remain nameless—he might get into big trouble if his family saw his name used in such a manner. I'll call him Tuna Nut. Well, Tuna Nut becomes unglued with any mention of bluefin tuna. If there is any possibility of getting into tuna, he's there. He has a house on Cape Cod and a boat large enough to chase fish, but the boat is on a trailer and launching it alone is more than a chore—it's just too big for one man, his age, to handle. Yet he will almost kill himself getting that boat in the water, and then run for miles just to follow a faint hunch of bluefin. One of the biggest problems is that Tuna Nut needs a hip replacement and has a very bad back. Both problems would make any sane man not even think about trying to chase, fight, and land a big tuna—and try to do it alone? Insane!

Over the last five years, Tuna Nut's job has taken a backseat, his health continues to decline, and his family wonders if he will come home alive. My wife and I get e-mails about where the fish are and how far he needs to run, and we just wonder what he is thinking. Given the way tuna move and how fickle they are, it can be tough to find fish with day-old information, but Tuna Nut will chase a week-old lead like it was two hours old. To his good fortune, he has found a friend to go with, so at least there are now two anglers on the boat. And with the coming of a new tuna season, although he badly needs to address his medical problems—he can hardly walk—Tuna Nut will be back out chasing the fickle bluefin.

I know other anglers, striper hounds, that are the same way. They fish all night and still try to stumble through work just to do the same thing the next night. I must admit that in my younger years, I was that bad.

I remember one group of Pennsylvania anglers that would go off the deep end for several weeks each autumn—sleeping, eating, and living around fish activity. This group would travel to Martha's Vineyard to fish the derby. They were so intent on catching fish and winning the derby that they would have breathed less if that would have helped them find more fish. Bad weather, darkness, hunger, or lack of sleep never dampened their quest to catch fish. They fished *hard*.

One night—their last on the Island, in fact—I fished with them at Lobsterville Beach, and the fishing was good. Around midnight we gathered around the cars, talking about tackle and the fine fishing we had just experienced. I was ready to hit the sack, but not these guys. They were planning to fish all night, saying they could sleep in the car on the drive home. I couldn't really blame them, because for most of them it was their only chance in a year's time to fish the sea. Living so far from salt water, they needed to pack a lot of fishing into several weeks.

It is one of the problems with chasing fish: Their habits do not always fit into our lifestyle. Part of trying to find time to fish is determining the best times to fish. I have always liked morning; first light or just before is a productive fishing time. And most anglers have time to fish before work, especially in spring and summer, when the sun rises early. But planning time is just one factor in catching fish—we must also know how and why they feed.

Knowing how a fish responds to different water conditions, bait, time of day, or time of year, as well as the way a fish feeds, swims, and lives, helps us determine the best way to fish for it. Knowing a fish's habits makes finding and catching that fish easier. But do not count on a fish always doing what it is supposed to—as with most encounters in nature, expect the unexpected.

Different saltwater species prefer certain types of water and bait and have favorite times to feed because these periods allow easier feeding in a suitable environment. Bass love to feed in rolling surf; bonito prefer open, sand-free water. Some areas do offer a variety of fishing opportunities. Water conditions, bait type, time of year, and time of day all influence tackle choice, fly selection, type of retrieve, and which spot within the location is best.

Throughout the chapters of the first section of this book, I inserted some miscellaneous basic information on some species' habits. In this chapter we will take a more detailed look at the habits of some gamefish and what makes them tick. If two fish are similar (like bonito and albacore), I will discuss them together, for even fish of different families have similarities.

Tides, though significant in fishing, are more important to the location than to specific species. Fish feed in all types of water, and moving water is generally most productive. But to say a certain tide is best for any one species is absurd. Tide makes the conditions in one spot good or bad, and the fish come to feed in these conditions or not. The same holds true for wind and weather.

Remember that fish are, well, fish, and unlike humans, who live to eat, they eat to live. Some saltwater fish need a constant source of energy just to exist. Stream and river trout live a different life; food is served to them from a constant flow—certain lies in some pools have permanent residents. These ideal locations keep the same fish year after year, sometimes for their entire lives, because they offer feeding with little effort. Saltwater fish are not so lucky. They must work for dinner, at times swimming miles to find food. Some locations do offer easier feeding, but never the luxury of sipping surface-floating insects. The only feeding conditions that are similar are hatches of worms, shrimp, or crabs that give saltwater gamefish easy feeding. But these events are sporadic and do not provide a long-term food source—they still must constantly hunt for food. This need to hunt for food makes unlike fish feed together in the ocean. In many cases, conditions have more to do with the way a fish feeds than does its species. Although two species may swim or eat differently, they still will feed on the same baits and they will still hit the same fly. They are fish—not rocket scientists. Too many anglers get hung up on theory, believing they need special tackle and techniques for different phases of fishing. This may be true at times, but stay with the basics, then go to a bag of tricks if it proves necessary. First, be an angler.

Striped Bass

The most popular saltwater gamefish is the striped bass, *Morone saxatilis*. It is often called rock or rockfish in the southern states—Delaware and below. The species is distinguished by seven or eight dark stripes (hence its other popular name, linesider) running along its powerful elongated body, and it has a separate spiny dorsal fin and a wide, thick-based tail. The color varies from a dark olive green to blue-gray back, blending to a white silvery underside. Fish in clear, light sandy areas tend to be lighter in color, while ones from darker rocky locations are deeper in shade.

The striper's heavy skin, hard scales, large fins, and large tail make the fish ideally suited for feeding in rough rolling water. These fish can swim under and through stormy water with ease. Bass and bluefish are the only two fish in the Northeast capable of feeding in heavy surf, and the striper is far more aggressive in penetrating the white water—only storm surf will drive the fish off because of sandy water.

Best Waters to Fish for Striped Bass

Because they are able to tolerate the most diverse water conditions, stripers have the widest distribution of all the saltwater gamefish species. Bass feed comfortably in the shallows, in rolling surf, and in the confines of a backwater: Expect bass to feed anywhere bait swims. Favorite holding waters are deep sections or rocky structure, any place the fish can stay undisturbed while they sit waiting for the next feeding time. A channel, even with boat traffic, holds bass if it is deep enough; loca-

The dark stripes along the side and sharp dorsal fin are characteristics of the striped bass.

tions of 20 feet or deeper at low tide are ideal. Stripers do stay in shallower places when waiting for a tide change to feed, but usually not for long periods.

Stripers can feed in water so turbulent that the novice would never think to fish it. They will actually flow with an incoming wave right up onto a beach, chasing bait, with their backs out of the water. However, it's the way they feed in rolling white water that makes them unique. (Never consider any water unfishable. Even waves over a shallow bar can hold fish unless that water is saturated with sand.) Stripers can feed in knee-deep white rolling water. Likewise, the strong rips that a bass can swim in will surprise the beginner. Stripers hold like trout, waiting to ambush prey from pockets along a rip. No rip is too small or too fast for them to feed in.

Other than in moving water, which is a favorite feeding location of all gamefish, bass feed by trapping bait against a shoreline or in a back eddy, or by attacking from below in deep water. Although they are slower-swimming than most other saltwater gamefish, stripers strike quickly and are able to turn and move in tight quarters. Using the powerful tail and large fins to accelerate rapidly, they are positive strikers, and the large mouth misses little that comes into range.

How Striped Bass Feed

Linesiders are both surface and subsurface feeders, particularly in low water. They do not "blitz" as much as bluefish, but when they do, it's wild fishing. Bass are masters of white water, feeding in rolling water other species could not survive in. This fascinating manner of dining makes the striper special. At times of heavy feeding, it will hit anything that moves. Yet with certain baits, such as sand eels and spawning worms, they can be very selective. When choosing flies, even for heavily feeding fish, size is the most important consideration.

Lacking large teeth, stripers usually take big baits by grabbing the head first, using a strong grip to hold and crush the prey. The large head allows them to inhale small bait, pulling it from several inches away, into the mouth with suction created from the gill plates. When taking a fly, stripers seem to give only a slight pull on the line. Don't strike too soon. Let the fish inhale the fly first. Fish are missed by striking too soon. Striped bass also react to poppers this way—swimming under the lure and dragging it down with a chugging sound. The strike may be explosive, but do not react to the sight or sound—wait to feel the take. To hook a striper successfully, let it hook itself. Many baits are sharp and bony, and bass generally grab, clamping down on their prey. The lure's feel does not bother them, as it does a trout, so there are few rejections. Wait until you feel the fish take the fly before you strike.

Stripers have a unique way of feeding that is uncommon for northern fish—they stand on their heads to grub bait from the bottom. Southern flats fish do this all the time, nosing food from the sand. Watching striped bass in low water, their tails flailing in the air, is a wild sight. I have witnessed fifty-pound fish performing this feat. They use this method to pull sand eels from their beds, and are hard to fool when feeding in this manner.

Best Time of Day to Fish for Striped Bass

Even large bass can turn up at any time in unexpected locations. Looking for small fish in Pleasant Bay on Cape Cod, I once took a fifty-two-pound bass on light spinning gear. The fish was holding on a mussel bar in 4 feet of water at 7:30 on a bright, calm morning. It rushed the small needlefish I cast, leaving a wake that looked like a sea serpent made it. On the first pass it missed the lure, but the next cast took the fish. I use spinning tackle, or the aid of a spin fisherman, to research water; this was one time it backfired, for the fish would have taken a fly. Bass offer this type of excitement, for they are unpredictable, and many good fishing spots go unnoticed because anglers are unwilling to divert from the norm.

Night and low-light periods are usually the most productive time for bass, particularly in the hot days of summer. Being a morning person, I prefer the hours before dawn for several reasons. One is that I'm alert, but mainly there is less fishing activity because most anglers are still in the sack. All-night angling is the best way to fish for bass, but early morning offers ideal fishing, with less hours to be invested. Both morning and evening as the light changes are the optimum times to fish, for the changing light confuses the baitfish, making easier feeding for most gamefish. Dark, rainy, overcast days are nearly as good as night for stripers: Fish them with confidence.

How Striped Bass Fight

Although stripers are not fast runners, the big ones are capable of powerful runs, using current and wave action to elude their captors. Good-size fish generally make one long run—and in a rip, several-hundred-yard runs are possible. But the run generally weakens the fish, and prompt landing helps keep the bass from regaining its strength for another run.

In a surf line, bass use the wash to aid the struggle, and wear down the tippet. Patience is needed when the fish is in the backwash. Use controlled pressure, because the fish combined with the water's force will overtax the leader. Slow, steady tension is the best method, and be ready to give ground if the fish surges with the wash.

Stripers are not known as jumpers; they do, however, thrash on the surface after being hooked. This is another time when the angler must show restraint, applying minimum pressure and allowing the fish to run—a thrashing fish might roll on the leader, cutting it with its armor plating. On occasions a jump or two will delight the angler, especially in shallow water—but tarpon this species is not.

Special Features of Striped Bass

The dorsal fin and back edges of the gill plates are sharp, capable of puncturing or cutting. Dorsal spines are not only keen but also toxic: Avoid contact with them. If keeping a larger fish, handle it by the upper section of the gill plate, where it joins the chin. Handle all stripers, even large ones, by the lower lip and support them with both hands when lifting. Grab smaller fish by the lower jaw, for their mouths have no real teeth, just a coarse sandpaper-like finish. Return all fish gently and quickly to the water. When releasing large fish from a boat, use a net and avoid bringing the fish aboard—unhook, revive, and release in the water. Revive by grasping the tail and slowly forcing the fish back and forth in the water. This forces water through the gills while allowing the fish to rest. Let the fish swim away—don't just drop it.

Since small bass do not have sharp cutting teeth, shock leaders are unnecessary when fishing for them. But use a shocker for large fish, because line wear and strain might occur after fighting for an extended period. A heavy shock tippet is overkill—I prefer thirty-pound test. Anything heavier only takes away from fly action, and in calm, clear water may decrease the number of strikes. In calm, clear conditions, a straight tippet is a better choice if fish are being fussy, for there are times when bass do become leader-shy. If casting to feeding fish without success, a lighter leader might make the difference.

Best Baits for Striped Bass

Any bait that swims, walks, or crawls is food for bass; they are versatile feeders, sometimes trying to eat things nearly as large as themselves. I once took a 14-inch fish on a 10-inch swimming plug. Without the presence of schooling bait, bass are content to eat whatever is available: crabs, cunners, small blackfish, and worms. Any bass hound knows how well eels work. Bigger baits generally attract big fish, but if bass are feeding on tiny foods, the large fish will go for small offerings. The striper's fondness for sand eels gives the fly rodder an opportunity to catch a nice fish on a small fly.

Although aggressive in their feeding, stripers can be selective, particularly with certain baits, which means fly length and body shape must be precise. Sand eels and spawning worms are classic examples of baits that make fish fussy; they may require not only close imitation, but also proper fishing technique. However, a totally different offering is worth a try if other methods are not working—bass may single out bigger bait when feeding on small foods.

When bass *are* on oversize baits—bunker, eels, squid, or mackerel—use the biggest fly possible. Or try a good-size popper, one that makes a hefty splash— enough commotion might overcome the small size. The fly angler must sell the pop, not the champagne bottle.

Best Time of Year to Fish for Striped Bass

Forty-eight degrees Fahrenheit is the temperature that nudges bass toward slow, deep feeding. Lying dormant much of the winter in large sanctuaries like the Hudson and Chesapeake Bay river systems, they first become active as the water reaches the high forties, but temperatures of fifty-five to sixty-four are peak feeding times.

Arriving in southern sections in mid- to late April, and mid- to late May above Cape Cod, the stripers' appearance varies each season. June brings the hot spring action from Montauk, New York, to Cape Cod—subtract two weeks farther north, add two weeks farther south. Fall feeding hits its peak along the Maine coast in early September, drifting south like a slow-moving snowball, gaining in size till mid-November. Along the New York coast the fish separate; some head into the Hudson River, while others continue south to the Chesapeake. Groups of fish linger, bringing fishing for the hardy angler until mid-December. Block Island has some runs of huge fish after Thanksgiving, as does Montauk, but only the hardiest souls enjoy it. Good runs of mixed fish also occur along New Jersey's shores into mid-December.

The fall run is unquestionably the best time to take bass along the coast. There are locations, "pockets," that at other times can be every bit as good as fall fishing because of ideal conditions. But the late-year migration erupts along the shore, affording everyone good fishing.

Striped bass offer fishing not witnessed in other locations. Their feeding habits make them ideal fly-rod fish. Working as they do along the surf line, next to structure, or up on a flat, bass allow even the wading angler, using just a short cast, to take a big fish. Few species around the world provide this opportunity. And compared to all other fish, more saltwater fly rodders fish for bass because they appear in so many different types of water. Though they lack the tuna's run or the bonefish's ghostly qualities, stripers are king, because they are "stripers."

Bluefish

"If bluefish grew to the size of bluefin tuna nothing could stand before it in the oceans of the world," writes A. J. McClane in *McClane's New Standard Fishing Encyclopedia*. This describes perfectly how bluefish live and feed: voraciously. They are one of the most aggressive-feeding fish in the ocean. Even juvenile "snappers" are savage feeders, growing an inch a week from midsummer to early fall. This is what makes the bluefish a wonderful fly-rod fish: It feeds so

Bluefish have a bright silvery blue-green side and sport a mean look.

much. And the bluefish rates high as a fighter. Though not known as a long runner, in the right water it will make good runs, and jumps are not uncommon. For its size, the bluefish's power is incredible.

The bluefish, *Pomatomus saltatrix,* often called chopper, has a slighter build than the striper both in width and depth. It tends to be bigger-shouldered in the fall, yet not as round, with less belly. The lines are straighter than those of a bass, tapering to a powerful, forked, thick-based tail giving speed and power. The slightly pointed front end has a protruding, toothy lower jaw—giving the fish a fierce look. The first dorsal fin has seven to eight sharp spines; the second dorsal fin is long, starting from about mid-body and tapering to the tail, with a matching lower fin. Bluefish range in color from blue-green on the back to silver-white on the underside. Akin to bass, their color varies with the environment—individuals are lighter-shaded in clear, sandy-bottomed areas. A closer look will reveal light shades of yellow and several shades of iridescent pink on the back and sides. These iridescent shades appear on bass as well, and only the good taxidermists capture it.

Bluefish now range from Maine to Florida, but they keep working farther north. In the mid-1960s they were infrequent visitors to New Hampshire and

Maine, but by the mid- to late eighties there were good numbers of fish up north. Of late, however, their numbers have declined. When they are plentiful throughout their range, bluefish are a popular and willing gamefish.

Best Waters to Fish for Bluefish

Like bass, blues frequent most waters, and only sandy water or too much freshwater mixed with the salt drives them out. Most rivers hold good concentrations of blues, unless heavy rains keep the fish from entering. Otherwise, they feed in all waters, preferring strong rips near deep water. Choppers are bolder than striped bass, feeding all day and venturing into shallow waters at any time. They do work the wash, feeding in the first wave, and sometimes run up the beach with their backs out of the water, but not as regularly as bass do.

Open water finds bluefish finning on top, primarily in the spring, and these fishing conditions can be great. The fish are visible on calm days as they spook from boat wakes. Rocky shorelines are also ideal in midsummer, with fish occupying bays, sometimes milling around large rocks right near shore. Both instances find the fish spooky, indicating a possible link to spawning, for these are the only times bluefish hold for prolonged periods in quieter water.

Fish congregate in large bays and sounds, holding there all season. These areas must provide deep water, 30 feet or more, to keep bluefish for prolonged stays. Once in these waters, they move around feeding, following bait for the easiest meal. Any location that would hold choppers for an extended period needs ample bait—feeding a bluefish is harder than feeding a linebacker.

The teeth of a bluefish are sharp, and the jaws are extremely strong.

How Bluefish Feed

In a feeding frenzy bluefish can turn water to a bloody froth—the sight and sound is awesome. One beach in Florida witnessed several feeding sprees of bluefish so violent that people in the water were attacked. A bluefish would never try to eat a person, but it will strike at movements when a frenzy occurs. This is why fishermen are never bitten, because they remain still and don't splash around as a swimmer would when running for the shore.

Blues and bass frequently dine together, and the bluefish's frantic feeding commotion excites the bass. Many times big bass start feeding because of the competition caused by the bluefish.

Rather than holding in one location, bluefish circle, attacking in packs. I once watched a school feeding off Nauset Beach on Cape Cod. From my camper's roof I observed them cornering bait next to shore. The fish would swim in, all facing the same way, then some would break from the school and attack. There were times when the group disappeared, only to appear again, repeating the routine. When facing shore the bluefish would hit aggressively, but when facing away they were reluctant to strike. Bluefish use the cornering method to trap bait, and once it's pinned, the attack begins.

Bluefish frequently feed on small gamefish. Along the Outer Banks beaches of North Carolina, they drive weakfish right onto the beach, and many of the frantic trout wash onto shore. Blues regularly bottle up members of the herring family along a beach or drive them into coves and harbors, feeding so violently that some baitfish die from lack of oxygen. Bluefish work schools of bunker in open water, and on a calm day the sound is like a wave breaking. This noise travels some distance, helping to lead anglers to the feeding fish. (Bass also feed in this manner.)

With other baits—sand eels, shiners, and crabs—blues can be as subtle as bass. At night the strike might be so slight, you would swear it was not a bluefish. In a feeding frenzy bluefish strikes are hard; otherwise, it's difficult to judge the fish by the strike.

Blues attack from the rear, biting their prey rather than swallowing it whole—although they do at times take small bait intact. This is why blues are hooked on the tail hooks of multi-hooked plugs, while bass are generally caught on the front hooks. Bluefish cut baits to pieces, eating the chunks. The reason other fish feed under feeding schools of blues is to pick up the sinking pieces. Sometimes blues nip at the tail of a fly several times before getting the hook.

Never strike at the sight of a bluefish. Wait to feel the hit. A bluefish slashing at a popper or surface fly is an exciting event. Some anglers might try to hook the fish before it has the lure, taking the fly away. As with bass, waiting to feel the take hooks more fish. At night, or when fishing subsurface, strike as you would a bass, with a straight pull of the stripping hand.

Best Time of Day to Fish for Bluefish

Expect to catch choppers at all times of the day or night, regardless of brightness, boat traffic, water conditions, or depth. They feed whenever possible, even driving bait into a crowded yacht basin on sunny afternoons in midsummer. The best times for shore or shallow-water fishing is during low light or at night. Having had so many encounters with blues at different times, I always count on seeing them. Isolated locations are better for daylight fishing because the fish are spooky if not feeding heavily, especially in low water.

How Bluefish Fight

Bluefish are fierce brawlers. But unlike bass, they are not long-distance runners. The larger ones will make decent runs—and in shallow water they can make the drag scream. But it's their strength and stamina that is so unbelievable; blues are surprisingly powerful. The large forked tail and flat sides give them incredible pulling and holding power. In rips, a bluefish might seem stuck to the bottom, for lifting them is difficult. The first bluefish will shock a sweet-water angler, for he or she will expect such a strong fish to be much larger.

Bluefish are best when caught in shallow water; they make good runs and numerous jumps. Without deep water to dog in, they must fight in the open, which brings out their best battling skills. Lifting them is work in deep water, requiring time and muscle, particularly in current, where blues can hold stubbornly and make you labor for every foot of line.

Special Features of Bluefish

The bluefish's teeth and biting power are incredible. Big ones can cut a two-pound bunker in half and break the tail on a plastic plug. Your flesh will offer little resistance, so remember to keep fingers away: Use pliers to remove hooks. A bluefish can see as well out of water as it can in, and bites can be aimed accurately. The snapping jaws can easily cut mono to fifty-pound, sometimes on the hit. Wire is best when blue fishing, but long-shanked hooks will suffice if working mixed fish where some species are leader-shy. Expect to lose a few flies, because some fish might take the lure deep or from the front.

Other than their mouths, bluefish have few weapons. The dorsal fin has smallish spines, but they are not as dangerous as those of the striper. There are no sharp gill plates or spines on the lower fins to worry about. Except for the lethal mouth, blues are easier to handle than are bass.

Best Baits for Bluefish

Bluefish prefer schooling baits, probably because they are so abundant; with their large appetites, ample food is necessary. Blues do feed on small baits, and they will grub the bottom for food, but large amounts of bait keep them feeding hard in one location. Sand eels are favorites of blues of all sizes, but the bigger fish prefer to feed on large baits. Spearing are great shallow-water baits, bringing blues into shore in low light. Deep-water baits are squid, mackerel, herring, and bunker, plus other schooling foods.

Best Time of Year to Fish for Bluefish

Choppers are thought to be warmer-water fish compared to bass; however, there seem to be several subspecies of bluefish that tolerate water as cold or colder than bass will. I have taken bluefish above Cape Cod in November. Feeding starts with water temperatures in the high fifties, with the mid-sixties ideal temperatures, generating good feeding.

Starting in the Carolinas around the first of March, bluefish move northward, following the bass migration up the coast, feeding as they go. Some schools peel off from the large group, staying in specific locations all season, as long as there is ample food. Bluefish summer from Virginia to Maine, with some schools holding in the bays and sounds while others roam the open waters out to blue water.

Fall brings the best fishing, and like bass, bluefish feed heavily as the water temperature drops and the days shorten. The late-season runs bring hot fishing as the gamefish start their journey south. Maine can be hot by mid-August, with Cape Cod, then Nantucket and the Vineyard holding fish until late-October storms drive the heavy concentrations south. The runs of fish at Race Point, Cape Cod, and Great Point, Nantucket, are something to behold, and although they're not always fishable with a fly, the action is fantastic.

Moving southward, bluefish feed from Rhode Island, running the Long Island shores, along New Jersey, meeting with the fish flowing from the Chesapeake Bay to descend upon the Carolinas in late November. Thanksgiving brings thousands of people to the Outer Banks for the annual bluefish run, but in the heat of a blitz, fly fishing is impossible due to the crowds. It's best for fly rodders to fish another week and work less-popular beaches.

The blue's insatiable appetite makes it ideal fly-rodding fare. In shallow water it offers the thrill of a jumping bonefish. Its powerful, never-ending fight will satisfy any angler. Tackle dealers love them because bluefish destroy so much gear—anglers love them for the same reason. Experiencing a good bite of a seven- to fifteen-pound bluefish is as exciting as any fishing in the world. But there is one difference—no $3,000 to $5,000 price tag.

Weakfish

Weakfish, *Cynoscion regalis,* is the trout of the sea, for when feeding in small creeks, its habits are similar to stream-born trout. *Cynoscion regalis,* also called the gray weakfish or squeteague from Rhode Island north, and trout or gray trout from Delaware south, do resemble trout with their large back fins. The body shape is that of a lean striper with a thinner, slightly forked tail. The mouth is large and lined with small sharp teeth, with several large canine

Here is a nice weakfish taken by Captain Bill Hoblitzell. The troutlike appearance and big canine teeth make this gamefish a special catch.

fangs along the front. The fish is brightly colored with a greenish blue to olive back fading to a mixture of copper, lavender, light green, and purple along its sides. The underside is a bright silvery white, with the same touches of iridescence scattered along the body that are found in bass and blues. Dark spots dot the upper portion of its body, giving it a trouty look.

The weakfish's range is south of Cape Cod to Florida. The two best North Atlantic locations are Peconic Bay to Gardiners Bay on Long Island in New York, and the Chesapeake Bay. During good years, runs of fish are found throughout the range, but these two areas concentrate the fish during spawning in the spring.

Best Waters to Fish for Weakfish

Shallow-water weakfishing is by far the most fun. Small creeks, flats, and shallow rips offer a pure fly-fishing adventure. Weaks feeding in small water is an experience every fly rodder should enjoy. It's light-tackle fishing at its best.

Other places to try are shallow reefs, shorelines, rolling surf, and still water. Many of the same waters that hold bass have weakfish, but they rarely work the surf line the way a bass does. They are not the powerful swimmer the striper is, and stay outside the first wave. Only when driven by bluefish, as occurs on the Outer Banks, do weakfish venture into the first wave, and this is only for survival. Weaks do work rocky shores, but prefer sand or hard, level bottoms.

Deeper waters, rips over bars, and reefs will hold weakfish if there is enough bait. Deep cuts, river mouths, and holes in bays and sounds might contain fish throughout the summer.

How Weakfish Feed

Weakfish feed in many of the same locations as bass, and the two species are frequently caught together with the same fishing methods. When dining in a small creek, weakfish take up feeding stations, holding to let the current bring food. A telltale pop hints that a weakfish is working a section of water. Bass feed like this, but less frequently. Weakfish will hold in one location for some time, and are one of the few saltwater gamefish species that repeatedly feed this way.

Weaks do sip food right on top, but I have never taken one with a popper, though a slow-worked popper at night would probably work. Sipping most of the time means the fish are feeding on shrimp or on baitfish as it floats near the surface. Weakfish do not have the speed, teeth, or biting power of a bluefish or the holding strength of a bass's mouth. They impale big baits with the large canine front teeth; smaller food is taken whole.

A weakfish's take is similar to that of a striper: a slow tightening of the line. And also like stripers, striking too quickly lessens the chances of setting the hook. Weaks are deliberate feeders, much like trout, and are not as spontaneous as a blue or bonito. They do at times strike hard when feeding on baitfish, hooking themselves in the process. But in most other situations, let the fish take the fly before striking.

I have never witnessed weakfish "blitzing," driving bait as bluefish do, although I have fished in heavy concentrations of feeding weakfish, with numbers of breaking fish working all around. Yet never was there panic. Weakfish do herd bait, but they do not work as a pack, as do other gamefish, attacking to create confusion. Feeding in pods when working small waters, they become more competitive when there are larger numbers of them. Larger schools are generally found in deeper areas, feeding in moving water. When finding big groups in the shallows, fishing, as with most gamefish, is easier because of competition. When not competing, weakfish can be selective feeders.

Best Time of Day to Fish for Weakfish

Small-creek fishing is strictly a nighttime game. Only on rare occasions have I taken weaks in shallow water when it was bright, and then mostly in the afternoon. Sometimes during periods of heavy feeding, weakfish will continue working into first light, but this is infrequent. The first morning call of a bird ordinarily spells the end to fishing. Unlike other gamefish that turn on in the shallows at first light, weakfish head for deeper waters to feed.

In water depths of over 10 feet, weakfish are catchable at any time and feed readily throughout the day. Find moving water over a reef or bar or through a cut, and weaks can be found feeding. Ocean beaches with wave action might have daytime feeding, particularly in the fall when the weakfish, bass, and blues mix. This, however, can be out of fly-tackle reach.

How Weakfish Fight

Weakfish are not weak, as the name implies, though they do have delicate sections along the mouth's corner that can tear, leaving a large hole. This might result in a lost fish because the hook could fall out. The roof and tongue areas are firm and hold hooks well, but compared to the striper, the weakfish's mouth is soft. This is the reason most anglers use less pressure, while keeping a good bend in the rod, for weakfish. The bend softens the strain and eliminates slack line.

Weakfish are head-shakers. When hooked they give several pumps before running. The small fish keep head-thumping right until landing, and if hooked in one of the soft areas, this shaking can throw the hook free. Not great fighters compared to other saltwater fish, weaks are not chumps either, and will fight hard for their freedom. Fish in the seven- to ten-pound range give nice runs—not fast, but respectable. When hooked on moderate tackle they are fine fly-rod fish—certainly stronger than any trout I've taken.

Special Features of Weakfish

Other than several big teeth in the front section of the mouth, which the angler must be wary of, weakfish are easy to handle. They have no spines, and without powerful jaws there is no danger from a bite; however, the teeth will cause punctures. Handle the fish by gently gripping behind the head when releasing, or by grabbing the gill plate if keeping the fish. Nets make landing easier from shore and boat.

Best Baits for Weakfish

Small baits are ideal. Classic fly rodding can occur when weakfish are dining in the shallows on shrimp and small baitfish—spearing and sand eels, worms and crabs. They do feed on numerous larger baits—squid, herring, bunker—but the smaller foods are best suited to fly tackle. When working deeper waters, fish different patterns until the proper one is determined. Long sand eel flies are usually my first choice for weakfish in deeper waters.

Best Time of Year to Fish for Weakfish

The spring run begins along the Northeast coast in the latter part of April to mid-May. Weakfish arrive in the Chesapeake and Delaware Bay systems at nearly the same time as they appear in Peconic Bay. Akin to bluefish, this possibly indicates an offshore migration rather than the fish working up the coastline.

Weakfish spawn in the spring, and the best fishing occurs then. Locations that concentrate the fish in their breeding areas are the best places to fish. After spawning, the weaks spread out, either staying in the bays or moving to other feeding locations throughout the region. The Peconic Bay area, one of the top weakfish locations, feeds the northern zone. The southern bays, Chesapeake in particular, retain more fish because of their size. Here the fish spread out around the bays, offering more sporadic fishing. In late fall, large schools of small fish are present off the Outer Banks, but seldom near shore unless driven in by bluefish. Yet small schools and groups appear along the beaches in the spring and fall.

In peak years weakfish are fishable all summer before they school up for the fall run. Unlike other fish, where the late-season runs are best, the weaks are king during the spring. Some good fall catches do occur late, but nothing like the early-season numbers.

Weakfishing is a unique blend of fresh- and saltwater angling, allowing the angler to combine trout tactics with a saltwater environment. Though not a spectacular fighter, the weakfish is a game, scrappy competitor. The thrill of fishing for it comes on a quiet night, when feeding pops fill the air, and the line tightens while eight pounds of weakfish explode in a small creek.

Unfortunately, the good runs of weakfish we had in the mid-seventies and early eighties are all but gone. Weakfish do run in cycles, but most of the problems today are due to overfishing. The commercial catch occurs in the spring during spawning. Taking fish before they spawn or while they are spawning is just poor judgment and unwise. I have never understood how people trying to make a living from the sea can be the least inclined to protect it.

Bonito and Albacore

Bonito and albacore are members of the mackerel family: They look alike, are similar in shape, and many times feed together in the same manner. Both fish are popular with anglers. There was a time when bonito far outnumbered albacore, but in the last eight to ten years the albies, in most locations, are caught in better numbers. Both species are famous for having lockjaw in the Northeast. They seem to take flies much more aggressively in the Carolinas than they do up north.

The Atlantic bonito, *Sarda sarda,* also called the green or common bonito, has a tuna-shaped body, though it is slightly thinner with more bulk in the center of the fish. The back is green to blue-green, fading to a silvery white belly with approximately seven dark horizontal stripes rolling from the fish's middle to the top of the back. The sides have a slight yellowish tint. Both species, bonito and albacore, change color rapidly after death. The forked tail has a small base and is built for speed.

Cooper Gilkes with a nice bonito he took on the east side of Martha's Vineyard. The bonito has darker lines across the body.

Albacore, or albi, is a local name for little tunny, *Euthynnus alletteratus,* also called false albacore or little tuna. Do not confuse this species with the long-finned albacore used in white-meat canned tuna. The body shape and general appearance are close to that of the bonito, with a taller dorsal fin. The back is blue-green to deep blue, with light silvery blue sides and a silvery white underside. The feature that distinguishes the albacore from similar species is a patch of markings located on the upper back. This section of dark, thick, spaghetti-like lines runs from behind the dorsal fin to near the tail base. The forked tail creates speed.

Best Waters to Fish for Bonito and Albacore

Both species are offshore fish that move inshore in late summer or early fall. In open waters look for surface action or bird activity. Trolling with conventional tackle is the normal way to find these fish in deeper offshore waters. In shallower locations (5 to 20 feet), fish the rips, because bonito and albacore prefer moving water. Great Point at Nantucket is a favorite albacore location, as is Cape Point at Hatteras. The strong rips bring the fish in to feed. Harbor mouths and saltwater inlets will have either speedster feeding at the entrances, and might have fish running inside if there is deep enough water. Open, deeper beaches often see these fish at low light, and they can be close. On these beaches a wind chop generally makes bonito and albacore strike better.

Neither fish tolerates sandy water or freshwater. Even moderate surf holds the fish offshore. Inlets mixed with freshwater hold fish at the mouths, but never inside. They prefer shorelines near deep water, and unlike bass and blues, seldom venture over shallow bars to feed near shore.

Rips over reefs, such as at Montauk, attract bonito and albacore, as does the water along Rhode Island's rocky coast. Here the fish generally hold just offshore, teasing the surf anglers.

How Bonito and Albacore Feed

Bonito and albacore are blitzers and lone feeders. Not that they travel alone, but they do spread out, feeding separately. They are schooling fish, and when attacking in groups both species can be as savage as bluefish, but with more speed. When blitzing bait, bonito and albacore strike quickly and leave just as quickly, frustrating the boater. They move much faster than blues. If breaking fish are moving too rapidly to pursue by boat, they are probably one or the other of these ocean speeders. While fishing in the Bahamas, Barb and I once chased a feeding school along a shoreline with a car. The road ran right along the shore, and even in an automobile, they were tough to keep pace with.

When spread out and feeding over a large, open area, bonito and albacore are much easier to catch. Here you can cast (from an anchored boat is best) and work singles and groups without chasing them. Anchoring allows you to experiment with different patterns and retrieves to find the proper combination for that day, tide, or light angle. Because these fish are fickle, the experts I know believe trial and error is the best way to catch them. There are no set rules to their feeding or to their preferences of fly type or retrieve style. Just keep working.

Most feeding is on the surface, but intermediate and fast-sinking sink tips often work best. At times bonito and albacore will take top-water flies fished with a floating line, and this is the most exciting way to fish. Crease flies will work, as will sliders. One advantage with a sink-tip line is speed—they cast with fewer false casts and cut through the wind better. One problem with any fast-sinking line is the dark color. You need to use a tapered leader of 8 to 9 feet in length when fishing for ocean speeders.

Bonito and albacore generally take hard, grabbing the fly as they turn. With such speed the line should tighten quickly, unless the fish swims toward the angler, creating slack. If the fish takes and keeps swimming toward the angler, the strike will be subtle. At times many gamefish will grab food and keep swimming to the next target. With a fast-swimming fish, you may not feel the take—this is when a very fast retrieve is effective. A fast retrieve may not be necessary to make the fish take, but it helps to detect the strike.

When feeding separately on the surface, both species make a chugging sound. This deep, single "gulp" distinguishes them from other fish and reveals

Very big albies like this one taken by Warren Marshall are hard to come by, but Harkers Island, North Carolina, is the best place to find them. PHOTO COURTESY OF CURT JESSUP

their presence. On calm water or days of light wind, this sound carries for some distance.

How Bonito and Albacore Fight

The speed and power of all the tuna-shaped species is incredible. The first run just screams the drag because these fish can cover 100 yards in seconds. There is little doubt when a bonito or albacore takes the fly, for their speed is twice that of other inshore fish in the Northeast. Line will fly from stripping basket or boat deck at a blinding rate. There is no time for untangling: The tippet will snap like a rifle shot if a snag occurs.

Even after the first run, the tail never stops beating. These fish bear down, requiring pressure to recoup line, and when you think you are winning, another fast run will make the reel smoke. Pound for pound, bonito and albacore are the strongest inshore fish we have. Although a bluefish might be more stubborn, it doesn't have that high-rpm tail. Both bonito and albacore are superb fighters, and a moderate drag and plenty of backing are necessary to fish for them.

Special Features of Bonito and Albacore

All tuna-type fish have a large, sharp, investigative eye. This makes bonito and albacore line- and leader-shy. Even though they have toothy mouths, a shock leader is off-limits. With good light they examine flies with the intensity of a diamond broker. At such times, precise imitations might be the factor that brings strikes. And just as important is leader diameter; you may need to drop down in size if fish are looking and turning off.

Neither fish has the fearsome bite of a bluefish, but each has sharp teeth. The forked tail and small tail base make both fish easy to grab, and hook removal is simple. If releasing, make sure to revive these fish. Most are spent after a fight and need help, plus a quick return, for survival.

Best Baits for Bonito and Albacore

Bay anchovies, also called rain bait, are one of the speedsters' important baits in the Northeast. These 2- to 3-inch-long wide-sided baits are tan to light green in color, and ball up in small to midsize schools. Sand eels are the favorite bait of both species, with spearing close behind. Any small top-water schooling bait, such as spike mackerel or squid, are also good bets.

Bonito and albacore seem to prefer the thinner-bodied baits and small baits to the bigger deep-sided herring-bunker baits. In Harkers Island, North Carolina, the albi capital of the Eastern Seaboard, 3- to 5-inch-long silver or striped anchovies are the major bait. This might be the reason why albies take flies better here than they do up north. There may also be more fish, so the competition makes the albies feed more aggressively.

Without the striper's large mouth or the blue's powerful cutting jaws, bonito and false albacore favor mouth-size foods. Even larger tuna feed on small baits—many tuna-trolling lures are tiny compared to the fish's size. Thin- to medium-bodied patterns tied 2 to 5 inches long cover most bonito-albacore fishing situations.

Best Time of Year to Fish for Bonito and Albacore

Bonito move inshore first around mid-May in the Carolinas, then work north, reaching Martha's Vineyard about mid-July. To the offshore angler they are available sooner, and in some locations are present most of the season. Fish holding near shore stay until the storms and cold fronts push them out. Apparently there is a certain temperature that chases them to deeper, warmer water, because their exit is always quick and final.

The oceanic bonito has a small patch of squiggly dark lines to the rear of its back, with dark lines that run from its tail to the pectoral fin.

Albacore move to inshore feeding grounds about mid-September, hitting the southern locations almost the same time they enter northern areas. But the albacore remain closer to shore longer in the southern sections, and I have hit fish after Thanksgiving below Hatteras, North Carolina. They leave the Vineyard with the bonito about the first week of October.

Bonito visit more locations than do albacore, but in recent years both species have been making good runs, even venturing into Long Island Sound, where for many years they were seldom seen. Their numbers are growing, and they show up in more inshore places each year. Inshore albacore are mostly confined to the islands of Massachusetts, the deeper waters of the Rhode Island coast, Montauk Point, and the beaches and points of the Outer Banks of North Carolina. Yet both fish are very popular offshore species, and abundant from several miles out into blue water.

These fast species add another dimension to saltwater fly rodding, particularly when found inshore. They even give the surf fisherman an opportunity to lock horns with offshore fish. They feed all day and are fast and hard-fighting, offering a unique, crafty opponent that keeps us guessing. Bonito and albacore are special fish.

Bluefin Tuna and Oceanic Bonito

When I wrote the first edition of *Inshore Fly Fishing,* bluefin tuna were seldom targeted by light-tackle anglers along much of the eastern coast. I'm sure there were a few who took fish, but nothing like the fishing we have experienced in the last ten years. The early pushes of smaller fish in the fifteen- to twenty-five-pound range got many anglers chasing these great fish. They're ideal for fly rodding. Most runs occur in mid- to late summer and into the fall, although I have seen surface-feeding bluefin outside Nauset Inlet off Cape Cod in May. Anglers that target bluefin often cover many miles looking for surface-feeding fish. If fish get locked into a location, it's much easier fishing.

Because of my boat's size, I am not what you call a serious bluefin angler. Most of my encounters have occurred while looking for other species. Weather permitting, I do target bluefin if there is a good run of fly-tackle-size fish within range. But if the fish are much over fifty pounds, unless I have another angler on board, it would be difficult for Barb and me to land a big tuna.

Bluefin tuna, *Thunnus thynnus,* and oceanic bonito, *Katsuwonus pelamis,* are two hardtails that seldom venture into shallow water and are usually found a mile to many miles offshore. Oceanic bonito, or skipjack tuna, are perfect fly-rod fish (like albies), ranging to fifteen pounds in the Northeast. Both bluefin and skipjack are members of the mackerel family, along with albies and

Al Conti with a good bluefin that he took while being our guide to the best bluefin fishing I will ever have.

Atlantic bonito, but they differ in the type of water they feed in. Bluefin do, on rare occasions, run through the Cape Cod Canal, and I once spoke to several anglers who watched a school of bluefin blitzing bluefish in Provincetown Harbor, but these are very infrequent events.

The best tuna trip I ever had was with Al Conti, the owner of Snug Harbor Marina. Al fished for swordfish off Rhode Island when there still was a fishery, so I don't need to say anything more about Al's experience. Also onboard was Pip Winslow, a coworker at Orvis, and Ed Hughes, a local guide who now guides in Central America. Al knew there were fish off the Mud Hole southwest of Block Island. On our way out, we saw some breaking fish just outside Block and we wanted to chase them, but Al said it was better to find the draggers, where the fish would be concentrated.

Al was dead-on right, and within several miles we came upon a floating city of boats. Many sportfishing boats were mixed in with the draggers that hauled up nets full of whiting. As Al explained, the tuna were feeding on spillage from the nets—it was like one big chum line. I spotted some birds working a location, and we motored to that spot. I don't know who hooked up first, but we were into fish immediately. Al started chumming with pieces of butterfish, and soon there were tuna all around the boat. We were constantly hooked up for over six hours.

At first there were several oceanic bonito mixed in with the bluefin, but once the tuna locked in, the bonito left. The tuna were thirty to forty pounds—an ideal size for our situation. We had 12-weight outfits, and fighting the fish from a dead boat was the only option. When you are surrounded by tuna, you don't move the boat. Hooking the fish took no skill—we just dropped the fly in the water, and it vanished in a huge swirl. If we would have put a hand in the water, it would have been eaten. It dawned on me that commercial fishermen could fill a boat with small tuna using short bamboo rods with a short line and a jig, just lifting them into the boat—it was that wild.

Hooking up was easy, but landing them was not. Lifting these fish with 12-weights took some work—a 14-weight would have been better. The real problem, however, was break-offs caused by the fish swarming around the boat. Holding fish close to the boat required a constant flow of butterfish pieces, and each piece landing in the water created chaos. We all broke off several fish when other fish whacked our backing or fly line below the boat. I learned a lesson about rigging tackle from this trip. Apparently the section of mono I installed between the fly line and backing acted as a shock absorber. Fish strikes on the line would break the leader, but the rest of the system remained sound. I was the only angler not to lose a fly line.

I hooked several fish on a popper. The fish could actually spot the lure in the air, and then crushed it instantly when it hit the surface. Most fish would sound, but I hooked one that ran away from the boat. My backing was "on fumes" when I stopped the fish, and after a long fight back, it made another run of perhaps 300 yards. When I finally landed the fish, it weighed forty-two pounds—the biggest of the day.

What really amazed us was the power of these fish. You would spend ten minutes of hard pumping to lift the fish up 100 yards, and they would take it back in several seconds. And what really hurt was when you were close to landing a fish and pop! Another fish hit the fly line, breaking the leader. Al, not being a fly angler, was surprised at the lifting power of a fly rod. That day we did a lot of lifting and pulling as each angler landed several fish, and we never broke a rod.

When I tell other anglers about this experience, they ask if I hope to ever have another day of tuna fishing like it. My answer is no. Back then I was in my late forties and still worked construction, but after that one day of fishing, I hurt for a week. It took forever to be able to straighten my right hand. I literally fought fish for over six hours without stopping. Perhaps now I would be wiser and take a break, but when fishing is that good, it's hard to stop.

Most fly anglers hunt tuna like albies or bonito. You look for surface-feeding fish, bird activity, or concentrations of boats. Often this sport requires long runs, and you must keep moving constantly, searching for action. But once you find action, be patient. There are times when fish keep popping up and a number of schools might be feeding in the same location. This can mean multiple shots at fish for several hours, or one school might surface every fifteen minutes. Leaving too soon, looking for that next pot of gold, can make for lost opportunities. One late morning south of Block Island, Barb and I kept working several schools of very small bluefin and oceanic bonito. Every so often they would pop up, feed, and then quickly disappear. One time we reached a school just as it sounded. As we watched, the fish seemed to circle about 20 feet below the boat. At the same time another school appeared several hundred yards away. We were tempted to move but held tight. Our patience paid off because the school surfaced right rear the boat, and we both hooked up with mushies. This happened several times, and I was also able to ace a tiny bluefin of about ten pounds.

How Bluefin and Oceanic Bonito Feed

I have seen hundred-pound-plus tuna feeding on 3- to 4-inch-long peanut bunker. And most of my hookups have been on 3- to 4-inch-long flies. You would expect bigger fish to feed on big baits, but this is not always the case. One important bait is the halfbeak, or ballyhoo, part of the Hemiramphidae family. They are less than a foot long with a round body, and range from just outside ocean beaches to well offshore. Halfbeaks are a favorite food of offshore bluefin and the ideal bait for the long rodder to match. A 7- to 8-inch-long Snake Fly or large sand eel pattern works well. Herring, squid, and large sand eels are other popular offshore foods. I have seen small, 3-inch-long baitfish that looked like anchovies holding under weed lines, and when this occurs, small flies are a good choice. Bluefish are one of the most aggressive-feeding gamefish, but for a big bluefin it's a favorite food—in the sea there is always a bigger, fiercer foe.

Tackle

For fish in the low-twenty-pound range, a 10-weight outfit will fit in a pinch, but a 12-weight is really a better choice. For fish over forty pounds, 14-, 15-, or 16-weight outfits are the smart choice, as their shorter length and heavy construction are built to lift fish. Even when chasing these fish in a boat where you can follow them once they sound, lifting power is important. Rigging up for tuna is different than for other species I have addressed so far—their sheer size and power are overwhelming. You can slide by with a fair to good backing-to-fly-line-to-leader system with other fish, but not with tuna. Chapter 17 contains a section on setting up a tuna system. This is a tested system that will work if you tie each knot precisely. There are other ways to rig a system that also will work, so choose one that you believe in, and make each connection like it was going to be holding a life hanging off a high bridge.

A reel for tuna must hold at least 300 yards of backing—I want 400. In most cases you can follow the fish with the boat, but extra backing will come in handy if two fish are hooked at one time, or if it takes extra time to get after the fish. A tuna will take 100 yards of line before you can say the first line of the Lord's Prayer. And if you get too far into the prayer before moving, the prayer won't help—the line will part like a pistol shot. Only the best reels with a strong drag system will work for the bigger fish. A twenty-pound tuna is like a big albi, so a good drag system is adequate. But when they hit fifty pounds and over, the pressure on the drag is tripled. This is where the best reels come into play. They have excellent drag systems, are well balanced, and are built with high-strength aluminum that prevents torque when lifting a big fish. Serious offshore anglers do not skimp on tackle—they buy the best. With what these anglers spend on boats and fuel and the long runs they make to find fish, tackle failure is not acceptable.

Other Species

So far we have discussed the major fly-rod species on the Northeast coast, ones that are numerous and popular. Other types of fish roam our waters, but for many reasons do not generate the interest of the previous seven fish. Some, like pollock, *Pollachius virens,* and Atlantic mackerel, *Scomber scombrus,* are numerous, but maybe not glamorous enough to interest anglers.

Pollock move inshore in late fall, feeding along rocky shores and in and around saltwater estuaries. Several locations south of Boston provide hot pollock fishing for me in mid-November. I'm sure there are numerous spots in Maine that also have great pollock fishing. I have taken numbers of scrappy two- to five-pound fish with small flies—it's a fun way to end the season. Bigger fish prowl deeper rocky areas, but this kind of pollock fishing is spotty.

Mackerel show in deeper water off New York in mid-April, moving north along the coast, and are fishable all summer in sections of Maine. When found near the surface, they take small bright flies well and are sporty, fast-swimming fish, ranging from one to three pounds. Spanish mackerel, *Scomberomorus maculatus,* are mixed in with bonito and albacore around Martha's Vineyard and Nantucket. They are an incidental catch, but are becoming more common.

Shad, *Alosa sapidissima;* sea-run brown trout, *Salmo trutta;* Atlantic salmon, *Salmo salar;* and coho salmon, *Oncorhynchus kisutch,* are mostly caught in freshwater. When found in salt water, salmon and even trout will take saltwater patterns. They do occur as odd catches when anglers work waters for other fish. Shad are a popular fish taken in freshwater locations, but they're seldom caught in salt water.

Many offshore fish—marlin, dolphin, and sharks—receive attention from fly rodders in many locations around the world. There is certainly no reason why the New England and mid-Atlantic bight angler can't do the same. Lefty Kreh's book *Fly Fishing in Salt Water* offers additional information on offshore saltwater fly fishing.

The red drum, *Sciaenops ocellata*, is a favorite fly-rod fish in many southern places, but it's seldom taken on fly even on the Outer Banks. In the Carolinas drum are popular gamefish, but few fly rodders fish for them there. Along the outer beaches fly rodding for redfish is still not popular, but fly fishing for reds is now taking hold in some of the inland waters in the Carolinas and Georgia.

The spotted sea trout, *Cynoscion nebulosus*, another popular fish, does occur from New Jersey south to the Gulf Coast. Similar to the weakfish, this species is often caught in the same way. Unlike the northern trout, spotted sea trout are daytime feeders, dining on small baitfish and shrimp. The best fishing locations are large shallow areas 2 to 5 feet deep. Work the dips or drop-offs in these locations, because they concentrate the fish at low tide. Basic small bait or shrimp patterns used for weakfish will also take sea trout.

The fish roaming our waters offer unlimited fly-fishing opportunities. The adventurous angler can catch ten species in a season without leaving sight of land. I can count nine that are possible from shore when fishing both southern and northern zones of the Northeast coast, with the possibility of a forty-pound fish taken from the surf. How many other areas offer such a variety of fish in so many different locations? The problem we have is trying to decide what fish to pursue. Now, that's a first-class dilemma.

20

Releasing Fish

Before going to the Island School in Eleuthera, Bahamas, I had been releasing fish for many years and believed I was handling them in a careful, safe manner. Well, I was wrong. After my visit to the school, it was time to improve the way I handle and release fish. This unique institution is doing valuable research on the best ways to release bonefish. But even more valuable, it is teaching young people about conservation and protecting the environment, and about life in general, better than any other program I have seen. Barb and I had a chance to spend some time at the Island School—and we came away completely impressed.

Many anglers release fish. We handle them, take pictures, and hold them up to show friends. And when we release them and watch them swim away, we believe that the fish will survive without problems. But after my visit to the Island School and talking to Dr. Andy Danylchuk, who at the time was the director of research at the Cape Eleuthera Institute, I totally rethought my approach to releasing fish.

Meeting Andy was a flashback in time. I had just lost a dear friend, Pete Laszlo, to cancer. Thirty years ago Andy could have been Pete's younger brother, even his twin—the same bright blue eyes, light-colored hair, and lean build, plus the same intense love of marine ecology and the environment. Andy's wife, Sascha, a researcher and scuba instructor at the school, possesses that same intensity.

Barb and I wanted to visit the school because we heard it was a fantastically run program; the bonefish catch-and-release project came to my attention from Terry Gibson at Florida Sportsman. It was a good excuse to see something new and perhaps learn more about handling bonefish as well as other species. After talking to Andy and Sascha for twenty minutes, I realized that I, like so many other anglers, had more to learn about handling and releasing fish.

Here are some of the topics the institute's researchers wanted to investigate: Does the length of time a fish fights affect its survival? How does the stress of handling a fish influence its short- and long-term behavior? How long does it take a fish to fully recover after release? Fish cannot breathe out of the water, so how long is too long for hook removal or taking photos? Predation in some locations is surely a factor. Hook damage can be a problem with smaller fish, and water temperature affects the time it takes a fish to recover.

One point that really hit home was that fish cannot breathe when out of water, and if the fish stays out too long, it could have long-lasting breathing problems. Our lungs make it possible to breathe; the gills of a fish do the same thing. The gill filaments, the red membrane under the gill plate, basically separate air from water. These filaments are fragile and begin to stick together when exposed to air. If exposed too long, the damage can be permanent. The short-term problem—with even one minute out of the water, one minute of not breathing—is a much longer time before the fish can evade predators and feed again. But another problem could be degenerative damage to the fish's respiratory system, which can affect its ability to feed, fight off infection or disease, or reproduce. Think of it this way: If a man lost 40 percent of his lung capacity, he could still live and function because he doesn't need to chase his food or evade predators. Yes, he would be limited in terms of physical activity, but he could still survive. For a fish that needs to escape predators and chase down food, however, it would be a death sentence.

A good way to photograph a fish is to leave it in the water.

Think about all those great cover photos with the fish out of the water. Did some of those fish stay out too long and perhaps were affected, even though they swam away? Good photos might come with a price—a dead fish. Sascha made a good point: When you lift a fish from the water for a photo or to remove the hook, hold your breath. This way you will know when you have held the fish too long. Better yet, shoot the fish in the water or lift it out when the person taking photos is ready, then put it back quickly. Another point that made an impression is that a fish that is weak and loses its balance (rolls on its side) is six times less likely to survive. I have watched anglers play a fish forever, either because they were afraid of losing it or did not know how to fight it. This is one point we need to convey to all anglers: Learn how to fight fish correctly, and use tackle heavy enough to put pressure on a fish, particularly as it starts to tire. Some anglers like to boast about light rods and light lines—they call it sport. But it might not be sport to the fish.

Another subject is the use of barbless hooks. I have been fishing with barbless hooks for over thirty years—even when using plug tackle. It does a lot less damage to the fish, and I think you land more fish as well. The other plus is that barbless hooks do less damage when we hook ourselves.

Andy explained that predation is a big problem in some locations in the Bahamas. The more remote areas that harbor large numbers of sharks and barracuda experience fish losses to these predators. I have witnessed this while fishing for bonefish on Andros Island, and now I'm seeing the same problem with stripers and bluefish in locations that have seal populations. The numbers of seals that have invaded the waters of Cape Cod and the islands of Massachusetts are steadily increasing. They actually follow anglers along the beach, waiting for them to hook a fish. I have lost fish when a seal attacked the hooked fish, and I have watched seals chase and eat fish that I released. There are places on Cape Cod where I will no longer fish because of the possibility of losing fish to seals.

Proper handling of a fish increases its chances of survival. The best way to handle and release fish is to use your hands and remove the hook carefully. Grabbing the fish with a device can damage its jaw. Andy tested gripping devices on bonefish and found that about half the bonefish grabbed with a device had jaw damage. I believe that bonefish have a more fragile jaw than stripers, and certainly bluefish sport an extremely

If you must lift a striper from the water, grab it firmly by the jaw.

powerful jaw. A jaw-grabbing device is fine for blues, and if you grab a striper by the jaw and handle it with care, there should be little damage, although with stripers just using your thumb and forefinger works well. Now that Andy is living in New England and working at the University of Massachusetts–Amherst, he and his colleagues plan to test lip-gripping devices on northern species.

If you lift a fish from the water, support it from the underside. When handling a fish, avoid contact with the red tissue under the gill plates. These are the fish's lungs and are very fragile. If a fish is hooked near the gills, try to carefully remove the hook using a small pair of pliers or, better yet, a set of forceps. Forceps are long, small, and smooth, and when used carefully, they can remove a barbless hook quickly and get the fish back into the water without too much harm. If the fish is bleeding from the gills and if it's legal, keep it because it will not survive.

There will always be some mortality when releasing fish. When a fish inhales the fly, there is always the possibility of harming the fish. But, if you are careful and spend the time to revive the fish properly, most releases will end with a healthy fish that will survive.

Fish Release Checklist

- Start with a barbless hook.
- Land the fish quickly.
- Handle the fish as little as possible.
- Keep the fish in the water or return it to the water quickly.
- Be sure the fish is strong enough to swim away with ease.

A successful fish release starts with landing the fish while it is still lively (see the fish-fighting techniques in chapter 15). A fish that is totally exhausted has little chance of surviving. Once the fish is close, apply good pressure to bring it to hand while it is still swimming well. The second leading cause of death, after hooking a fish in a sensitive area, is fighting a fish to exhaustion. A fish that is lively will often bolt away after release.

If the fish is upright but not lively, hold the fish by the tail, or jaw if it's a striper, and move it back and forth in the water. This will get the water flowing through its gills. It might take some time, but be patient and be sure that the fish can swim before releasing it. Fish that revive well will often pull away once they are ready to go. When holding a striper by the jaw, the fish will often begin to grab your fingers when it is ready to swim.

Remember, fish that are kept in the water and receive little handling are more likely to swim away and return to the sea unharmed. When releasing hardtails, try quickly moving the tail back and forth sideways through the water with your hand. This seems to work better than pushing the fish head forward and then pulling it back as you would with most fish. I have had hardtails just come to life and bolt from my hand when using this technique.

I found that holding a hardtail by the tail and moving the fish quickly through the water with a sideways motion seems to revive them quickly.

As of this date, solid scientific catch-and-release facts are not available for many species of fish. Whether all fish are affected in the same way, and whether some fish can survive out of water longer than others, is not entirely known. But the facts we do have are food for thought. Treating each fish like it might die if it is left out of the water for longer than thirty seconds is certainly a good practice that could lead to a healthy future for sportfish populations.

PART FIVE

Tides, Water Conditions, Weather, and Safety

21

Tides

The rising and falling of ocean water depth is what creates the tide. This force is unstoppable and relentless but predictable, with two highs and two lows each day. To the angler who has never experienced a tide, the initial encounter must be strange: to look at a place at high tide, then to come back six hours later and see, in some locations, completely different-looking water. Unlike lakes and rivers, which need rain or winter runoff to change their water levels, the ocean rises and falls to a steady beat. Yes, severe weather will affect the sea for short periods, but not with the impact it has on a river.

What Causes Tide?

The sun and moon are the principal forces creating tides, and the moon's effect is 2.17 times greater than the sun's. Full moons and new moons create higher

It's low tide at this ocean beach location.

Here is the same section of beach at a higher tide. In big tide locations high and low tide can look dramatically different.

tides, or "spring tides," and stronger currents. Half-moon tides, or "neap tides," are the smallest tides. When either a full or a new moon occurs at perigee, there will be a higher tide and a stronger current. Tides and currents are not as strong when full and new moons occur at apogee. Also at a new moon, the midday tide is higher than the night tide. At a full moon the opposite is true, and the night tide is the larger.

Tides, both incoming and outgoing, do not rise or fall in one steady flow, but move in three stages. The tide begins to rise, then slacks for a short period, ebbs or recedes slightly, and starts to rise again, repeating this process several times before reaching the high. Then it reverses this process on the falling tide. A drop in flow does not always mean the end of a tide. Boatmen and waders should always consult tide charts and watches.

What Alters Tide?

Both weather and wind affect tide. When the barometer is low, tides during both high and low water are higher than normal. With higher than normal pressure, tides are lower. When a major storm brings very low pressure, high water and flooding can occur and currents will be extremely strong.

In the Atlantic, tides increase in size and flow later when the wind blows strong to southward or eastward. When winds are northward or westward, tides are lower than normal and occur earlier. Wind can change water depth and currents in back bays and sounds. Give strong winds serious consideration if water depth and sea conditions can hamper your angling.

How to Predict Tide

Tide changes advance approximately fifty minutes per day; thus, if stripers move into a location, or a creek starts running out at midnight, you can expect this movement to occur at about 1:00 a.m. the following morning. This fifty-minute change depends upon the time of year, moon phase, and local conditions or surroundings, and might be altered somewhat by wind, particularly in smaller waters.

The only sure way to predict tide accurately is with a tide chart, which is accurate to several minutes. Tides are the saltwater fly rodder's river flow; they move water, which moves bait, and therefore moves the gamefish. The sweetwater fisherman has no tide to cope with, but when fishing salt water he must learn to forecast and understand tides. A good saltwater angler can predict by the tides the best times and locations to fish. This is why knowing a particular area is so important. Being able to determine when a current starts flowing, or when it is strongest, makes finding fish easier.

Reading a tide chart seems simple, and for many locations it is. Most coastal open waters have predictable tides that will coincide with a tide chart without adjustment. One large area will have approximately the same tide. For example, from Rockland, Maine, to Monomoy Point off Cape Cod, there is only one hour's difference in the tides, and the tides in between can be predicted from a Boston tide chart. Yet Wasque Point and Menemsha can be well over a two-hour difference and are only 30 miles apart, on opposite ends of Martha's Vineyard.

River systems, bays, islands, and outlets will confuse the novice. Fishing the small creeks around Shelter Island is one example of why you need to learn a location. All the creeks are excellent with an outflowing current. Someone fishing there for the first time might look at a tide chart and say, "Okay, it's high tide at eleven o'clock, I'll try at eleven-thirty." But at the creek the water is still flowing in, and may continue to do so for two hours after the high. Because the creek mouth is so small, it takes longer to fill the larger backwater.

Places like Great Point in Nantucket can be confusing, with both high and low tides and an east and west current flow. Great Point can be high at twelve o'clock, but the current will already have been flowing west for more than an hour, and will continue to flow west until an hour before low. Tides and current flow do not always coincide.

Wind affects tide, and in some locations this can be significant. I have seen the tide's flow change in speed and size as a result of wind. An area like Nantucket is where a "bayman's" knowledge is very important. The years I fished Nantucket, I always relied on a tide chart. Even then, it took time every year for me to become accustomed to the different tide phases because of the lag-time changes due to wind. Some fishing locations—outflows, back bays, and river systems—have a lag time in tide or tidal flow affected by wind. Predicting lag time and wind influence takes experience and local knowledge. Lag time does change depending on the tide size. A bigger than normal spring tide creates a longer lag time. Adding wind effects to this calculation further confuses it. The only real way to predict flow in some locations is through firsthand experience—and then flip a coin. If current direction or time of water flow is critical to a spot, always plan to arrive there early. Those places having short time spans of good fishing require that you hang around, because wind or big tides will alter the time of flow.

The *Eldridge Tide and Pilot Book* is my bible, a friend that helps me understand tides. The book covers tides from Nova Scotia to Key West, Florida, with tide charts and tide sizes, current flows and speeds, moon phases, sun rising and setting times, and wonderful information on tidal effects. No traveling angler should be without it.

A logbook is also useful, to keep exact records for each regular fishing spot. And after reading all the books, daytime research is probably the best way to learn new waters.

Is There a Best Tide?

Everybody always wants to know what the best tide is. Some areas are good at all tides. During slack tides fishing may be slow, although sometimes that is the best time to fish certain spots. Some locations only have a slack high, and at low tide still have water flow. This is particularly true at the mouths of large bays and estuaries. If I had two hours to fish on each tide, I would either choose high outgoing, the first two hours after high tide, or low incoming, the first two hours of the rising tide. These two tide periods have been the most successful ones for me, though there are certain areas where an hour or an hour and a half during a tide are the best fishing times. But each section of water is different, and **time on the water** is the only way to gain the know-how to fish it well.

The best tide in some locations might depend on the time of year. Outflows that empty large bays or ponds flush out warm water in the spring and fall. Even small outflows attract fish because of the warmer water. Fish congregate at these places for the warming effect as well as the ample food source.

A rising tide distributes fish, moving them onto flats, into beaches, and into back-bay areas. A coming tide makes fish bolder, diminishing their fear of being stranded. Fish will frequent waters on a rising tide that they would not venture into on a falling tide. Likewise, fish are concentrated by a falling tide as they seek deeper water. Cuts and drop-offs along large flats are prime examples of locations that collect fish at the end of a tide.

Remember that bait is a prisoner as well as a beneficiary of currents created by tide. The mass movement of bait in the tide is a continuous occurrence in the ocean. Some baitfish have the same fear as gamefish of being trapped, and move from certain locations on a falling tide. Big baits like bunker and herring need to move from constricted areas; being trapped in confined quarters leaves them vulnerable to attack by gamefish. The outlets of rivers and harbors are prime locations at outgoing tides because these big baitfish are flushed out then. Many outlets create hot fishing on an outflowing tide. Certain baits, such as worms, crabs, and shrimp, bloom on high outgoing tides, either spawning or hatching.

Here are some thoughts on different locations and what tides are best. Remember, these suggestions are general and not set in stone. In big tide locations, on big flats, the last two hours of outgoing and the first two hours of incoming are often the most productive. The fish are concentrated along the edge, and the lower water levels make these locations accessible for wading. Outflows are best as the tide first begins to move out, and this might last for several hours. The start of the flow into the outlet is good if there is enough water to hold fish. Again, this can often be productive for several hours. This is also true with offshore rips, when the beginning of the flow is best on both the rise and drop. Ocean beaches can be good on all tides, but the last two hours of incoming and first two hours of outgoing are normally better. Choose a falling tide when fishing places that require long-distance wading on reefs or on big flats. This gives ample time to fish the tide and find land if the fog sets in.

Checking locations at low tide can help to find the best fishing spots.

However, part of the fun of fishing is bucking the trend and catching fish at the wrong time. If you have the time and the tide is wrong, go fishing anyway—you might be pleasantly surprised.

Tides affect every facet of saltwater fishing. Without tides the sea would be a huge lake, requiring weather to add motion. Tides give the ocean character and movement—a constantly changing appearance and feel. Tides not only make fishing better, they also make it more interesting, because somewhere there is always flowing water because of the tide.

22

Wind, Weather, and Temperature

There are many factors that affect our fishing. Some—the tides, moon phases, and changing seasons—are predictable events. Others—wind, temperature, and surf activity—are caused by weather and are unpredictable. Severe weather fronts and major storms can influence fishing. Some will be of slight significance; others are very important. Factors like weather can change a fish's feeding patterns or drive it to other areas. Tide, which creates water movement, is very influential, and perhaps the most meaningful of all the factors in a saltwater fish's life. These effects can not only change a fish's patterns, they can change yours as well. The saltwater fly fisherman must learn to understand and cope with such factors in order to be successful.

Many years ago I had an opportunity to see how weather modified fish behavior. A hurricane hit the coast of New England, and being a pesky youngster of ten with several years' fishing experience, I talked my dad into fishing after the hurricane subsided. The weather was just starting to clear, and a gusty wind was still blowing. There was a good sea running, especially for Long Island Sound. My father said we were wasting our time, for there would be no fish, but to please me we went to try a favorite spot in Westport, Connecticut. One look at the riled-up water should have discouraged us, but we persisted. As we parked the car and headed to the small jetty near Southport, even at my young age I could see my father's point, for the water was roiled and dirty. We rigged our light and medium spinning gear and walked out onto the jetty. Both of us were bucktail jig fishermen who used surface poppers sparingly.

Checking the water, we started casting from the jetty as the waves rolled heavily onto the shore. I thought I had several bumps on the first cast but said nothing, feeling my dad would think I was imagining things. Then my father leaned back, hooking a fish solidly, and at almost the same moment I too was into a fish. We both played and landed school-size stripers. My dad's was bigger, as his heavier tackle enabled him to cast farther, reaching the bigger fish. After releasing the fish, we continued taking fish, and the action was almost continuous for several hours. We were both beginning fishermen, not realizing the effectiveness of swimming plugs. Had we used them, we probably would have taken much larger fish, although we took a few fair-size bass to ten pounds. With the rough conditions, the fish were some distance from shore, and fly fishing would have been tough.

However, the next morning we came back early and had the same action. The weather and wind conditions had changed, dropping the swell and bringing the fish closer to shore. The fishing was fast and hot, and fly rodding would have been great because the fish were so close. I also had the pleasure of saying "I told you so" to my dad, and he thanked me for being such a pain in the rump. The next time we experienced the same storm conditions, there would be no hesitation: We would go fishing.

Only later did I find out why the weather change helped us. The storm had gone through, and because it was so violent the fish moved into deeper water and held without feeding. Probably they had fed before the storm and waited for the weather to subside before starting again. Before and after a storm are times fish feed vigorously. This is not only true of saltwater fish, but of freshwater species as well. Here is one situation that can help you get fish.

Weather

Moderate weather systems, especially a good rainy front, will start fish feeding. Dark rainy days are excellent for fishing. Bluebird days are enjoyable and ideal for sight fishing, but overcast, rainy, foggy days are more productive times to fish. During foul weather, stripers feed at all hours, even in the summertime, when they usually feed at night. Fish might feed all day because of dark, rainy conditions. When the weather is bad, fishing is best.

Cold fronts, even when not associated with rain, can affect fishing. In the spring they might turn fishing off for several days. In the fall, however, they often trigger heavy feeding, especially later in the season when fish are on the move. A cold front will often turn on albies and bonito. When that northwest wind kicks up in mid- to late September, it seems to make these fish feed vigorously for several days.

But take note: Bad weather brings danger. High winds or fog can pose problems for wading and boating. Avoid thunderstorms, especially when using a graphite rod, which is an excellent conductor of electricity. Planning to take a boat on an extended trip offshore, or running the beach with a buggy, requires knowledge of weather conditions. Check local weather stations or the National Weather Service for reports.

Fog can set in quickly. Be ready to move if you are in a location where the wind or tide might create a dangerous situation.

Weather is important to fishermen because pressure changes start fish feeding. Weather also moves fish and bait and gives action to water by causing waves and increasing or enhancing rips. Knowing and understanding the ways that weather alters a fish's environment helps the angler find fish. Both wind and surf are products of weather systems. The fly rodder is sometimes a prisoner of the wind, but by using proper casting techniques, wind can be used to the angler's advantage.

Wind

Onshore winds along open beaches or even large bodies of water bring waves or rough surf, and tough fishing. However, this wind also puts fish on the beach. This is especially evident in areas like Cape Cod, the Vineyard, and Nantucket in Massachusetts, Montauk Point in New York, and Block Island off Rhode Island. A good southwest blow can turn Cape Point at Hatteras on the Outer Banks into a melee of feeding fish, but this may not be suited for fly fishing because of the crowds.

Any beach or rocky shore that accepts ocean waves can be good with an onshore wind. Wave action only disrupts shallow locations, places with soft bottoms where rolling waves would cloud the water. When the wind is blowing in your face, the fish are at your feet. This also holds true for bay and sound areas, where the wind pushes baitfish onto a shoreline and the gamefish follow. When the wind is offshore, fishing and casting are easy, but the wind might move the bait out too. Wind affects large bodies of water, like Great Bay in New Hampshire, the Chesapeake, and Barnicut Bay in New Jersey, as it does open beaches. In bays, wind pushes bait from side to side, or traps it into a corner, or blows it into pockets, concentrating fish along a windward shore. But remember, strong winds might render some locations unfishable.

Remember too that wind, especially strong winds, affects tide. Wind can influence water level as well, particularly where it blows up against a shoreline, causing flooding conditions. A good rule of thumb is that when onshore winds occur, the water is higher than normal and remains higher throughout the tide. Offshore winds drop the water level and cause a lower low tide. Some rips flow better in certain wind conditions. Bear in mind that wind against the tide creates a good chop, making fishing better, but it also makes boating dangerous. Some areas become hazardous in strong winds.

When wading, consider both tides and weather for fishing and safety, especially when walking reefs, offshore bars, or flats that require you to cross deep water to get to a fishing area. Remember, when the tide starts coming, unless you know the place well, it's time to leave.

Weather is also a major factor when wading long distances. If fog begins to roll in, leave while shore is still visible. Fog sets in quickly, and I have had several scary experiences with it. One morning I fished a reef in Long Island Sound that extends out about a mile. The reef was exposed, and I waded out off the west side and started fishing. In a short time I noticed the fog rolling down the sound, from the east. Fish were feeding in the shallows, and I gave the fog

When the wind is blowing like this, you need to find a fishable shoreline or back bay.

little thought because there was a bright sun overhead. I hooked and landed a fish and started casting again when the fog engulfed me. I still did not worry, for the incoming tide had just started and I had two hours to get back in. I kept fishing, feeling the fog would burn off. It didn't. Then the tide began coming, and I started back to find the reef. With the reef now covered with water, I lost my bearings, and everywhere I walked the water got deeper. A place that I knew well seemed suddenly like the moon's surface. With my heart starting to pump hard, I stopped and listened. The reef's light-station foghorn seemed to be coming from everywhere. But I could faintly hear the thruway traffic, and by watching the current flow I finally found higher ground. Slowly I made my way in, tacking back and forth until I hit the reef's dry part. If I hadn't known the reef well, I could have had a frightening experience. I'm a very good swimmer, so I'm sure I could have eventually made dry ground. However, I learned my lesson well. When you are fishing areas unfamiliar to you, caution and safety are the first and most important considerations.

Fishing Moon Tides

Moon phases are important, for they affect tides. Both full and new moons create larger than normal tides, causing rips and currents to flow more strongly. Some anglers believe a full moon brings better fishing. The bright moon does eliminate the effects of the phosphorus, a tiny sea creature (and/or jellyfish) that glows when your line and fly come in contact with it. (This phenomenon is called fire in the water.) Fish can be uncooperative when there is phosphorus in the water on moonless nights.

I have experienced mixed success during full moons, and would not plan a trip around them. For the angler who is unaccustomed to fishing in darkness, a bright moon is a welcome friend and a good way to learn night fishing. I prefer a dark moon, less than a quarter, particularly in shallow, clear water, where fish might be spooky.

Temperature

Temperature changes influence fishing, altering how a fish feeds. They also affect your ability to fish. During periods of very cold weather, fly fishing is miserable—wet, freezing fingers can discourage even the hardiest angler. Many times temperature changes accompany a weather front, and both alter fish activity, sometimes drastically. Not that the fish quit feeding, but they may move, sometimes heading into deeper water.

The saltwater fly rodder's season is divided into three parts: the spring run, the summer doldrums, and the fall blitz. Depending upon where you fish, these three occur at different times. Spring runs start earlier in the southern areas and then move north. Then, in the autumn, the fall run reverses this sequence. The early season brings some species of fish out of hibernation and on the feed. Other types of fish move up from their southern haunts, hungry after their long journeys. The spring run can bring hot fishing up and down the coast.

Summer brings a slowdown period to warm-weather inshore waters. Requiring less food, some species grow sluggish and turn exclusively to night-time feeding. However, the angler who works will take fish all summer. Cold-water areas like the Cape and farther north can be excellent in midsummer. Hot weather will begin the offshore fishing season. The Gulf Stream blossoms and continues to bear fruit until late fall. By late September the fall migration starts fish feeding heavily, because some species must store fat for the winter hibernation, others for a long southern journey. Whatever the reason, the hot fishing makes the fall season my favorite fishing time. If only there were two Octobers and two Novembers.

We are prisoners of our environment; fish are more so. They are in the elements every minute of their lives, enduring under adverse conditions. The ones that survive learn to use home ground wisely, capitalizing on tides and winds to make feeding easier. Fly anglers must do the same to make their fishing more productive. Learn the fishes' habits and how their environments affect them, and your angling success will triple.

23

Safety and How to Drive on Beaches

Most accidents that occur to anglers are minor. Hooking yourself is probably the most common. Handling fish when unhooking them can land a hook in a finger, hand, or arm. Barbless hooks will prevent any serious damage, unless the hook is driven into the face. Most serious hooking problems are from casting—often at night. One way to prevent possible face or eye damage is to watch your backcast or the rod tip as you cast. If you keep following the rod tip with your eyes, the only area that can be hooked is the back of your head. And a barbless hook will slide out with little damage, and just a slight injury to your pride.

Heavy rolling surf demands respect from even the most experienced surf angler; even a small wave can knock an angler down, causing at least a dousing or lost gear. A large wave can kill. I've surfed ocean waves for over thirty years and have been caught in undertows, pounded to the bottom, and tumbled like a rag doll in a large roller. Even when I anticipated the blow, in the daytime with proper swimwear, it was scary. Being dragged unexpectedly, at night, into a wave's backwash on a steep beach with full fishing gear can spell trouble.

Being caught by the surf is a rare event if the proper precautions are taken. But if it does happen, don't panic. If you can't hold bottom, try to get away from shore to keep from being slammed onto the beach, then dragged repeatedly into the backwash. Shed all the gear that hinders swimming and try to work your way to the side of the hole, where the beach is not as steep. The hole's center is not the place to be because it contains the roughest water. At the hole's sides the waves should help push you in to the beach, with less undertow. Tide rips can be strong and may start to carry you into open water. Don't fight the flow, but swim to one side to reach the wave rolling over the bar, which will carry you to shore. At night, being tumbled in rolling surf is no fun, but it's not as bad as it sounds if you keep your cool and don't fight the water. The waves, if used properly, will help put you on a safe section of the beach.

Prevention is worth a pound of cure. Do not venture too close to the water's edge, even in medium surf. Never turn your back to the surf, but keep watching it in the event two waves double up or a large set forms. During big surf at high tide, avoid getting caught against a high bank in the steepest and deepest part of the hole. Here a big roller can trap you with no escape. Observe the surf for several minutes to get a feeling of its size and action—do this while you're checking to see how to fish the water. In the event a wave catches you, immediately back up the beach, walking with the wave flow, to gain as much height as possible. Then, as the wave starts to pull back, plant your feet and stand sideways to lessen the water's pull.

If knocked down, the angler must try to quickly gain a foothold to keep from being pulled into the wash. On a shallow beach a wave may knock you over, but other than giving you an unwanted bath, there is little danger. Sections of steep beaches have waves that race up with tremendous force and return to the sea with the same power, carrying with them anything in their path. In all my years of fishing the rolling surf, I've witnessed only a few close calls. Luckily, these turned out to be only good, wet lessons of what the sea can do to even the strongest person. Enjoy it, but respect the sea's power.

Safety Tips for Flats and Reefs

When wading long distances in shallow areas on an incoming tide, be aware of three things: where you walked out, how deep the water was there, and the number of dips you must cross to reach shore. In the heat of battle we all forget how much time has passed, then realize with a jolt that the shoreline is a long distance away and the tide is rising by the minute, leaving no time for guesswork in finding the path to shore.

Unless you know an area well, once the tide starts in, begin working toward shore. If there are several bars between you and shore, check on the way out to see if there is a gradual deepening after each bar. In this case work to the next bar, continuing to cast, for the fish will also move in with the tide, searching for food. A good bet, when the fishing is hot, is to walk to shore, find the deepest spot on the way there, mark it on your waders, then walk back out. When the water starts to get near that mark, it's time to head to dry ground.

Most mistakes on small tide flats just mean getting wet. I have tiptoed off several times with my waders filled, but was never in fear of drowning. Anglers who are not swimmers may want the assurance of a flotation device, but it's best to be smart enough to leave at the proper time.

I fish a hole on Cape Cod Bay that requires about a 0.75-mile walk over sand flats to reach. There are several deep troughs to cross en route to the spot, which is good on a low incoming tide. Once the water starts to cover the first bar, it's time for me to leave, no matter how good the fishing is. With a 10-foot tide, the water might outrun me, and with the distance I have to travel and the cold water, the situation could get out of hand. Locations like this demand special research and savvy, plus safety gear like a compass and a flotation vest. A compass is a good idea for any area where the angler is wading over 100 yards from shore, where fog could set in and eliminate any visual contact with shore. Being lost in fog, wading an incoming tide, is a frightening experience. I've had it happen several times, and if the surroundings had not been familiar, I would have been in trouble. When you are in thick fog without a compass, sound is the only reference you have, and even this can be distorted if the noise is too close. A distant rumble like that of a highway or a train can be music to one's ears, and I have used this several times to find shore.

Deal with any approaching fog bank immediately by heading toward the closest dry ground leading to shore. In a boat, unless you are lost, the situation

Fishing any rocky structure in big surf can be dangerous. Pick only the high flat rocks to fish from, and keep watching for rogue waves.

is not life threatening as long as the craft is operated in a slow, safe manner. Boats that operate offshore or in dangerous water need special equipment: radar, GPS, and good ship-to-shore radios. All boats should be equipped with a fixed compass.

Safety Tips for Fishing Cliffs

When fishing cliffs in heavy surf, watch the location for several minutes to be sure it is safe—in really big surf, spend at least ten minutes. Choose only the higher places, and never fish a spot that requires climbing down to reach it. If a rogue wave appears, you could be trapped. If a set of waves looks threatening, back away to higher ground until it looks safe. Never fish cliffs at night—never. When changing flies or leaders, move back away from the water's edge. Avoid crossing a low area to reach a spot. Move slowly, don't take chances, and never stop watching for big waves. If a spot look questionable, find a safer place.

Venturing out onto dark, slime-covered rocks is foolish. Even with a slight downward grade, you could slide off the rocks. I experimented once with sneakers and a wet suit on a waveless day, and walked out onto slick rocks—and skied down the wet surface as if on ice. At least on ice I may be able to dig in, but there was no give to the rocks' surface. With felts and studded shoes, traction is undoubtedly better, although once the angler falls, there are no handholds to stop the slide. And even with good studs, a hard rock with a slope that is too steep can cause a fall.

Although cliff fishing sounds dangerous, it's really not. Even with all the angling hours put in rock-wall fishing by fly rodders, some inexperienced, there has never been, to my knowledge, a serious accident. Just don't take chances when doing any type of fishing.

Running the Beach

Some areas allow anglers to run the beach with motor vehicles, opening miles of fishable areas to the four-wheel-drive owner. A few areas are passable without a four-by-four, with the right tires and tire pressure, but the driver better be skilled in running the beach. (I don't advise it.) Running on sand is not difficult to learn. Just refrain from doing anything crazy and stay in the track, the set of tire tracks made by other vehicles. Keep above the water line and off the dunes.

Tire pressure is important. Most vehicles can run about seventeen to twenty pounds of tire pressure. Hard tires chew up the beach, making it difficult for others to follow, and add stress to your vehicle. Always drop tire pressure down on soft beaches.

When turning around in sand, back up into the higher section of the beach: Backing downhill can cause a hang-up. If stuck, try to reverse direction or dig out—do not keep spinning the tires. Unlike driving in snow, there is no bottom to the sand. Avoid the steeper sections by keeping to the flat areas. In the event the beach is washed out, find a way around it, because saving your vehicle is worth the extra time you'll spend; the sea claims vehicles every year.

Beaches like Nauset and Provincetown on Cape Cod require safety gear to run them, but the last time we ran the Outer Banks in North Carolina, there were no equipment requirements. Basic safety equipment is helpful when driving any beach. A shovel, tire gauge, and towrope are good for starters; add a jack, jacking board, full-size spare tire, and fire extinguisher. On isolated beaches an anchor and come-along can pull you out of most hang-ups.

Running a beach not only allows easy, fast travel, but it also means your extra gear is only a short distance away. Long lengths of shoreline will be accessible, and you can reach feeding fish quickly. But at night or when no activity is evident, use the buggy only as a means of getting to a certain place. Cover the water carefully—don't race from place to place, spot-casting. I prefer to park near the shore and walk to it, rather than drive right to the edge with my lights blazing, as some anglers do. Usually I fish several hundred yards of beach without moving the buggy. Use the lights sparingly; don't shine them into the water. Run with just parking lights unless safety is sacrificed by doing so. Lights along a beach may not always drive fish away, but they might push fish to deeper water, beyond fly-rod range.

Running beaches is fun and adds another dimension to Atlantic coast fishing. If done with care, it's safer than driving on the road. And it sure beats walking great distances of soft sand in waders. It's always wise to contact the state or town associated with the beach you plan to run for information about it and what rules must be followed. Each beach is different, so don't just assume that a beach is open to traffic.

Appendix One—Conservation

Conservation is essential to preserving a sound fishery. Not only should anglers try to keep their impact on a fishery as low as possible, but fishery management agencies need to establish and enforce rules that keep the fisheries sound and growing. Unfortunately, in too many places, this is not happening.

The once-abundant striper populations are rapidly diminishing. I have witnessed the fishing quality on Cape Cod go steadily downhill in the last five years. From the late 1990s to about 2003, there was great fishing that was hard to beat. You could just go out and catch fish—they seemed to be everywhere. Now the outer beaches of the Cape are like a morgue. The fishing in Cape Cod Canal runs hot and cold, and along Cape Cod Bay it's nothing compared to the fishing of ten years ago. There are still some pockets of fish, but compared to the late nineties, it is just bad. One telltale sign that the fishery is in serious decline is the lack of out-of-state anglers. They used to pack the Cape and

Handle every fish as carefully as possible.

Islands in the fall; there were buggies loaded with anglers and gear at all the hotels, on the roads, and at every beach. In the parking lots you would see license plates from as far away as the Midwest. But now there is a conspicuous lack of out-of-state anglers.

The fishing in Long Island Sound and on the northern Jersey Shore is better, with some hot runs of fish—but this might be due to the stocks of Hudson River stripers being stronger. Long Island Sound and locations around the mouth of the Hudson mostly contain fish from the Hudson River. Much of Rhode Island, Massachusetts, and farther north contain Chesapeake Bay fish, which supply the lion's share of stripers from the Carolinas to Maine. The fishing in the rips south of Monomoy to east of Nantucket are also good, but this location held good numbers of stripers even during the bleak years of the moratorium. Actually, this area is a sanctuary for stripers because it gets little fishing pressure: No commercial fishing is allowed in much of the water, and the area is so vast.

I know anglers in Maine, on Nantucket, and on Martha's Vineyard who are also seeing low numbers—the surf fishing and inshore fishing are tough. Some say it's a lack of bait and there are still plenty of gamefish. But if that were true, why didn't they fill the 2009 commercial striper quota in Massachusetts even after extending the season? Yet, instead of reducing the number of fish harvested, an increase in the quota is being discussed. And the commercial fishery targets bigger fish, 34 inches or larger.

The fishing regulations for recreational anglers are also a problem. (Be sure to check the rules for the state you are fishing in. Some southern states have very complex regulations.) In the six coastal states from New Hampshire to New Jersey, current regulations allow an angler to keep two fish a day over 28 inches. Any charter boat taking six anglers can keep two fish per angler, plus two for both the captain and mate. And any angler fishing from either boat or shore can do the same day after day. The numbers add up fast, undermining the foundation of the fishery—we are killing off the breeding stock and the females, because often the biggest fish are females. An eight-year-old female striper is just reaching prime breeding age—that fish is about 29 inches long. Why not have a slot limit and not kill fish over 28 inches? This would protect fish that reach spawning age, allowing them to reproduce.

In Florida the breeding stock of many fish are protected. The current high quality of that state's snook fishing is a prime example of how to protect and improve a fishery that is in trouble. Keep the taking of fish at a safe level, have

This scene is a bluefish blitz at Cape Point in Hatteras, North Carolina. There was a time when this happened every year; unfortunately now this event is only a memory.

a slot limit to prevent the killing of larger breeding fish, monitor the numbers of fish, and react quickly if these numbers decline. Florida took a snook population that was in serious decline and built it into a top-notch fishery that anglers travel a great distance to fish. I know anglers that even label it a world-class fishery. The Northeast and mid-Atlantic fisheries are totally different, with their very liberal limits and no enforcement. Perhaps the biggest problem is the number of states involved that govern the fish. It's like government everywhere—too many opinions. One state, Florida, controls the snook population, and they do it right.

There are also diminishing numbers of bluefish. These great gamefish are strong and feed with a vengeance that makes them an exciting foe even on heavy tackle. The fall runs of blues all along the outer Cape, from Herring Cove to the tip of Monomoy, and the action at Great Point, Nantucket, could be nonstop for hours. The legendary Thanksgiving bluefish run at Cape Point in Hatteras, North Carolina, drew a huge gathering of anglers, mostly fishing bait or plugs. Actually, there was no room to fly fish, but that didn't matter because it was enough just to witness this event, to see what seemed like a thousand anglers all catching bluefish—big bluefish—on a run that went on for several days. The beach buggies could be thirty deep at the point, but even with crossed lines and anglers tangled up, there was never a harsh word. It was a fun event for the whole family. But sadly, this run and the runs to the north are gone.

I know that bluefish are cyclical, but it's been many years and there still is a shortage of bluefish compared to the eighties. Is it lack of bait? Are we taking too much of the important foods like menhaden and sea herring that gamefish need to survive and maintain good numbers? Something is wrong and we need to fix it. Again, this leads back to fish management, which does not seem to be getting the job done.

To give one example, in Massachusetts in 2010 they shortened the fall sea bass season. Sea bass are a favorite bottom-feeding food-fish, and a great fish to introduce kids to fishing. If there is a problem with a declining sea bass fishery, why not close it in the spring or early summer until they spawn? In the spring these fish are loaded with spawn. Why not determine when they spawn and have a limited take, or have a closed season until they complete their spawning cycle, then open the season in the late fall? This is similar to the plight of stripers—not protecting the reproduction, the one element that maintains a species. There is a reason why our hunting seasons for the most part open in the fall—the young are born in the spring.

Anglers who care about their fishery must keep abreast of its problems and voice their concerns to the politicians. It's your fishery, and it's up to you to help protect it. Phone calls, letters, and e-mails carry weight—the politicians do listen, and it does not take many complaints to get their attention. Stripers Forever is a not-for-profit organization that wants to give stripers gamefish status to prevent commercial harvesting of the species. This organization is all volunteer and there are no membership fees—they just need your support, and will keep you informed.

Remember, we all need to protect our fisheries. This begins with fighting fish properly, handling them carefully when releasing, and not overharvesting. By nature, fly anglers are not a problem for most fisheries. We use small, single hooks that do less damage, and most fish are put back safely into the sea to keep reproducing. If we have a fault, it is using tackle that is too light or not using the proper techniques to land fish quickly. It's up to each of us to do our part to ensure that every fish we catch and release is healthy when it swims away.

Appendix Two—World Records

I believe at one time I held a record for weakfish, but I never really spent time chasing records—it takes work and planning. I did, however, witness and help a good friend catch a really big striped bass that was an official record before it was broken by an angler on the West Coast. Captain Pete Kriewald landed a forty-five-pound striper on an August evening nearly forty years ago. We had been into fish for several days and had seen other anglers take several big stripers. As we approached a school of feeding fish, we both cast into the mayhem. I hooked a bluefish while Pete stepped on his line and saw his cast land close to the boat—but it was the right place to drop his popper. A monster striper inhaled his offering. After seeing the fish take, I quickly broke my fish off and started the boat. Pete worked the fish for about twenty minutes before getting it to the boat. He didn't see the fish take, so he didn't realize how big it was. I only told him it was a nice fish, since I didn't want to get him too excited. Only after the fish was in the net did he realize how big it was.

Pete was not prepared to hunt for a record. His leader was just a section of monofilament with no shock tippet. Luckily it was long enough, and it was under the pound test limit of the record that he submitted the fish for. And we followed all the proper rules to hook, fight, and land the fish. It was a great day and just as exciting for me as it was for him. Pete is now in another place fishing better water, but it is good memories like these that keep him in our thoughts.

Catching a quality world-record fish gives an angler a good feeling of accomplishment. There are several records that I would enjoy having, but I'm not dedicated enough. My dream has always been to catch a record surf-caught striper, where it's just me and the fish. That would be a record that would have real meaning to me. I have no interest in catching a two-pound fish on a twenty-pound tippet just for a record, but there are anglers who do, and there is nothing wrong with it. Chasing world records is a personal quest. It's important to be aware of both the IGFA leader requirements and the rules of the chase. Most record-seeking anglers target a certain species on a given pound test.

Anglers that seek records should join the IGFA, study the rules, and be sure that the leader is built to the proper dimensions. Be aware that the break strength on the labels of some leader materials may not be correct. Do your own testing, or get leader material that is known to be accurate. Then go out and have fun, and perhaps someday your name will appear in the record book.

Appendix Three—The Changing Structure along the Coast

The environment in which a fish lives usually affects how it feeds and acts more than any other factor. Fish will feed in the same manner along a sandy beach in Maine as they would in New Jersey as long as the beach's slope, wave size, and available bait are similar. Fish feed differently because their surroundings dictate how they must eat to survive. How fish act and feed along a rocky, wave-battered cliff might be totally different from how the same fish feed along a quiet beach. And certain species, like stripers, will do well in heavy rolling surf, while bonito are seldom found in rolling discolored water. I believe that bait, a constant food source, is vital to producing and holding a good fishery. It is why some beaches, river systems, bays, and outflows constantly have fish, while other locations are only good for short lengths of time.

The shoreline from Maine to Montauk Point is a changeable mixture of sand and gravel beaches, rocky and sandy points, jagged cliffs, and boulder-strewn

The rugged parts of the shoreline between Maine and Montauk are a sharp contrast to the beaches from Long Island south.

shorelines. Added to this are vast estuaries, big and small river systems, off-shore rips, and rocky reefs. These areas also have vast flats, both sheltered and located along big bays. But once you start to travel down along the south shore of Long Island, the character of the water changes. The beaches are mostly sand with some jetties mixed in. There is less slope to the beaches, and the holes and troughs are not as deep as the beaches of Cape Cod.

The Outer Banks of North Carolina, including Cape Point, boast some good holes and steeper beaches, but not the clear water that you find up north. A unique feature of the Outer Banks is the Diamond Shoals, which extend from shore 12 miles into the Atlantic and are the closest spot to the Gulf Stream along the Eastern Seaboard. The Shoals are the meeting place of the Gulf Stream flowing up from Florida and the Labrador Current flowing down from Greenland and Nova Scotia. These two currents create ideal fishing conditions for many species, from marlin to tarpon to flounder. Depending on the time of year, the variety can be outstanding.

Bait types vary from north to south. Mullet are a major bait from the Carolinas to New Jersey, with some runs spreading farther north. But these runs are made up of smaller-size baits, from 3 to 6 inches long. Sand eels take over where the mullet leave off, ranging from New Jersey to Maine. Atlantic menhaden are an important food source along the entire coast. While they are less abundant in northern waters because of overfishing, they are essential to quality fishing. Other big baits like herring and alewives are also important foods that can be found throughout the Atlantic. Spearing is a major food source inside estuaries and along sheltered beaches. Plus, there are many other bait types that intermix with the major food sources.

The tide also influences how a fish feeds. From Penobscot Bay in Maine to Cape Cod Bay in Massachusetts, the tide is quite similar in both size and time. It ranges from about 8 feet to 12 feet, and high tide in both places is within a half hour, yet these locations are close to 200 miles apart. Yet less than 10 miles away in Nantucket Sound on the south side of Cape Cod, the tide ranges from 2 to 4 feet, and from one end of Martha's Vineyard to the other, the tide can be completely different. The Vineyard requires a special tide chart that should be checked for each location—do not assume or guess what the tide will be.

The normal range for the northern tides from Maine to Cape Cod is 8 to 10 feet. From the south side of the Cape down into Rhode Island, tides average 2 to 4 feet. Along the outer beaches the bigger tides start just off Chatham and increase as you go north. This is also the line where the colder water begins.

The tide in Long Island Sound averages about 7 feet, but from Shelter Island Sound south to Cape May, New Jersey, the average tide is 2 to 5 feet. Delaware Bay runs about a 5-foot tide, but once you head south from Indian River Inlet along the coast to the Outer Banks of North Carolina, the tide averages 1 to 4 feet, with most of the tides running about 2 feet.

The topography, water temperature, and bait type are factors that influence how a fish feeds and acts, not the name of the state.

Maine and New Hampshire

These two states have similar water and share two major species of fish: striper and bluefish. The offshore bluefin tuna fishery is also very good. Both states feature cliff fishing and vast river-estuary systems like the Kennebec River and the other rivers around Bath, as well as the Piscataqua River and Great Bay that enters the sea in Portsmouth, New Hampshire. These estuary systems would take years to fish, and I don't think that you could learn them all in three lifetimes. There are also good beaches and small clear-water rivers and creeks that offer great sight fishing. Locations with less brackish water are very clear on incoming tides, with fishing akin to the tropics. The major bait types are sand eels, spearing, herring, menhaden, and alewives.

Massachusetts and Rhode Island

By far these two states offer the best variety of fishing water along the Atlantic until you hit Florida. And even then, they have large areas of structure that southern states do not. The section of water from Monomoy Point to east of Nantucket Island and west to Muskeget Island harbor more rips and holding water for fish than any other location in New England. This water ranges in depth from a few feet to 50 feet, plus has rips that stand 6 feet tall on a calm day. The water from Point Judith to Watch Hill, Rhode Island, and the rips and reefs ranging from Fishers Island to Watch Hill include holding water and feeding areas for a mixture of many different fish. I hooked and landed several bluefin within a mile of the mainland in both Block Island Sound and Cape Cod Bay.

The outer beaches boast excellent fishing, and locations like Cape Cod Bay and Narragansett Bay offer miles of productive shoreline. The number of ponds, harbors, and outflows of these bodies of water and the small creeks that flow into open water make Massachusetts and Rhode Island a fly-fishing haven. And many of these locations are ideal for sight casting, with their clear, shallow water. The three big islands—Nantucket, Block, and Martha's Vineyard—offer excellent fishing. The Vineyard is a fly-fishing mecca, perhaps the most popular striper location in the world. It is also one of the best locations to chase false albacore and bonito from shore. For the kayak angler, there are many small bays, harbors, and ponds to explore; and shore access for the wading angler is excellent. There is much more water than I have space to mention here.

The major gamefish species are striped bass, bluefish, bonito, false albacore, weakfish, and offshore bluefin tuna—it could be the best bluefin fishery for small boats. Major bait types include sand eels, spearing, herring, menhaden, alewife, and bay anchovies. (*Fly Fishing Boston* by Terry Tessein is a good guide for information on fishing locations from Rhode Island to the southern coast of Maine.)

Connecticut and New York

Long Island Sound is a unique fishery, with most of the stripers coming from the Hudson River. The Hudson is an important spawning area for stripers, and most of the water around the mouth of the river contains Hudson River fish. Along the Connecticut shoreline, most of the water is discolored because of the heavy influence of the many river systems. The Long Island side has clear water and not as much structure, while the Connecticut side has heavy structure, reefs, large points, and sheltered beaches. There are a lot of protected areas that are ideal for fly fishing. The Norwalk Islands are a tangle of rocks, reefs, and structure that offer good boat angling and good shelter. Many estuaries and two big river systems, the Connecticut and the Housatonic, have early-season fishing.

Just around the corner from Orient Point are Great Peconic Bay and Gardiners Bay, both of which at one time had vast runs of weakfish. This sheltered water is ideal for fly fishing, and the water in some locations is crystal clear. The water from Southold, Long Island, to the Race and on to Fishers Island, then out to Montauk, is a hot fall bonito and albacore location. The bluefin tuna run is a little farther offshore than in Rhode Island and Massachusetts.

Montauk Point is perhaps the most popular fishing location in the Northeast, but much too crowded for shore fly fishing. The water all around the point is a popular fall boat fishery. The area just down from the point and south offers good beach fishing. This is where the structure ends and the sand begins. The beaches along the south shore offer good fishing, as do the bays from the

Hamptons down to Raritan Bay. Many of the beaches are not as steep as the northern outer shorelines.

The major gamefish include stripers, bluefish, weakfish, bonito, and false albacore. The major bait types are sand eels, spearing, herring, menhaden, alewives, and bay anchovies.

New Jersey and Delaware

The shoreline and backwater are a continuation of Long Island's, with flatter outer beaches and miles of backwater bays. The difference is that the Jersey shoreline faces east, while the Long Island outer beaches face in a more southerly direction. Sandy Hook offers good shore access and hot late-fall fishing. Point Pleasant down to Island Beach are popular fly-fishing haunts, both spring and fall. Like all the outer beaches from Maine down to Maryland, stripers and bluefish are the main draw for fly rodders. In the fall the bonito and albies mix in, feeding along the shore. As off Long Island, anglers who want to chase tuna often need to run farther offshore. Jersey and Delaware are changeover states, with different bait and a much longer season, and weakfish are more abundant in the backwaters. When you look at these two states, they are similar to Rhode Island—small states with large amounts of water.

Delaware Bay is a large piece of open water. Like most big marsh-estuary-type bays, boat fishing is popular because shore access is limited. In some locations, the grassy sod banks that make up the shoreline of the marsh and the many creeks that empty into the main body prevent walking long distances.

Major bait types include spearing, herring, anchovies, menhaden, mullet, and alewives. Crustaceans like shrimp and crabs also become more important as a food source. Fish up north also feed on crustaceans, but they are less important. As we move south, the fly rodder finds a treasure in this food source because they can match the crustaceans easily.

Maryland and Virginia

Chesapeake Bay, the largest area of backwater in the country, sits sandwiched between the two states. There are miles of shorelines with creeks, rivers, and bays, and the larger rivers like the Potomac are important spawning areas for striped bass. The Bay is the major source of stripers in the Atlantic. It is also an important spawning area for blue crabs and a breeding area for many baitfish like menhaden as well as numerous other crustaceans. Over 200 miles long and 30 miles wide in some spots, the Bay offers fly-fishing opportunities for many anglers. This is truly a boater's paradise. However, it is a large body of water, so anglers fishing from small boats or kayaks must watch the weather. Stripers are the major fishery, but bluefish and weakfish also offer good fishing. Like all backwaters, the shallows, small creeks, and marsh banks are ideal fly-rod locations. And if the fish are feeding on crabs and shrimp, it plays right into the fly angler's game plan.

The Assateague and Chincoteague Island National Seashore offers miles of over-sand access for fishing; contact the National Park Service for information. This area of outer beach has spring and fall runs of stripers as they migrate along the coast. The boat fishing at the mouth of the Bay and along the Virginia shoreline gives access to the many small islands that dot the coast. There can be good runs of blues along the beaches as the fish migrate north in the spring and south in the fall. And there is a much longer fishing season for bluefish.

The major baits are spearing, herring, menhaden, mullet, alewives, shrimp, and crabs. Major gamefish types include striped bass, bluefish, bonito, false albacore, weakfish, sea trout, and redfish. Offshore fishing also offers an assortment of species, but it's big water with long runs requiring big boats.

North Carolina

The barrier islands that run from the Virginia border to Cape Lookout, North Carolina, offer a fishery that is next to none for shore access. Many of the beaches are open to four-wheel-drive vehicles, and there are plenty of places that are only a short walk to good water. These islands also form Albemarle and Pamlico Sounds, whose combined area nearly rivals Chesapeake Bay in size. For all the great outer-beach access, however, fly fishing is not popular like it is up north. When there are runs of fish, the beaches tend to be crowded with spin and bait anglers, and there are fewer opportunities to pick up fish during slow times. The better locations for fly tackle are the protected waters of the sounds. Here you can find weakfish and sea trout, and at times redfish.

I have only fished this water at certain times and not for very long, but it just amazes me that there can be such beautiful beachfront and good-looking water yet the fly fishing can be so tough. However, it's a location that I love to fish, and I will keep coming back. Perhaps it is the lack of small bait close to the beach— there is nothing to draw the gamefish into fly-casting range. Mostly when bait does hit the beach, it's driven by schools of fish. Shore-bound fly anglers need places that have small to midsize foods close to shore. Locations where big baits are driven to shore but then leave often have feast-or-famine fishing.

There is decent boat fishing for stripers around Oregon Inlet. And the one incredible fly fishery that draws anglers from all over is Harkers Island, near Cape Lookout. In the fall the runs of false albacore are world-class. Not only are there lots of fish that aggressively take a fly, but they are also big. When conditions are right, it could be the best fall albi fishery along the Atlantic.

Major bait types include spearing, anchovies, herring, menhaden, mullet, alewives, shrimp, and crabs. The major gamefish are striped bass, bluefish, bonito, false albacore, weakfish, sea trout, and redfish. Offshore fishing also offers a vast assortment of species, particularly out on the Diamond Shoals, but it's big water with long runs requiring big boats.

Glossary

attractor fly: A fly pattern that does not match any one bait type but can suggest several food types.

bar: Any formation of matter that creates a rise along the bottom. Bars are formed from sand, gravel, or a mixture of many materials, even shellfish, like oysters or mussels. Sandbars along ocean beaches shape much of the outer coastline.

bird activity: Any time birds are sitting in groups, feeding, or become excited. The presence of terns feeding or gulls just standing along a beach can be a sign of possible fish activity and a sure sign that a food source is present.

blind casting: Casting to sections of water that are inviting-looking but without the visible presence of fish. Blind casting is prospecting for fish.

breachway: An outflow that runs into the ocean, with rock jetties guarding both sides of the entrance. Often both the incoming and outgoing flows are very strong. In Rhode Island the term *breachway* is commonly used to describe an outflow that drains a salt pond.

breathe: Term used to describe the movement of a fly. Fly-tying materials like marabou, ostrich herl, and saddle hackle produce a lifelike movement even without retrieving the fly. Adding in flash can enhance the movement, making the fly look more alive.

casting angle: Casting at a different angle to the current, or to the flow off a beach or rocky cliff.

casting stroke: The arm and body motion that produces and sets up the cast. Pulling backward during the backcast and pushing forward during the forward cast are significant parts of the casting stroke. The West Coast casting style uses a shorter casting stroke, while other casting styles employ a much longer casting stroke.

cinder worm: Also called worm hatch. The spawning of *Nereis* worms, commonly called clam worms or sandworms. These worms transform, swarm, spawn, and die within a time frame of about six hours or less. These swarms often occur at full or new moon.

covering water: Blind casting to reach as much water as possible. Casting and moving along a beach or casting from a drifting boat are examples of how to cover water.

current flow: See **flow.**

cut: Most often used to describe the deeper section of water that forms between sandbars around ocean holes. It can also be a deeper section of water that runs along the edge of a flat or along a river mouth.

dead-drifting: Letting the line and fly swing, flow, or move without retrieving. The line is held tight but not moved toward the angler.

drift and swing: Casting either across or quartering downcurrent and letting the line and fly swing, using enough retrieve to keep contact with the fly.

drift fishing: Drifting in a boat down a rip or in a flow along a beach while casting to cover as much water as possible.

drop-off: Any place where there is a distinct change in water depth. The edge of a channel or reef, the edge along a flat, and the backside of an offshore bar are all examples of drop-offs. Some drop-offs can be severe, but even a slight change in water depth is called a drop-off.

edge: Any change in water depth where there is a visible edge.

feeding lane: The calm section of water that forms just below the junction where an outlet spills into flowing water. A common term used in freshwater to describe the good holding water just downcurrent from a small stream that flows into a river.

feeding line: Also called slipping line. After casting, an angler might need to feed more line when working a hard flow by letting line slip through his hands. This technique allows the fly to drift with a fast flow—it's effective when fishing an ocean beach, working a flow off a cliff, or in a fast current.

feel: See **touch.**

finning: When fish are swimming on or near the surface and you can see the fins or tails above the surface of the water. Even just a wake on the surface is sign of fish activity.

flow: Also called current flow. Water movement created by tidal flow or wave action.

flow off a beach: After each wave hits the beach, it runs up the slope, stops, and then flows down the slope. This flow creates movement close to the beach. In big surf the flow can be very strong and sometimes large.

hardtails: Term used for fish in the mackerel and tuna families, which have small hard tails. Bonito, false albacore, oceanic bonito, and bluefin tuna are called hardtails, but the term is mostly used when discussing bonito and false albacore.

Hi-D lines: Another term for a very fast-sinking line sometimes associated with lead core lines.

holding line on the tip: Using the rod tip to control the loop and hold the line during the casting stroke. This allows the caster to make adjustments and makes perfect timing less critical.

lifelike fly: A fly pattern that precisely matches a food type.

line control: Managing the fly line and fly to flow into locations that might hold fish. Controlling the depth, swing, and drift while keeping the line tight enough to feel strikes.

loading the rod: Putting a bend in the rod during the first part of the casting stroke makes the rod work better and saves wear and tear on the casting arm. If the rod does not have a good bend when beginning the casting stroke, your casting technique is poor.

loop control: Throwing a tight (small) loop is the proper way to fly cast for most line types. Casters who can control the size of their loop will have good casting form and control.

mending line: Manipulating a section of the fly line by throwing a U-shaped bend in the line either during the cast or after the cast lands on the water. This is an effective way to alter the fly's depth or change the swing. Mending upcurrent allows the fly to settle and reduces the swing angle.

mung: A fine brown to reddish weed that collects along the shorelines of ocean beaches after storms or steady, strong onshore winds. This weed can make fishing impossible.

natural-density fly: A fly pattern that suspends in the water when just drifting and not moving forward.

ocean hole: The deeper section of water that forms along some ocean beaches. These sections are odd in shape and keep changing in size and shape when wave direction and storms pound the beach.

outflow: Any opening that flows into a larger piece of water. A small creek flowing into a bay or a big opening that flows into the ocean are outflows.

pocket: A section of deeper water that might hold fish or bait.

point: A section of land that protrudes out from a shoreline along a beach consisting of sand, rocks, or gravel, or a combination of these materials.

quartering: Making a cast or fishing a flow when the line is at an angle to the current. Most often this technique is used when fishing downcurrent at a quartering angle to the flow.

release anchor: An anchor with a float tied to the end of the anchor line, permitting an angler to throw the line and float overboard and follow the fish without the time-consuming need to pull up the anchor.

rip: A fast-flowing section of water formed when tidal flow is condensed or restricted. Reefs, sandbars, and points block water flow, creating rips.

rip line: The choppy ripple line that forms just at the drop-off below a rip.

rolling water: Any moving water associated with wave action where there is bubbly and tumbling water.

sight fishing: Casting to fish that you can see in clear shallow water. Most often sight fishing means actually seeing the fish but it can be casting to fins, tails, or surface wakes on a shallow flat.

single-handed retrieve: Holding the rod with one hand and using the other hand to retrieve.

sink-head fly line. See **sink-tip fly line.**

sink-tip fly line: Also called sink-head fly line. A fly line that has a fast-sinking front section that is usually 15 to 30 feet long. The running line can be floating or intermediate, and some lines have a rear taper in the running line. Another type of sink-tip line is a floating fly line with a clear intermediate tip section that is 10 to 15 feet long. Fly-line manufacturers use various wording to label this family of lines. Depth Charge, Quick Descent, Wet Tip Express XXT Fast-Sinking Fly Lines are just a few of the many different names for sinking tip lines.

slick: A patch of oil that forms on the surface of the water just after gamefish have fed on baitfish. A slick can also form from oil that seeps from some baitfish. In a wind chop, the patch will show up well.

slipping line: See **feeding line.**

slope: The angle or contour of a beach. Some ocean beaches can have very steep slopes at high tide.

slough: Also called trough or wash. Pocket of water just off an ocean beach where the waves spill down the beach and form rolling white water—a perfect feeding zone for some gamefish. During periods of little or no wave action, this section of water is also a good feeding location for cruising fish.

smelling fish: The scent of feeding fish or bait can alert an angler to fish activity. This scent can smell like melon or cucumber.

spey rods: Spey rods range in length from 13 to 15 feet long. They require special casting techniques and are ideal for locations calling for a long cast.

strike zones. Also called **sweet spots.** Locations that are the best feeding places for fish. A drop-off along a reef, a trough along a beach, or a mouth of a small creek are places where fish like to feed.

stripping basket: A device that holds the fly line while fishing. Most are plastic box-shaped baskets with something in the bottom to eliminate line tangles. Used mostly by wading anglers when fishing jetties or rolling surf and when standing in flowing water.

sweet spots. See **strike zones.**

switch rods: Switch rods, also called two-handed rods, are 10 to 11 feet long, giving the angler more casting distance with fewer false casts and better clearance for backcast height.

tidal flow: The water movement caused by the rising and dropping of the tide.

touch: Also called feel. Feeling the take of a fish. It can be a slight bump, or a gentle tightening of the line, or the sense of weightlessness if a fish takes the fly while swimming toward the angler. Also, being able to feel what the line and fly are doing during the retrieve. Anglers that develop a good sense of touch catch more fish.

trough: See **slough.**

two-handed retrieve: Putting the rod under one arm, holding it by the rod's handle near the armpit, and using both hands to retrieve.

wash: See **slough.**

water column: The location in the water depth to find fish or to work a fly. On deep offshore rips fish are often holding near the bottom, well down in the water column.

wave action: Movement created by a breaking wave. Breaking waves form the water flow behind a bar and create the flow in an ocean hole.

weedless fly: Any fly with a device like a piece of mono or wire that guards the fly's hook to prevent snagging on weeds or catching on the bottom.

weed line: A line of weeds often consisting of sargassum weed. Weed lines hold bait and can have fish holding under or near the line.

white water: Bubbly water created by breaking waves. A trough along a beach, the backside of outer bars, and areas with cliffs and ledges are places that create white water after a wave breaks.

worm hatch: See **cinder worm.**

Selected Bibliography

What follows is a list of the books I use as references for my fishing. I am always learning something new from them.

The Book of Fly Patterns, Eric Leiser. New York: Alfred A. Knopf.

Casting with Lefty Kreh, Lefty Kreh. Mechanicsburg, PA: Stackpole Books.

The Edge of the Sea, Rachel Carson. Boston: Houghton Mifflin.

Eldridge Tide and Pilot Book. Published by Robert Eldridge White: 64 Commercial Wharf, Boston, MA 02110.

A Field Guide to Atlantic Coast Fishes of North America, C. Richard Robins and G. Carleton Ray. Boston: Houghton Mifflin.

A Field Guide to the Atlantic Seashore, Kenneth L. Gosner. Boston: Houghton Mifflin.

Fishing Knots, Lefty Kreh. Mechanicsburg, PA: Stackpole Books.

Fly Fishing, Joe Brooks. New York: Outdoor Life Books.

Fly Fishing in Salt Water, Lefty Kreh. New York: Lyons & Burford, Publishers.

Flyfishing Knots & Leader Systems, Dave Chermanski. Portland, OR: Frank Amato Publications, Inc.

The Hook Book, Dick Stewart. Intervale, NH: Northland Press.

McClane's New Standard Fishing Encyclopedia, A. J. McClane, ed. New York: Holt, Rinehart and Winston.

Practical Fishing Knots, Lefty Kreh and Mark Sosin. New York: Lyons & Burford, Publishers.

Salt Water Flies, Kenneth E. Bay. New York: J. B. Lippincott.

Saltwater Fly Fishing from Maine to Texas, Don Phillips, ed. Portland, OR: Frank Amato Publications, Inc.

Salt Water Fly Patterns, Lefty Kreh. Fullerton, CA.: Maral, Inc.

World Record Game Fishes. Fort Lauderdale, FL: International Game Fish Association.

Index

A

albacore
  best time of year to fish for, 309–11
  best waters to fish for, 306–7
  cliff fishing, 121
  feeding habits, 307–8
  fishing estuaries, 51–52, 55, 56, 58
  fishing flats, 97
  fishing jetties, 63, 66, 67
  fishing ocean beaches, 101
  fishing shorelines, 12, 15
  handling, 191
  hooking, 171
  how they fight, 308
  night fishing, 144
  open water fishing, 129–30, 131, 133, 139, 143
  overview, 305–11
  preferred baitfish, 258, 260, 309
  and rips, 35
  special features, 309
Allen, Farrow, 270
Apte, Stu, 228
Atlantic mackerel, 136, 315
Atlantic salmon, 315

B

baitfish
  alewive, 39, 259
  anchovies, 135, 259–60
  bait identification, 47–48
  bay anchovy, 135, 259–60
  blackfish, 61, 76, 120, 262
  blueback herring, 39, 259
  bottom fish, 261, 262
  bunker, 38, 57, 58, 76, 89, 259
  crab, 47, 57–58, 76, 120, 261
  cunner, 61, 76, 262
  eel, 261, 262
  flat-sided baitfish, 259–61
  halfbeak (ballyhoo), 262
  herring, 38, 39, 57, 58, 76, 175, 259
  killies, 22
  mackerel, 38, 57, 76
  menhaden, 39, 175, 259
  mullet, 259
  pogy, 259
  sand eel, 22, 23, 38, 47, 61, 76, 89, 175, 257–58, 261
  sandworm, 22, 261
  shrimp, 22, 23, 47, 57–58, 97, 261
  silver anchovies, 260
  silversides (shiners and spearing), 22, 23, 38, 57, 76, 258–59, 261
  smelt, 259, 264
  squid, 33, 38, 76, 260–61
  stickleback, 259
  striped anchovy, 260
  and tides, 328
  worms and worm hatches, 23, 39, 40–41, 47, 57–58, 89, 97, 261
Bay, Ken, 270
beaches. *See* ocean beaches
Berkley tackle company, 220
bird activity and finding fish, 4–5, 38, 80, 133–34, 140
Blanton, Dan, 222, 265
bluefin tuna, 129, 143, 262, 311–15
bluefish
  best time of day to fish for, 299
  best time of year to fish for, 300–301
  best waters to fish for, 297
  cliff fishing, 117, 126
  and diminishing numbers of, 343–44
  feeding habits, 298–99
  fishing estuaries, 49, 51, 55–56
  fishing flats, 82, 96, 97
  fishing jetties, 66
  fishing ocean beaches, 102, 103
  fishing open water, 130, 131, 134, 135, 136
  fishing reefs, 71, 76, 80
  fishing shorelines, 12
  handling, 191, 192
  hooking, 179, 180
  how they fight, 299
  night fishing, 148
  overview, 295–301
  preferred baitfish, 258, 259, 261, 262, 300
  and rips, 33, 38
  special features, 299–300
  and tackle, 196
boat fishing
  depth finders and recorders, 48, 80, 133

fighting, landing, and handling fish, 184, 188–90
fishing creeks, 25
fishing estuaries, 44–45, 47, 48, 49, 54, 56
fishing flats, 86–88, 90, 91
fishing jetties, 61
fishing ocean beaches, 114–15
fishing open water, 127–43
fishing protected waters and shorelines, 12–13
fishing reefs, 70, 72, 73–75, 77–80
night fishing, 147–48
and points, 77
and rips, 31–38
safety issues, 338–39
sea kayaks, 56
bonefish, 82, 171
bonito
    best time of year to fish for, 309–11
    best waters to fish for, 306–7
    cliff fishing, 121
    feeding habits, 307–8
    fishing estuaries, 51, 52, 55, 56, 58
    fishing flats, 97
    fishing jetties, 63, 66, 67
    fishing ocean beaches, 101
    fishing open water, 129–30, 131, 133, 139, 143
    fishing reefs, 71
    fishing shorelines, 12, 15
    handling, 191
    hooking, 171
    how they fight, 308
    night fishing, 144
    overview, 305–11
    preferred baitfish, 258, 309
    and rips, 35, 37–38
    special features, 309
    tackle for, 198–99
The Book of Fly Patterns (Leiser), 270
Brooks, Joe, 167, 214, 254

C
Cameron, Angus, 10, 184
Cape Cod, MA
    beaches, 5–6, 103, 184
    Buzzards Bay, 114
    Cape Cod Bay and Cape Cod Canal, 341
    Nauset Beach, 100
    Pleasant Bay, 39, 51, 52, 95
    present fishing quality, 341–42

saltwater estuaries, 51
seals, 319
casting and retrieving
    backcasts, 154, 157, 158, 160–61, 163–64, 165
    blind casting, 16, 89, 140, 171
    casting a switch or two-handed rod, 164–65
    casting for surface-feeding fish, 175
    casting large flies and poppers, 161
    casting sink-tip/sink-head lines, 161–62
    cliff fishing, 123–25, 126, 176
    to different sections of water, 7–8
    fishing creeks, 24–25, 152
    fishing estuaries, 40, 43, 44, 45, 46, 54
    fishing flats, 86, 87, 88, 89, 90, 91, 92, 94, 97
    fishing jetties, 64–65, 67–68, 69, 152
    fishing ocean beaches, 101, 103, 104, 106–7, 108, 109, 111, 112, 113, 114
    fishing open waters, 130, 132–33, 134–35, 137, 139–40
    fishing reefs, 72–73, 76–77, 78–79
    handling too much line, 163
    importance of roll casting, 166
    making a good fly cast, 154–60
    night fishing, 8, 144–47, 165, 171
    practicing, 2
    retrieving in calm water/top water, 174–75
    retrieving in flowing water, 173
    retrieving in slow water and faster water, 172–73
    retrieving up- and downcurrent, 174
    rips, 28–30, 34, 37
    rods, 197–98, 199
    rolling surf, 175–76
    saltwater fly casting/overview, 152–66
    from shorelines, 13–14, 15
    shorelines with light surf, 13–14, 15
    sight casting, 4, 81
    the two-handed retrieve, 28–29, 167–72, 174
Chase, Herb, 116
Chesapeake Bay, 39, 43, 49, 184, 198
chest packs, 217
coho salmon, 315
compasses, 216, 338
The Complete Book of Fly Fishing (Brooks), 254
Connecticut
    fishing waters, 349
    Housatonic River, 89, 90
    Norwalk Islands, 178

Penfield Reef, 70
    Saugatuck Shores, 82
Connecticut River, 43
Connecticut Salt Water Fly Rodders, 177
conservation issues, 341–44
Conti, Al, 223, 312–13
Cook, Seth, 138

D

Danylchuk, Andy, 317, 319, 320
Danylchuk, Sascha, 317, 318
Dean, Gordon, 254
Delaware and fishing waters, 350
Delaware Bay, 55, 127
dolphin, 143, 315

E

Eldridge Tide and Pilot Book, 327
estuaries and estuary marsh systems
    backwaters, 41, 43, 46, 52
    bays, 41, 49, 57, 58
    characteristics, 39
    cut banks, 44, 46–47, 48, 53
    drainage outflows, 44
    eelgrass, 53–54
    larger creeks and deeper areas, 44–45
    marsh banks, 47
    saltwater estuaries, 50–58
    working an estuary system, 47–49

F

Falky, Joe, 23
feeding lanes, 41–42
Fishing Knots (Kreh), 229
fishing lines
    and backing, 220–23, 226
    Berkley Big Game, 222, 226
    Berkley XT, 227
    Bluewater Express, 223
    braided-mono, 212, 228
    choosing, 208–11
    Dacron, 221, 222
    fast-sinking, 209–10, 211, 212
    floating lines, 209, 211
    fluorocarbon, 184, 225–26
    Gelspun or braided lines, 210, 221, 223, 224
    intermediates, 209, 211
    lead-core, 35, 212
    Leviathan, 223
    and line control, 106
    line system and knotting system, 220–29

    management of, 197
    Mastery Billfish, 223
    Maxima, 222, 226, 227
    Micron, 221
    monofilaments, 184, 222, 224, 225–29, 231
    offshore lines, 210
    running lines, 210, 212, 226
    shooting head systems, 161, 211–12, 226
    sinking lines, 35, 65, 73, 211, 212, 226–27
    testing, 231
    top-water lines, 35, 53, 76, 77
fishing locations
    checklist, 8–11
    choosing, 3, 7
    selections for the novice, 2
fishing skills and techniques
    blue-water fishing, 138–43
    catch and release, 191–93, 317–21
    choosing sections of water, 7
    cliff fishing, 116–26
    developing a routine, 6–8
    finding fish, 3–8, 11
    fishing creeks and streams, 18–25
    fishing estuaries, 39–58
    fishing flats, 81–97
    fishing jetties, 59–69
    fishing ocean beaches, 98–115
    fishing open water and chasing fish, 127–43
    fishing reefs and rocky points, 70–80
    fishing shorelines and light surf, 12–17
    handling fish, 190–93
    hooking and fighting fish, 177–93
    landing fish, 185–87
    learning and practicing, 2–3
    mixed fresh- and saltwater systems, 41–49
    night fishing, 8, 15, 16, 89, 144–49, 165, 171
    rips and moving water, 26–38
    saltwater fly casting, 152–66
    stringing fish, 193
fish scents, 101, 110
flats
    big tide locations, 90–91
    boating the flats, 86–88, 90, 91
    deeper flats, 90
    fast-water flats, 92–93
    fishing flats, 83–86, 95–97
    low-light fishing, 88–90
    night fishing, 91–92
    ocean flats, 93–94
    and rips, 92, 93
    sight fishing, 84–86

flies, fly patterns, and lures
    alewife, 264
    anchovy, 270, 274
    attractors, 3, 254, 255
    basic working fly collection list, 270–86
    blackfish, 265
    Blondes, 139
    bluefish, 135
    bottom fish, 265
    bucktails, 64, 262, 265
    bunker, 264, 265
    choosing, 257, 262–63
    chum, 256, 265
    Clouser, 255
    Clouser Deep Water, 266
    Clouser Minnow, 264, 285–86
    crab, 265
    Crystal Hair, 64, 262, 263
    D. L.'s Crab Fly, 272–73
    D. L.'s Gold Bug, 273–74
    D. L.'s Spearing Fly, 282
    D. L.'s Wiggler, 274
    and dead-drifting, 28–29
    deer-hair-headed, 79, 113, 265–69
    Enrico's Bunker, 265
    Enrico's Sea Fiber, 264
    EP Adult Bunker, 274–75
    EP Bay Anchovy, Tan, 282
    EP Crab Tan, 278
    Epoxy Sand Eel, 284–85
    EP Tuna Killer, 280
    Eric's Epoxy Sand Eel, 278–79
    Eric's Inverted Sand Eel, 282–83
    Eric's Small Baitfish Fly, 283
    finger mullet, 264
    fish hammer, 135
    Flashabou, 262, 263
    and fly boxes, 216, 269, 271
    and fly hooks, 266–69
    foam-headed flies, 14, 255, 256, 269
    Glow Squid, 265
    Gray Ghost, 254
    Gurgler, 174, 264, 277
    hairbugs, 264
    herring, 264, 270
    and imitating baitfish, 257
    jelly worms, 74
    Krystal Flash, 262
    Lefty's Deceiver, 58, 255, 264, 269, 270, 279
    making your own, 271–86
    marabou, 64, 262

    Mega Mushy, 275
    Mickey Finn, 254
    mullet, 264
    Mushmouth, 259, 265, 280
    poppers, 14, 35, 66, 79, 174–75, 264, 269
    pulsating flies, 14, 28
    purchased flies, 271
    saddle hackle, 64, 262, 264
    saltwater fly starter list, 270–71
    sand eel, 38, 58, 258, 263, 265, 269
    Sand Eel Fly, 286
    sandworm, 265
    shiners, 264, 265
    shrimp, 22, 265, 286
    Shrimp Fly, 286
    slab flies, 269
    sliders, 66, 79, 264
    smelt, 264
    Snake Fly, 3, 14, 41, 58, 263, 264, 265, 269
    snapper blue, 264
    spearing, 58
    spiked mackerel, 264
    squid, 265
    stickleback, 264
    streamer, 23
    surface bugs/top-water, 14, 35, 49, 66, 79, 126
    Tabory's Glow Squid, 280
    Tabory's Slab Side, 265, 276
    Tabory's Pop-Hair Bug, 277–78
    Tabory's Snake Fly, 280–82
    Tabory's Surfboard Foam Fly, 278
    Tabory's Worm-Snake Fly, 283–84
    Tan Crab, 274
    trolling lures, 142
    weedless, 14, 54, 76
    Whistler, 265, 276
    worm, 40
    worm hatch, 265
Flies for Saltwater (Stewart and Allen), 270
floats and float tubes, 23, 25
A Fly Fisher's Guide to Salt Water Naturals and Their Imitations (Rogers), 262
Fly Fishing Boston (Tessein), 349
Fly Fishing in Salt Water (Kreh), 263, 315
fly hooks
    barbless, 255, 266
    Daiichi, 266
    Eagle Claw 254SS, 266
    flat mill file, 269
    Gamakatsu, 266

keeping hooks sharp, 267–69
Mustad 34007 and 34011, 266, 267
Shur Sharp Sharpener, 268–69
stainless steel, 266
Tiemco, 266
Foley, Dave, 50
footwear, 61, 119, 217
Frech, Jack, 180, 255–56

G
gaffs, 186, 189
Gallasch, Bill, 254
Gartside, Jack, 174, 264, 277
Gibbs, Harold, 254
Gibson, Terry, 317
Gilkes, Cooper, 200
gloves, 217
Goddard, D. L., 271, 272, 273, 274, 282
guides and guide services, 37, 38, 130

H
hooking, fighting, and handling fish
applying drag, 182–84
barbs and barbless hooks, 181, 255, 266,
319, 320, 336
catch and release, 191–93
and clearing the line, 178–79, 181
fighting and landing fish from a boat,
188–90
handling fish, 190–93
landing the fish, 185–90
landing tools, 189
and preparation, 177, 178, 179
pumping the fish, 184–85
the run/fighting the fish, 182
setting the hook, 179–81
short-range fighting, 185
and the two-handed retrieve, 169–70
using enough tackle, 187–88
Huff, Steve, 167
Hughes, Ed, 312

I
IGFA records and requirements, 37, 220,
224, 345
insect repellent, 216
Island School, Eleuthera, Bahamas, 317

J
jaw-grabbing devices, 320
Jaworowski, Ed, 270

Jeans, Fred, 88–89
jelly-worm fishing, 74
Jessup, Captain Curt, 127–28
jetties
anatomy of, 60–63
fishing a jetty, 63–68
landing fish, 68–69
rips, 62–63, 64
sandbars, 64
team fishing, 69
Johnson, Paul, 268

K
knots and knotting system
Albright, 223, 227, 228, 244–45
attaching backing to reel, 253
Bimini Twist, 219, 222, 223–24, 227, 228,
240–41
blood knots, 228, 243
clinch knots, 222, 224, 226, 235, 237
connecting leader or backing to fly line,
247–50
double nail knot, 222, 252
double uni-knot, 222, 251
figure-eight knots, 228, 234
haywire twist, 228
Homer Rhode loop knot, 228, 235–36
improved blood knot, 243
improved clinch knot, 237
joining Dacron and Micron to mono,
251–53
knots for attaching fly to tippet, 232–38
knots to form double lines, 239–41
knots to tie line to line and line to leader,
242–45
line and knotting system, 220–29
loop knot, 238
loop splice, 222
loop-to-loop connections, 226
making a loop in line, 246
nail knots, 220–21, 222, 223, 224, 226,
247–50, 252, 253
necessity of, 218–20
non-slip loop, 224
offset nail knot, 222, 253
speed nail knot, 249–50
spider hitch, 223, 227, 239
and superglue, 224, 226, 231
surgeon's knot and loop, 222, 223, 224, 227,
228, 242, 246
testing knots, 231

three-and-a-half-turn clinch knot, 235
twice-through-the-eye clinch-trilene knot, 233
uni-knot, 232. *See also* double uni-knot
wind knot, 227
Kreh, Lefty, 154, 205, 228, 263, 264, 270, 315
Kriewald, Captain Pete, 74, 138–39, 177, 345

L
Laszlo, Pete, 214, 317
leaders
    basic IGFA leader system, 224
    and leader materials, 225–26
    lengths, 226–27
    materials for, 225
    mono leader system, 223
    shock leaders, 227
    and tippets, 125, 184–85, 210, 216, 220, 223–28, 232–38
    two-leader systems, 223–24
Leiser, Eric, 9, 270
lights, 22, 87, 148, 149, 216
lines. *See* fishing lines
Long Island, NY
    Gardiner's Bay, 21
    Great South Bay, 51
    Montauk, 80, 114
    and outlets along the shoreline, 67
    Peconic Bay, 21
    and saltwater estuaries, 50
    Shelter Island, 198
Long Island Sound, 12, 70, 127, 130, 342
Loving, Tom, 254

M
Maine
    coast, 119
    fishing waters, 348
    Kennebec River, 39
    present-day fishing quality, 119
marlin, 143, 315
Martha's Vineyard, MA
    Cape Poge Gut, 51
    Chappaquiddick Bridge, 43
    creeks, 19
    Dogfish Bar, 81
    Edgartown harbor, 52
    estuaries, 51
    Lobsterville Beach, 12, 52
    Menemsha Bight, 52, 56
    ocean beaches, 114

offshore rips, 31, 37
Ponds, 51
present-day fishing quality, 342
Tashmoo Pond, 261
Maryland fishing waters, 350–51
Massachusetts. *See also* Martha's Vineyard, MA; Nantucket, MA; Nantucket Sound
    fishing waters, 348–49
    Tuckernuck Island, 32, 33
McClane, A. J., 222, 295
McClane's New Standard Fishing Encyclopedia (McClane), 222, 295
McNulty, Copp, 177
Merwin, John, 196
Meyer, Deke, 270
Murray, Joe, 82

N
Nantucket, MA
    creeks, 19
    estuaries, 51
    Great Point, 27
    ocean beaches, 103, 114
    offshore rips, 30–31
    present-day fishing quality, 342
Nantucket Sound, 30–31, 114
nautical charts
    and cliffs, 119
    and creeks and ponds, 19
    and estuaries, 43, 51
    and jetties, 61
    and ocean beaches, 100
    and reefs, 71
    and rips, 32
nets, 189–90
New Hampshire
    fishing waters, 348
    Great Bay, 184, 261
New Jersey
    Barnegat Bay, 12
    fishing waters, 350
    and outlets along the shoreline, 67
    present-day fishing quality, 342
New York. *See also* Long Island; Long Island Sound
    fishing waters, 349
    Hudson River, 41, 49
    Montauk, 80, 184
North Carolina
    Cape Point, Outer Banks, 100
    fishing waters, 351–52

Harkers Island, 130
and ocean beaches, 103

O

ocean beaches
  flat water, 111–12
  getting below the bait, 114–15
  ocean holes, 100, 103, 104, 105, 110, 111,
    112
  reading an ocean beach, 103–5
  rips, 101–2, 110, 112
  rocky areas, 112–13
  sandbars and points, 103–4, 108–9, 112
  the wash, 105–10
  water depths, 99, 100
  weeds, 100–101
oceanic bonito (skipjack tuna), 129, 139, 143,
  311–15
open-water fishing and chasing surface feeding
  fish
  blue-water fishing conditions, 140–43
  blue-water tactics, 138–43
  fishing techniques, 131–37
  and temperature fissures, 141
  trolling and chumming, 138–40
Orvis Company, 215
*The Orvis Pocket Guide to Saltwater Baits and
  Their Imitations* (Tabory), 262

P

Peluso, Angelo, 270
Peterson, Eric, 263, 271, 278, 282, 283, 286
Piscataqua River, 43, 348
pliers, 216
pollock, 315
Pond, Bob, 49
Pop Flyes (Popovics and Jaworowski), 270
Popovics, Bob, 270
Posh, John, 3, 10, 41–42, 74, 178
Puglisi, Enrico, 259, 265, 271, 274, 278, 280,
  282

R

Rajeff, Steve, 160
red drum, 315–16
reefs
  fishing a point, 76–77
  fishing deep reefs, 77–80
  rips, 76, 80
  shallow reefs, 72, 75–76
  sunken reefs, 72
  types of, 72–75

reels
  choosing and recommendations, 206–7
  drags and drag systems, 203–6
  recommendations, 206–7
  resistance to salt water, 204
  setting and checking the drag, 205–6
  types, 202–3
releasing fish, 317–21
Rhode Island
  breachways, 67
  coast, 67, 114, 116, 119, 184, 261
  Cuttyhunk, Block Island, 115
  estuaries, 50, 51
  fishing waters, 348–49
  Narragansett Bay, 127
  Newport, 185
  ocean beaches, 114
  rocky cliffs, 116, 119
  rocky shore, 184
Rio Line Company, 223
rips
  and drop-offs, 36
  and estuaries, 48
  and fishing conditions, 37–38
  and flats, 92, 93
  and jetties, 62–63
  and ocean beaches, 101–2, 112
  offshore rips, 30–38, 110
  and open water, 140
  overview, 26–28
  and reefs, 76, 80
river systems, 41
rods
  building rods, 199, 201
  choosing, 200–202
  lengths and weights, 197–200
  switch rods, 164–65, 197
  two-handed spey rods, 164–65, 197
Rogers, George V., Jr., 262

S

safety issues
  and boat fishing, 115, 132
  and cliffs, 339
  driving on beaches, 339–40
  and flats and reefs, 337–39
  and hooks, 336
  safety equipment, 338–39
  and the surf, 336–37
  and water locations, 8, 121, 337–38
  and the weather, 331

Salt Water Flies (Bay), 270
Saltwater Flies (Meyer), 270
Saltwater Flies of the Northeast
    (Peluso), 270
Salt Water Fly Patterns (Kreh), 270
Salt Water Fly Tying (video), 270
Saltwater Fly Tying (Wentink), 270
Schober, Frank, 218
Scientific Angler, 223
The Scientific Angler (Johnson), 268
sea bass, 344
sea-run brown trout, 315
sea trout, 316
shad, 315
sharks, 143, 191, 192, 315
shoals, 71–72
Simroe, Ted, 201
Skok, Dave, 259, 265, 271, 274, 275, 280
Slater, Jim, 214
Smith, Frank, 177
Smith, Ray, 116, 119, 125
Spanish mackerel, 315
Stewart, Dick, 270
striped bass
    best time of day to fish for, 292–93
    best time of year to fish for, 295
    best waters to fish for, 291–92
    cliff fishing, 117, 126
    diminishing numbers of, 341
    feeding habits, 292
    fishing creeks, 21
    fishing estuaries, 49, 51, 55
    fishing flats, 82, 94, 97
    fishing jetties, 61, 66, 67
    fishing locations, 4, 32–33, 39, 43
    fishing ocean beaches, 101, 102, 103, 113
    fishing open water, 131, 135–36
    fishing reefs, 70–72, 76, 80
    and gaffs, 186
    hooking and flies, 171, 179, 180
    how they fight, 293
    landing and handling, 189, 190, 192
    night fishing, 148
    overview, 290–95
    preferred baitfish, 258, 259, 261, 262, 294
    and rips, 32–33, 38
    special features, 293–94
    and tackle, 196
Stripers Forever, 344
stripping baskets, 61, 214–16
Swiderski, Captain Roger, 127–29

T
Tabory, Paul, 59–60
tackle
    choosing, 197
    knots, 218–53
    lines, 207–12
    overview, 314–15
    recommendations for three tackle
        outfits, 213
    reels, 202–7
    rods, 197–202
tarpon, 167, 179–80, 181
Tessein, Terry, 349
tidal estuaries, 43
tide charts, 27, 326, 327
tides
    altered tides, 325–26
    best tide, 327–29
    and boat fishing, 13
    and cliffs, 119–20, 121
    and estuaries, 43, 44–45, 48, 52–53, 56
    and finding fish, 4, 7, 8–9
    and fishing locations, 290
    and flats, 87, 90–91, 93, 95
    and jetties, 61–62, 66
    and moon phases, 334
    and ocean beaches, 101, 111
    and open water, 130, 136, 140
    predicting tides, 326–27
    and reefs, 72, 76
    and rips, 26, 27, 28, 31, 32
    and shorelines, 17
    and small creeks, 18
    and water flows, 21
    what causes tides, 324–25
trolling, 138–39, 140
tuna, 129, 139, 142, 143, 171, 189

V
vests, 217, 338

W
water flows, 18, 19–21, 41, 44, 48
wave action
    and cliffs, 120, 124, 125
    and estuaries, 56
    and fighting fish, 186
    and flats, 93, 95
    and jetties, 61, 62, 66, 67
    and ocean beaches, 105, 106, 107, 108,
        110, 112

and reefs, 79
and rips, 27, 31
and shorelines, 16, 17
and wind action, 332
weakfish
  best time of day to fish for, 303
  best time of year to fish for, 304–5
  best waters to fish for, 302
  feeding habits, 302–3
  fishing creeks, 21
  fishing estuaries, 49, 51, 55
  fishing flats, 97
  fishing jetties, 66
  fishing open water, 136
  fishing reefs, 71, 74, 76
  handling, 191
  hooking, 180
  how they fight, 303–4
  night fishing, 148
  overview, 301–5
  preferred baitfish, 258, 261, 304
  special features, 304
  and tackle, 198
weather
  and fishing locations, 290
  and fog, 331, 333–34, 338

and the influence on fishing, 330–32,
  334–35
National Weather Service, 331
and rips, 38
and temperature changes, 334–35
Wentink, Frank, 270
wind action
  and casting, 160
  and estuaries, 56, 57
  and finding fish, 4, 7
  and fishing lines, 209
  and fishing locations, 290
  and flats, 96
  and the influence on fishing, 332–34
  and jetties, 62, 73
  and ocean beaches, 108, 110
  and open water, 130–31, 136–37, 141–42
  and reefs, 79–80
  and rips, 27, 28, 31–32, 37
  and tides, 327
Winslow, Pip, 312
world records, 345

Y
yellowfin, 143

About the Author

Lou Tabory has given more than 1,000 talks and demonstrations on marine fly fishing over the past twenty years. His articles have appeared in *Field & Stream, Salt Water Sportsman, Fly Fisherman, Sports Afield, Saltwater Fly Fishing,* and elsewhere. This is the second edition of his first book. Lou and his wife, Barb, live in Ridgefield, Connecticut.